GEORGE HARRISON

Behind the Locked Door

For my mother, Kathleen, and the other Fab Four: J, K, L & M

GEORGE HARRISON

Behind the Locked Door

GRAEME THOMSON

OVERLOOK OMNIBUS

This edition published by Omnibus Press and distributed in the United States and Canada by
The Overlook Press, Peter Mayer Publishers Inc, 141 Wooster Street, New York, NY 10012. For bulk
and special sales requests, please contact sales@overlookny.com or write to us at the above address.

Copyright © 2015 Omnibus Press
(A Division of Music Sales Limited)
14/15 Berners Street,
London, W1T 3LJ, UK.

Cover designed by Fresh Lemon
Picture research by Jacqui Black

ISBN 978.1.4683.1065.8
Order No. OP56155

Printed in Malta.

A catalogue record for this book is available from the British Library.

Cataloguing-in-Publication data is available from the Library of Congress.

Visit Omnibus Press on the web at www.omnibuspress.com

Contents

Prologue

Be Here Now
New York, August 1, 1971

It was 40 years ago today – give or take a week. It is July 2011 and Ravi Shankar is remembering the Concert For Bangladesh. Ninety-one-years-old, frail but sharp and magnificently silver-bearded, his recollections are fresh and clear as mountain air. "It became something so big that I couldn't believe it," says India's greatest classical musician of the modern age. "It was," he smiles, "a momentous thing."

Few would argue. Momentous not just musically and culturally – though it was both; and momentous not just for the thousands of refugees and war children whose plight received worldwide recognition and who, later, perhaps gained some small crumb of material comfort thanks to the music played that day. It was also a momentous landmark for the man Shankar calls "my brother, my friend and my son, all together."

Rock music's first *en masse* act of philanthropy was the symbolic pinnacle of George Harrison's career – solo or otherwise. The two concerts, staged at Madison Square Garden on the afternoon and evening of Sunday, August 1, 1971, and starring Harrison, Shankar, Bob Dylan, Eric Clapton, Leon Russell, Billy Preston and Ringo Starr, were a perfect synthesis of everything the former Beatle stood for at the moment of his greatest potency. Through its founding humanitarian impulse; its daring attempt at cultural cross-fertilisation; its undercurrent of benevolent spiritualism, and its genuine and crusading desire to open hearts, eyes and minds to the East, the concert both embraced Harrison's personal passions and sought to perpetuate, without any great cosmic fuss, the wider idealism of the Sixties. And then there was the music, a bubbling brew which further reflected Harrison's expansive outlook, placing the sounds of the sitar, sarod, tabla and tamboura alongside a kinetic mix of rock, blues, soul, folk, pop, gospel and R&B. In so doing, the Concert For Bangladesh was a flesh-and-blood incarnation of the soulful quest for spiritual enlightenment and uplift that had made his debut solo album, *All Things Must Pass*, such a fiercely impressive statement the previous year. On record, and now on stage, Harrison seemed like a new breed of emotionally evolved rock star for a new era.

Such a thing would have seemed highly unlikely even 12 months earlier. Harrison was historically the Beatle with the lowest profile. He was never The Quiet One – that was a shallow, simplistic label – but he was the least flashy, the least brash, the one who was drawn least to the spotlight. After the band split officially in April 1970 there was no shortage of observers who half expected him to disappear to an ashram and never return. Instead, in August 1971 he was enjoying by far his most fertile period as a musician. A triple album, *All Things Must Pass* had been released at the end of 1970 and had stayed at number one in the UK and US for close to two months. At the same time, its lead single, 'My Sweet Lord', was also number one on both sides of the Atlantic. It would become the best-selling song of 1971 in Great Britain, but sales and statistics can only tell you so much. These were colossal records, charged with a powerful spiritual current which connected to the most generously idealistic impulses held over from the late Sixties.

Look more closely and Harrison's quiet rise to prominence makes sense. He was the Beatle who, during the band's lifespan, travelled furthest from his prosaic origins and became the first to seriously question and challenge their *gestalt* relationship. All four men experienced a highly accelerated evolution – Fab years were akin to dog years: one

vii

equalled four or five of the human equivalent – but as the youngest and initially the least worldly, Harrison "went on the longest journey of all The Beatles," says Bill Harry, founder of the influential early Sixties Liverpool pop zine *Mersey Beat* and a close friend of Harrison and the other members in their formative years. "He was the one who became more stretched than the others." By the late Sixties he was "stretched" tight, still only in his mid-twenties and travelling fast, at last acutely aware of his potential and intent on fulfilling it. Harrison ended the decade on a roll. Having recorded two of his greatest songs, 'Here Comes The Sun' and 'Something' during The Beatles' final sessions for *Abbey Road*, he was the only band member who could reasonably be said to have walked away from the group with his songwriting and profile in the ascendancy. During the dark days of 1970 and 1971 he seemed to keep his head – and largely his own counsel – while Lennon and McCartney tore strips off of each other in public. He was the only Beatle who, in the general public perception at least, entered the Seventies still swaddled in their unique force field of idealism, optimism and innate warmth.

For a brief spell, it seemed easier for Harrison to be a Beatle outside of the band than in it. That would change, but for now their legacy gave him kudos as a solo artist without imposing any of the creative restrictions he'd had to endure over the previous decade. "I do think he was overshadowed by John and Paul in the band, but he really came into his own when they split up," says Glyn Johns, who all but produced *Let It Be* in 1969 and worked with Harrison on several Apple albums. "I thought the way he handled his career and himself at that moment was astonishing, and I came to be an enormous fan. He certainly held his head as high as any of them as a solo artist after The Beatles broke up. He cast his net outside of the norm and the comfort zone and had huge success, and more power to him."

The impulse behind the Concert For Bangladesh was far too urgent for it to be a mere coronation, but none the less it became the crowning moment of a remarkable 12 months. He certainly looked the part: heavily bearded, extravagantly maned, emanating grace. Dressed in a simple woollen shirt and waistcoat during his introductory speech, Harrison looked like a noble toiler of the soil plucked from some work of late 19th-century Russian literature; later, scaled-up a little for the performance, he was brilliant in a white suit, benevolently Messianic for those who looked for their rock stars – and ex-Beatles – to be such a thing, and plenty did.

Crucially, the music was rich and raggedly powerful. He played three of his most famous Beatles songs, recorded in either 1968 or 1969: 'Something', 'While My Guitar Gently Weeps' and 'Here Comes The Sun', downsized to a humble folk strum. By doing so he acknowledged The Beatles' weighty legacy with a light touch, incorporating his past into the wider context of his own solo work without being suffocated by it. He would struggle to pull off that particular trick again, but for now these songs simply felt like part of him, merging seamlessly with his new solo music.

Everything sounded mighty and joyous. A song of creative frustration and ultimate emancipation, 'Wah Wah' was an escalating thrill, almost out of control, the twin drummers Jim Keltner and Starr thumping down the groove behind massed ranks of vocalists and the sprawling band: horns blaring, organ vamping, guitars flashing. 'My Sweet Lord' was already a classic, a hymn of naked need and humility set to a campfire symphony of rattling acoustic guitars. The cool, fluid beauty of 'Beware Of Darkness'. The gospel-rock of 'Awaiting On You All'. Each one connected to the moment and the man and the message. And at the centre of it all was an artist who seemed finally to have found his place in the world, happy to stand back as Billy Preston and Leon Russell shamelessly stole the spotlight, or decorously backing Bob Dylan on his wonderful mini-set. If the Concert For Bangladesh was, as *Rolling Stone*'s Jon Landau observed, apparently with a straight face, "rock reaching for its manhood," then it was just as clearly Harrison's personal coming of age.

But looks can be deceiving. Simply playing the concert at all was a severe test of mettle. Having come to loathe and indeed fear live performance by the time The Beatles quit touring, Bangladesh was his first up front, spot lit, official concert appearance since August 1966. According to Pattie Boyd, who first met Harrison early in 1964 and was married to him between 1966 and 1977, he was "*extremely* nervous. He had to really steel himself to do it." Shankar recalls that "he seemed to be a little worried, after such a long time," while his second wife, Olivia Harrison, told me in 2009 that "George playing at Bangladesh was a very courageous move. That really was his contribution, overcoming his self-consciousness to do that." It was a generous gift, but in the wider narrative of his career it proved a fleeting triumph rather than the bold new leaf it may initially have appeared. His reticence would ultimately claim him.

One reason why the mere idea of the Concert For Bangladesh captured the public imagination and resonated so far beyond the walls of Madison Square Garden was because it united those two lightning rods for Sixties idealism – Bob Dylan and, in the form of Starr but most significantly Harrison, The Beatles – at a time when both had retreated from the trenches. It may have been 1971, but as a cultural phenomenon the Sixties had not quite ended. The *Woodstock* film had ensured the spirit of that age had spilled over into a new decade, and rock music was still – just – regarded as a force powerful enough to challenge established orthodoxies. At first Bangladesh looked like the crest of a new wave for the icons of the Sixties, providing a new lease of life replete with possibilities. In fact, it was closer to a final hurrah for the promise of that decade and, in many ways, for Harrison's brief tenure as a solo superstar as well. The sadness that frames the brightness of the Concert For Bangladesh is the knowledge that Harrison would never again connect so directly and powerfully with the times.

The promise of his first year as a solo artist was quickly spent. It supplied sufficient momentum for another – more austere – hit album, as well as one further huge hit single, but his energy was already waning. His ill-starred US tour at the end of 1974 provided final confirmation that Harrison was no longer a genuine contender. Indeed, were you to draw a graph denoting the progress of his career in the ten years post-Bangladesh it would look like a very swift descent down a very steep Alp: lawsuits, increasingly lacklustre albums, gloom, illness, drink and hard drugs, domestic discord, spiritual confict, retreat. By the end of the decade he was, creatively and culturally, an irrelevance. An old fogey by his mid-thirties and thoroughly disenchanted with the industry he had been a part of for almost 20 years, the greater his distaste for the cut and thrust of the fray the more his career couldn't help but be defined by his time in The Beatles, a Catch 22 which would drive him to periods of deep bitterness. Playing live was not on the agenda, and he was happier at home tending his garden than making records. With the exception of a spirited renaissance in the late Eighties and a brief Japanese tour in 1991, it would remain that way until his death in 2001. Not so long after the Concert For Bangladesh Harrison essentially became the musical equivalent of the gentleman farmer, with no appetite for the spotlight and no real urge to push himself to greatness.

It was not just a slow artistic decline, though it was certainly that. It was more obviously a very conscious and deliberate turning away. One of the contributory factors was the aftermath of the Concert For Bangladesh itself, which as well as underlining his lack of appetite for live performance was a complex and frustrating business; organising the film, the album and the money it raised took up huge amounts of his time and left him even further disillusioned with the Machiavellian machinations of the record industry.

But there were numerous other causes for his flight away from the rock and roll frontlines. He struggled with the legacy of being a former Beatle ("recovering Beatle" may be a more apt description; like an alcoholic with the bottle, no Beatle was ever freed from the grip of the Fab Four) and it engendered suspicion, anger and a deep-rooted need for privacy. He came to describe his time in the band as "a nightmare, a horror story. I don't even like to think about it."[1] Except he *had* to think about it, because he was forced to talk about it every time he raised his head above the parapet.

If The Beatles ended up becoming a largely negative current pulling Harrison away from music, there were also positive forces behind his retreat. Many of them originated from the man who inspired Harrison to organise the Concert For Bangladesh in the first place, and who died in December 2012. Though he engaged with numerous other gurus and teachers, Ravi Shankar remained Harrison's spirit guide through much of his explorations. "It was a very important relationship for George, Ravi was a bit of a father to him," said Olivia Harrison. "Sometimes they were like brothers, sometimes father and son. They always played music and were always discussing ideas about things they could do together."

The impact of Shankar on Harrison was that of a pebble thrown into deep, still water, and the ripples spread through his entire life. "Something about Ravi opened a door in George," says Pattie Boyd. "And I don't think he really knew what he was getting himself into."

The pair first met in the summer of 1966 and retained an extraordinary bond until Harrison's death. The Indian musician arrived in his life at a time when the Beatle "realised that nothing was actually giving me a buzz any more. I wanted something better. I remember thinking, I'd love to meet someone who would really impress me. And that's when I met Ravi..."[2] Nearly 50 years later, his hunger for change and meaning remains palpable.

Their relationship was fluid and complex and richly rewarding. On that July day, when I asked why he thought Harrison had spent the second half of his life in thrall to the culture and spiritual philosophy of the East, Shankar said, modestly enough, "I am one of the causes maybe. It was through my music that he came to me and we met. Then he went to India. We were together for a few weeks in Kashmir and Bombay and I started teaching him, and that was the period when he started getting really interested not just in the music, but in the books I gave him along with the music. Through my music and through his visit there he really got so deeply interested in our path. Not just the religion, but the old Vedic philosophy. He got so deeply interested, and proceeded with more and more reading and being attached to India and our music."

Indian music was the catalyst for Harrison's lifelong explorations, and it was Shankar who placed the key in his hand. From there, door upon door opened to endless rooms, to Bhakti yoga and transcendental meditation, Rishikesh and the Maharishi Mahesh Yogi, His Divine Grace A.C. Bhaktivedanta Swami Prabhupada and Krishna and the Concert For Bangladesh itself; to glimpsed moments of bliss and oneness and transcendence, but also to periods of doubt, confusion, pain and fear; to the irregular rhythms of red-hot fame followed by retreat, the eternal pendulum of privileged excess and devoted denial. And each footfall took him a further step away not only from The Beatles, but from childhood certainties and very often the people closest to him. "It did make life more complicated," says Boyd. "Once you open any door that lets in more information on life and why we're here, you pursue that and it opens up other doors, and it's just endless: ancient knowledge, history, everything there is. There is too much to learn, actually, and once you start on that path and you have opened that door you can't close it. The mystery and intrigue is always there and you have to follow it."

He followed. He followed and he found something more nourishing and enduring and complex than fame and pop concerts and the charts. In time it became clear that Beatle George, and that glistening solo superstar heading a cast of legends at Madison Square Garden, were pale reflections of a man made up of numerous parts, many of which were almost comically contradictory. The routine paradoxes evident in most humans seemed in Harrison to be amplified, just as the success of The Beatles was itself riven by extremes. The searcher, looking east and inside for simplicity, peace and enlightenment, had garages full of the fastest and most expensive cars on the planet. The eccentric, extravagant grandeur of his home at Friar Park in Henley-On-Thames at times bounced between the dry asceticism of a monastic retreat and flesh-and-powder excesses more suited to the Chateau Marmont. He was just as likely to follow the Grand Prix circuit as it jetted its decidedly unspiritual way around the world as he was to spend time on his knees tending to his plants. The quick-witted Liverpudlian with a pitiless tongue and child's sense of mischief, the man who happily slipped into the chorus line to play a lumberjack during a *Monty Python* show, could also be found earnestly endorsing Yogic Flying as a key policy issue in the 1992 general election.

When Beatles producer George Martin was sick Harrison arrived to see him in his brand new McLaren F1 sports car, which could reach speeds of 230 mph. At Martin's bedside he presented the former Beatles producer with a small statue of the Hindu god Ganesh. Good health and wisdom, Harrison said, derives from finding pleasure in the smallest, simplest things. He then drove off in his million-dollar jet-car at something close to the speed of sound, leaving the cosmic contradiction trailing in his wake.

Somewhere in the space between these truths lies the essence of a complex man. "I think his increasing obligations and responsibilities clashed dramatically with the kind of austerity associated with a spiritual path, particularly an Indian one," says John Barham, his friend and the string arranger on his earliest and best solo records. "On the one hand he wanted to cross over from the material world into a spiritual world, and on the other hand he was caught in the net of his great wealth and possessions. I think he experienced anguish."

His was not a simple life. The path to transcendence was riddled with very earthly obstacles: lust, ego, temptation, jealousy, pride, anger. Prickly and temperamental, Harrison was no stranger to the sense of entitlement that all rock stars carry with them like a cross between a medal and a scar, yet he was also sensitive, conscientious, thoughtful to a fault to his friends, funny, smart, a born worrier, and a man who found that fame limited his opportunities to enjoy the very human kind of interaction with others that he often craved. He believed man had the capacity for deep enlightenment, to hold heaven within his own consciousness, and yet he remained immensely fearful and suspicious of its capacity to wound and destroy. And, as it turned out, rightly so.

He was, ultimately, peculiarly ill-suited to fame, never mind superstardom. Though at times he slipped back into the role of Beatle George, tempted by the ease and access it offered, he spent significant parts of his adult life trying to escape the limitations of his physical self and his public persona, and instead looked inward. While John Lennon at times frantically hopped from cause to cause in the hope that if he could change the world he *might* just have a chance of changing himself, Harrison approached fulfilment from the other end of the telescope: he believed that if he could only change himself he would already have changed the world. It became – perhaps admirably – his life's work, and very probably the work of his next life, too. It could be fun, and interesting, and he generally retained a keen appreciation of the absurdity of existence and his privileged place in it. But it was rarely a smooth ride.

CHAPTER 1

All Those Years Ago

In the mid-Seventies George Harrison stood outside the building in which he was born and thought: "How do I come into that family, in that house, at that time – and who am I anyway?"[1] These may seem, at first glance, a strange set of questions. Most people revisiting their childhood home might be more inclined to notice that the current occupants had painted the door purple, or put in new windows. Elevated musings about "nipping through the astral plane,"[2] however, were entirely in keeping with the man Harrison had become in the near 30 years since he had lived at 12 Arnold Grove, Wavertree, in the south-east of Liverpool.

He was thrown into the heat of superstardom following an upbringing defined by its utter normality, and always seemed somewhat suspicious of the transaction. Unlike his friend Bob Dylan, who saw his conventional beginnings as a blank canvas on which to daub all kinds of colourful legends and myths, and ultimately paint himself anew, Harrison simply came to regard his origins with puzzlement. In the years immediately after Beatlemania had turned his life on its head he often struggled to square his quotidian childhood with the extraordinarily exalted position in which he now found himself.

The issue birthed some elemental questions. Why me? Why now? And, yes, who am I anyway? "He really couldn't understand why he was such a famous worldwide musician," says Pattie Boyd. "It was always a bit confusing to him. He started looking at himself and started to question why he, this boy from Liverpool who was probably destined to be in some quite lowly job, had been thrust out there to become so well known."

Post-fame, the urgency of those questions accelerated. Later, having drank deep of the laws of karma, fate and reincarnation, he came to understand that no matter where he had physically entered this particular world on this particular occasion, "there's no way I wasn't going to be in The Beatles, even though I didn't know it. In retrospect I can see that's what it was – it was a set-up."[3]

This *fait accompli* offered some crumb of comfort to a man with a lifelong quest for meaning. It also served to further distance him from his roots. Physically, Harrison left Liverpool behind early in his life; first in 1963, aged 20, when he moved to London with the rest of The Beatles, although since his first visit to Hamburg in 1960 he had lived an increasingly peripatetic existence. As the youngest band member with the tightest family unit, "[initially] he probably went home more than the others," says Tony Bramwell, a childhood friend who later worked for The Beatles. "He used to go back a lot to see his mum and dad." The Harrison family moved from Liverpool to nearby Warrington in the mid-Sixties, and as early as 1966 Harrison had, at least mentally, also moved on. "I get a funny feeling when I go back to Liverpool," he said. "I feel sad, because the people there are living in a circle – they're missing so much. I'd like them to know about everything – everything that I've learned by getting out of the rut."[4] A year later Pattie Boyd would observe that "George doesn't miss anyone."[5] A year after *that* he would declare that his true roots were in India.

He cut his ties even more profoundly in 1970, the year his mother died. He moved his two brothers (his elder sister had been living in America for several years), to live in and around his Friar Park estate in Henley-On-Thames. "He went back to see his mother, but after she died I don't know if he really went back much at all," says Chris O'Dell, a former Apple employee and later a close friend who lived at

Friar Park with the Harrisons in the early Seventies. She is the subject of his song 'Miss O'Dell'. "He might go to see his father but mostly everyone would come to him at that point." For the last 30 years of his life contact with Liverpool was sporadic – he brought his new girlfriend and future wife Olivia Arias for a nostalgia tour in the mid-Seventies, but physically, spiritually and emotionally he found very little of himself there.

"You grew up wanting to go somewhere else," Paul McCartney said of The Beatles' collective attitude to coming of age in Liverpool[6]. Harrison was perhaps more honest about honouring that feeling into his adult years than anyone. While he was alive there were no chummy returns to his old schools, no nostalgic gigs at the Cavern, no ribbon-cutting photo ops. He refused the Freedom of the City in the mid-Eighties. Posthumously there have been no peace memorials. He does not have an airport named in his honour. Of all The Beatles, he is the one who has most stubbornly resisted deification by his home city.

He also left very little trace of Liverpool in his music. Once you start looking for it, there is a quite striking lack of sentiment in his songs for the place he came from: no 'Penny Lane', no 'In My Life' or 'Strawberry Fields Forever', not even a 'Liverpool 8'. His view of the city and the childhood he spent there was never susceptible to easy nostalgia, nor even to much discussion. "Liverpool was always okay," was about as expressive as he got[7]. As his spiritual self evolved so the ties of his physical origins became less and less meaningful. He came to believe that his real home was a long way away, that he was not really "from" Liverpool; his eternal spirit, born and reborn over and over again, simply re-entered "a body" at that particular place and that time. "It was quite clear to me that he believed that in a prior life he was Indian," says Chris O'Dell. When Harrison sings of being "such a long, long way from home," on 'World Of Stone', he is most assuredly not talking about Merseyside, or indeed any earthly place.

Which begs the question. How much of the man can we see in the Liverpool boy? And how much of the Beatle?

★ ★ ★

The childhoods of the most globally successful or truly pioneering artists are frequently defined by what Tom Waits once described as "some kind of wounding early on."[8] They mostly conform to one of a handful of archetypes: those which are scarred by parental absence or loss; those which are privileged but lonely, loveless and achingly miserable; and those which are chaotic and peripatetic, in which adults and juveniles periodically reverse roles until nobody is quite sure which is which.

Seldom are they absolutely solid, warm and unremarkable. Harrison had by far the strongest domestic foundations of any Beatle; of all four, his was the only traditional family unit which remained intact into adulthood. John Lennon, raised by his aunt Mimi, wrestled lifelong with the legacy of an absentee father and a mother who first left him and was then killed when he was 17 and only just beginning to establish a bond with her. Ringo Starr's parents divorced when he was three and he barely knew his father. Paul McCartney's mother died when he was 14. Harrison, by contrast, was enveloped in a large family which offered unconditional love and support. His maternal grandmother lived just around the corner from Arnold Grove. As the youngest he was the most indulged, and always remained the undisputed golden boy. In The Beatles, the baby of the family was not such an exalted position; at home, it awarded certain privileges. "George being the youngest, as often happens in families, was utterly adored by his mother, and his father as well," says Boyd. His mother would recall, "George never gave us any cheek but he always got round us."[9]

His music would often – too often, perhaps – end up sounding as solid and undramatic as his upbringing. He possessed none of the turbo-charged drive or ambition so often bequeathed to artists by a childhood defined by an unstable home life or a dead parent. As a musician he was committed and conscientious but he was never, he admitted, "of the competitive nature."[10] As a Beatle he craved more creative input but never sought the lion's share of the spotlight; as a solo artist he was always most comfortable being a prominent part of a collective rather than the front man. From the day he was born he already had, without even trying, the indulgent attention of those closest to him, and he had little of that demon urge to seek adulation or approval from another source.

The last of four children, George Harrison was born on February 25, 1943 (much, much later he told *Billboard* magazine that he was actually born very late on February 24). His parents had married in 1930. His mother Louise was of Irish stock, from Wexford, and a practising Catholic, though never devout. She worked in a local greengrocer's shop before her children started to arrive: first Louise, in 1931, then Harold in 1934, Peter in 1940, and finally George in 1943. By the time the two youngest boys were born their father, Harold, had long returned from sea, where he had worked as a first-class steward on the White Star Line between 1926 and 1936. Back on dry land, he got a job first as a bus conductor, and then as a driver.

Money and indulgences were always scarce. Harrison was born at the height of World War II and grew up in the days of rationing, an austerity measure which wouldn't end completely in the UK until 1954; every shilling counted, and *was* counted. None of The Beatles, aside from perhaps Lennon, displayed a particularly *laissez-faire* attitude towards money, and in the early days of the band's success it was Harrison who kept the closest eye on how much they were making and where it was going. It was a fascination which later led to a sometimes sour sense of injustice, expressed in 'Taxman' and 'Only A Northern Song'. "They understood the value of what their father's did," says Tony Bramwell. "George knew his dad only earned a few pounds [a week] so he saw no reason why anybody working for him should earn more than that. None of them were very lavish."

Harrison's grammar school, the venerable Liverpool Institute, was remembered by his fellow pupil Paul McCartney as a "Dickensian old place,"[11] and indeed the Liverpool of his childhood is as far from us now as the age of Dickens was from the Forties and Fifties. It was a city and a time defined by the immediate aftermath of war. The bombs that fell on the port came too early for Harrison to recall; what he did remember were the bomb sites that scarred the city for decades afterwards, the dingy cobbled lanes with slaughterhouses at the end, the sharp humour and the savage put-downs, the weird pavement dramas: escapologists in the streets, men and women enacting loud and sometimes bawdy public pantomimes, the hustle and the bustle and noise and dirt and clamour of a huge port, trams cutting across pedestrians, steamers and ferries and freighters massed in the water.

Many of the houses that provided the backdrop to it all are still standing, though the city and the times have shifted almost immeasurably. Twelve Arnold Grove hasn't changed so much. Part of an old fashioned cul-de-sac of traditional terraced homes with an alley – or "jigger" – running along the back, then as now it was a tiny house sited towards the end of the row, boxed in tight on either side by identical properties. Facing the terrace from the road there is a door to the right, a window to the left and another above it. You can walk its entire width in four paces. Inside it was small, dauntingly cold, with no bath or toilet and no heating except for a small coal fire in the kitchen, the room where everyone tended to congregate. The living room at the front, by contrast, was chilly and unwelcoming, reserved for special occasions. The house was a cramped space for two adults and four children; the kind of home where a family becomes either tight or murderous for the lack of any alternative. For the Harrisons it was the former. All in "he had really fond memories of his childhood," Olivia Harrison told me. "He had a pretty stable home life." Harrison remembered it, wittily, as a period of "relatives and absolutes."[12] Pattie Boyd's impressions of the family dynamic when she first met her future husband were that they "had a very close relationship. They were a very tight family, and very loving. He was very secure within himself, and you only really get that security from a very tight and loving family as a child."

Initially he hardly knew his sister, Louise. Twelve years his senior, she had gone away to teacher training college, then married when he was ten and moved to Scotland. She later settled permanently in the United States. Her memories of him as an infant were of a boy who "was always the one who tried to please. When the fire needed more coal, he would always say, 'Mummy, I'll do it. Let me get the shovel.' Or, when we'd be going to church, George would polish everyone's boots."[13]

His eldest brother Harry, nearly a decade older, was off doing National Service, then working, and married in his mid-twenties. Peter was three years older, and the only one of his siblings with whom Harrison tended to play and share interests, including music. His father was the breadwinner but his mother was the heart and soul of the household. "His mum was lovely," says Bramwell. "A proper mum, Lou. She'd let you call her by her first name. His dad worked on the buses and he was always cheerful. If we got on his bus we didn't have to pay for it. [His sister] Louise was nice, but she disappeared off to the States when we were quite young. His brothers were good lads."

The family had been on the Housing Association waiting list for years, and when Harrison was six they were finally moved from Wavertree to a council house at 25 Upton Green, Speke. Their new home was a step up: much more room, modern, with an inside toilet, part of a community of similar houses built around a neat central green. Despite the amenities "George's mum hated moving to Speke," says Bill Harry. "Even though the house was nicer and they had a bathroom and all that, she missed the Wavertree and the people, and the communication with the people."

Speke was something akin to a social experiment. Situated eight miles south-east of the city centre, it was developed in the Thirties as a satellite town, with its mixture of prefabs and new council houses. The airport – now John Lennon airport – was built in the area at the same time. The new influx was a mixed bunch, a democratic blend of families shipped in from respectable areas and less reputable characters relocated from slum clearances. Harrison recalled some "nasty moments after we'd moved to Speke. There were women whose husbands were running away and other women who were having kids every ten minutes. And men were always wandering around, going into houses – shagging, I suppose."[14]

"Speke was a vicious place, believe me, more dangerous than Liverpool," says Bill Harry. "Where [George] was living was okay, but some of the nasty elements from areas in Liverpool, in the areas they were put into in Speke there were lots of fights and beatings. It was built as a new town but they didn't build any cinemas or places of entertainment. The kids would come in to [Liverpool] in the evening, come out of the pubs or the cinema and there would be no buses, so they would steal cars to get back to Speke." Bramwell, who lived about a quarter of a mile away from the Harrisons in Hunt's Cross, recalls "some real budding Teddy boys who used to terrify the daylights out of us."

★ ★ ★

Shortly before moving to Speke, Harrison had started at Dovedale primary school, near Wavertree. John Lennon was a pupil, three years ahead of him, but given the gulf in age the two were never aware of each other. He was a sporty boy, particularly keen on football and swimming. He joined the Cubs and later he would go to watch the sports car races and the British Grand Prix at Aintree, the start of a lifelong love affair with speed and automobiles. He would write to the British Racing Motors team and receive pictures of all the latest models. Though perfectly able to occupy himself, he was never short of friends. One Dovedale schoolmate, Rod Othen, recalls Harrison as a "quiet sort of guy, wicked sense of humour, always in mischief, always – certainly at Dovedale – in trouble for doing all sorts of things: pulling girls' hair, climbing up onto the old air raid shelters, throwing paper balls around and passing notes in class."[15] Even at this early age he "didn't suffer fools gladly,"[16] yet he already possessed an acute moral compass when it came to what he saw as the mistreatment of others. "If he saw anyone being bullied George tended to step in," says Othen. "He didn't like people bullying people."[17]

He tended to have distinct friendships. His primary school was a long way from Speke, where he ran with a different gang. "There was about five or six of us," says Bramwell. "We didn't run wild, we just did the things that kids can do. We were very innocent until we got into skiffle and rock music."

Situated near the crooked southern elbow of the river Mersey, not long before it narrows at the point where Widnes faces Runcorn and starts drifting inland towards the north-east, Speke was a scrubby mix of the industrial and the rural, bordering onto a kind of urbanised country park. Close to Liverpool airport there was open land and railway tracks. Harrison and his friends would play in the fields and farms, build dens with hay bales, pretend to be Robin Hood or Cowboys and Indians, make rope swings over the pond. There was an old Tudor building, Speke Hall, ripe for exploration, and lots of factories: Bryant & May, Dunlop and Meccano, where the boys would hop over the fence to grab any badly pressed toys that had been discarded. Further to the east were woods, marshlands and farmland which could be explored on foot or on bicycle. Early on in his life he already acknowledged a desire to escape from the hustle, to find the kind of landscape that matched a deep inner need for calm. He would go down to the Oglet shore and tramp along the muddy riverside, and walk for hours along the cracked cliffs of the Mersey when the tide had gone out. "There's a part of me which likes to keep quiet," he said in the mid-Sixties, when his life was very unquiet indeed. "I do prefer wide, open spaces to traffic jams."[18]

He was content to be quiet when he had nothing much to say, but he was no pushover. In the official Beatles biography, first published in 1968, Hunter Davies described Harrison's parents thus: "Mrs Harrison is ... jolly, very friendly and outgoing. Mr Harrison is thin and thoughtful, precise and slowly deliberate."[19] Marry the two descriptions together and it's a fair representation of Harrison's basic nature. His sister-in-law Irene, wife of his brother Harry, remembered his parents as "tolerant, sensible, loving people. They were so warm and brought you into everything."[20] He learned the gift of inclusion, hospitality and thoughtfulness from them, the idea that "you mustn't disappoint people who are counting on you."[21] He also inherited a stubborn, undeviating streak. McCartney, a schoolmate and childhood friend who came to know the family well, spotted something a little more stern and stubborn in his parents' demeanours which was also passed along to their youngest son. Of Harry, he recalled in 1987: "[He] was always great fun, but forthright and very straightforward... I remember always being a little disturbed by the hardness in his character. Now Louise was lovely, but quite a hard lady, too, in some ways, but soft as toffee on the inside... She'd always tell you how she felt, Louise."[22]

This particular Apple didn't fall far from the tree. Like any child, his personality at this time is provisional, subject to almost constant shifts and evolutions, yet it's notable how little the essentials would change into adulthood. However much Harrison may have left his home city behind in body and consciousness, in his character he remained very Liverpudlian. It was there in his mix of cheek and charm and forthrightness, his dry wit, love of wordplay, his dislike of the "bullshit" which he, in later times, seemed to smell almost everywhere. His sense of humour, described by Bill Harry as "surreal and bizarre", was wry and a little bleak but never far from the surface. However much he changed, right up until his death he remained identifiable as that boy: stubborn, wickedly funny, irreverent, thoughtful, brooding, inclusive, independent, oddly embittered, cocky, lustful, a playful glint rarely far from his eye.

For those who put their store in astrology – and certainly Harrison later did – he was by his own estimation a classic Piscean: black and white, yin and yang, hot and cold. In certain company he could be loud, extrovert, aggressive and confrontational. Paul McCartney's earliest impressions were of "a cocky little guy with a good sense of himself; he wasn't cowed by anything."[23] At other times he would be thoughtful, with a shyness that could be both soulful and surly. One schoolmaster recalled him as "a very quiet if not even introverted little boy who would sit in the furthest corner and not even look up. I'm not saying he was unintelligent, but [he] hardly ever spoke."[24]

He was capable of a kind of blissful clarity of thought and perception often only accessible to a child, although through his life he frequently struggled to articulate it to his own satisfaction; he also had a similarly childlike knack for uncomfortably straight-talking. He seemed to have the truth gene implanted into his DNA long before his consciousness was expanded by drugs and spiritual awareness; fame and adulthood failed to politely polish his rough edges. There was not always a great deal of clear blue water between honesty and plain rudeness. "Oh yes, he was *pretty* blunt!" says Bramwell. Allan Williams, who booked The Beatles at his Liverpool club the Jacaranda and later took them to Hamburg, describes Harrison as "nice to get on with, but he wouldn't suffer fools. He always had a sharp tongue. Crikey, yeah! He didn't put up with any bullshitters."

He was encouraged to be independent from an early age. His parents were not, recalled his sister-in-law Irene much later, "the sort of people to stop their children being themselves."[25] He demanded that his mother stop walking with him to primary school; he was sent on errands to the shops alone at a young age; and when he hit double figures he benefited from their relaxed attitude to alcohol and tobacco – at least that was how he told it. It's not hard to detect the whiff of bravado and exaggeration in his claims that he was allowed to stay out all night and could drink when he wanted, but it's true that he was afforded an unusual amount of trust and leeway which he rarely seemed to abuse.

Life was certainly less of a struggle for him than it was for the other Beatles. There was nothing much for him to rail against at home, so he railed – or, more often, brooded and raged internally – at authority. Any "wounding" was either deeply implanted at birth or grew from experiences outside of home, primarily through a dawning awareness of the constrictions and rote expectations of society at large. His experiences in The Beatles exacerbated it, but what friend, filmmaker and *Monty Python* animator Terry Gilliam calls his "weird kind of angry bitterness about certain things in life"[26] was evident from an early age. It's hard to place its origins – it seems almost like a traumatic response to coming face to face with the true nature of reality. "Our parents were so honest that we grew up being able to trust what they told us and knowing that we were secure in what was happening," said his sister Louise. "When we got out into the regular world, it was something completely different."[27] Beyond the security and support of the family unit Harrison's teenage years slowly revealed a violently anti-doctrinal streak which never left him.

Although a judgemental, didactic seam runs clearly through his own songwriting – there's no shortage of "I want to tell you" jabs and lofty "I look at you all" sermonising – he tended to regard similar sentiments as insufferable in the mouths of anyone else. Religion was a formative, if relatively casual part of his early upbringing which he independently chose to reject. He attended non-denominational schools but he was christened at Our Lady of Good Help, the church around the corner from Arnold Grove, which closed in 2011 after more than 100 years' service. He would go to Mass with his mother and siblings even after the family moved to Speke, but it never really stuck. He took First Confession and Communion but when it came time for his Confirmation in his early teens he thought, with characteristic clarity, "'I'm not going to bother with that, I'll just confirm it myself later on.' From then on, I avoided church."[28]

He was suspicious of the culture of priests making the rounds of Liverpool's working-class neighbourhoods to collect half-crowns in their "sweaty little hands,"[29] although friends often thought him a soft touch when it later came to doling out funds to his own spiritual causes. His lapsed Catholicism was made explicit in his music. In 'Awaiting On You All', from *All Things Must Pass*, he dismissed all formal religious dogma and in particular a Pope who "owns 51 per cent of General Motors" and is qualified only to comment on the Stock Exchange. Much later, the posthumously released 'P2 Vatican Blues (Last Saturday Night)' was an even more direct denouncement of the Church of Rome. The Irish writer and director Neil Jordan, who worked with Harrison on his 1986 HandMade film *Mona Lisa*, recalls that he had become quite virulently anti-Catholic later in life. "He hated the Pope, and he said he would pay me any amount of money if I would make a movie that would tear the Catholic church to strips. Quite recently I made [TV series] *The Borgias*, and he would have paid for that, I'm sure. He would have loved it, actually."

Those early, sceptical brushes with Catholicism were not insignificant. Right at the end of his life, while making *Double Fantasy*, John Lennon would tell the drummer Andy Newmark, with typically barbed candour, "You know, George is a frightened Catholic: God one day, coke the next. He gets so high he scares himself back to church." By then church was no longer the imposing physical edifice of his youth but a more fluid, internal point of connection to the spirit. And yet an attraction to some kind of God figure – and the accompanying confusions and contradictions it exposed – may well have been ingrained at an early age.

His real venom was reserved for school. Although Harrison was a reasonable student at Dovedale, given his subsequent academic achievements – which amounted to precisely zero – there must have been some surprise when he passed his 11-plus exam in the summer of 1954, a feat which entitled him to attend a grammar school rather than a far less prestigious technical school or secondary modern. "He was really chuffed to have passed the exam to get into the Institute," said Rod Othen. "It was the best school in Liverpool, no doubt about it."[30]

The move to the Liverpool Institute from Dovedale in September 1954 was a significant fork in the road. In such circumstances some pupils rise to the occasion; others deliberately disappear and look for escape routes. Grammar school saw Harrison's good nature and general mischievousness harden into something which regularly presented itself as being more angry and cynical. "The Institute was a pretty strict grammar, a top school," says Bramwell. "Very mixed social strata, but they were all bright. Masters and prefects wore gowns, you wore uniforms and caps; the masters would teach up on a raised platform." Corporal punishment was regularly doled out, some of it via the aptly named master, Frank Boot. "The teachers were very slipper-happy: bend over the desk and get hit."

From the top of the tree as a popular final year pupil at Dovedale, Harrison was demoted back down the pecking order. He didn't take it well. "The worst thing was leaving the junior school and going to the big grammar school," he said. "That's when the darkness began... where my frustrations seemed to start. You would punch people just to get it out of your system."[31]

This was not an exaggeration. McCartney, in the year above Harrison at the same school, recalls introducing him to an older friend called Ritter. "I remember we'd been standing around [the] playground and I'd tried to introduce George to Ritter, introduce him to my peer group... And we'd been sitting around and George suddenly head-butted this friend of mine. I thought, Fuckin' hell. Now I'm sure he had a very good reason to do it... What might have been construed as good old-fashioned rudeness I had to assume was ballsiness."[32]

Already McCartney was shaping up to be one of nature's diplomats, pouring oil on troubled waters. Harrison was less inclined to play nice when his mood dictated otherwise. He later described the move to the Institute in elemental terms, the emotional climate taking a sharp turn for the worse. While it "was very pleasant being little and it was always sunny in the summer,"[33] by the time he was 11 the barometer recorded that it was "raining and cloudy, with old streets and backward teachers."[34] He was dragged from the simple blues and yellows of a post-war spring back to the rutted, charcoal-streaked gloom of some eternal Dickensian winter. For Harrison, these shift in moods changed the very nature of the cosmos. It would ever be thus. He had a gift, or perhaps was cursed, with the ability to take the micro and make it macro: his bad moods were universal downpours; his moments of bliss enveloped the entire world. Mood swings were expressed as psychic storms, with the knowledge that, as he expressed later in 'Blow Away' and 'All Things Must Pass', "a mind can blow those clouds away." These hurricanes and sunbursts came to be fully expressed in his music and, often, his sometimes erratic treatment of those around him.

To sum it up: "I didn't like school. I think it was awful; the worst time of your life."[35] He would later describe being in The Beatles in almost exactly the same terms.

He rapidly lost interest in his studies and quietly slid down the academic scale, falling into the lower C-stream of poorly performing pupils. He would spend his lunch money at the pictures, or knock off classes and go around to Harry's girlfriend, Irene, to say hello while his brother was off doing National Service, with the strict instructions that she didn't tell his mother.

His English teacher was George "Cissie" Smith, who was married to Lennon's aunt Mimi and took an extremely dim view of his cheap blue suede winkle pickers in particular, and his entire dress code in general. The most obvious means of rebellion in the Fifties was via clothes rather than deeds. Harrison did his bit. He was a ratty looking kid, a flash Ted with big, sticky-out ears, a baby face, and an impressively precarious quiff slicked back with Vaseline into what was described as "a fuckin' turban" by Arthur Kelly, his Wavertree friend and a schoolmate at the Institute. He had a slow, slack Scouse drawl which marked him out, in John Lennon's words, as "a real wacker"[36]; in other words, an authentic working-class Liverpudlian lad. When Harrison first met Mimi, a very proper and rather severe lady who set great store in her social standing, she was utterly horrified and wouldn't let him in the house.

For school he devised many ingenious variations on the official uniform: he tapered his trousers on his mother's treadle machine until they were skin tight; he wore a bright yellow waistcoat, alternated with a jet black one. He would wear his school badge on a safety pin so it could easily be flipped inside the pocket when he was out of school. It was home-made rebellion on a post-war ration. "George was already wearing drainpipe trousers, he had narrowed his tie and was wearing a quiff," says Bramwell. "He was a semi-juvenile delinquent; in his lunchtime!"

He was a devoted habitué of the school's smokers' corner. "It started off on Woodbines and then we got exotic, things like Passing Clouds," says Othen. "It wasn't just a place where he went and smoked... there were more talk and ideas and people's experiences shared in that smoky corner than in many other places in school."[37]

It provided some relief to what was happening inside. School, with its "fascist"[38] teachers, was his first realisation of life as a rat race, apparently bent on recruiting an army of drones sitting behind desks being fed the same information. It seemed to strike a genuine horror within him that never left. "That's when things go wrong, when you're quietly growing up and they start trying to force being part of society down your throat," he said. "All those things annoyed me. I was just trying to be myself."[39]

A combination of Youngest Child Syndrome – "he was the golden boy, absolutely," says Pattie Boyd – and a family who were generously inclined towards independence and self-expression ensured that he never quite aligned himself to the notion of being told what to do. There was never a huge amount of that kind of thing at home. He relished even less being told what to think; when he was given the opportunity to find his own path to his own interests, he eagerly soaked up knowledge, but he was not given to forced instruction. From an early age he seemed to possess an alternative perception of normality, one which didn't include school, National Service, the army cadets, exams and algebra. "I always knew there was something I was not going to get from school," he said. "I was fortunate enough to feel there was an alternative."[40] Like a million disaffected kids before and since, that alternative was music.

Be Here Now
Liverpool, July 1958

It is high summer 1958, and yet another young man is bargaining on his guitar providing a passport to immortality. He has left his home on the southern edges of the city and travelled on the bus with his friends – they are not *really* a group, despite history's subsequent attempts to make them seem so; this is something more fluid and provisional, in the way that teenage music-making almost always is – to the home of Percy Phillips, who runs the rather grandly titled Phillips' Sound Recording Services from the living room of his terraced house at 38 Kensington in the centre of Liverpool.

The five boys are herded into a booth and in the time it takes to play them they record two songs from their limited repertoire live into a single microphone: one is a cover of Buddy Holly's 'That'll Be The Day'. They all love Buddy Holly. The other is – rather boldly – a song of their own. It is a spirited but unremarkable three-chord country blues with a passing but not quite litigious resemblance to Elvis Presley's 'Trying To Get To You'. It is called 'In Spite Of All The Danger' and it is performed by John Lennon, Paul McCartney, Colin Hanton, John Lowe, and George Harrison. The latter sings background vocals and plays a neatly constructed little solo, for which he receives a songwriting credit. He is still only 15.

For 17s/6d the five young men have the tape of their two recordings pressed onto ten-inch shellac. They have just made their first record, though they only have one copy to share between them. They each take turns looking after it for a week before passing it on. In time any unlikely dreams of recorded glory recede. The songs will not be released to the public for almost another 40 years. When they are, it will be a quarter of a century since Harrison stopped playing with the group which slowly evolved from that summer's day recording session. By that time the 15-year-old will not only have achieved immortality, he will have lived several other lives all at once. But to his eternal ambivalence and even regret, what started at 38 Kensington will come to define him.

CHAPTER 2

Plug Me In

Not long after his life disappeared down the world's longest helter skelter, Harrison could be found, not surprisingly, clinging onto absolute certainties: hard wood; solid body. "I believe I love my guitar more than the others love theirs," he said. "For John and Paul, songwriting is pretty important and guitar playing is a means to an end. While they're making up new tunes I can thoroughly enjoy myself just doodling around with a guitar for a whole evening. I'm fascinated by new sounds I can get from different instruments I try out. I'm not sure that makes me particularly musical. Just call me a guitar fanatic instead, and I'll be satisfied."[1]

It's seems a simple point but it's significant. Harrison didn't grow up wanting to be a pop star, or a singer, or a songwriter. He just wanted to play guitar. It *was*, of course, partly a means to an end: money, girls, a better life, a bigger house. But above all it was an end in itself, a direct route to some very simple but profound source of pleasure. "George just never put the guitar down from the age of about 12 or 13," says Tony Bramwell. "It was constant – on the bus, at home, when he was doing his butcher's delivery round. He would drop the guitar at my place, do his rounds, then be back at my house to fiddle around with it. He was absolutely devoted to it."

His love affair with the instrument went through occasional cooling off periods during the subsequent 45 years, but it was never under any serious threat. Even in the long, fallow years when he released no music, he would still be playing, either for fun or from force of habit. Percussionist Emil Richards, who toured with Harrison in 1974, played on several of his solo albums and remained a lifelong friend, says that "I always thought of him as a musician, not a singer. That was my strong impression of George: how well he could play and how often he would put a guitar in his hand. He had his guitar in his hand all the time: touring, at [his home on] the [Hawaiian] islands, singing old songs, new songs he was working on - just playing all the time. It was almost annoying at times! Music, music, music..."

Even before he moved to Speke, at Arnold Grove Harrison would listen and sometimes stand on a chair to sing along with the songs he heard drifting from the radio or played on the wind-up record player his father had brought back from New York when he was a seaman. It was a mixed bag. In those days of limited choice one listened to almost everything that came within earshot: Irish tenor Josef Locke, big bands, music hall, the crooners Bing Crosby and Mel Tormé, cheesy novelty tunes like 'I'm A Pink Toothbrush, You're A Blue Toothbrush' and Vaughn Monroe's 'In The Middle Of The House', jazzy pop singers Kay Starr and Teresa Brewer, pre-rock 'n' roll jivers Johnnie Ray and Frankie Vaughan, the country music of the early Fifties: yodelling Jimmie Rodgers and Slim Whitman, doomed Hank Williams, and the folk-blues of Big Bill Broonzy. Some of the songs on heavy rotation – Josh White's 'One Meat Ball', Hoagy Carmichael's 'Hong Kong Blues' – stayed with him forever. He recorded the latter for his 1981 album *Somewhere In England*.

He and his brother Peter, he later recalled, "would play anything."[2] Like all The Beatles, in later life Harrison could draw upon musical tastes that travelled far beyond rock 'n' roll, but it was rock 'n' roll that really stuck: first Fats Domino, then Elvis Presley, Gene Vincent, Buddy Holly and Little Richard, alongside their UK equivalents: Tommy Steele, Billy Fury, Marty Wilde and Cliff Richard. Beggars couldn't be choosers. They soaked up everything. "We started getting records," says Bramwell.

19

"We both had elder brothers and they were getting records before us, but we would nick them and swap with each other, listening to them over and over again." In many ways Harrison's earliest musical heroes remained his most enduring. Not just Elvis, Buddy and Little Richard, but Nashville country guitarist Chet Atkins, the harder-rocking Carl Perkins, who wrote 'Blue Suede Shoes', and The Everly Brothers.

Mostly it was an obsession experienced from a distance – often the most fatal kind. He had to content himself with going to the cinema to see Bill Haley & His Comets playing 'Rock Around The Clock' in the classic 1955 movie *The Blackboard Jungle*; a ticket to see Haley in person at the Odeon in February 1957 proved beyond his modest means. Watching Buddy Holly perform live on television's *Sunday Night At The London Palladium* was as close as he got to another hero, but some acts were more accessible: Danny & The Juniors, The Crew Cuts, and home-grown skiffle king Lonnie Donegan all came through Liverpool. He saw Eddie Cochran perform, just before his death, at the Empire in 1960 and spent much of the time watching Cochran's fingers, more interested in how he played the guitar than the songs he was playing on it.

By the time Harrison hit his teens he had become enthralled with the instrument, so much so that he was inclined to conjure one out of thin air. He would spend his time in class drawing pictures of guitars with fancy f-holes and cutaways; he also expended significant amounts of effort unsuccessfully trying to make his own guitar out of plywood. Finally, when he was 13, his mother gave him the £3 10s he needed to buy a used Egmond steel strung Spanish-style guitar – proudly advertised by the company as "the cheapest model in our range!" – from Raymond Hughes, a former school friend at Dovedale. He would stay up until the small hours consulting his manual to learn the shapes of the basic C, F and G chords, sometimes worrying away at the thick strings until his fingers bled. "It was," he recalled, "the only thing I really liked."[3] One day, overplayed, the cheap guitar simply outlived its usefulness. "It wasn't very good," Olivia Harrison told me. "He said he took the neck off and it fell apart, so he hid it and six months later he gave it to his brother, Peter. Then he got a better one."

Once again it was his mother who saved the day, paying the not inconsiderable sum of £30 for a Hofner President, an acoustic with those all-important f-holes and a single-cutaway with a sunburst finish. It was much more like the real thing, and a lot more money. Louise gave him constant support, financial and moral. "At the back of my mind I remembered all the things I wanted to do as a girl, but nobody encouraged me," she said[4]. His family were helpful in other ways. His father organised some valuable instruction from a friend named Len Houghton, whom Harrison would visit for a couple of hours every Thursday night in his flat above his off-licence shop. "He would show me new chords and play songs to me like [the Harry Akst number] 'Dinah' and [jazz standard] 'Sweet Sue', and Django Reinhardt and Stéphane Grappelli sort of tunes."[5] His introduction to the great gypsy guitarist Reinhardt in particular gave Harrison an extra dimension to his playing that many of his contemporaries would lack. He also learned bits of Bach. Olivia Harrison remembered that "his father had a friend, and that's why George knew all these jazzy chords, because his father's friend knew all these old songs and taught them properly. George was obsessed with playing the guitar and did everything he could to learn."

He also picked up tips from his peer group. "At the Institute there was a guy called Colin Manley who was a very good guitarist," says Bramwell. "He could play Chet Atkins and The Shadows and The Ventures, and he showed George a lot of those tricks. He was a big influence on George and his playing. He became more than three-chord proficient. [Plenty of people could do] Lonnie Donegan or Bert Weedon *Play In A Day*, but he could play proper tunes."

For a long time Harrison was more interested in proficiency than creativity. He liked the detail: the specifications, the technical side of the instrument, the nuts and bolts, learning chord inversions. He was slow and methodical, and never a great improviser. Years later, pondering the idea that he might just, well, make something up, Harrison said, "Oh no, that's too mystical. I wanna know where we're heading."[6] "George was always very precise, he was that way all throughout The Beatles – very precise solos, very worked out," says Jackie Lomax, a contemporary in Liverpool's early rock and roll scene. "He could do the solo the same as Buddy Holly on the record, and so on. There was no blowing, there was no blues in it – you know what I'm saying? He was that way all the time, and that impressed me."

Nevertheless, he was self-deprecating about his talents. "George never thought he was any good," his mother said in the Sixties. "He was always saying that, telling me about all the people who were so much better than he was."[7]

Once you reach a certain level of proficiency, however, you want people to know. The skiffle boom, in full swing by 1956 and 1957, was the war babies' equivalent of punk. It required precious little proficiency: most songs were based around two or a maximum of three chords, and there was an encouraging DIY aspect to the rudimentary instruments. Skiffle's main practitioner, Lonnie Donegan, was "a big hero" to Harrison.[8] Presley might have been more impressive, Cochran may have been the essence of rock and roll when viewed in the flesh, but a lanky, adenoidal Anglo-Scot singing a decidedly ramshackle version of 'Rock Island Line' may well have been the first musician whose success suggested to Harrison that this was something he could actually do for a living.

★ ★ ★

It's tempting to overstate those earliest performances, to build them, brick by brick, into the wider narrative of The Beatles myth, and in doing so over-emphasise the significance of every chord and front room jamboree. In truth they were unremarkable, inauspicious and routine, the same tentative baby steps taken by millions of aspiring musicians before, at the time, and ever after. Even the name of the first "band" was appropriately generic: in the age of Brando and Dean, The Rebels was a moniker adopted by earnest young musical revolutionaries up and down the country. Harrison's version consisted of his brother Peter and school friend Arthur Kelly, who had stumbled on a guitar in someone's garage. All three played guitar, and a couple of other likely lads were recruited on mouth organ and that skiffle staple, the tea chest stand-up bass.

They played precisely one gig, at the British Legion club on East Damwood Road, just around the corner from Upton Green. It was an audition which became a public performance by accident when the headlining band failed to arrive. They played two songs – by some accounts, several times – and arrived back home breathless with excitement, a little ale on their tongues, and triumphantly clutching ten bob each.

It was nothing. It was everything. It was a start. The next morning Harrison talked proudly about what had happened the night before to the boy with whom he had recently struck up a friendship. Paul McCartney, nine months older, was in the year above him at school and also lived in Speke. It seems surprising that the pair hadn't at least spotted each other around the area. Bramwell recalls that "Paul used to come [out playing] occasionally, but his dad didn't let him out as often as our parents."

They were nearly neighbours, but their allegiance stemmed from being grammar school boys stuck out on the outskirts of town, travelling back and forth on the no. 86 bus every day on the long journey to and from the Liverpool Institute on Mount Street in the city centre. McCartney got on first, and Harrison hopped on at the next stop. It was during these two-hour round trips that the pair got to know each other and discovered not only that they both loved music but were also blossoming musicians. McCartney initially played trumpet. The first musical collaboration between the two was the unlikely combination of guitar and trumpet on 'When The Saints Go Marching In'. "On and on," Harrison laughed, "Always 'The Saints'!".[9] McCartney rapidly switched to guitar, and the two would make time to get together and play – "not in any group," said Harrison, "just listening to each other."[10]

Even after the McCartney family moved from Speke in 1957 to a new home in Forthlin Road, Allerton, about 20 minutes' bike ride away, the pair continued to meet at each other's houses. They mastered The Vipers 'Don't You Rock Me Daddy O', a hit early in 1957, dissected the records of the Everly Brothers and Buddy Holly, plonked around on a bit of Bach, and genially indulged the entreaties of McCartney's father, Jim, to play Gershwin's 'I'll Build A Stairway To Paradise'. It was a fast friendship but never quite an equal relationship: the age gap, which diminished as they grew older but never lost its significance, was especially pronounced at this time. "I tended to talk down to him because he was a year younger," said McCartney. "I know now that that was a failing I had all through The Beatles years. If you've known a guy when he's 13 and you're 14, it's hard to think of him as a grown up."[11]

But they were mates, and in time McCartney began to champion Harrison to the other members of the band he had recently joined. The Quarry Men were a skiffle group named after Quarry Bank Grammar, the local school attended by John Lennon, the 17-year-old leader of the band who operated a more or less revolving door policy of friends and acquaintances lurching in and out. People tended to be recruited because of specific abilities: pianist John Lowe was brought into the fold because he could play the intro to Jerry Lee Lewis' 'Mean Woman Blues'. Right now they needed a guitarist who could solo. McCartney, still fresh-faced himself and shot by nerves on stage, was prone to "sticky fingers"[12] at the crucial moment. Harrison, on the other hand, could play 'Raunchy', Bill Justis' 1957 instrumental hit which swiftly became his party piece. Impressed, McCartney made a case to the group leader. "I know this guy. He's a bit young, but he's good."[13]

The first meeting between Harrison, McCartney and Lennon has become another dramatic vignette to be overplayed in The Beatles movie. In reality, it was simply one of those things: it may have been in a chip shop, or at a local basement gig, or on the top deck of a bus, or at 25 Upton Green. Harrison couldn't quite remember, so it's unlikely anyone else can. What is significant is that, prompted by McCartney, he informally auditioned for The Quarry Men by playing 'Raunchy' and everyone was suitably won over. For Lennon, however, it wasn't just about the music. "George was the youngest, and it was obvious," says Tony Bramwell. "He looked very young, even younger than his years. John Lennon didn't particularly like him and didn't want him in the band. He regarded him as too young, a kid, but Paul was pushing for him." Says Bill Harry, who observed these opening skirmishes, "George did have a strong personality but he was a bit cowed in the presence of John Lennon, because John had this overbearing presence about him which seemed to intimidate people."

Few 17-year-olds relish the thought of having a 14- or 15-year-old tagging along beside them, the abrasive Lennon least of all. He felt Harrison's age would adversely affect the band's cool quotient by several degrees. "It was too much, too much," he said. "George was just too young. I didn't want to know at first. He was doing a delivery round and just seemed like a kid."[14] Harrison was very obviously doe-eyed around Lennon – "I was very impressed by John," he said[15] – and his alluring aura of reckless maturity. Lennon had already left school and was now studying at the Liverpool College of Art, had had sexual relationships, was drinking and fighting and very much his own man: aggressive, charismatic and unpredictable. Smitten, Harrison would often pop up at his house out of the blue. "He came round once and asked me to go to the pictures with him but I pretended I was busy," said Lennon, adding that "I didn't dig him on first sight."[16]

More exasperating was his habit of hanging around when Lennon wanted some private time with his new girlfriend, Cynthia Powell. To Powell, Harrison was like a particularly persistent and annoying kid brother. He would sometimes tag along when they went to the cinema, or appear whistling from around the corner when they were out for a walk. When she had her appendix removed and Harrison turned up at the hospital hot on the heels of her boyfriend, Powell burst into tears. Harrison was undeterred. To Lennon he said, "I think Cyn's great, but there's one thing wrong. She's got teeth like a horse."[17]

This kind of blithe disregard for social convention was not uncharacteristic. There was no gloss, no guile and no embarrassment in the way he approached people he liked and his embrace of new things. Just as he had no qualms about airing his sometimes cutting points of view, he would also offer friendship openly, defences down, particularly with people a little older and more worldly than he was. He formed an endearingly direct attachment to his future sister-in-law Irene, engaged to Harry and several years his senior. While his brother was off doing National Service he would amble over to her house uninvited and they would go on day trips, or get something to eat, or visit the cinema, or go to see Lonnie Donegan. He was, said Iris, a "funny little fellow,"[18] and not easily daunted by any sense of awkwardness.

In the end his place in the band came through sheer, stubborn perseverance as much as his repertoire of licks. He would show up at Quarry Men rehearsals, play 'Raunchy' or 'Guitar Boogie Shuffle' by Bert Weedon during a break in proceedings, and wait his chance or for someone else not to show up. Eventually he was officially in. Aside from his age and a certain gauche quality, he offered plenty of positives. In terms of stage presence he was no threat: he wasn't flash, and he was unlikely to hog any of the limelight. He was a nice guy, amenable without being dull, funny but committed, willing to throw in ideas but generally happy to defer. Musically, his attributes were obvious. He knew interesting chords and brought with him new material to expand the band's core repertoire of Elvis, Buddy Holly, Gene Vincent and Chuck Berry numbers: The Coasters' 'Young Blood' and 'Three Cool Cats', Carl Perkins' 'Your True Love' and some guitar instrumentals: 'Guitar Boogie', 'Ramrod' and the ubiquitous 'Raunchy'.

He was competent and organised, and his quiet diligence brought a steadying influence to the music. When he joined The Quarry Men, Lennon's guitar had only four strings. "George was the only one who could tune his guitar," says Bramwell. "John had no idea, he tuned it like a banjo."

Harrison also offered a readymade rehearsal venue. "My mother was a big fan of music and she was really pleased about me being interested in it," he said. "She was really happy about having the guys around,"[19] Mimi wouldn't have the frightful looking Harrison in the house so Lennon would often come around to Upton Green; Louise would, on occasion, give him and her son a little glass of whisky as they rehearsed. "George told me that the other Beatles would prefer to come to his parents' house rather than the others' houses to rehearse at the beginning," says Pattie Boyd. "These were the parents who understood the whole thing from the start."

They weren't just supportive, they were active agents in the few informal bookings The Quarry Men managed to get. After Harrison joined in February 1958 they could barely scrape any gigs together for a year and a half. "Ah, the legend of The Quarry Men," laughs Bramwell. "In the original line up they hardly ever played, and they were pretty poor." On December 20, 1958, the band played at the wedding reception of Harry Harrison and Irene, at 25 Upton Green. "Just one of those occasions where they thought they would practise on people and see what happens," recalled his elder brother wryly. "They were not exactly what the people there expected."[20]

A couple of weeks later, on New Years' Day, 1959, they played at the belated Christmas party of the Speke Bus Depot Social Club, of which his father was the chairman, at Wilson Hall in Garston. Harold arranged for the manager of a nearby cinema, The Pavilion, to come and see them, but during the interval the band got legless on free pints of Guinness and cider and made an abject embarrassment of themselves in the second set. Although Harrison was the one member to stay sober, his father was furious.

At this point they were a band more in their own minds than in any tangible sense. They would show up at art school parties, people's houses, the odd all-nighter where the only entry criteria was to bring a bottle of wine and an egg for breakfast. The Institute was next door to the College of Art, and they would duck in on their break, check out the girls, smoke and generally revel in an atmosphere of grown-up lassitude. Harrison tried his best to fit in. "I think [John] did feel a bit embarrassed about that because I was so tiny," said Harrison. "I only looked about ten years old."[21]

Bill Harry, a student at the art school and a close friend of Lennon and Lennon's friend Stuart Sutcliffe, recalls them playing in the college. "George and Paul used to come to our canteen, and to our Life rooms to rehearse. They were booked for the college dances, and we just referred to them as The College Band."

Their most pressing activities involved hanging around at clubs like the Jacaranda and doing the rounds of cafes, chip shops and pubs. But although to all intents and purposes nothing was happening, it was a potent, critical period which saw Harrison make the mental adjustment to being part of a group, reinforcing the idea that he could stand apart from the crowd. The rudimentary recording they made in July 1958 at Percy Phillips' house was part of the same evolution, an exercise in giving this inner sense of otherness some tangible shape – and what can be more real than making a record with your voice and guitar on it which you can hold in your hand? It might almost be enough to convince yourself, and perhaps others, that you're not completely wasting your time.

'In Spite Of All The Danger' wasn't released until 1995, when it appeared as part of the vast retrospective *Anthology* project, credited to McCartney-Harrison. Because of this – and another of their very earliest recordings, the Shadows-struck instrumental 'Beatle Bop', renamed 'Cry For A Shadow', which they recorded in Hamburg in 1961 and which was credited to Harrison-Lennon – there have been rather fanciful attempts to position Harrison at the vanguard of the band's early songwriting attempts. In fact, those early credits were primarily a case of smoke and mirrors. He had precious little to do with 'In Spite Of All The Danger'. "[It] was actually written by me, and George played the guitar solo," McCartney later said. "It was my song. It's very similar to an Elvis song. It's me doing an Elvis. I'm a bit loath to say which! It was one that I'd heard at scout camp when I was younger and I'd loved it."[22] Harrison was given a credit because he wrote the solo and, in their youthful naivety, the rest of the band believed this merited some kind of recognition. That kind of generosity wouldn't last long. "I can well remember even at the rehearsal at his house in Forthlin Road, Paul was quite specific about how he wanted it played and what he wanted the piano to do," said John Lowe, who played piano on the song. "There was no question of improvising. We were told what we had to play. There was a lot of arranging going on even back then."[23]

'Cry For A Shadow', meanwhile, was an instrumental which evolved in Hamburg after Lennon and Harrison had tried to play 'Apache' by The Shadows and failed miserably, "but we liked it and used it in the act for a while."[24] Neither song suggested a budding songwriting talent being thwarted by his two band mates. Harrison's early years are notable for the subsequent lack of scraps and juvenilia they have thrown up: there are no lost gems, discarded lines of poetry or lyrics, tantalisingly half-formed ideas or hints at classics in embryonic form. It was a lick here, a riff there, the occasional run of chords strung together. He wasn't writing in any meaningful sense.

★ ★ ★

28

The Quarry Men drifted, particularly after the death of Lennon's mother Julia in a car accident in July 1958. Louise remembered that for a time afterwards Harrison was "terrified that I was going to die next. He'd watch me carefully all the time."[25] She sent her son around to see Lennon and offer his condolences, a gesture which was appreciated, although a consequence of the death of Julia was bringing Lennon closer to McCartney, whose own mother Mary had died of cancer in 1956.

Initially, Harrison's friendship with McCartney had been the stronger. The pair went off on short breaks during the school holidays, hitchhiking to Hale Village, near Manchester, or venturing further afield, to Devon and then to Wales, heading north back to Merseyside after a couple of weeks. Photographs show them looking absurdly young, carefree and dapper. "We had hardly any money and we used to take haversacks filled with tins of Ambrosia creamed rice and a little portable meths stove for cooking with," McCartney recalled.[26] They stayed in cheap B&Bs and occasionally found a couple of girls to keep them warm.

For Harrison, sex was more of an idea – or perhaps a dull, persistent ache – than a reality. Although he was not short of girlfriends, it was all relatively demure. "I think he was quite innocent before he went to Germany," says Bramwell. "There might have been a bit of fondling..." When it came to girls, the connection was often musical. "My first girlfriend was Rory Storm's sister, Iris Caldwell," he recalled in the late Sixties.[27] Storm was the *nom de plume* of local musician Alan Caldwell, whose mother's house, known as Stormsville, was the hub of much social and musical activity. There would be songs and games in the front room, while in the cellar the family opened a skiffle club called The Morgue where bands, The Quarry Men among them, would come to play. Harrison would tend the cloakroom at The Morgue with Storm's younger sister Iris. "I met George at the ice rink when I was 12 and he was 14," she said. "Every night he would come around to our house after school. He used to play guitar and wanted to get into Rory's band [The Texans], but Rory said he was a bit young. We went out for ages, but it was a totally different concept to boyfriend and girlfriend today. We'd walk down Lilly Lane, which was like a lovers' lane, and kiss and cuddle."[28]

Her mother recalled, "George used to come and watch TV three times a week. He and Iris used to sit there holding hands. It was the first time either of them had ever taken any interest in someone of the opposite sex. At Iris's fourteenth birthday party, I remember George turned up in a brand new Italian-style suit covered with buttons. As in most teenage parties, they kept on playing kissing games and somehow or other, George and Iris always ended up together."[29]

"She was really nice and had cotton wool in her bra," said Harrison. "She probably didn't ever think she was my girlfriend. You never know when you're young; you just fancy somebody, or someone's in the same room as you, and you end up thinking they're your girlfriend."[30]

They split up after Harrison, never one of nature's born diplomats, insulted Caldwell's best friend at her birthday party, after rolling in late with Arthur Kelly. "We were playing a game where all the girls were named after fruit," she remembered. "The boys would come in and mum would ask if they wanted pears or apples, and whoever was that girl got a kiss. George didn't find his choice that attractive. When my mum asked, 'Do you want lemons or pears?' George just said, 'I'm not hungry'. I was so upset. He had insulted my friends. I said I never wanted to speak to him again."[31]

Later Caldwell dated Paul McCartney, saying "Paul was charming [but] George had something else,"[32] which seems a pithy observation on a number of levels. Harrison, like many a testosterone tormented teenager before and since, wished it had all been a little different. "In the late Fifties in England it wasn't that easy to get it," he recalled. "The girls would all wear brassieres and corsets which seemed like reinforced steel. You could never actually get in anywhere."[33] In strict contravention of Leonard Cohen's later advice, he invariably did go home with his hard-on, following hours of necking, groping and dancing. "Not getting any relief... that was how it always was."[34]

He was friendly with other girls, such as Jennifer Brewer and, later, around the age of 16, Ruth Morrison. Girls were important – especially if they looked like Brigitte Bardot, which in the late Fifties was regarded by Harrison as the Holy Grail of female attainment – but male friendships at that time tended to be more significant. During the band's hiatus the bond between Lennon and McCartney strengthened. They were brought closer not only through the dreadful shared experience of losing their mothers, but also through the creative union of writing songs together. It was a joint endeavour which placed them apart from Harrison, who was happier doodling alone, and it seemed to clarify something elemental regarding his role as the junior member of the trio.

He was keeping his options open. With The Quarry Men, "nothing seemed to happen for a while, I think we broke up,"[35] so he joined the Les Stewart Quartet. Musically, Harrison was a natural joiner. In the early days he was happy to fall in with whoever might have him. Later, as an exalted Beatle, he embraced the essentially democratic impulse of playing with the likes of Delaney & Bonnie, and later The Traveling Wilburys. Lennon and McCartney were wired a little differently. They were instigators, leading men. Harrison was always happier as supporting artist.

Les Stewart worked in the same butcher's shop where Harrison earned pocket money as a delivery boy. Stewart played banjo, mandolin and guitar. Harrison joined as guitarist and occasional singer, augmented by Geoff Skinner and Ken Brown. Harrison and Brown had learned that the Casbah Coffee Club, a new venue run by Mona Best in the cellar of her large Victorian house at 8 Hayman's Green, was looking for an act for its opening night. Brown hustled along and secured the Quartet a booking each Saturday for the next two months. Then, with 300 hundred tickets sold for the opening show, the band had a huge row and he and Harrison walked out on them.

"I had promised to have a band for the opening night, and here I was with only George," said Brown. "It's a start, but we needed to do something. It wasn't unusual then to have a group and no drummer, so that was okay. It was then that George told me about his two friends who he had played with, and he gave them a ring. That, of course, was Lennon and McCartney. I went to see Mo [Best] and told her what had happened and that George had a couple of friends who could help us out. So they came down and we had a few practices in the Casbah to be ready to open in a couple of weeks' time."[36]

The Quarry Men – now Lennon, McCartney, Harrison and Brown – were rapidly resurrected for a series of weekly spots between late August and mid-October. They shared a single microphone in a stifling basement room – it even looked like a sauna, with its lack of windows and sweating wooden walls – with minimal amplification. The Casbah was both a beginning and an end. They still didn't have a drummer and, after a falling out with Brown one night over their fee, by the end of the run they were reduced to a three-piece and had finally decided to dispense with the name The Quarry Men.

The obsession with music, combined with his longstanding disaffection, had effectively scuppered Harrison's schooling. In the spring of 1959 he flunked all but one of his mock GCEs (he passed Art), and when the time came to sit his final exams he didn't bother. By the summer he was 16, out of school and out of work, borrowing money from his parents. It was not easy to hold true to his course, although Louise was unwavering in her support. "His mother had always encouraged him in his passion for music, and if she didn't totally adore him she wouldn't have been so *colluding* with him in trying to get to what he wanted to do, which was just play guitar," says Pattie Boyd.

Negotiating the hopes and expectations of his father was a little more complex. When he had left his job as a seaman in the Thirties Harold had been unemployed for over a year before getting work on the buses. He viewed a "trade" as a passport to lifelong security. His youngest son, however, shuddered at the prospect. Never one for dutifully toeing the line of least resistance, he saw his father devote his life to the routine of a steady job, and while he respected his dedication he quickly decided that it wasn't for him. Harold had other ideas. When Harrison – the only one of the three boys to go to grammar school – showed no inclination to knuckle down, his father arranged for him to sit an entrance exam at the Liverpool Corporation. Harrison failed it. Eventually he did get a job, earning 30 shillings a week as an apprentice electrician at Blacklers department store in the city centre, where he learned to lay cable, clean the lights and keep a watchful eye on Santa's Grotto. This bolstered paternal hopes. With his two eldest sons now holding down steady trades – Harry as a mechanic, Peter as a panel beater – Harold's fervent wish was for Harrison to become a full-time electrician; the men could open a garage together and start a family business. For Christmas 1959 his father gave Harrison a set of screwdrivers and a tool kit. He looked at his sister-in-law Irene and said, 'Does he want me to stick at this? I think he does.'

It was relief, then, that by early 1960 some progress musically could be reported. Stuart Sutcliffe, a gifted artist with a mean-and-moody James Dean image, and one of Lennon's closest friends from the College of Art, was persuaded to spend a windfall on a bass guitar and join the band. He wasn't very good but he just about got by, and the four of them began playing under a slew of new names. They had already appeared at a regional talent show billed as Johnny & The Moondogs. Once Sutcliffe joined they were The Silver Beatals, the Silver Beatles, the Silver Beats. What's in a name? Surviving recordings from this time, many taped in the McCartney family bathroom, reveal a rudimentary band: shaky, provisional, enthusiastic but inconsistent, with no real dynamic. Harrison's guitar soloing on things like 'Cayenne' is both proficient and painfully stiff, every note carefully measured and placed in the song, although he hits a decent stride on Brenda Lee's 'I Will Always Be In Love With You'. "Colin Manley and Brian Griffiths were the best guitarists in Liverpool," says Bill Harry. "He wasn't as good as them, basically, but he was very diligent. You could tell that by the fact he took all the time and effort and patience and perseverance to learn the guitar."

As legend has since conveyed countless times, their modest big break came through an audition arranged by the squat, pugnacious Welshman Allan Williams, whom the band knew as the owner of the Blue Angel club and the Jacaranda cafe. A genial hustler on the local music scene, Williams was helping music agent and showbiz entrepreneur Larry Parnes find local talent to provide backing for his solo acts when they toured up and down the country; few artists in those days had their own band. The Silver Beatles rolled up. With disinterested stand-in drummer Johnny Hutchinson just about keeping the beat they were, said Harrison, "a bit of a shambles... pretty dismal."[37] They impressed Parnes sufficiently, however, to secure a seven-date tour of Scotland in May as the backing band for young hopeful Johnny Gentle.

With this glimpse of the big time in his sights, Harrison decided to ditch his job at Blacklers. He asked Peter's advice. His brother advised him to give it a go. His father, to his credit, also put aside his misgivings, agreeing that he was young enough to at least see what might happen by pursuing music seriously. In many ways Harrison carried all the unfulfilled dreams and longings of his family with him: his elder sister Louise had possessed a flair for drama but had not been able to pursue it, partly because her parents had baulked at her going to live alone in London to study acting; her mother had always felt an attraction to the spotlight. However much his parents worried, they did everything they could to help him achieve his goals. "This is what I was told by George in Hamburg," says Roy Young, the rock and roll pianist who almost joined The Beatles in 1962. "He said that his father was always saying to his children, 'Listen kids, whatever you do in life, never give up.' I saw George years later in a club and he put his arm around my neck and said, 'Never give up.'"

Aged 17, Harrison became a full-time musician, and "nine-to-five never came back into my thinking."[38] It's debatable whether it had ever figured much in the first place. Quitting Blacklers simply sealed the deal. Aware of Harrison's later tendency to wail about the "horror" of being a Beatle, Tony Bramwell suggests that, all in all, "it was probably better than being an apprentice electrician. It dragged us all out of Liverpool."

★ ★ ★

The Johnny Gentle tour was a short, sharp dose of reality. They toured draughty dance halls in the north of Scotland: Peterhead, Forres, Fraserburgh, as far from the hot spots as it was possible to travel without falling into the sea. They slept in shabby boarding houses and sometimes the van, argued, bonded, scuffled for their individual space in the band, were royally ripped off for the first time and made, by all estimations, an absolutely abysmal noise on stage. But it was a start, and after they came back to Merseyside at the end of May they felt a little more like a grown-up band and Harrison a little bit more of a man.

On their return things began to happen. With Allan Williams now acting as their booking agent, they spent almost all of June and

July playing around Liverpool with a series of temporary drummers, improving incrementally. Williams' initial impression of the band dynamic was that "George was the baby of the group. He didn't have much say within the band at that time. It was John's group and he looked up to John, but George was growing up very fast." Harrison recalls that around this time he began consciously to be aware of the need to assert himself a little more, to fight for every inch he could get in the band. "He was a very nice person but he wouldn't take any nonsense," says Williams. "Being the youngest and being told what to do, he had a bit of a chip on his shoulder."

Musically, the sudden sense of something bubbling away, albeit at a low heat, spurred him on; he acquired his first solid-bodied electric guitar, a sunburst Futurama III, an inferior copy of a Fender Stratocaster made in Czechoslovakia. Then came a sudden breakthrough. First, they got a booking in Germany. Next, they secured a permanent drummer. Mona Best's 18-year-old son Pete had been given a kit the previous Christmas, and had been playing with a band called The Black Jacks until they had broken up. Best was sounded out, offered the job, and joined the band now known simply as The Beatles on August 12, 1960. Less than a week later Harrison was in Hamburg – and life begins.

Be Here Now
May 1961, Hamburg

Mid-afternoon on the Reeperbahn. The sinful heart of Hamburg, which tends to come alive only as darkness falls, is restful. Roy Young, new in town, is looking for his Beatle friends. He walks the four flights to their basic attic room above the Top Ten Club to see if they are in residence. All is quiet.

"I knocked on the door, and as I walked in it looked empty," says Young. "There were four bunk beds in the room where they slept. There was no noise, and so I went over by the beds to look out the window to see if I could spot them in the street.

"Suddenly a pair of arms came out from under the sheets and wrapped around my neck. It was George. He squeezed my neck so hard he almost broke my Adam's apple. He was pulling me into the top bunk bed, hitting my head against the bed. He was drugged, stoned out of his head, or getting over a lot of drink. I had to almost break his arm to get loose. When he sat up in bed, I said, 'What the fuck are you doing?' He said, 'Oh, I was just playing, man, how are you doing?' He really didn't seem to know what he was doing.

"The funny thing is, you really couldn't see him in the bed, because he was so thin it was like there was no one in there under the sheets. Like a ghost."

Young pauses and laughs. "I mean, you went out to Hamburg and you were *done*. There was no going back."

CHAPTER 3

Life Itself

The welcome Hamburg extended to Harrison was unceremonious. His first ever home away from home was a filthy storeroom behind the screen of a seedy cinema at 33 Paul-Roosen Strasse, just off the Reeperbahn in St Pauli, the city's red light district. The Bambi-Filmkunsttheater, known as Bambi-Kino, specialised in sex films and old Westerns. After late nights playing in the neighbouring clubs, Harrison would wake up to the sound of frantic panting, or gunfire, galloping hooves and John Wayne. Outside he found a more modern version of the Wild West.

He shared his room with the rest of The Beatles. Shunted into an alcove off a dark corridor leading to the fire escape, it had bare concrete walls, no windows, no wallpaper, no heat and no furnishings except for two sets of bunk beds. It was lit by a bare light bulb. If he wanted to wash, clean his teeth or shave he had to do it in the washbasin of the ladies toilet, situated right next to their room. The stench from the lavatory was endemic, and Harrison didn't smell much better. "I never used to shower," he said. "I don't think we bathed or showered at all when we were first there."[1]

Everything before Hamburg was a rehearsal. He arrived in the city at the optimum age for adventure and was given daily lessons in every aspect of life, particularly the realities of sex, drugs, and, most significantly, rock and roll. Between August 1960 and the end of 1962 he grew up there. So did the band. "A lot of people say The Beatles were created in Mathew Street, which wasn't true," says Allan Williams. "They were created in Hamburg. Seven days and nights a week for months. It would make or break any band, and it made them. Before that, in Liverpool, it was church halls and things like that."

Hamburg was, as has often been observed, Germany's very own Liverpool: a large, northern, working-class port sited on the Jutland peninsula on the river Elbe. St Pauli could be found down by the river, a throbbing hub of prostitution, strip joints, sailors, soldiers, transvestites, gangsters, murky bars, nightclubs and cheap cafes. Something was always happening and it was usually vaguely nefarious. And if St Pauli was the heart of Hamburg's darkness then the Reeperbahn was the dark heart of St Pauli. Harrison went abroad for the first time and landed straight in the belly of the beast.

It was "the naughtiest city in the world"[2] and he loved it. Hamburg was "the best thing we'd ever seen," said Harrison. "Clubs and neon lights everywhere and lots of restaurants and entertainments. It looked really good. There were seedy things about it, obviously...."[3]

"He was very innocent when they went," says Williams. "There was nothing like it in Liverpool where, when the last tram left Lime Street, the town was dead. In Hamburg it was only beginning to happen at midnight. They were very exciting days, and very enjoyable."

By the summer of 1960 a thriving trade had developed in British rock and roll bands heading over to the clubs lining the half-mile strip of the Reeperbahn. Local impresario Bruno Koschmider had been at the vanguard of several slightly dubious characters making scouting trips across to the UK to find acts to fill his venues. One of the first were The Jets, led by singer and guitarist Tony Sheridan, who made such a splash that soon the nightclubs were bursting with British groups – good, bad and indifferent. "I guess we were, for a German audience, authentic," said Sheridan. "We didn't look at ourselves as being that authentic, but in Germany they certainly accepted us straight away, and that just exploded overnight. And this really got the Hamburg thing off the ground, because the moment some British artists were there, the whole scene started blossoming and clubs were opening on every corner, almost."[4]

One of the earliest groups to make the trip was the Jacaranda's steel band, led by Lord Woodbine, aka Harold Philips, a Trinidadian calypso singer and Liverpool promoter who was a friend of The Beatles. "I had a group working in Hamburg, and I thought The Beatles were good enough to go there," says Williams. "So I suggested it. I even drove them there. Hired a minibus."

Harrison arrived on August 17, 1960, having spent the past day and a half in a Green Austin van with no seats, jammed in with the rest of the band, now a five-piece following Pete Best's swift recruitment. Accompanying them were Williams, his wife Beryl, her brother Barry Chang and Lord Woodbine. They stopped off in London to pick up a tenth passenger, Herr Steiner, an Austrian working in the Heaven and Hell coffee shop on Old Compton Street who had been hired as Koschmider's interpreter. They headed for Harwich, caught the ferry to Holland, and finally crawled into Hamburg.

Harrison's entire presence in the country was predicated on a number of clear falsehoods. First, Williams "had to lie a bit to his parents, saying that Hamburg was like a holiday resort when it was actually the most evil place in Germany. Sin City. I talked to Louise and Harold because I wanted [The Beatles] to go over and they wanted to go over." The group didn't have time to get their travel visas organised in Liverpool, so they had to bluff their way onto the ferry at Harwich by pretending to be students going on a trip. Documents signed on August 25, 1960, show that the band did eventually get some official paperwork organised in Hamburg; however, Harrison's was fraudulent. "You had to get a visa so I lied, him being underage," says Williams. "I gave him a different date of birth, which wasn't very difficult. Nobody challenged it. I had to tell a few lies to get him over, I sure did."

Nobody studied Harrison's passport closely enough at that time to spot the error. But Koschmider, who had contracted the band to work at the Indra Club, knew that he was underage, which would have major repercussions. Not only was he not old enough to work in Germany,

Harrison was not even old enough to *be* in the Reeperbahn legally. The authorities enforced a curfew at ten o'clock every night – the police would come into the premises and it would be announced from the stage that anyone under the age of 18 must leave the area immediately. They would routinely check passports. Holding a guitar, Harrison was hiding in plain sight: somehow he was never spotted.

Within hours of arriving they were on stage at the Indra Club. Like his band mates, Harrison was paid 30DM (£2.50) per day, handed over every Thursday. It wasn't a fortune, but it was more than their fathers earned. For that sum they were contracted to perform for a total of four-and-a-half hours each weekday night between 8 p.m. and 2 a.m. On Saturdays it was six hours, between 7 p.m. and 3 a.m. Sunday hours were 5 p.m. to 1.30 a.m.

The Indra was the bottom of the ladder. It was small, with no dance floor and poor amplification. Nobody knew who they were and they started nervously, hunched around the microphone and huddling together for comfort. They had barely ever played for more than 20 minutes in the past. Now they had to claim the audience and hold them for an entire night, take requests, interact with them. Both Williams and Koschmider told them in no certain terms to loosen up and put on more of a show. Away from home and with nothing to lose, they soon shed their self-consciousness. They would eat and drink on stage, smoke, swear, mock the audience in pidgin German, throw food, argue. They became more confident through sheer necessity – with no template to conform to and a captive audience, they could take risks as long as the customers kept coming, drinking, dancing and paying. "Before Hamburg, we didn't have a clue," said Harrison. "We'd never really done any gigs. We'd played at a few parties, but we'd never had a drummer longer than one night at a time. So we were very ropey, just young kids. When we arrived we started playing eight hours a day. It was pretty intense."[5]

When the Indra Club was forced to close down after a month due to noise complaints, The Beatles were moved by Koschmider to the larger Kaiserkellar. A step up, the Kaiserkellar had a dance floor, a better PA, and another band on the bill to take some of the weight; although, because they had to start earlier and finish later, they ended up playing for six hours most nights.

The Beatles in Hamburg was a pure expression of experience – life as lived poured onto the stage. They grabbed material from anywhere, improvising, adding solos, sometimes extending songs to well over ten minutes, and mixing rock and roll standards with songs their parents loved and things they remembered from shows and films. "At first we played the music of our heroes - Little Richard, Fats Domino, Chuck Berry, Buddy Holly, The Everly Brothers, Ray Charles, Carl Perkins – anything we'd ever liked," said Harrison. "But we still needed more to fill those eight-hour sets. Eventually, we had to stretch and play a lot of stuff that we didn't know particularly well. Suddenly, we were even playing movie themes, like 'A Taste Of Honey' or 'Moonglow', learning new chords, jazz voicings, the whole bit. Eventually, it all combined together to make something new and we found our own voice as a band."[6] It was, he said, "probably the most important times of our lives. It was our apprenticeship, we worked so hard. We got a lot of rehearsing in, we got the group going."[7]

Their rapid progress was noticeable to everyone, not least the band themselves. It was like an old bone-shaker transformed into a throbbing motorcycle. Stuart Sutcliffe wrote a letter to his mother saying, "We have improved a thousand-fold since our arrival and Allan Williams, who is here at the moment, tells us that there is no group in Liverpool to touch us." That prophecy would soon come true. It wasn't just a significant period in their improvement as musicians. The early days in Hamburg fostered their sense of being apart – and a cut above – the more synchronised, synthetic bands of the day. "Rory Storm & The Hurricanes came out here the other week, and they are crumby," Harrison wrote home to Arthur Kelly. "He does a bit of dancing around but it still doesn't make up for his phoney group. The only person who is any good in the group is the drummer." The drummer happened to be Ringo Starr.

But Hamburg was about much more than music. McCartney, Sutcliffe and especially Lennon had already got their feet wet in the shallows of adult experience back home; Harrison, by contrast, found himself diving straight in at the deep end. Where the cast-iron underwear of Liverpool's young ladies had proved a staunch last line of defence, the spoils of Hamburg were considerably more accessible. Harrison lost his virginity in a bunk bed in an airless room with the other band members within touching distance. If they weren't watching, then they were acutely aware of what was going on, and applauded when he had finished. He was the last Beatle to cross the threshold, something which did little to counter his designated role as the band's babe in arms.

Sex was plentiful in Hamburg but Harrison later tended to play down some of the more lurid myths that grew up around their time there. It wasn't "one big orgy";[8] he didn't sleep with a stripper, though he couldn't account for anyone else's proclivities. None the less, it was a case of famine to feast, and the learning curve was steep. "Of course, all the girls threw themselves at the groups, especially if they were English," says Williams. "Most of them came back with a dose of gonorrhoea. They used to come to me and say that had a sore prick, so I'd make them piss in a glass. I'd hold it up and it would be full of what looked like Shredded Wheat. I'd have to send them to the clinic. I was known as the pox doctor. Not just The Beatles, all the bands got a dose. God, there are some stories. All those strippers and prostitutes. It was quite an education for George, even if he got a sore prick."

"You could go with a girl every night and get laid," says Roy Young, who befriended the band on their second stint in Hamburg in spring 1961. "Not one girl, you could find three or four in the one night. It was no problem. It was a dream land for young guys getting paid for playing music. George was very enthusiastic!"

There was also an abundance of the other accumulations of the rock and roll life. Living on a precarious diet of milk, cereal, pancakes, hamburgers and egg and chips, most of their money went on having fun. Harrison discovered the joys of whisky and coke. On weekends the entire populace of St Pauli seemed to be drunk and living reverse hours, getting up in the afternoon for breakfast and escalating steadily into the small hours. Harrison recalled "wandering around in the broad sunlight, pissed as newts, with no sleep."[9] To keep their energy levels high during shows they were given uppers by friends and the club's waiters and owners. Harrison, "frothing at the mouth," would sometimes stay awake for days after taking Preludin and Dexedrine. Lying in bed, he would "start hallucinating and getting a bit weird."[10] Presumably it was on one of these jittery morning-afters that he strangled Roy Young half to death.

★ ★ ★

He was almost grown. As if to prove the point, he even went through a physical spurt. "In the early days when I was still at school, I was really small," he said. "I sort of grew in height when we were away in Hamburg."[11]

Almost grown, but not quite. The Beatles became a gang in Hamburg, a tight-woven collection of friendships, volatile but united and protective of one another. The exception was the recently arrived Pete Best. Taciturn and rather remote, he tended to keep himself to himself and was less keen on embarking on hedonistic sprees. Among the other four it was more than just a musical bond. They "did everything together, really," says Young, and the shared personal experiences of sex, drink, drugs, and the intimacy that came from working and living together forged an awareness of their collective power as a unit that would – regardless of the numerous feuds and falling-outs which followed – never be breached. It also flicked a switch in their conceptual understanding of who they were and what they could be. "They were more intelligent than most of the other groups in the town," says Williams. "They had all had pretty good educations, while most of the other groups had no intellectual tastes. And they had arty friends."

Their "arty friends" were crucial in underlining and shaping this newfound awareness of their own otherness. Quite quickly after arriving in Hamburg they fell in with a graphic artist, Klaus Voormann; his girlfriend, art student Astrid Kirchherr; and Jürgen Vollmer, a photographer at the Institute for Fashion. Talented, hip, intellectual, upper-middle class and consciously apart from the crowd, they were in their early twenties and defined themselves as "Exis" after their interest in Jean-Paul Sartre's existentialist philosophy. All three became close friends with The Beatles, and both parties influenced the other. The

Exis' arty European aesthetic – which encompassed not just Sartre but Juliet Greco, Man Ray and the neo-Gothic writer and artist Jean Cocteau – met and merged with the band's love of American rock and roll imagery. In time their greased back Teddy boy haircuts would be replaced by forward-brushed Parisian cuts, and The Beatles haircut would be born. For now, they all ditched the conventionally "showbiz" lilac suit jackets that a neighbour of McCartney's had made for them as stage wear, and which they had brought in the van all the way from Liverpool. In their place came black T-shirts, leather jackets, black jeans, biker or cowboy boots. The Beatles, said Kirchherr, possessed "faces I'd always dreamt of taking pictures of, they had so much personality,"[12] and looking at the strikingly soulful photographs taken by Kirchherr and Vollmer, the band instinctively understood the spirit that was being reflected back at them.

The Exis put a modernist, arty, inclusive twist on their evolving brand of rock and roll. It impacted on some more than others. Lennon and Sutcliffe were their true muses. They never had much time for McCartney, which annoyed him. And Harrison? Harrison was more of a beloved man-child, a mascot, "little George, a lovely little boy."[13] If the kinship between The Beatles and their Hamburg friends was based on art, intellect and mutual attraction, sexual and emotional, Harrison was viewed in a more maternal fashion. They loved him for his sincere wonder at this new world he was in, for his guileless fascination with the beautiful Kirchherr in particular, with her short blonde hair and her black-painted bedroom, and for his dry, often self-deprecating humour. They didn't love him for the brilliance of his mind or the depth of his insights. "We never thought about George's intelligence one way or another when we were talking about them," said Kirchherr. "We knew he wasn't stupid, but he was just such a lovely young boy. He was just so sweet and open about everything."[14]

Kirchherr was 22 and Harrison still just 17. "She seemed so much older than me, and so grown up," he remembered.[15] Age enforces its own hierarchy, but it is not immutable, as McCartney was beginning to find out. At this stage, however, Harrison had neither the creativity, the confidence nor the frame of reference to force his way up the pecking order. The "slight superiority complex"[16] he felt from McCartney and particularly Lennon was not just about age; it had an underlying intellectual dimension. Like them, he had benefited from a good schooling, but he was not yet someone who thrived on the absorption and application of ideas. "George was the least educated, in a way, of the ones who went to grammar school," says Bill Harry. McCartney was now reading Steinbeck, Shakespeare, Dylan Thomas and, with his thoughtful, clear-eyed ambition, was starting to understand that all these influences could somehow feed into the band. Lennon was a discerning and ambitious reader, knowledgeable about art, and already writing songs, stories, plays and poems. He had a hustler's ability to straddle the Teds and the art school crowd. Sutcliffe was perhaps the most artistically gifted and self-aware of them all.

Harrison was far from stupid, but by comparison his creativity and intelligence was much rougher around the edges, a little less consciously artful. When they had backed Johnny Gentle in Scotland they had all chosen stage names; though tongue-in-cheek, each one is quietly revealing about how each member saw himself and their role in the band: McCartney, as "Paul Ramon", and Sutcliffe, as "Stuart de Stael", both wore their pretensions firmly on their sleeves. Harrison, by contrast, was plain old "Carl Harrison", after Carl Perkins. Lennon always maintained that he stayed as himself.

Harrison was sufficiently savvy to be aware of his status, and self-aware enough even to make jokes about it. Kirchherr gave each member of the band Christmas presents. After watching Lennon open an Olympia Press edition of a book by the Marquis De Sade, Harrison picked up his present, still wrapped. "What's in mine then, comics?" And although the garrulous, cocky McCartney may have asked Kirchherr and her friends most of the questions – Who's this, then? What's that? Why did you do this, love? – Harrison was listening intently to the answers. He was not daunted by the company he kept, or in any sense apologetic for being there. "He was calm," said Voormann. "He looked you straight in the face."[17]

Yet to everyone they met in Hamburg, on this initial visit and the next, he was very clearly the junior partner. His actions would often betray the fact. He would look up to the older musicians also playing the clubs, like Tony Sheridan and Roy Young, watch them and ask for advice. "He was the younger member of the family," says Young. "I almost treated him like a son, in a way, and he would treat you a bit like a dad. It was good for him to have people around him who gave him that comfort zone. He looked up to John, very much so. John and George were very close."

Sheridan fulfilled a similar role; part musical mentor, part big brother, although Harrison was a little wary of the older man's gift for trouble and his penchant for getting into fights. "We were all practically kids," said Sheridan. "It wouldn't be wrong to say we were kids, especially George, of course. George was very keen on learning anything he could. And there was practically nobody else that he could look up to, to get that sort of crash course training. I was slightly older, and so I knew a bit more, and I was into weird chords and things... One of the nicest things for me was to hear a particular chord or harmony that I'd taught George. To hear these suddenly coming through one of The Beatles' tracks... was quite gratifying, 'cause I knew where he got certain things... George was not looked upon by the others as being especially good, although they liked his image, and they liked the way he stayed in the background a bit."[18]

The Beatles was not an arena which encouraged mutual appreciation or moral support. It was a competitive environment and compliments were few. "In The Beatles his job was playing guitar," says Bramwell. "That was it. No one ever turned around and said, 'Bloody hell, that was a great bit!' It was just his job to do it. Nobody ever said he was amazing."

He wasn't amazing yet, or anything like, but the point stands. While Lennon and McCartney were already pushing out in front as the main singers, personalities and – soon – performing songwriters, Harrison's less ostentatious contributions were largely taken for granted. "The rivalry was between Paul and John," says Sam Leach, a prominent Liverpool promoter at the time. "They had their sights set on each other." Out on the sidelines, Harrison was not even given the compliment of being regarded as a threat. He and McCartney tended to argue about everything, not least, a little later, over who was going to drive. "I've got the keys," said McCartney. "Well, I've got the wheel," replied Harrison, sitting stubbornly in the driver's seat. It's a cute image but as a metaphor for the way the band functioned it falls well short. In truth, McCartney and Lennon had both the keys and the wheel, and Harrison was in the back seat. For a long time it was simply assumed that he was not going to be a part of The Beatles brains trust, or at the very most would be toiling on the factory floor rather than calling the shots in the boardroom. Hamburg solidified a complex dynamic and a defined internal hierarchy which would serve The Beatles through much of their career. It was subject to periodic revisions, alterations and allowances, but it would be many years before it truly began to shift.

Despite his youth and his low-key presence, those viewing Harrison from outside the band already sensed that his boyish exterior disguised inner depths. Vollmer felt "he had this melancholy feeling that I identified with,"[19] while Roy Young remembers him tuning in and out, moving between self-contained silence and more extrovert behaviour.

"He'd be sitting there and you'd think he was miles away, then he'd say, 'You know what we could do...' and bring up things. He was a deep thinker. He was quite a quiet character but there were moments when he would suddenly spark off and go into this loud, outspoken guy, and then – whoops – where has *he* gone? Back in his shell a bit. I think because he was younger he didn't feel he had the right to speak out quite as much as John and Paul, because they were older. Then again, having them around him all the time gave him an older outlook in life, and made him more grown up. I was guess he was leading a bit more of a life than the normal guy of his age, but the other side was: 'I'm not allowed to speak out because I'm only a young boy' – more of a psychological thing."

★ ★ ★

It was his youth that scuppered Harrison's first spell in Hamburg. At the end of October, in breach of their Kaiserkellar contract, The Beatles starting playing extra shows for another Hamburg promoter, Peter Eckhorn, at the nearby Top Ten Club. Eckhorn offered better money and a bigger PA. Koschmider – "Not a very nice man," says Williams with admirable understatement – took his revenge by informing the authorities that Harrison was underage, and "when he was found out he was more or less deported." The official notice read: "I the undersigned hereby give notice to Mr George Harrison and to Beatles' Band to leave on November 30, 1960. The notice is given to the above by order of the Public Authorities who have discovered that Mr George Harrison is only 17 (seventeen) years of age."

Though the band's travel expenses to Hamburg had been paid by Koschmider, their contract stipulated that the cost of the return trip was their own responsibility. It was left to Kirchherr and Sutcliffe to take a forlorn Harrison to the station – "little George, all lost" – and, like some orphaned Dickensian waif, fortify him with a bag of apples for the journey. He hugged them both – an atypically direct demonstration of affection, but one which he would grow into – and embarked on a 24-hour odyssey back to Liverpool, via Holland and London, by train, ferry, train, taxi and train again. He arrived bedraggled, a little fearful and thoroughly depressed. "He was scared to be by himself on such a long trip," Voormann recalled. "He was scared to fall asleep, in case 'somebody nicks my guitar.'"[20] It was a huge blow. Just as the band were stepping up a gear, the youngest member had ruined everything by being sent back to Liverpool – for being too young. It looked as if Lennon's qualms about having him in the band had been well founded.

For the first few days of his return he simply assumed The Beatles would find another guitar player and carry on without him. In addition, he had spent all his money getting home and had nothing tangible to show for his time there, other than his deathly pallor and skeletal frame. He felt, he said, "ashamed, after all the big talk when we set off for Hamburg. My dad gave me a lift to town one night and I had to borrow ten bob off him."[21]

His silver lining lay in the misfortune of his friends. Unknown to him at the time, McCartney and Best had also been thrown out of Germany for taking their revenge on Koschmider by starting a small fire in the Bambi-Kino after lighting a condom as a prank. It was hardly a towering inferno, but Koschmider was keen to see the back of them. Lennon also returned to Liverpool shortly afterwards.

Sutcliffe, who had fallen in love with Kirchherr, stayed on with his new girlfriend to study art. After being deported Harrison had written to him in Hamburg. There was no drama, and no ceremony. Typically, the talk soon turned to music and guitars:

"Dear Stu, I hope you are going on ok there with Astrid. I arrived ok (24 hours exactly), but spent a packet on porters, taxis, etc... If you aren't coming home for awhile, can you send some money to keep Frank Hessy* laughing. I want to get an Echo for Christmas, £34, or £6 down, the rest when Frank catches me, so if all my other stuff is up to dak [sic] I will probably be able to get it with no guarantee. I believe Gerry has one, only he ruins it by using it on every number. I bought Eddie's *Singing To My Baby* LP, 'Man Of Mystery', 'Lucille', 'Only The Lonely', 'Like Strangers', (Everly's new one), 'Perfidia', (Ventures new one), and may buy an instrumental called 'Chariot'."

★ ★ ★

After reconvening they were quickly back in business. The Beatles may have returned to Liverpool rather less than triumphantly, but they had become a new band in their time away. Gone was the stiff, rather woody amateurism of only a few months' earlier; in its place was a hard, lean, electric rock and roll band. Nobody was prepared for the change in their look, their sound, their confidence. Allan Williams put them in touch with Bob Wooler, a compere and booker on the dance-hall circuit, and on December 27, 1960, they played the Town Hall Ballroom in Litherland, billed by Wooler as "Direct From Germany". Loud, fast, cocky, muscular, and with that powerful sense of unity they had picked up overseas, "they were just amazing," says Tony Bramwell. "They were such a shock compared to what we listened to in those anodyne poppy days. This scruffy lot, jeans, cowboy boots, leather jackets, grubby T-shirts, doing rock and roll differently than we had ever heard it before."

★ Hessy's was a music shop located at 62 Stanley Street, at the corner of Whitechapel, in Liverpool.

Such was their strangeness, and such was their low profile before they went to Hamburg, several people came up to them afterwards and complimented them on how well they spoke English. "They didn't know us in Liverpool, and there was a big gig at the Town Hall [and] so many people really dug the band," said Harrison.[22] "We went down a bomb."[23]

Local promoter Sam Leach first saw them a fortnight later, at Hambleton Hall on January 10. "I knew them [from before they went to Hamburg] and they weren't very good," says Leach. "[Afterwards] you couldn't believe what they were like, the actual charisma coming from them in this horrible little hall, even the Teddy boys stopped fighting. You could see the charisma, and this incredible sound. It didn't go over your head, it went right through you."

As they got more bookings outside Liverpool they became a more professional unit, on and off stage. Neil Aspinall came on board as driver, roadie, human shield and all round helping hand, a role that would be finessed over the years but would remain essentially the same for the next four decades. A veteran of smoker's corner at the Liverpool Institute and a trainee accountant, the wiry Aspinall was a good friend of Pete Best (and would shortly father a child with Best's mother, Mona).

In Sutcliffe's absence, some reorganising was required. Both Harrison and Lennon refused to take on the bass; the former may have been the youngest, but the one thing that was not negotiable was his attachment to his instrument. He was also particularly against the idea of getting anyone new into the band, so McCartney switched from six strings to four, leaving Lennon to play rhythm guitar and Harrison to play lead. There remained a feeling, however, never quite shaken off, that McCartney was a Beatles guitar player in everything but name. Indeed, both the musical and personal dynamic of the band was partly defined by the fact that Harrison was a lead guitarist who leaned instinctively towards the solid, unflashy bottom line more common to a bassist, while McCartney was an exponent of a highly melodic and occasionally ostentatious bass style which made the kind of impact more traditionally associated with lead guitar.

As the sound was coalescing so was each distinct part. Harrison may not have been headline-grabbing but he was slowly becoming the right guitar player in the right band. "He wasn't that great a guitarist," says Leach. "He was good, I seemed to think he played a bit more rhythm than lead, but as a band together they were fantastic."

As a musician he was still learning, focused on getting his parts right, putting the emphasis on diligence rather than sparky creativity. "He was somebody who wanted to do everything perfectly," says Young. "He was very much like that." Williams agrees: "He improved every day. He was very meticulous, he took his playing very seriously." In 1961 Harrison ditched his Futurama III and bought his first Gretsch guitar, a 1957 Duo Jet. It cost him £75 and underlined the evolving air of professionalism.

Meanwhile, everyone in the band was given a shot in front of the microphone. In Hamburg Sutcliffe sang 'Wooden Heart' and Best battled manfully through 'Matchbox'. Harrison fronted several songs in the set but his voice wasn't yet his own. Always an imperfect and somewhat limited instrument technically, in later years it relied on its soulfulness for its impact, and his deep connection to the words he was singing. There was none of that in 1961. His version of Bobby Vee's 'Take Good Care Of My Baby' was merely competent imitation. Had it not been, he would have pronounced "curr" with a long, flat Liverpudlian vowel sound, just as he would a decade later on 'Beware Of Darkness'.

He could rustle up a decent rasp on his designated rockers – 'Roll Over Beethoven', 'Everybody's Trying To Be My Baby', 'Reminiscing', 'Sheila', 'Nothin' Shakin' (But The Leaves On The Trees)' – but, unlike Lennon and McCartney, there was little evidence of a distinct personality or any attempt at nuance. He seemed most at ease on the more jokey material: the Twenties novelty hit 'The Sheik Of Araby', which was still in their repertoire over a year later, and 'I'm Henry VIII, I Am', an old music hall number. Both had been recorded recently by Joe Brown, of whom Harrison was a big fan. In the Eighties they became neighbours and close friends. "'The Sheik Of Araby was rubbish," says Sam Leach, not without due cause, "But 'Henry VIII, I Am' was a good one. He sang that the first night I saw them. It was a novelty number, comic relief almost, but it was fun."

Harrison's voice was used to far greater effect on the three-part harmony singing which was already a significant factor in making their sound unique. "We'd always loved those American girl groups, like The Shirelles and The Ronettes," he said. "We developed our harmonies from trying to come up with an English, male version of their vocal feel."[24] "They were one of the few bands that had harmonies, and they picked the right stuff, like [The Marvelettes'] 'Please Mr Postman'," says Jackie Lomax. "If they hadn't had the harmonies in the background it wouldn't have made so much sense."

They were playing almost every night, and often afternoons, too. Their first appearance at The Cavern was one lunchtime in February 1961, after which the club rapidly became their second home. They played there almost 300 times during the next two-and-a-half years. It was a dank basement boasting a proud range of health and hygiene hazards, and their appearances at the Mathew Street venue came to define their time in Liverpool as a band; and not just retrospectively – this was history being made as it happened. It also shaped how each one of them was viewed as a distinct personality by their growing fan base, most of whom were female and who throughout 1961 became increasingly devoted: screaming, falling on their knees in front of the band as they played on stage, and splitting into fiercely competitive factions dedicated to a particular band member. Every Beatle had his own fan club. No one was left out, although sometimes it engendered a competitiveness which teased out jealousies and could become unpleasant. When Harrison discovered in 1962 that Lennon was sleeping with one of The Beatles' most dedicated fans, Patricia Inger, behind Cynthia's back, he was incensed. "When George found out about John and me he took it really badly," said Inger. "In fact, he slapped my face."[25]

Before his first trip to Hamburg, Harrison had been seeing Pauline Behan, who lived near him in Hunt's Cross. "George had a very nice girlfriend, it got quite serious but nothing ever came of it," says Williams. "She wasn't a tart or anything like that, but it just didn't happen." The pair stopped dating early in 1961 after Gerry Marsden got hold of Harrison before a lunchtime Beatles show in the Cavern and told him he was "in love with your girl". Given his escapades in Hamburg,

Harrison could hardly complain that Behan had been enjoying other company while he was away, but he dutifully gave her an ultimatum: me or Marsden. She chose the latter. They parted on good terms and saw each other frequently on his returns to Liverpool later in the Sixties.

He wasn't short of other options: backstage, after hours at the Blue Angel sipping a scotch and Coke, quick opportunities out of town. "By the spring and summer of 1961 girls quite literally seemed to fall at The Beatles' feet," Tony Bramwell remembered.[26] Harrison was not an obvious heartthrob. He was "still a spotty teenager who ... had the worst skin problems," said Bramwell,[27] and was not above plastering over his acne with Max Factor Panstick. But he was the guitar player in a popular band. That fact, aligned with his dark eyes, lop-sided grin, vaguely vampiric teeth, dry wit and youthful soulfulness, attracted many admirers. "All the girls wanted to mother him," says Leach. "He had plenty of girls. He was always the smartest, dress wise, and he was the funniest, in a dry sense. It just wasn't so obvious."

He wasn't shy of making a speculative approach, either. Long after he had split up with Iris Caldwell he was still chancing his arm. "When I was going out with Paul [McCartney] and we'd had a row, George would still phone up asking if he could take me out," said Caldwell. "I don't think there was any rivalry over me. It was all good-hearted."[28] Perhaps. Perhaps not. Remembers Leach: "When I got engaged, George said to my fiancée, 'If you pack in Sam will you go out with me?' She said no, but he was still always after her."

The confidence that comes from being a member of a band on the rise is a mighty thing. Each subsequent return to Hamburg over the next 18 months was a line in the sand, a measuring point of how far they had progressed in the intervening period. On their second trip, during which they were contracted to play Peter Eckhorn's Top Ten Club for three months between April and July 1961, billeted in the attic upstairs, they felt like old hands, taking newcomers under their wing. "They would tell you everything about Hamburg, what to do and what not to do," says Roy Young. "It was great information, because it was a pretty rough area, and you had to be careful." On stage, says Young, "they were pretty well-equipped, and they did stand out. They weren't really into writing their material then, but they were playing strange songs: I mean, 'Your Feet's Too Big' by Fats Waller – where did that come from? Their musical taste was extraordinary, really. And on stage George was coming out of his shell, for sure. He was quiet but he was full of fun and mischief."

Collectively, The Beatles could be trouble. Young had a car, and they were always trying to persuade him to take them to the beach. He declined, knowing that "if I got them in the car they would break it all up, because they were like that." One day they sent Harrison out as a decoy. "I got on the street and George was standing there, and he said, 'Hey Roy, why don't you and I go to the seaside? Come on, it will be just the two of us.' As we went down the street towards the garage there was John, Paul and Pete, they jumped out and grabbed me. I couldn't get out of it." When they got to the beach the band – fully clothed – jumped into the water, and later tried to push Young's brand new vehicle into the sea. "By the time we got back to Hamburg the car was completely wrecked."

During their second visit they made some recordings for Polydor Germany, backing Tony Sheridan, with whom they frequently played at the Top Ten Club. The results, made on June 22 on a converted stage at Friedrich-Ebert-Halle, covered no one in much glory. At the time, only 'My Bonnie' and 'The Saints', a ramped up version of 'When The Saints Go Marching In', saw the light of day on a single credited to Sheridan and The Beat Brothers. Harrison's fills on 'My Bonnie' are nervy and lacklustre, although he raises his game a little for the break, which is a rough prototype of the template followed by many of his early Beatles solos. The rest of the sessions were released after The Beatles became famous, including two songs recorded without Sheridan: 'Ain't She Sweet', sung by Lennon with a faltering break by Harrison, and their own 'Cry For A Shadow', the instrumental which had evolved after Lennon and Harrison had tried aping The Shadows and found that the tune veered off somewhere else. A lively surf roll with a catchy motif and a witty ending, it had charm but quickly ran out of both steam and ideas. They were not yet a recording band; enthusiasm far outweighed experience and expertise.

None the less their exploits were now being reported back home. The Sheridan session was front page news in the second issue of *Mersey Beat*, published in July, 1961. Had the band unearthed a new songwriting talent? "I mentioned that The Beatles had done an original composition by George Harrison," says Bill Harry. "That was the first mention in print of a Beatles original. When all the Lennon/McCartney stuff started coming out, I used to meet George at the Blue Angel club at night and every time I saw him I'd say, 'What's happened to your songs?' And he seemed a bit as if he couldn't get anything in with [John and Paul]. I'd go on and on to him: 'Why the hell aren't you writing songs?' He did one with Ringo but I don't know what happened to that. He told me he did write one." In those days, and perhaps for some time after, "he didn't push all that much," says Harry. "He was a person that really needed to be pushed, but he didn't really want to be pushed."

★ ★ ★

The manner of The Beatles' return in July from their second spell in Hamburg could hardly have been in greater contrast to their first. They played a crammed 'Beatles Welcome Home' session at the Cavern and continued to grow in popularity. On November 10, 1961, they headlined Operation Big Beat at the Tower Ballroom in New Brighton, billed above Gerry & The Pacemakers, Kingsize Taylor & The Dominoes, Rory Storm & The Hurricanes and The Remo Four. Around 4,300 fans showed up. By this point, says Jackie Lomax, "I don't think anyone would have doubted that they were the best band in Liverpool." And the biggest.

At the same time they came to the attention of Brian Epstein, a 27-year-old local businessman who ran the record department in his family's North End Music Store (NEMS) in Liverpool. He had become aware of the band through *Mersey Beat* and local promoters like Sam Leach selling tickets to their shows, as well as the recently released 'My Bonnie', which he stocked in NEMS.

Epstein was well-off, well-heeled and almost terminally bored. He detected something intangible in The Beatles which sparked his interest, the same kind of rough-hewn, soulful yet sexually resonant otherness the

Exis had picked up on. He wasn't at all sure if he liked the music, but he was magnetised by them. In November 1961 he came to see the band at The Cavern and visited backstage afterwards. "And what brings Mr. Epstein here?"[29] asked Harrison, whose first impressions were of a "posh rich fellow."[30] Further meetings were arranged. At one, when Epstein expressed some consternation at the news that McCartney was going to be late because he was having a bath, Harrison piped up: "He may be late, but he'll be very *clean*." They might have had more in common with the local movers and shakers – Allan Williams, Sam Leach, Bob Wooler – who laid claim to them at various times, but they knew that Epstein was the kind of man who could take them places. Because of his age, Harrison needed parental consent to sign the five-year contract which eventually made Epstein their manager in 1962.

The band which made its third trip to Hamburg, from mid-April to the end of May 1962, was an impressively professional proposition. They not only had a manager, they were playing original songs like 'I Saw Her Standing There' and 'Ask Me Why' to packed audiences at the Star Club, "a big place, and fantastic because it had a great sound system," said Harrison.[31] It was a bittersweet return. Stuart Sutcliffe had died of a brain haemorrhage on April 10. He had visited The Beatles in Liverpool shortly beforehand, and had come around to Upton Green. Harrison remembered later that "there was something really warm about his return, and in retrospect I believe he was finishing something... We didn't go to the funeral. That was it."[32] He and Lennon did, however, visit Kirchherr in her Hamburg flat when they arrived in Germany, and Harrison offered quiet support and understanding to Lennon, the Beatle closest to Sutcliffe, who was devastated by his death.

The fact that they were staying in a hotel on this trip rather than a glorified broom cupboard was commensurate with their growing status back home. They had topped the *Mersey Beat* poll of best local bands, published on January 4, 1962, just three days after they had made an audition tape for Decca at their studios in West Hampstead, in north London. This was Epstein's first bold move.

The tape included some of the songs Harrison was currently singing in their stage act including 'Three Cool Cats', 'Take Good Care Of My

Baby' and, bizarrely, 'The Sheik Of Araby'. It was essentially the pick of their Cavern set, and showed minimal awareness of how the band should be presented as a recording act. They set up their amps, played live, bashed through 15 songs in little more than an hour, and headed back out into the snow. Nobody had any inkling that it was going to be their big break, and Decca duly turned them down. In moments of disappointment, Harrison was often the main motivator. "There was a feeling we all had, built into us that something was going to happen," he said. "I felt extremely positive."[33] Lennon later recalled that "it was only Brian telling us we were going to make it – and George."[34]

The rest of 1962 was a blur of shows brought into focus by their repeated returns to The Cavern, which drew them back again and again. The major drama within the band was the sacking of Pete Best in favour of Ringo Starr, an act of treachery for which many observers at the time implicated Harrison in a leading role. "George was very instrumental in that," says Bill Harry. "It was a bit of a dirty trick, and it was mainly George. He was the main person, and he got Paul to back him up. They knew Rory Storm & The Hurricanes [the band with which Starr drummed] from the clubs and after hours drinking, and of course in Hamburg." Harrison later admitted that "I'd been instrumental in talking them into getting Ringo into the band."[35]

There have been all manner of conspiracy theories over the reasons behind Best's dismissal. There were rumblings that they were jealous of his smouldering good looks and the attention he got from their female fans, but no Beatle was particularly deprived on that score. In the end it seemed have been partly about his playing, but mainly about his personality.

In terms of performance, the stakes had been raised. It was no longer just about keeping the shopgirls and office boys at The Cavern happy; it was about selling their sound. After the Decca rejection The Beatles had finally signed a record deal with EMI offshoot Parlophone in May 1962, and on June 6 had recorded their first session for the label with EMI producer George Martin. Martin raised some concerns about Best's drumming. Although at the time it was standard practice to use a session drummer in the studio (indeed, even after Starr joined, Martin would use Scotsman Andy White as the drummer on the re-recorded version of 'Love Me Do', released on The Beatles' first album), his reservations did not go unnoticed by the band. These may have confirmed their own misgivings about Best. Roy Young, who ended up playing piano with The Beatles in 1962 and was allegedly invited by Epstein to join permanently, recalls that "George was a perfectionist, and Pete couldn't play the way George wanted the music to be."

The crux of the matter was the fact that, as Sam Leach says, Best "was a good drummer, but he wasn't a good Beatle." The band were already well aware of the importance of their personal chemistry, and Best had never really added much to the equation. "Pete was too taciturn, he didn't have much to say," says Harry. "Ringo had this great sense of humour, he was very relaxed. George really enjoyed Ringo's company, and he was one of the top drummers." Says Bramwell: "Pete was never with the other three as one of the lads. He would go home straight after the shows, we'd all go for a drink or a Chinese meal and Pete would go home. Ringo was always around the clubs at night, drinking and chatting and being funny. He was a more natural Beatley person."

It was left to a reluctant Epstein to do the dirty work, telling Best on August 16, almost exactly two years after he had joined, that "the lads don't want you in the group any more." The Beatles fulfilled their gigs for the next two nights with Johnny Hutchinson, before recruiting Ringo Starr for his first show, at Hulme Hall, Birkenhead, on August 18. The picture finally snapped into focus. "They could be very tough and ruthless," says Allan Williams, who had fallen out with the band after they refused to pay him his commission on their second trip to Hamburg. "There was no sentiment in them."

Harrison didn't escape scot-free for his part in the reshuffle. Epstein had arranged for The Beatles to be photographed for the cover of *Mersey Beat* just prior to leaving Liverpool airport on September 3 to fly to London for their next EMI session. When the picture ran, Harrison could clearly be seen sporting a gleaming black eye. "I was there the night George got a black eye," says Jackie Lomax. "Eppy fired Pete and the band turned up with Ringo to play The Cavern – we were all in the dressing room and this fairly big lad came to the door and said, 'Where's

Pete Best?' And George said, 'Oh, we sacked him.' And this guy hauled off and punched him right in the face, and gave him a big black eye that was swollen by the time he was on the stage." Bill Harry recalls it was "Bruno, a West Derby guy who liked Pete. I think people knew that [George] was one of the main architects of Peter's dismissal. We ran a piece in *Mersey Beat* saying that he had gone around to Ringo's [house] to ask if he would join the band, but Ringo had gone to Butlins."

There was significant disquiet from fans over Best's departure, but it didn't last long. George wrote to one: "Ringo is a much better drummer and he can smile – which is a bit more than Pete could do. It will seem different for a few weeks, but I think that the majority of our fans will soon be taking Ringo for granted." And he was right. "Ringo was a member of the band," said Harrison. "It's just he didn't enter the film until that particular scene."[36] It was fate.

★ ★ ★

By the time of their final two trips to Hamburg, playing the Star Club in the first two weeks of November and again in the last two weeks of December 1962, Starr had bedded in and they had released 'Love Me Do', their first single on Parlophone, on October 5. It progressed, slowly and erratically, to a chart peak of 17 in late December.

If Harrison was on his way to becoming a fledgling pop star on a national scale, his status as a local hero was already sealed. For his mother it was a special kind of vindication, and she took to the reflected glory like a woman who has spent her entire life waiting for the opportunity. She was often seen in The Cavern, sitting with the fans and singing along. On the sole occasion Lennon's aunt Mimi was persuaded to visit the club she crossed swords with Mrs Harrison, who nodded at the stage and smiled, "Aren't they great?" "I'm glad someone thinks so," came the tart reply. "We'd all have had lovely peaceful lives but for you encouraging them."[37] One imagines Louise felt inordinately pleased that Mimi might think so.

In Hamburg, Harrison now stayed in hotels and had his own room. On stage, too, the gradual gentrification of The Beatles had already begun. Epstein had taken them out of their leathers and put them into shirts, ties, and matching suits. For The Beatles as a live band, the best had already been and gone. "Our peak for playing live was in Hamburg," said Harrison. "At the time, we weren't famous and people came to see us simply because of our music and the atmosphere we created."[38] In many ways life would never be quite so simple, or so much fun, ever again.

Be Here Now
Bournemouth, August 20, 1963

The first song George Harrison writes for The Beatles is pieced together in a hotel room during a six-day, 12-show run at the Gaumont Cinema in Bournemouth. Dressed up as a meat-and-potatoes broken-hearted lament composed by a man with a bad head cold, this "exercise to see whether I could write a song"[1] has an unmissable subtext. Arriving in August 1963 as the insatiable appetite of Beatlemania is really beginning to bite, 'Don't Bother Me' is the first of many acts of equivocation by the author concerning the reality of fame: "Don't come around, leave me alone, don't bother me," he sings, and, more pertinently, "I know I'll never be the same".

It is not, as Harrison would quite quickly acknowledge, a very good song. But as with all of his most memorable work with the band it is at least a song one senses is written out of sheer necessity, rather than as an opportunity to chase down and snare some idle, trifling thought. Harrison would never be much inclined to float off and write about "newspaper taxis" or "Maxwell's silver hammer", but he would always be rather adept at writing about himself.

"If I was going to write a book about George I would print out every lyric he ever wrote, and I guarantee you would find out exactly who he was," says Glyn Johns. "Beginning with 'Don't Bother Me'. It's all there, as plain as plain can be."

Bournemouth doesn't easily lend itself to a destiny-shaping role in The Beatles story, but it plays its part. Harrison is not the first Beatle to write Beatles songs, but he is the first Beatle to write songs about *being* a Beatle. Sometimes subsequently it would feel as if he could write about little else. Few, if any of them, are lit from within with a sunny sense of joy and gratitude. Even now, when life is filled with fun and laughter, the clouds seem to be hovering.

CHAPTER 4

Beatle: Red

Fame came as a friend. Later it would orchestrate a mugging, later still a mauling, but following the release and minor success of 'Love Me Do' Harrison was in the sunny uplands of his life as a Beatle. The thrill of making music – and money – and the experiences it yielded far outweighed any potential negatives.

His part in the recording of 'Love Me Do', a modest piece of work to begin with, had been negligible. George Martin had broken down the song in the studio and pieced it back together again, asking Starr to sit out on the re-recording and paring down Harrison's parts to a bare minimum: singing backing vocals and strumming one of the two Gibson J-160E acoustic guitars that he and Lennon had recently acquired from Hessy's. The simple hook came courtesy of the foggy harmonica blast and McCartney's melody line on the title phrase.

George Martin would take some convincing of Harrison's attributes as a musician. Famously, the guitarist initially made an impression by other means. When the scrupulously well-bred producer attempted to put the band at ease in the studio by asking them to "let me know if there's anything you don't like," Harrison responded, "Well, I don't like your tie for a start." The first of many oft-repeated Beatles one-liners to go down in the annals, this one may even have happened.

It set the tone for an extraordinarily bountiful working relationship which was to last for the next seven years and which would, from that pointedly humorous start, be a meeting of equals. The Beatles would be no one's subordinates and, similarly, Martin was there to do much more than merely press the buttons.

In early October Harrison stayed up late at Upton Green to listen to 'Love Me Do' on Radio Luxembourg and "went shivery all over, [it was] the best buzz of all time."[1] He was in that happy stage of life defined by a series of firsts, the golden – and by definition unrepeatable – period when nothing feels tired and no one feels jaded: the first flush of success and attention, the first record, the first big interview, the first broadcast. In February and March 1963 The Beatles embarked on another landmark, their first ever national tour, supporting 16-year-old pop singer Helen Shapiro around England. Harrison spent his 20th birthday performing at the Casino Ballroom in Leigh, Lancashire, and would very probably have chosen to be nowhere else.

By the end of the tour Shapiro was still closing the show but the momentum had switched. Having started propping up the bottom of the bill and opening the concert, come early March The Beatles were closing the first half and had become headliners in all but name. Their second single, 'Please Please Me', had reached number one on February 22, sealing their status as bona fide national pop stars and "the most talked-about group on the British beat scene."[2] Even at this modest altitude, they had already begun to feel a reduction in the air pressure: the crowds at the stage door were growing and they had to wait in the car while a path through them was cleared. Their visits to British towns often left behind visible collateral damage, while the screams that greeted them when they appeared on stage grew louder and more uninhibited.

In comparison to 'Love Me Do' Harrison was much more prominent on 'Please Please Me'. His guitar riff was written to order when George Martin requested he come up with something more potent to hold the song together. Played on one of the Gretsch Country Gentleman guitars that became his signature instrument during the early years, it is the first great Beatles hook. He and McCartney also contribute the rising, punchy "come on!"s which bring each chorus to its breathless climax.

The song gave its title to their debut album, recorded at Abbey Road on February 11 during a break in the Shapiro tour. Eight of the 14 tracks on *Please Please Me* were Lennon-McCartney originals. Harrison's most visible contributions were his two lead vocals, on 'Chains' and 'Do You Want To Know A Secret'. The former, a song recorded by Little Eva's backing band The Cookies the previous year, was one of Gerry Goffin and Carole King's less memorable works, and its inclusion on the album was the sign of a band plucking filler material rather randomly from their current live set. The whole thing is sharp and shrill where the original is warm and loose, and Harrison's vocal is committed but ragged.

'Do You Want To Know A Secret', which bore a passing resemblance to The Stereos' 'I Really Love You', a song he would record nearly 20 years later on *Gone Troppo*, was given to him to sing because, said John Lennon, "it only had three notes and he wasn't the best singer in the world."[3] The evidence provided by his wobbly, rather weedy falsetto tends not to contradict Lennon's ungenerous view. Indeed, Starr's stirring lead vocal on 'Boys' raises more heat, as does Harrison's solo on the same song, driven on by the drummer yelling, "All right, George!"

It was 12 hours' work. The studio was a brief pit stop from relentless touring. After ending their dates with Shapiro they went straight out again later in March, with Chris Montez and Tommy Roe, when Harrison sang 'Please Please Me' for three shows while Lennon recuperated from 'flu, and then again in May with Roy Orbison. During that brief window their first album was released, staying in the Top 10 for 62 consecutive weeks. 'From Me To You' became their second number one single.

The Orbison tour was Harrison's first encounter with his future fellow Traveling Wilbury. They talked country music and, it transpired, also both enjoyed a lie-in. "We missed the bus a lot," Orbison later recalled. "They left without us."[4] Lennon's offhand remark to a journalist that Harrison liked jelly babies (another subtle piece of rank-pulling, perhaps?) led to him being deluged by notes and gifts from fans, and showered by the sweets on stage. Fun at first, but an enormous pain when it was still happening a year later and he had to firmly ask a journalist to print his request for fans to please – *please* – stop throwing them.

Around this time the human shield surrounding the band hardened. Mal Evans, the giant doorman from the Cavern, was hired full time to bolster Neil Aspinall's position as stagehand, roadie, driver, dogsbody, all-round human buffer zone and, very often, post-show procurer of female company. The pair became the first line of defence for the remainder of The Beatles' lifespan, and in certain scenarios long after.

"At first, when we went out on the road as a famous group it was good fun," Harrison said.[5] Travelling around the UK, he would usually room with Lennon, twin beds in modest digs. They would eat badly at roadside cafes, go for a Wimpy after the concert, perhaps stay up for a couple of drinks in the hotel bar. Girls came and went, of course, but the Sixties were not yet swinging. Yet there was a sense of excitement and camaraderie as they each observed their trajectory and tried to make some sense of it.

In between the Montez and Orbison tours Harrison had managed to snatch a holiday in Tenerife with McCartney, Starr, Astrid Kirchherr and Klaus Voormann, staying at a house belonging to Voormann's parents. McCartney recalls, in the first flush of something like stardom, being annoyed because nobody on the Spanish island knew who they were. Be careful what you wish for, might have been the lesson. In photographs Harrison is a beach Beatle: white shirt on, shades in place, skinny white legs disappearing into black swimming trunks, ciggie constantly on the go, playfully trying his luck with the blonde, beautiful Kirchherr.

He was free from Liverpool, striking out and savouring the freshness of it all. Though nominally still living with his family, sharing a twin bedroom with Peter, the amount of touring Harrison was doing, and the frequency with which he had to be in London to record, tape TV and radio shows, or appear in concert, required a base in the capital. For the first half of 1963 The Beatles could be found living in the Royal Court Hotel in Sloane Square, or the President Hotel, just off Russell Square, or the Russell or the Imperial on the square itself. This was old school London, genteel and slightly scuffed at the edges, and a different world entirely from Liverpool.

When an opportunity presented itself he would try to get back home, though there had been changes there too. The Harrison family had recently moved to 174 Macket's Lane near Woolton Golf Club. It wasn't far from Speke but it was a more modern and upmarket address, and was soon beseiged by fans. When he came home Harrison would move around on his hands and knees to avoid being spotted through the window. His father put up a blackout blind in the front room.

Ringo Starr quickly noticed that his family "treated me like a different person" after The Beatles initial success.[6] A similar thing, almost inevitably, happened to Harrison. "My family changed, but in a nice way," he said. "They were so knocked out with the whole idea of what was happening... everybody likes success, but when it came on that scale it was ridiculous."[7] Although he maintained in 1964 that "I haven't grown away from my parents at all,"[8] the whole family began to look at him in a different light. He had always been the golden boy. Now that he seemed to have fulfilled that promise on a national scale he belonged to everyone, and there was a palpable shift in perception. Their worlds began to orbit around his sun. "In some respects, honestly, they had the same kind of reaction that other people had," says Chris O'Dell. "He had gone on and done all this amazing stuff, so to some degree he held the power." In 1964 he told his father he would pay him three times his current weekly wage to stop working. Harold didn't have to be asked twice. Shortly afterwards he and Louise left Liverpool, moving into a bungalow with a substantial garden which Harrison bought for them in the village of Appleton, near Warrington.

While still at Macket's Lane, when her son was absent, rather than shoo them away or hide behind the net curtains, Louise welcomed the fans into her home. They became almost extended members of the family, cooking in the kitchen, helping out with the ironing (they were especially keen to do Harrison's shirts) and tidying up. She would invite some of them into his bedroom, showing them the contents of his wardrobe and giving them tokens as gifts. The quintessential hands-on mother, she embraced his stardom with a zeal which bordered on the disquieting. "The family used to come around the [*Mersey Beat*] office and [George] did some radio shows with his mum from The Cavern," says Bill Harry. "His mum would reply to all their letters personally, hundreds and thousands of them. She gave out photos of him as a kid. She was just a very proud mother." Across the Atlantic, long before The Beatles made it to the States, his sister would be badgering local DJs to play her brother's band.

Harrison himself hadn't changed much. He was still largely without airs and graces, happy to help those he liked whenever he could, and bluntly dismissive of those he had little time for. When home he would take out family and old friends in his first car, a dark blue Ford Anglia, swiftly to be replaced by newer, far more expensive models. They would head off on day trips to the Transporter Bridge, which linked Runcorn and Widnes, or to the pretty town of Frodsham, or other local beauty spots. "When they first cracked it George still used to come round to our house and take my mum out for a drive, take her to Chester for tea or something like that," says Bramwell. "Very sweet."

In the city he would visit old haunts like the Blue Angel club, and perhaps check in on the girlfriends he regarded with affection and treated with kindness and gentle civility, no matter what he got up to when he was away. But already Liverpool was too small, and many diehard fans resented The Beatles' success. They couldn't go to the pubs, or watch other bands because their safety and privacy could no longer be ensured. Everything had to be run past Epstein for approval. Though they had long since outgrown it, they kept their promise to play one final gig at The Cavern on August 3. Not long afterwards they all moved to London, sharing flat "L" at 57 Green Street, Mayfair, near Hyde Park, for £45 a week. The major talking point was the fact that they had a bathroom each.

Harrison wasn't remotely domesticated. The couple who lived downstairs would cook for him, while the floor of the flat was strewn with overflowing ashtrays and scattered record sleeves. Music would play constantly from the hi-fi in the corner. He would wake late, potter around, then head out for lunch. Already he was described as "looking around for fans and seems both annoyed and pleased when one of them finally asks him for his autograph in Park Lane."[9]

Lennon, now married to Cynthia Powell and the father of a baby son called Julian, and McCartney, who had moved in with the family of his new girlfriend Jane Asher, soon departed Green Street. Harrison and Starr weren't far behind. Late in 1963 Brian Epstein bought the top floor apartment of Whaddon House, a five-storey modern block in William Mews, a small, secluded street near Harrods in Knightsbridge. In the spring of 1964 Harrison and Starr followed him, moving into Flat 7, a fourth-floor apartment in the same building.

London, for McCartney and Lennon, fostered the next phase of their artistic development: new plays, foreign films, modern art galleries, writing, reading, hanging out at the new satirical hotspot, The Establishment club. Harrison did not tend to join them in their discussions on Cartier-Bresson, Norman Parkinson, Colin Blakey, Peter Cook and Jean-Luc Godard. He was not a particularly active participant in what he described as their "intellectual phase."[10]

For Harrison the capital meant the Ad Lib and Annabel's, a silver E-Type Jag, girls, a smart West End pad and four good bespoke suits. There is a wonderful innocence, a fresh and honest relish, to those earliest days of fame. In interviews in the music papers McCartney and Lennon are by far the dominant voices. Harrison, when he speaks, is both funny and absolutely straight. There is no side, no try-too-hard regard for what impression he should be making or what image he should be projecting. A 'Life Lines' piece in *NME* in February 1963 ran the rule over the personal preferences of each Beatle. Harrison reveals that his ultimate ambition is to design a guitar. His favourite food is lamb chops and chips, his favourite singers Little Richard and Eartha Kitt. His favourite actress is Brigitte Bardot (but of course), while Duane Eddy and Chet Atkins get special mentions as musicians. For hobbies he wrote "driving, records, girls." Not yet quite 20, he was young and acted even younger. In another early interview he talked about how much he enjoyed go-karting and playing "gear" practical jokes with Gerry Marsden.[11]

These were the sincere and unsophisticated expressions of a man whose only responsibility in life at this point was to play guitar in The Beatles and be rewarded handsomely for it. His ambitions were modest, indeed almost the stuff of infant story books: a house with a swimming pool, a bus for his father, a fancy car. Then again, he also exuded grounded common sense. He indulged in shopping sprees but would like, he said, "to invest money and perhaps branch out in different show business ventures."[12] Any sense of unease was only faintly visible around the edges, and then only really apparent in hindsight. By August 1963 he is already dreaming of "a bit of peace and quiet. Sitting around a big fire with your slippers on and watching the telly. That's the life!"[13] It was a joke but also, as it transpired, not a joke at all, and a rather poignant attempt to cling on to some semblance of the life which was rapidly disappearing in the rear view mirror as he was carried at top speed in the opposite direction. By the end of the year it would have all but vanished completely.

★ ★ ★

Beatlemania was not an instantaneous affliction. It came in a series of escalating waves. It began to build seriously with 'She Loves You', recorded on the first day of July 1963 and released in mid-August, spending all of September at number one. It was The Beatles' motherlode in 140 seconds: the thrillingly irresistible "yeah, yeah, yeah" chorus, sung in lusty unison in the manner of a group of friends returning home late from the pub; the sassy sixth ringing out from Harrison's guitar; the daring falsetto "ooohs" accompanied by the visual hook of Harrison and McCartney shaking their mop tops with comic abandon as they sang them. The combined impact captured what writer Jonathan Gould described as "a kind of common voice that was expressive of The Beatles' own collective persona; the musical equivalent of an editorial *we*."[14] It cemented in sound the sense that The Beatles were, in Mick Jagger's phrase, a "four-headed monster", of one mind and almost mystically unified. This subtext coursed through 'She Loves You', and it was an immensely powerful and persuasive one. It changed everything.

"'She Loves You' was when it really exploded," says Bramwell, who was now working for NEMS and would assist Evans and Aspinall on the road. "[Until then] it had been pretty crazy, but that was just the sort of thing that happened to pop stars. But then it turned into total mass hysteria – on stage, off stage – and by normal human beings, not just teeny bopper girls." One of the first effects of superstardom is that opportunities expand but the arena in which they can be enjoyed rapidly narrows. "On tour it was like, 'Did anyone see anything?' 'Did anyone go on the beach, did anyone get to Snowdonia?' No. Maybe they'd get to the swimming pool. Everyone loved it for the first six months or so, then it just got tiresome. And George was the first to get tired a little, hence 'Don't Bother Me'."

As 'She Loves You' was sending the nation into phase one of Beatles meltdown, the band were already busy working on their second album at Abbey Road. The really significant piece of business for Harrison was the recording of 'Don't Bother Me'. His first song, or at the very least the first statement about which he ever felt sufficiently exercised to express publicly, was an unambiguous expression of his need for privacy, and his jittery sense, ever growing, that life was about to lurch completely out of control.

Written at the age of 20, 'Don't Bother Me' seems in hindsight prophetic: dour, grumpy, stubbornly protective of its author's sense of solitude, musically a little sour. It provides embryonic evidence of a stark, wintry aspect to Harrison's natural worldview, and one which bled into his writing style: bars are snapped off prematurely, time signatures are often complex, key changes jar, minor chords fall like shadows, dissonance is frequent and drones run the length of songs like chains. Here was our first, albeit modest, encounter with a new, not altogether welcoming side of The Beatles' musical personality. "The first proper song he wrote ... was a protest song before anyone here had really heard of Dylan or John [Lennon] had thought of it," says Bramwell. "George wrote the first protest song." This statement is true only in the sense that it was the first of many songs Harrison wrote complaining about his lot as a pop star rather than, say, an electrician, but it does identify the enduring tendency in his make-up to see his glass as half-empty.

Bill Harry, an early champion of Harrison as a songwriter, insists the intent behind 'Don't Bother Me' was more prosaic. "I went to see them at the ABC Blackpool, [on July 19] 1964," says Harry. "I was chatting to George and he said, 'By the way, I want to thank you.' 'Why?' He said, 'The last time I was in Liverpool at a club I suddenly thought, Oh God, if I bump into you you're going to go and on about writing bloody songs again, you're going to bother me and hassle me.' That gave me the inspiration to write 'Don't Bother Me', and I've just received £7,000 in royalties, so thanks very much!'"

The money, indeed, would have been a major factor. Having seen what his two friends were earning in publishing royalties, Harrison's impetus to compose was not merely creative. Always the Beatle most interested in the band finances, when Lennon and McCartney were questioned about money they would reply: "Ask George – he's the only one who asks the questions and finds out where it's going."[15] Epstein agreed. "George is the only one who asks questions," he said in 1964. "He's the only one who takes an active interest in the business aspect of The Beatles. He wants to know how I book them, how the discs are distributed, and everything that has to do with the financial working."[16]

Though insisting that he was "no more money-mad than the others,"[17] he kept tabs on it as much as he could. Perhaps he already sensed that The Beatles were largely an earning machine for other people; probably he also realised that this kind of success rarely lasted more than a couple of summers. Harrison later noted that in 1963 he earned £72,000 gross income but only saw £4,000 of it, after Epstein, NEMS and – several rungs down the ladder – Evans, Aspinall *et al* got their slice. The same year he dug out an old recording contract The Beatles had signed in Hamburg and took it to his publisher to see how much they were owed in royalties. Helen Shapiro, just 16, had noticed that while Lennon and McCartney were busy composing 'From Me To You' on the tour bus in March, Harrison was grilling her about the pounds, shilling and pence. "George asked me lots of show business questions," she said. "He's the keenest to know all the mechanics of the music industry."[18]

"I am interested in money," he said. "I suppose I spend plenty by some standards. On the other hand I hate the idea of just getting rid of money because it's in your pocket. I like to keep as small a wallet as possible in case I'm tempted to waste cash on unnecessary things. I haven't got a very good business head, but if my life had been entirely different and I'd only had a little savings in the bank, I reckon I'd have made a success of some small business by taking advice from somebody.

I'd have asked what I ought to do with my saved-up money to make it grow."[19]

He was canny with his cash but he was never destined to be anyone's working-class hero. "I never thought because I was from Liverpool I shouldn't live in a big mansion house myself one day," he said.[20] He recognised early on the distancing effects of fame and fortune and seemed to actively welcome them. "People say, 'Don't you miss going for a bus ride like any normal bloke?' The answer's no. What? Get some dirty old man breathing down your neck?... I used to stand in bus queues and think about how great it would be to have a car."[21] Yet he was also the Beatle with the most conscientious approach to the music and the deepest appreciation of the fans. He wanted the shows to be right and would apologise if they came on late or performed below par. He was all too aware that the only reason he could buy a flash car or a Savile Row suit was because people were willing to come and see the band and buy their records. As an avid music fan himself, he understood the essential interaction that took place every time someone bought a record or a ticket. "An artist who did well and then wanted to forget about his fans might as well forget about his fame at the same time," he said.[22]

There is plenty of evidence to suggest that the other Beatles didn't take 'Don't Bother Me' terribly seriously. "It's your turn now," said Lennon to Harrison in the control room just prior to them beginning to record it; you can almost see him smirk and rub his hands together as he adds, "I'm looking forward to this..."[23] "The first take wasn't too successful," recounted the *NME* journalist on hand to report on the session.[24] The first takes of Harrison songs generally weren't. His would often be the ones which proved the most stubbornly resistant to being recorded successfully. Even the modest 'Don't Bother Me' took what was, for 1963 at any rate, a fairly excessive 17 attempts spread over two days. Later, takes for Harrison compositions would stretch into three figures.

It would be almost two years before a second Harrison song appeared on a Beatles album. Instead, in the manner of parents trying to occupy a restless child, he was given a weekly column in the *Daily Express*, for which he was paid £100. It was ghost-written by the journalist Derek Taylor, who would shortly become The Beatles' own press officer and a lifelong confidante. The column, said Taylor, was regarded as "a nice thing for George, give him an interest in life because the others have their songwriting and Ringo is rather new."[25] Harrison, characteristically, took more of an interest than perhaps anyone expected. Objecting to some "phoney" utterances attributed to him in the first column about his father's green bus, from thereon he collaborated with Taylor to ensure that the stories portrayed him if not always entirely accurately, then at least honestly. "He was anxious to please," said Taylor. "If he is committed to something he does it with enormous thoroughness." Taylor added, in his customary charming manner, that "he has a rather straight-ahead way."[26]

★ ★ ★

While his three band mates and their partners went on holiday – Paul and Ringo to Greece; John (with Cynthia) to Paris – after finishing the bulk of *With The Beatles*, Harrison travelled to America, becoming the first Beatle to set foot – and indeed play – in the United States. He and his brother Peter visited their sister Louise, who was now living at 113 McCann Street in Benton, Illinois, a small mining community near St Louis where she had recently moved with her Scottish husband Gordon, a mining engineer.

Already a star in his home country, he was unknown in the States and seemed quite happy to be so. He had no qualms about sitting in with the local band, The Four Vests, and played with them twice. First, at the VFW (Veterans of Foreign Wars) Hall in nearby Eldorado, where after the interval Harrison was introduced, perhaps a little mockingly, as "the Elvis of England" and joined the band on a set which included 'Roll Over Beethoven', 'Johnny B Goode', 'Matchbox' and 'Your Cheatin' Heart'. He also performed with the group at the Bocchi Ball Club in Benton.

It was relaxed and fun, although there was a missionary motive behind the trip. He gave The Four Vests a selection of Beatles records, which they seemed reluctant to learn; in the end they mainly stuck to playing rock and roll classics and Hank Williams songs. More successful was a two-mile hitchhike he and Louise took to WFRX-AM radio station in the neighbouring town of West Frankfort, clutching a copy of 'She Loves You'. The station played the single, just as they had also played – with heavy persuasion by Louise – 'From Me To You' in June, very possibly the first time a Beatles song had ever been aired in the US. He noticed that Cliff Richard's *Summer Holiday* was playing second feature at a drive-in in St Louis. The British Invasion was not a phrase rushing to anybody's lips.

At the Fenton Music Store on South 10th Street in Mount Vernon, Harrison bought a fireglo red Rickenbacker 425 guitar for $400. According to Gabe McCarty, the member of The Four Vests who drove him to the store, "he just had to have one."[27] He asked for it to be refinished in black, because "all the other guys [in the band] had black instruments"[28] – which wasn't entirely true, but the respray would make his new guitar the same colour as Lennon's, and anyway, red might have been construed as a little ostentatious. He also returned to the UK with some new records. "I bought Booker T & The MGs' first album, *Green Onions*, and I bought some Bobby Bland, all kind of things," he later remembered.[29] He also bought a "really terrible"[30] James Ray album which had one saving grace: a song called 'Got My Mind Set On You', which in substantially altered form would relaunch Harrison's recording career in 1987.

Harrison and his brother travelled to New York for a couple of days, taking in a trip to the Statue of Liberty, before returning to Britain on October 3. His new Rickenbacker was put through its paces the next day, during The Beatles' first ever appearance on the new TV pop show *Ready, Steady, Go!*. "How many guitars do you use, George?" asks guest compere Dusty Springfield. "Just one at a time," he replies, before showing her his latest acquisition which, he promises with an innocent smile, he made himself.

After a short Scottish tour came the final sessions for *With The Beatles*. Aside from 'Don't Bother Me', Harrison's showpieces were slight. He tackled 'Devil In Her Heart', an obscure song by girl group The Donays, without any great ceremony, but made a more spirited fist, as one might expect, of Chuck Berry's 'Roll Over Beethoven', which he had been singing on stage for some time and would still be playing at his last ever concert almost 40 years later. His solo was the same as the one heard at the Star Club over a year earlier.

In general, however, the way the band now worked tended to play against his intrinsic desire to take his time honing his parts. Negotiating a fearsome tour schedule, McCartney and Lennon would set aside perhaps a week to write songs for a new album; often the first time Harrison would hear the results would be in the studio at 10 o'clock on the morning of the session, allowing him very little time to come up with his part. It made it all the more impressive that he was able to quickly reel off the crackling guitar break in 'All My Loving', setting aside his usual studious approach for something a little looser which tipped its hat to Scotty Moore, Carl Perkins and Chet Atkins while giving the song an added burst of energy; the ear-catching sixth chord in 'She Loves You' was Harrison's idea, something he had picked up from Fifties country records. Martin didn't like it; the rest of the band overruled him. As writer Ian MacDonald later observed, "beyond the basic words and music lay the vital work of arranging, at which juncture The Beatles became not a duo but a quartet."[31]

With its Exis-lite black and white cover photograph by Robert Freeman, *With The Beatles* was released in November, by which time the band had gone from a success to a craze to a full-blown phenomenon. Their four-song set on the prime time variety TV show, *Sunday Night At The London Palladium*, on October 13 had completed the transformation into a mainstream, headline-devouring media story in the days before pop stars ever got near the front pages of newspapers. Four more songs played at the televised *Royal Command Performance* on November 4 had simply sealed the deal, as Lennon prefaced a raucous 'Twist And Shout' with his famously mischievous quip: "For our last number I'd like to ask your help. The people in the cheaper seats clap your hands. And the rest of you, if you'd just rattle your jewellery."

It was a joke born of a degree of disgust. They refused to ever appear on the show again. Beneath the suits, toothy grins and ragged charm lay genuine contempt for the establishment. Despite Epstein's very successful makeover of The Beatles for mass consumption, Harrison always saw himself as being part of a non-conformist band, from outside the London showbiz clique, and was driven by a need to prove a point. Despite the occasional lofty and rather patronising piece by a 'weighty' music critic talking about their "Aeolian cadences" and "submediant key switches," The Beatles were not generally regarded as a serious proposition musically. Most of the media tattle centred on their hair, their looks, the screaming girls, their accents and exotically déclassé slang. The *Herald-Tribune* described them as "75 per cent publicity, 20 per cent haircut and 5 per cent lilting lament," adding that they were "a magic act that owed less to Britain than to Barnum." "The *Herald-Tribune*," said Harrison, "is fucking soft."[32]

"Although we didn't openly say, 'Fuck you!' it was basically our thing," he said. "'We'll show these fuckers.'" The attitude went back to his schooldays, to the teachers who "expected nothing of me and didn't have it in them to be able to give me anything."[33] The Beatles' success was as much an achievement of sheer will, determination and self-belief as an artistic and creative one.

★ ★ ★

Life became a blur, with no time to put a hand on the railings to staunch the dizziness or catch his breath and bearings. Whenever the urge descends to sigh over Harrison's seemingly unending complaints about Beatlemania and the fact that he "gave his nervous system for The Beatles,"[34] it's instructive to be reminded of how fast and unforgiving his life had become. When The Beatles returned from a short Swedish tour at the end of October 10,000 fans were waiting at the airport in London. They then immediately embarked on an autumn UK tour from November 1 through to mid-December, then a series of TV and radio appearances. Between December 21 and January 11, which roughly coincided with 'I Want To Hold Your Hand' occupying the top of the charts, they were committed to appear almost every night as part of *The Beatles Christmas Show*, a variety production featuring pantomime, comedy and music. It was Epstein's idea, and one which involved Harrison donning a housewife's headscarf and participating in doggedly sub-par sketches. They had Christmas Day off, flying back to Liverpool by private jet to spend a little over 24 hours with their families, before returning to London early on Boxing Day morning. Immediately after the end of *The Beatles Christmas Show*, from mid-January until February 5, they were in Paris, playing a rather trying extended run at the Olympia Theatre. On January 17, at the George V Hotel, they discovered to their astonishment that 'I Want To Hold Your Hand' had reached number one in America. That same week they wrote and recorded their next single, 'Can't Buy Me Love', at EMI's Pathé Marconi Studio in the French capital.

Within 48 hours of leaving France they were in the United States, dealing with a further massive, head-spinning escalation in attention: they discovered that everything in America is indeed bigger, even Beatlemania. They arrived back home on Saturday, February 22, spent the Sunday taping a TV show, and on the following Tuesday started recording their next album at Abbey Road. The Sunday session finished sometime after 10 p.m.; by 8 a.m. the following morning they were gathered at Paddington Station to begin shooting their first film.

Shoehorned between all those commitments were numerous other recording sessions, TV and radio appearances, photo ops and interviews. Just reading their itinerary over this period is exhausting. Actually having to do it was numbing. And this was while it was still, by and large, fun.

The barely credible schedule was endurable while there were still some firsts to be ticked off the list, new territory to be conquered. Their first trip to the US as a band couldn't fail to excite, not least because the success of 'I Want To Hold Your Hand' now ensured they were going as conquering heroes rather than wannabes. America had the added incentive of being the home of most of their musical heroes: from early loves like Elvis and Buddy Holly to Bob Dylan and the new Tamla-Motown artists with whom they were currently obsessed.

Harrison had become ill on the plane over with a fever and sore throat and took to his bed when he arrived at the Plaza Hotel on Central Park South, where they occupied the entire wing on the fifteenth floor. It was touch and go as to whether he would be well enough for The Beatles' historic appearance on *The Ed Sullivan Show* on February 9.

Aspinall acted as his stand-in during rehearsals but Harrison made it, partly down to the administrations of his sister Louise, who had travelled from Benton to see him and was deemed the only woman in a ten-mile radius who could get close enough to nurse him without hyper-ventilating.

"We got him to see the hotel doctor, Dr. Gordon," said Louise Harrison. "He said, 'This is a very sick kid. He's got a 104-degree temperature and has strep throat.' He was given some shots and vaporizer treatments, and I was in charge of watching over him. George was told to use his voice as little as possible. That's why at all the press conferences he was so quiet, and so the press thought he was the quiet one."[35]

He was certainly routinely underestimated. Harrison "doesn't have the maturity of the others, so he tends to play it a little safe," a member of The Beatles' entourage was heard to say. "It's as if he is the baby of the family."[36] Firebrand New York DJ Murray The K, who thoroughly annoyed Harrison by seeming to be everywhere he turned, added, as though referring to a particularly challenged child, "You have to be very careful of what you say to George. You have to be sure that every word means what you want it to mean. He takes what you say very literally." Though some may have construed this trait as a sign of unintelligence, it was in fact the precise opposite. Harrison measured his words carefully, said what he meant when he felt the need, and expected others to do the same. If not, he would tune out. In New York he had a transistor radio constantly in his hands, and the volume at which the music played during a conversation was indicative of his level of engagement. In his suite at the Plaza, journalist Al Aronowitz kept asking the below par Harrison the same question: "What's bugging you, George?" It now seems remarkably astute.

They were kings, and everything and everybody was delivered to their court. Sweating out his fever in the Plaza he bought a new 12-string electric Rickenbacker for $900. On his return to the UK he promptly used it on the sessions for their third album, the soundtrack to the movie they were just about to make. In many ways *A Hard Day's Night*, named after a classic Starr malapropism, provides the first definitive, indisputable proof that The Beatles were operating at a level far beyond the standards demanded of pop ephemera.

The first seven songs, side one in old money, would all feature in the film; the remaining six would not. The qualification barely mattered, for this was hardly a standard soundtrack, but instead a gloriously unified album which, in exactly half an hour, managed to capture the sheer energy and excitement of Beatlemania while perfecting the art of crafting smart, thoughtful pop music. *A Hard Day's Night* bristled with exuberance, confidence (cockiness, actually – and with good reason) and a sense of uncomplicated accomplishment, effortlessly upping the stakes without making a great fuss about it. Fittingly, it starts with the sound of The Beatles' embracing their own myth. The dramatic clang prefacing the title track, a shifting mixture of Harrison's bright Fadd9 chord played on his new Rickenbacker, Lennon's Gibson acoustic, Hofner bass and Steinway grand, was added post-hoc as a deliberately ear-grabbing opening statement. It is a sound which, like The Beatles themselves, cannot quite be unstitched into its component parts, the cosmic gong announcing the beginning of the most imperious of all imperial phases.

There is some evidence on *A Hard Day's Night* of Beatles-by-numbers, not least the doggedly formulaic 'I'm Happy Just To Dance With You', which you suspect was given to Harrison to sing because neither Lennon nor McCartney would have entertained for a moment the idea of singing it themselves. Though very much still the junior partner in terms of songwriting and singing, Harrison was starting to blossom as a lead guitarist. As McCartney later acknowledged, Harrison's doleful acoustic hook on 'And I Love Her' all but makes the song. He introduced his distinctively ringing and soon-to-be hugely influential 12-string guitar sound on the solo to 'I Should Have Known Better', and to the hard, tight riff to 'You Can't Do That'. He added biting fills to Lennon's 'Any Time At All', and a dazzling modern outro on the title track, which hints at a multitude of sonic riches yet to come. Although Harrison was always chiefly concerned with being at the service of the song, and few would ever do it better, his playing became more muscular, more exuberant, and a little more willing to turn heads. Fellow musicians were starting to sit up and take notice, not least because the film gave a worldwide audience the chance to see him play at length.

"I had heard George's playing on the records, but I hadn't seen him play before I saw *A Hard Day's Night*," says the former Byrds singer and guitarist Roger McGuinn. "I picked up some tips from him, like playing the G-string up and down the neck for lead guitar because it gave more punch to the lead line. And of course he played the Rickenbacker 12-string and that was a big influence on me, but I even liked to watch his Gretsch playing. He did a lot of barre chords – John and George used barre chords almost exclusively, whereas coming from the folk tradition I used lots of open chords. With The Searchers and The Seekers, you could hear some of that 12-string out there, but primarily it was The Beatles. I know George influenced us a lot."

The film itself is, of course, an improbable joy, and Harrison came out of it rather well for someone who had no real interest in acting. His was a pleasingly deadpan comic presence, particularly during his scene with Kenneth Haigh's superbly obnoxious advertising executive, in which he underplays nicely against Haigh's eye-swivelling contempt and – via scriptwriter Alun Owen – gave the word "grotty" to the world.

Harrison celebrated his twenty-first birthday during the filming and recording of *A Hard Day's Night*, partying upstairs at The Ivy. There was a film crew present, to whom he revealed that he had received "52 sacks of mail containing thousands of cards," although those from his band mates apparently were not among then. He later said that "the fellas kindly forgot about [my birthday],"[37] which did not go down well. "He would get really narked off if people forgot his birthday," says Bramwell. "He liked that whole thing, Christmas cards and birthday cards, those gestures." As if to compensate, in Liverpool seven truckloads of mail arrived at Macket's Lane. It took weeks and weeks to dispense.

★ ★ ★

Early on during the filming Harrison met Pattie Boyd, a 19-year-old model who had been given a bit part in the movie after working with director Richard Lester a couple of months previously on a Smiths crisps television commercial. Harrison had hardly been starved of female company in the time since The Beatles had begun to make a national impact; few were more than ships that passed in the night.

Bernadette Farrell was his last serious Liverpool girlfriend, whom he dated through the early months of 1963. "It was no big, raging love affair, but George was my boyfriend," she says. "He was a lovely, lovely man, a caring, private person. A lot of people said he was quiet but that's because they didn't get to know him. He was actually quite lively and humorous, always making dry quips. He was not shy, but he was happy to stand back and only speak when he thought it was relevant."[38] When The Beatles were given their first silver disc for 'Please Please Me', Harrison brought it around to the Farrell family home to show everyone. "He was very proud. My mum asked him if we could put it on the record player! It was just a short relationship that ended when he went to London... They left Liverpool almost overnight and he just didn't have time to see me."[39]

In London, when there was time, there was plenty of fun to be had with the capital's population of young aspiring dancers, singers, models and budding actresses. When he first moved south, Harrison dated Ann Marie Guirron, who worked as a model and later married Justin Hayward of The Moody Blues. He also had a fling with Estelle Bennett of The Ronettes. On January 28, 1964 he and Lennon attended a party held by the influential BBC disc jockey Tony Hall and his wife Mafalda, who also lived on Green Street. Phil Spector and The Ronettes were staying with the couple, and Ronnie Spector later recalled Bennett and Harrison "pairing off." They continued to see each other on and off over the following months until it fizzled out.

Touring was characterised by a more frenzied kind of sexual activity. Hamburg on wheels. "Man, our tours were like something else, if you could get on our tours, you were in," Lennon would say later, perhaps exaggerating. "Wherever we went, there was always a whole scene going. Derek's and Neil's rooms were always full of junk and whores and who-the-fuck-knows-what... They didn't call them groupies then, they called it something else, and if we couldn't get groupies we would have whores and everything, whatever was going."[40]

81

"After every concert the best-looking female fans would be given instructions as to how to get back to the hotel," said NEMS general manager Alistair Taylor, who became The Beatles' Mr Fixit. "The boys liked their perks. They had this amazing power to point and say, 'You, you, you and you...' and lovely young women would arrive at the hotel simply begging for sex."[41] Tony Bramwell sounds a note of caution amid tales of constant and unfettered copulation. "They obviously had more opportunity of [sexual] adventure, [but] they weren't always allowed to take advantage of the position they were in," he says. "They were guarded, and no one wanted to be embarrassed, they didn't want their mums to read about it in the *Daily Sketch*. There was obviously some crisis management, and things being brushed under the carpet, but not as much as there could have been."

Pattie Boyd was one of four models chosen to play schoolgirls in the train scene in *A Hard Day's Night*, which was filmed on the line between Paddington Station and Cornwall. Blonde, petite, with big, blue innocent eyes and two prominent front teeth, Boyd was a boarding school girl from a broken home who was several rungs up the class ladder from Harrison. Bright, well-spoken and independent, she was only just beginning to make her name as a model, at the vanguard of the look which Mary Quant described as "naive sophistication", that skinny, waif-like sensuality that came to define the Sixties pin-up. She had one line – "Prisoners?" – in the movie and can be seen during the sequence for 'I Should Have Known Better'. How typical of his life as a Beatle that the occasion on which he met his future wife would be captured forever on film.

Almost as soon as he clapped eyes on her Harrison asked Boyd out to dinner, but she declined because she had a steady boyfriend. They met again on the set at Twickenham Studios on March 12. Harrison asked how her boyfriend was; she told him she had dumped him. He grinned and asked her out again. They went to the Garrick Club, with Epstein acting as chaperone to these two "very young, very shy people."[42] And that was it. "We were almost immediately attracted to each other," said Boyd. "He seemed to be very carefree and light-hearted. I think [he] hadn't quite realised what had happened to [him]."[43]

He was just such a lovely young boy. He was just so sweet and open about everything." – Astrid Kirchherr. A rapidly evolving Harrison in Hamburg, April 1962. K & K ULF KRUGER OHG/REDFERNS

"He was very secure within himself, and you only really get that security from a very tight and loving family as a child." – Pattie Boyd. The baby of the family, second right, with, from left to right: Peter Harrison, Louise Harrison and Harry Harrison.

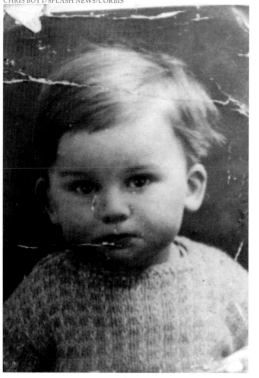

"Who am I anyway?" The Baby Beatle, left, and the Beatle Boy, right.

There's a part of me which likes to keep quiet. I do prefer wide, open spaces to traffic jams." The teenage Harrison, already finding solace in retreat. CHRIS BOTT/SPLASH NEWS/CORBIS

"George was obsessed with playing the guitar and did everything he could to learn." – Olivia Harrison. Aged 13 with his first guitar, a used Egmond steel strung Spanish-style guitar bought for £3 10s. KEYSTONE PICTURES USA/ALAMY

"He was slowly becoming the right guitar player in the right band." Harrison, with his new Gretsch, taking a break at the Cavern. KEYSTONE/GETTY IMAGES

Above and below: "On stage George was coming out of his shell, for sure. He was quiet but he was full of fun and mischief." – Roy You[n]g Harrison spreading his wings at the Top Ten Club in Hamburg in 1962, with Roy Young on piano. COURTESY OF ROY YOUNG

lot of people say The Beatles were created in Mathew Street, which wasn't true. They were created in Hamburg." – Allan Williams.
arrison, second right, with, left to right: Paul McCartney, Pete Best, Stuart Sutcliffe and John Lennon, performing live in Hamburg,
'61.

The best buzz of all time." The Beatles receive a silver disc for 'Please Please Me' from their producer George Martin.

"He would get really narked off if people forgot his birthday. He liked those gestures." – Tony Bramwell. Harrison, flanked by the joint secretaries of The Beatles fan club, celebrates his 21st birthday upstairs at the NEMS offices, Argyll Street, London, February 25, 1964. DAILY SKETCH/REX FEATURES

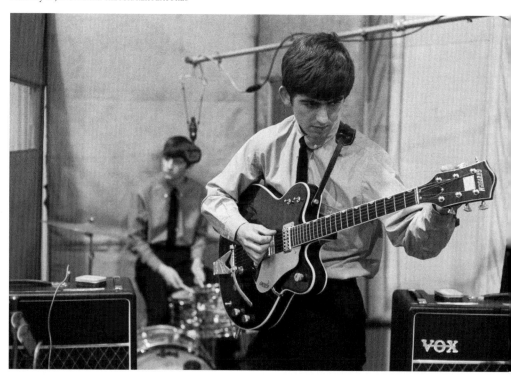

"What he came up with was really precise and always what was required for the piece of music." – Glyn Johns. Harrison tuning his Gretsch in Studio 2 at Abbey Road during the recording of 'She Loves You', July 1, 1963. TERRY O'NEILL/GETTY IMAGES

suppose we'll stay doing this stuff for a couple of years. I mean, naturally we won't be able to stay at this level." An obviously amused arrison meets Princess Margaret at the Royal Variety Performance on November 4, 1963. MIRRORPIX

was all so wonderful and very novel – and then it really started to grate on him." – Pattie Boyd. In the belly of Beatlemania, John F. ennedy Airport, New York, February 7, 1964. TOM GALLAGHER/NY DAILY NEWS ARCHIVE VIA GETTY IMAGES

"We were almost immediately attracted to each other. He seemed to be very carefree and light-hearted." – Pattie Boyd. Harrison and his future wife on the train to South Molton, Devon, while filming *A Hard Day's Night*, 1964. MIRRORPIX

"Girls managed to get into the garden, even into the house. It became a bit of a nightmare." – Pattie Boyd. Harrison surveys his new home, Kinfauns, at 16 Claremont Drive in Esher, July 17, 1964. MIRRORPIX

At 21, he embarked on the first serious relationship of his life. Within days he was meeting – and charming – her parents. Within a couple of weeks they were off to Ireland with the Lennons for the weekend, and in May the same foursome went island-hopping around Tahiti for a month. Harrison travelled as Mr Hargreaves, Boyd as Miss Bond, but by the time they had flown from London to Honolulu, via Amsterdam and Vancouver, their cover was already blown. They were so besieged at the Royal Hawaiian Hotel in Waikiki that they were forced to sleep elsewhere.

It was remembered by all as an idyllic time – "it felt as though we did nothing but laugh," said Boyd[44] – but as they flew off from Hawaii towards one of the remotest dots in the Pacific in search of some peace and privacy, Harrison let loose a rather plaintive cry at the gathering throng of reporters and photographers: "Why don't you leave us alone?"[45]

Be Here Now
Hollywood, August 25, 1964

One crazy scene in a thousand. Two days after their concert at the Hollywood Bowl in Los Angeles, The Beatles are persuaded to leave their vacuum-packed Bel Air sanctuary to play celebrity smile-and-snap with Jayne Mansfield at the Whisky A Go-Go nightclub on Sunset Strip. They are told that privacy and security will be taken care of. They forget for a moment that normal rules for such things no longer apply.

"When John, George and Ringo met with the glamorous star, there was mass pandemonium, noise and panic, and the meeting ended in complete disorder," Derek Taylor later reported.[1] Trapped in a gaudy booth designed to look like a monstrous satin clamshell, surrounded by paparazzi, with a fading Hollywood actress clamping her hand to his groin, a highly-strung Harrison snaps, throwing his glass of melted ice at a photographer and pushing his way to the exit. He never even gets a proper drink.

"It was hell," he said. "We left town the next day, and I remember sitting on the plane, reading the paper and there was the photo of me throwing the water."[2] The picture reflects back to the reader a gaunt, uptight, harassed-looking young man. It wasn't Beatle George; this was George Harrison. A few days later he sent a letter home to Liverpool. "You can see why we don't usually bother going out now," he wrote.

CHAPTER 5

Circles

Harrison first fell for Bob Dylan early in 1964. The Beatles played his second album, *The Freewheelin' Bob Dylan*, over and over again in their rooms in the George V hotel in Paris, and were seduced. On their second trip to America in August of that year they met him for the first time, smoking grass with Dylan and his entourage in the Hotel Delmonico on Park Avenue. Less than 12 months later he had already mutated from reluctant folk prophet to harrying electric hipster with the release of 'Like A Rolling Stone'. Its "how does it feel?" refrain seemed to capture something of Harrison's growing ambivalence as The Beatles dragged themselves around the United States for the second summer in a row.

How did it feel? At some point between early 1964 and the middle of 1966 being a Beatle for Harrison became "a horror story... awful... manic... crazy, a nightmare," an experience defined by "madness", "panic" and "paranoia." This terrible litany of fear and despair says as much about his own complex psyche as it does about the unprecedented experience he and his three band mates went through. Being in The Beatles was the opportunity of anyone's lifetime, but the attendant mania was a trauma which Harrison spent his entire life alternately trying to blank out and comprehend. Right up until his death it could make him shiver just to recall it, as though it had contaminated the entire experience of being in the band. "In later years, I was hanging out with him and Olivia at Tom Petty's house in Los Angeles," says Roger McGuinn. "I started playing a couple of Beatles songs and he was kind enough to indulge me, but Olivia said, 'George, what are you *doing*?' 'Well, Jim [Roger McGuinn] here wanted to play these songs...' I got the feeling from him that it was a bad memory, something he didn't want to go back to."

It's important not to turn Harrison's time as a Beatle into a three-act tragedy. His language tended towards extremes, and for every remembered "nightmare" there were just as many recollections of laughter, silliness, camaraderie and love. He was immensely privileged and for a long time, according to Pattie Boyd, "he enjoyed it, and the exclusivity that we enjoyed: always having the best table, clubs being open to us, it was all so wonderful and very novel. He was a very happy person and he loved so many things. He loved going out, driving his E-Type Jaguar, and we were having a very wonderful and fulfilling life. But then it really started to grate on him."

Being a Beatle was most enjoyable when it still seemed destined to be a fleeting moment in the sun. "I suppose we'll stay doing this stuff for a couple of years," he said in 1963. "I mean, naturally we won't be able to stay at this level."[1] They were all waiting for it to end, for surely this kind of white-hot success was merely a preface for the long, slow cool to come. That's what made everything more exciting. "It's great at the beginning," said Starr. "Things are bigger, things come to you faster, all that is great. Then you really want that to end. But it never ends. That's the deal."[2]

And so the world changed, and they changed. The northern premiere of *A Hard Day's Night*, held in Liverpool on July 10, 1964, became a kind of royal homecoming, but it also had the unmistakeable feeling of a final farewell, marking a conclusive break with what Lennon called "the cocoon of Liverpool. All the things there we dropped. It was like going to the next class in school."[3] "They had gone through a door and it closed," says Bill Harry. "In the early days it was really great. There was something so refreshing and exciting about them, but they became different people – they became more suspicious of the world, they realised they were living in a different world to what had been."

When the realisation struck that this was not a passing craze, that this was instead going to overtake and reshape their lives, Harrison found himself increasingly discomfited by the idea, a man stranded at the top of a very high mountain who could see no discernible way down. He was in an awkward position, still in his early twenties and trying to define his own identity within this hydra-headed monster. He had to contend with the full force of Beatlemania without the regular release of songwriting, and without the luxury of being able to steer the creative development of the band. He was a guitar player who valued his proficiency yet increasingly couldn't be heard; a man with plenty to say who was dismissed as The Quiet One, a funny haircut dispensing dry witticisms. He was sharp enough to already find it a highly constrictive niche.

Troubled by the disconnect between who he was and the image of Beatle George, he likened himself to a pools winner. Fame was something that happened to him, almost as though he was not an active participant. "Physically I'm the same bloke," he said. "I feel odd when people look up and point at me onstage."[4] "It was odd for him," said Olivia Harrison. "[Later] he'd look at photos of himself and say, 'That's Beatle George'."

There was another complication. Measured against the likes of Smokey Robinson, Tamla-Motown, The Byrds and numerous other favourites, he regarded his own band as no better than adequate. He absolutely adored Dylan, and the act of turning onto *Freewheelin'* and marijuana (which Harrison had smoked once before in Liverpool without, apparently, knowing what it was) put his own 'pop' career into a rather dim light. Soon, and for ever more, during interviews he would start reciting Dylan's lyrics as though they were scripture, often prefaced with a humble "as the man says". It was a lifelong habit. "George could always find a Dylan quote to fit just about any situation,"[5] said Tom Petty. "He who isn't busy being born is busy dying," from 'It's Alright Ma (I'm Only Bleeding)', was a particular favourite. "Money doesn't talk, it swears," another.

By comparison, The Beatles seemed just a tad juvenile. Harrison couldn't quite work out why they mattered to people as much as they did. He never saw them as anything special, just "typical of a hundred groups in our area. We were lucky, we got away with it first."[6] On their initial arrival in America Al Aronowitz fancied that Harrison played guitar with "a look of unconcern that seems to reflect a desire to be strumming elsewhere. 'Well,' he says, 'the songs that Paul and John write, they're all right, but they're not the greatest'."[7] His own guitar playing "was okay as far as he was concerned, but why was he suddenly world-famous," says Boyd. "He always wanted to find out, why him? He never grasped it."[8]

In this context, it's little wonder that the escalation in Beatlemania on each successive tour magnified a widening chasm between reality and perception. Despite the constant adulation and money, Harrison had hardly any creative respect, reward or input to show for it. The result: the higher he got, the worse he felt.

When did it stop being fun? Not all at once, naturally, and not ever, completely. The tour of Hong Kong, Australia and New Zealand in June 1964 was a turning point of sorts. At the time Harrison described it as "the biggest drag of all time" in one of his letters home and, 15 years later, as "another hassle altogether."[9] He hadn't wanted to go at all, partly because it was too far, partly because he'd had a bust up with Boyd just beforehand, and partly because Starr was ill and would have to miss some of the dates. He was told he had to go, the kind of stern, schoolmasterly instruction at which he instinctively bristled. "I really despised the way we couldn't make a decision for ourselves," he said. "It was just, 'Off you go'."[10] Stand-in drummer Jimmy Nicol took Starr's place. At each show they played for 27 minutes and, at some, had eggs and sweets thrown at them, apparently in appreciation. In Sydney's Town Hall they had to walk down the aisle to get to the stage; Harrison was manhandled by fans and ended up punching a policeman who was shoving him, an expression of fear and panic transmuted into blind rage. In New Zealand they were badly underprotected and had some heart-stopping moments trying to get past their fans; one 13-year-old threw herself in front of their car in Christchurch.

The crowds were unbelievable. Three hundred thousand people lined the roads as their motorcade took them from the airport to Adelaide's city centre. At least 30,000 blocked the area around the City Hall while three Beatles and a bemused Nicol looked down on them and waved, like the Queen on the balcony of Buckingham Palace or the Pope at St Peter's Square. For their own protection they were confined to their hotels where, as ever, girls were rounded up and paraded for their pleasure. Travelling to Sydney airport to catch the flight to New Zealand, Harrison said, "It seems wrong to come so many miles and still see nothing," a statement which could double as a motto for his entire Beatles touring experience, both literally and metaphorically. "Somehow we've come to accept being stuck in our hotel rooms. It just seems part of the job, part of being professional. To be honest, we were not looking forward very much to our Australian trip."[11]

Elsewhere, he admitted to one of the film cameras that followed them everywhere that he had no idea what day it was. The immediate past would vanish like water over the falls. There was no context, just perpetual forward motion and a kind of psychic travel sickness. "I don't like travelling even if it's on a holiday, you know, or anything," he said. "The travelling bit is terrible, but you've got to travel to get there."[12] He would get through the flights by taking uppers and drinking whisky and coke. He was never naturally happy being away from home. Decades later, his memories of this time focused almost entirely on the horrors of aeroplanes, airports, cars, crowds. "The Beatles was a big pressure," Olivia Harrison told me. "If you ever look at a map of their tours they just went zigzag across the country, it was crazy. There's only a small group of people who have ever had that experience, and theirs was probably the most intense."

Round and round they went. Each year for three years they arrived in America in August, and each time it got more wired and claustrophobic. The thrill of meeting their peers, heroes, film star crushes – and they met them all: from Dylan, Muhammed Ali, Elvis and The Byrds to Burt Lancaster, Fats Waller, Julie Christie and Jayne Mansfield – soon wore off, and paled in the face of death threats, bomb scares, astrologist's curses, endlessly risky flights, mob scenes and provocative police escorts.

Barely nine months after Kennedy's assassination, Harrison vetoed a cavalcade through San Francisco. "I was getting very nervous," he said. "They kept planning these ticker-tape parades and I was saying, 'I absolutely don't want to do that.' I didn't like the idea of being too popular. I think in history you can see that when people get too big, something like [Kennedy] can very easily happen."[13]

He would write back home to his parents, calm, thoughtful letters recounting the cordon of police and security around them, the accidents and madness that afflicted the kids trying to get to them, their kamikaze escapes from venues. "Don't worry," he'd say, "No one can get near us." In reality, "all the time, constantly, I felt frightened by things."[14] By November 1964 he was telling the press that "personally, I'm a bit fed up of touring. Not so much in England, but particularly in America."[15] He had only done it once; perhaps it felt like more. It was easy to get lost, particularly as 1965 came to mirror 1964: another film occupied the first few months of the year, then recording the soundtrack, then more touring. More chaos.

Everywhere they went suggested a scene of imminent catastrophe. In Houston they landed and the plane was besieged by fans on the runway, climbing on the wings, staring in the windows. After another flight their pilot discovered fresh bullet holes in the metalwork. Playing to 55,600 fans at the Shea Stadium, home of the New York Mets, in August 1965 was a rare thrill, a genuine event for them all. You could see it in their faces when they played – Harrison and Lennon in particular are having a fine time. But when they returned to Shea in 1966 the experience was meaningless. "When we were making *Anthology* I asked George a question about when they played Shea the second time," says Geoff Wonfor, Harrison's friend and the director of *Anthology*, the definitive 1995 television series on The Beatles. "He said, 'We didn't do it twice.' I said, 'Yeah, you did.' He said, 'No, we didn't.' Eventually he said, 'If you say we did then fine, but I don't remember.'"

As the world around them went insane it pushed them closer together. The laughter they shared – and there was still a lot of it – became gradually more loose and hysterical. They spent three years hiding: in bathrooms, in bedrooms, in dressing rooms, in cars, armoured vans and ambulances. "He'd phone home or write me lots of letters, saying 'We're stuck in our rooms'," says Boyd. "Every so often they would be invited out on someone's boat, say in Florida, and they could get away from everyone and they could have a nice time. But most of the time they couldn't go out, and the audience couldn't hear them, and it all started to seem a little pointless."

Crucially, the satisfaction they had once gained from performing had all but vanished. The realisation that nobody was listening and that musically they were going backwards demoralised them all, the diligent Harrison perhaps most of all. He had been singing 'Roll Over Beethoven' and 'Everybody's Trying To Be My Baby' for what seemed like half a lifetime, while The Beatles were still playing 'Long Tall Sally' after they had recorded 'In My Life' and 'Tomorrow Never Knows'. They were all stuck. Beneath the surface noise they were still capable of being a pretty hot little band, but compared to Hamburg it felt more and more like an act. "George didn't want to know the touring, and touring was no good for them," says Bill Harry. "It wasn't really The Beatles, they were doing these short sets that no one could hear. It wasn't like when we used to watch them when it would be an hour and a half on the Cavern stage – a few feet away, hairs [up] on the back of the neck. That was their best period, for sure. On the tours they were doing 20 minutes and you couldn't hear them. What's the point? They were basically just standing there for people to look at them."

"I wanted to stop touring after about '65, actually," said Harrison.[16] Perhaps he should have. The world tour of 1966 would prove to be truly nightmarish.

★ ★ ★

As the shows got more and more perfunctory and unsatisfying so the records became more sophisticated and rewarding, the gap between the two widening to the extent that it was almost like they had become two different bands. The Beatles made some of their greatest ever music in the years between 1964 and 1966, particularly on *Rubber Soul* and *Revolver*, and Harrison played his part. He brought the exotic sounds of the sitar, tabla and tamboura into the band's orbit, while at times his guitar playing was truly dazzling, evolving beyond his Chet Atkins and rockabilly roots to encompass something a little more crisp and modern. His dappled, sun-bright solo on 'Nowhere Man' is glorious, while the meticulously planned and executed guitar part on Lennon's 'I'm Only Sleeping', a ten-second flash of inspiration sparking against technical innovation, remains one of the band's most genuinely hair-raising recorded moments. The detail involved was characteristic, and painstaking. Harrison first worked out his part conventionally. He then asked Martin to transcribe it back to front, after which he played and recorded it that way. He then dubbed the results onto the song with the tape playing backwards. The result was an eerie, smudgy, sonic smear, like water running against its natural flow. It was beautiful and disquieting, and somehow deeply spiritual. His labyrinthine guitar run on 'And Your Bird Can Sing' is the art of Escher given shape in sound, a pure mathematical joy, and evidence of he and McCartney working in an almost telepathic kind of tandem. He grabbed 'Drive My Car' by the scruff of the neck, writing the bass part and turning it into a crunching, Otis Redding-style soul stomp.

And yet there were many other times when he felt undermined in his primary role in the band. McCartney took the lead guitar on 'Paperback Writer' and Harrison's own 'Taxman', and Harrison didn't even appear on 'We Can Work It Out'. On 'I Feel Fine', the innovative squall of feedback at the beginning, and the riff itself, came from Lennon.

His friend and fellow guitarist Peter Frampton recalls hanging out with Harrison in New York in 1971. "I said, 'Can I put on some Beatles tracks and ask you about them?' And he said, 'Sure.' I'd put on 'Paperback Writer' and say, 'I love the guitar on that', and he'd say, 'Oh, that's Paul.' I put all these other tracks on... 'Oh, that's Paul.' I was embarrassed. I said, 'I'm sorry,' and he said, 'It's okay, it's okay.' He was very sweet about it, but it wasn't until that particular moment that I realised he was stifled. Paul had written a song, he had a vision for what he wanted it to be, and he could do it himself rather than telling someone else what to do. I'm sure it was a very frustrating thing for George, and it would be a very insecure situation trying to do something for the guy who has written the song that would please him."

Leon Russell had almost exactly the same conversation with Harrison. "I would listen to some Beatles records with George and say, 'I like the guitar on that record,' and he would say, 'Oh, that was Paul.' That was interesting."

He persevered with his songwriting, though it didn't come easily. "It was, I think, quite hard for him, but he was really determined to write songs," says Boyd. "There were lots of them, he would write constantly. He would always play his guitar, and the way that he would write would be to play guitar until he would find a really nice little riff that he enjoyed, and then he would write the music. He did feel [overawed by John and Paul], but he was very determined not to allow that to hold him back."

After throwing his hat into the ring with 'Don't Bother Me', it is conceivable that Harrison was expecting some help from his band mates, that the songwriting process would become more collaborative. If so, he was quite wrong. There was never any suggestion that either Lennon or McCartney would deign to write with him. "I guess George was a kind of loner, really," said George Martin. "John and Paul had each other to play against, their collaboration was much more of a competition. George was the sole guy, he had no one to work with."[17] The pair still shuffled awkwardly around the idea of him writing at all. They loved him, but they didn't want to have to carry him, and they certainly didn't offer any encouragement. "There was an embarrassing period when George's songs weren't that good and nobody wanted to say anything," Lennon later said. "He just wasn't in the same league for a long time – that's not putting him down, he just hadn't had the practice as a writer that we'd had."[18]

The available evidence doesn't necessarily contradict such an analysis. In 1964 he had brought 'You Know What To Do' to the studio to be swiftly recorded and equally as swiftly rejected. Even considering the relative paucity of good original material on *Beatles For Sale* it wasn't deemed strong enough for inclusion on their fourth album, probably correctly. It sounds like Harrison is straining against his nature to write a breezy hit single, and the lyrics are dire, although he does come up with a pleasantly descending middle eight. As a consolation prize, he got to sing Carl Perkins' 'Everybody's Trying To Be My Baby'.

The two Harrison songs included on *Help!* were more pleasing, if similarly slight. 'I Need You' is very simple, very straight, a mid-paced Merseybeat stroll with a classic Harrisonian dart into the melodic shadows just before the bridge. Like Lennon's far more weighty 'Yes It Is', it employs – rather crudely – the volume pedal on the guitar as an effect in itself, and ultimately seems longer than its two-and-a-half minutes. 'You Like Me Too Much' is simplistic boy-meets-girl fare, a carefree shuffle bolstered by some pleasing barrelhouse piano from George Martin.

These are Harrison's baby steps, evidence of him learning on the job. You can tell how little Lennon and McCartney thought of his songs by how little effort they expended on improving them. They weren't above airing their general sense of superiority in public. A sharp little scene captured in *Melody Maker* in 1965 illustrated Harrison's sometimes over-eager tendency to want to be included, particularly when it came to Lennon, and the brisk manner in which he could be summarily dismissed.

> *George wandered over [mid-conversation]:* "Who should have been more sensible, John?"
> *Lennon:* "What do you want?"
> *Harrison:* "What are you talking about?"
> *Lennon:* "Mind your own bloody business. Got a ciggie?"
> *John helped himself to a cigarette from George's top pocket before Harrison could reply.*
> *Exit George*[19]

George Martin wasn't averse to talking down to him either, sternly informing Harrison in the studio in front of guests that he "should be coming in on the second time every time instead of the fourth." "Oh, I see," Harrison said.[20]

Boyd observed first-hand how these attitudes affected him. "I know that it was quite difficult when they were recording," she says. "It was quite rare for John and Paul to allow George to play what he had been writing, or for them to listen to it. Like a little brother, he was pushed into the background quite often. Occasionally he would tell me how annoying it was for him, that they were so wrapped up in themselves and their songs that they didn't have time for him. That really got to him, actually. It was mean. He'd say, 'They're allowing me *two songs* on the next album!' Gosh! He was annoyed."

"Paul and John were obviously talented and they were a great duo, but they also had massive egos which left little room for others," he said much later. "I felt ignored and undervalued for years."[21] At the time he tended to take out his frustrations on those around him rather than any culpable parties in the band. "George could be very cutting," says Boyd. "Most definitely. He always had that." Bill Harry adds: "There was this powder keg of frustration inside of him. A creative person, with all these songs, and he couldn't get any headway. There were two dominant people in it, so it was as if he was being pushed to the back, rather than being an equal partner. It wasn't an equal band, was it? And at times that came out in his attitude."

On *Rubber Soul* he once again was allowed two songs: 'Think For Yourself' and 'If I Needed Someone', "the song generally accepted as George Harrison's best composition to date," according to a live review in the *NME* in December 1965. A jangly pop song with an underlying drone, it was based around harmonic variations on the D chord and partly inspired by The Byrds' 'The Bells Of Rhymney'. A cover version by The Hollies reached number 20 in the singles charts.

His most muscular yet melodically confident piece of work to date, 'If I Needed Someone' was one of several songs written during this period which, though essentially juvenile in their expression, hinted at quite complex feelings about Pattie Boyd as their relationship evolved. On July 17, 1964, Harrison had paid £20,000 for a white, modern, Z-shaped, ranch-style bungalow at 16 Claremont Drive in Esher, not far from where Lennon and Starr now lived in the sedate Surrey stockbroker belt. The house was called Kinfauns, and he took no longer choosing it than he would getting measured for a good suit. "It was the first one I saw," he shrugged, "And I thought, That'll do." Forty-five minutes down the A3 from London, Kinfauns had four bedrooms and had only recently been built in what had previously been the walled vegetable garden of Claremont Girls School.

It was part of a private estate owned by the National Trust. Turning into an entrance on the main road, the visitor drove through peaceful wooded parkland before eventually arriving at the house. There was a high wooden fence around the property, a curving driveway and a path leading diagonally to the front door through nearly an acre of grounds, but it was hardly grand and not as secluded as he had hoped. Fans soon sought him out there, perhaps alerted by his new silver Aston Martin DB5, or his little summer run-around the Mini Moke, parked outside. He left the bedroom window open for his cats Rupert and Corky to come in and out until he and Boyd awoke one night to find two girls hiding under their bed.

Honouring a long term promise to himself, almost the first thing he did when he eventually moved in was install a heated swimming pool in the courtyard at the back of the house. He turned up late for the session for 'I Feel Fine' on October 18, 1964 after being delayed in Esher with the workmen, announcing to George Martin when he arrived, "Here, Mr. Martin, I've got a gear swimming pool."[22]

By 1965 Boyd had moved in and at the end of the year Harrison proposed – though not before checking with Brian Epstein first. They were married on January 21, 1966, in a ceremony at the Registry Office in Upper High Street, Epsom, with Paul McCartney as best man. Apart from McCartney's presence it was all family, and a low-key affair, again at Epstein's instigation. The Beatles' manager also organised a press conference, at which a reporter asked Harrison about starting a family. "I don't want children yet," he said, "but I'd like some a bit later on, two or three." The journalist thinks to ask his wife her opinion. "Do you agree?" "Oh yes!" She was 21 and he still only 22. It was, he said, "the normal age for people to get married. That's when a petrol pump attendant gets married, though he hasn't got all these people looking at him."[23]

Later, the couple went on honeymoon to Barbados, one of the few times they were ever truly alone. Marrying a Beatle was a little like marrying into the mafia. "There were always so many people," says Boyd. "I don't know why, it was just how it was. It was a huge family and there was a pecking order, and one just stayed within the confines of it." It could be a hazardous as well as a frustrating lot. Boyd was often the target of verbal and sometimes physical attacks by jealous fans. She was hemmed in outside Hammersmith Odeon at the end of 1965, kicked and punched and spat at. If she saw a group of young girls in the street she would cross the road.

'I Need You', 'If I Needed Someone' ("I'm too much in love") and 'You Like Me Too Much' reflect the emotional rhythms of his first two years with Boyd. They are at once breezily confident and slightly vulnerable. As both a Beatle and an unreconstructed product of the times, Harrison held orthodox views about who should rule the roost when it came to marriage. When she came to live at Kinfauns, Boyd's two Dalmatians had to be packed off elsewhere because they bothered his cats. He didn't like her modelling and asked her to stop. However enlightened one aspired to be, this was a pre-feminist age. "He had that old fashioned Liverpudlian idea that your wife doesn't go out to work," says Bramwell. "So she didn't go out to work. He'd rather have her at home cooking."

Asked if his attitude to women was old-fashioned, Boyd replies, "Oh yes, absolutely. Very conservative. I went along with it. That was the traditional, conservative point of view of marriage, which I had as well, but I'd had the dreadful experience of my mother divorcing twice, so I was always slightly suspicious of marriage and men remaining faithful."

On that score her fears were well founded. Dating Boyd had been no barrier to Harrison's promiscuity. In America the US gossip columns sniffed around his relationship with the young movie starlet, Joey Heatherton. "Are you going to take Joey Heatherton to a ball in New York?" he was asked late in 1964. "I don't even know him, whoever he is," Harrison replied drily, in his own droll way perhaps protesting too much. And in all those endless hotel rooms, the pursuit of some kind of distraction from the mania went on unabashed, in city after city, country after country. "Yeah Australia," Lennon later said. "Just think of [Fellini's] *Satyricon* with four musicians going through it. We had to do something and what do you do when the pills wear off?"[24] Jimmy Nicol, parachuted into this madhouse, was boggle-eyed at the antics behind the scenes. "George was not shy at all, as the press had tried to paint him," he said. "He was into sex as well as partying all night with the rest of us. I was not even close to them when it came to mischief and carrying on."[25] "He didn't mind going off with other women," says Bill Harry. "There are stories there that will never be told. Some of them were pretty close to the bone."

Boyd was not exactly oblivious, though she tended not to want to dwell on the details. "Being with George could be very, very difficult," she says. "He would get glorious outpouring-of-love letters from fans, and then all the girls in the office were madly in love with him. And of course we weren't allowed to go on tour. Brian Epstein wouldn't dream of allowing me to go on tour. George was loved wherever he went; this is not very good for somebody [like me] who is slightly insecure. It was a battle, you see. I battled with myself. I thought, if I let him know it will just make it even more difficult. It wasn't as if he was in a position to stop people writing to him or adoring him."

On the other hand, he was in love with Boyd and there were certain emotional readjustments to be made in light of the fact that he was with a woman who had her own successful career, her own public profile, her own group of fashionable friends, and more than her fair share of admirers, one of whom happened to be John Lennon, who "had always made a thing of fancying Pattie Harrison," according to his biographer Philip Norman, and once made a play for her in front of Cynthia.[26]

Boyd was, says Bramwell, "a flirt", who was capable of making Harrison "wildly jealous and possessive."[27] He wanted her to be at home while he was working late in the studio. She was in her early twenties and would, understandably, rather be out. There were sometimes pleading late night phone calls between Abbey Road and the house telephone in the nightclubs of the West End. A promoter on the Australian tour, Kevin Ritchie, recalled Harrison "wandering around the hotel feeling desperately homesick"[28] after he and Boyd had fought just before he left the country.

Whatever the mutual struggles, they were a good match, playmates as much as lovers, and for a time a happy fit. "He and Pattie were joined at the hip," says Bramwell, and in interviews he was keen to emphasise the equality of their relationship and her influence on him. "I've got a lot of my taste off Pattie," Harrison said.[29] She was given carte blanche to decorate Kinfauns, filling it with black leather sofas and modern furniture from the Habitat store that Terence Conran had recently opened on Fulham Road. The centrepiece of the living room was a huge circular brick fireplace. There were no gold discs on the walls, no flash. It was very much the home of a young, modern couple.

Marriage and Kinfauns led to a more domesticated lifestyle. Maurice Milbourne, the gardener, and Margaret, the housekeeper, looked after the basics, although Boyd usually shopped and cooked. Harrison ate sparingly: coffee and fried eggs for breakfast, or porridge, and often no lunch. A man of set tastes, he talked about "branching out into the avocado scene,"[30] but his favourite homecoming meal was macaroni and cheese.

At night they might drive into town to Parks restaurant in Beauchamp Place, or to Cubby Broccoli's private viewing theatre to watch the latest films, or to drink good wine at familiar haunts like Annabel's. They might just as happily stay in, entertain family and close friends, smoke a joint or two, watch television and listen to music. "When they all moved out of London, Paul was really the only one that socialised," says Bramwell. "To go clubbing or to the theatre was too much hassle, it was a two-hour drive to get anywhere. After George got married he didn't really go out a lot, apart from after recording sessions, when they might go to a club. But if they weren't in town he didn't come out and play." "George didn't want to meet new people or go to new places," says Boyd. "He was happy to visit my old friends and our families, but he was wary of newcomers."[31]

★ ★ ★

As life became deeper, richer, more confusing, more complex, it was clear that Harrison had things he wanted to say. Yet his plain-speaking nature seemed to wrong foot the lyricist in him. "My main trouble is the lyrics," he said of writing songs. "I can't seem to write down what I want to say."[32]

"The difficulty was putting words to it," Boyd agrees. "Almost always. Occasionally I would help, or we would play around with it and have fun. At times the words would just come to him, as if he knew exactly where he was going with the song, but it usually worked very gradually. He was a bit of a perfectionist."

For a man who did not have a natural affinity with the written word, lyrics could be a painfully drawn out process. The trouble lay in bridging the gap between blunt thought and poetic expression. It is overstating the case to say that Harrison was incapable of lying in a song, but he certainly channelled his feelings directly, if not always gracefully. "Writing a song is like going to confession," he once said[33] – and there is indeed something of the confession box, and the pulpit, about his writing, a sense of an unburdening of some heavy weight, which is not infrequently passed on to the listener. He struggled in the beginning to write for the craft or even the joy of it. It took the experience of Beatlemania to really seed the need in him to say something about the world he was now in and how he felt about it, but the art of snaring his feelings in three verses and a chorus didn't come easily. He tended towards first person expression rather than narrative, and he lacked an easy gift for metaphor or imagery. By 1965 he had "thrown away about 30 songs. They may have been all right if I'd worked on them, but I didn't think they were strong enough."[34]

As he tried to stretch in the mid-Sixties he often found himself singing about his own struggles with inarticulacy and the process of writing itself. There is a lot of preamble and frustration in his early songs. "I want to tell you," he sings, or "I could speak my mind", or "I've got a word or two to say," but for all the throat-clearing build-up, what he is actually trying to communicate often remains opaque. 'Think For Yourself' was surely written as a rebuke to sheep-like Beatles fans – "everyone was behaving the way they had heard they were supposed to," he said[35] – but this jabbed finger into the listener's chest feels more like a note to self, a prod of encouragement for Harrison to act on his own private convictions. 'I Want To Tell You' is even more obviously a song about his inability to communicate, his difficulty in honing his thoughts into a coherent point: "I feel hung up but I don't know why," he sings, and "my head is filled with things to say". Yet in fact he says almost nothing. It is a telling song, a study in disaffection, inertia, ineloquence and ultimately a kind of

Zen acceptance. Like so many of his subsequent compositions, the addressee could be a woman, The Beatles, his fans, himself, or God. The music is similarly conflicted and unresolved, but compellingly so, and ends on a glorious triple harmony from Harrison, Lennon and McCartney on the line "I've got time," where suddenly all seems wonderfully well with the world and within the band.

He was beginning to find both his feet and his style. The fact that he generally looked inward is perhaps the defining characteristic of Harrison's writing. This inability to sing from too far outside his own direct personal experience or emotion made him perhaps the most soulful of all The Beatles, though at times it could render the going rather heavy. It also made him perfectly placed to write the no-frills story of the band in song. Both pre- and post-break-up, Harrison stitched together an almost uniformly bleak counter narrative to The Beatles' fairytale romp as directed by Dick Lester. We hear the queasy reservations of the budding star ('Don't Bother Me'), the lot of the embittered millionaire ('Taxman'), the demeaned band member, both heart-heavy and mightily pissed off ('Not Guilty', 'Wah Wah', 'I Me Mine', 'Isn't It A Pity'), the sad seer of their break up ('All Things Must Pass'), and the cold-eyed documenter of the financial and emotional fall-out on the bitter 'Only A Northern Song' and 'Sue Me, Sue You Blues'.

Each one in its own way is an essay in disaffection. Only after the dust had long settled and John Lennon murdered was he able to cast a kinder eye on his old band, on 'All Those Years Ago' and 'When We Was Fab', but as late as 2002, on his posthumous album *Brainwashed*, there was 'The Rising Sun', on which he remembers being "crippled" by boundaries, "programmed" into guilt, and having his nervous system skewed off its axis. He had, he sang, worked all his life on the "avenue of sinners". Plenty of other musicians who travelled that road saw nothing more sinister than a path paved with gold, or at least a scattering of bronze and silver.

'Taxman' is the first significant chapter in this intriguing narrative. After years of rather muddled circling its merciful flash of clarity came almost as a shock. 'Taxman' is, on the one hand, a fine slice of dry wit, absolutely true to its target and roving into the realm of absurdist humour to make its point. On the other hand, it's a remarkably sour piece of glass-half-empty whinging from a man in the most successful pop group in the world.

It is quintessentially Harrison, amused and amusing, yet cured in a simmering resentment. You can see his point, however contradictory and simplistic it may have been. At this point the Labour government, still grappling with the pressures of a limping post-war economy, was charging a top rate of 95 pence in the pound. It would drop to 91.5 per cent the following year. Still a working-class man at heart, he believed he should not be relieved of the bulk of his earnings, however much they were, and – presumably – no matter to what social benefit they were to be put.

"He didn't think he had money," says Boyd. "We weren't lavish spenders, and Brian Epstein seemed to take care of everything, and I suppose it made George think that perhaps he didn't really have much. He wrote 'Taxman' because he realised that the Labour government was charging [95 pence] in the pound. He sat down and worked out how much a packet of cigarettes would actually cost him, and from there he thought, My God, it is costing an absolute fortune just to live in England, and he worried that he didn't have the money." It's worth noting that however much he belly-ached about the tax rate, he never became a tax exile. Unlike The Rolling Stones and countless other rock stars, the quality of life trumped the balance sheet.

And goodness, that resentment created a great song. Sharp, crisp and modern. Lennon later claimed to have, reluctantly, had a hand in writing the words. "I threw in some one liners to help the song along because that's what he asked for," he said. "He came to me because he couldn't go to Paul McCartney because Paul wouldn't have helped him at that point. I didn't really want to help him. I thought, 'Oh no, don't tell me I have to work on George's stuff.' But because I loved him and didn't want to hurt him, when he called I just sort of held my tongue and said okay."[36]

The very definition of an unreliable narrator, in this case it seems that not only does Lennon's memory accurately convey the manner in which Harrison was disregarded as a creative force by his two band mates, but also the means by which 'Taxman' came together. It's not hard to spot Lennon's shaping hand. The lyrics have a tightness, a coherence and clarity which none of Harrison's songs till now had possessed; everything is honed to a fine point. The band also, for once, put their back into recording it. The basic song structure is simple, a three-chord blues sharpened by sevenths, but it is enlivened principally by McCartney, who brings not just the wildly inventive bass line but also the ferocious guitar solo, as jagged and abrasive as anything heard on a Beatles record at that point. The backing vocals, with their tittering references to the Prime Minister Harold Wilson and opposition leader Edward Heath, are witty and full of character, and Starr's skittering drum fills propel everything forward. Ushered in with its *Goons*-like audio-vérité introduction, it makes a more than worthy opening track for the audacious *Revolver*.

Writing for the band was not just about purely felt creativity. Mammon played its part, too. At the beginning of 1964 Harrison's ambition, he said, was to retire with "a whacking great pile of money.... as long as I get an equal share of the money, I'm willing to stay anonymous."[37] But he wasn't getting an equal share of the money and he was very far from being anonymous. A bad deal all round.

Since 1963 the band's collective earnings had been filtered into Beatles Ltd., with NEMS' 25 per cent share taken off the top. Earnings from Lennon and McCartney's compositions, published by Northern Songs, were treated separately. They each owned 15 per cent of the public company's shares, while Harrison (and Starr) owned just 0.8 per cent. Once the two principal writers had realised the size of the pie they were reluctant to share it, yet another reason for keeping Harrison at arm's length. Northern Songs' profit for 1965 was a reported £621,000; Harrison would have seen a little under £6,000 of it. He formed his own publishing company, Mornyork, in 1964, swiftly renamed Harrisongs Ltd. Unbeknown to him at the time, in doing so he had signed over the majority share of his song rights to Dick James, the London publisher who also owned more than half the rights to all the work on Northern Songs.

Everywhere you looked, Harrison was losing out. "John and Paul as co-owners and directors and shareholders in Northern Songs earned almost as much as George Harrison did from his songs and that caused resentment," says EMI historian Brian Southall. "George felt he had been conned and it is true that he wasn't given any independent advice. Seemingly, every lawyer and every accountant who advised The Beatles was retained by NEMS, which was Brian Epstein's management company."[38]

It was a matter of perception as much as money: in the eyes of the law as well as in the eyes of the band, Harrison was a designated bit part player in The Beatles story. Little wonder that rather quickly his sights as a songwriter turned away from the government and settled on targets closer to home.

★ ★ ★

There may have been some consolation in the fact that he was beginning to realise that money was not going to provide a shortcut to genuine fulfilment. His material appetites were, if not sated, then at least being satisfied at any early age, which was "good really," he said, "because we realised that that wasn't it."[39]

Playing music on stage wasn't going to be "it" either. Shortly after *Revolver* was released in the first week of August 1966 The Beatles ground to a halt as a live band. On June 30 they had landed in Japan in the immediate aftermath of rioting at the decision to allow them to play the Nippon Budokan Hall, considered by many a sacred shrine and suitable only for martial arts, rather than pop concerts. Just before he arrived, while The Beatles were playing in Germany, Harrison received a letter saying he wouldn't live beyond a month. On landing they were taken straight to the Tokyo Hilton, where snipers lined the roof. During their stay in the city they were protected by 35,000 security personnel. "I did not set foot outside of the Hilton except for doing the concerts," he recalled.[40]

From Japan they travelled to the Philippines. Always highly attuned to the atmospheric mood music, Harrison was immediately put on red alert by the "the guns and cars and violence."[41] The concert was dangerously oversubscribed. Worse, the promoter had told President Marcos that The Beatles would meet him and his wife Imelda in an official reception at the palace. Except nobody had told the band, and their refusal to alter their plans – especially for the notoriously corrupt Marcoses – was broadcast on national radio and television, almost instantly creating a wave of national anger. By the time they arrived at the airport to leave the country the same security goons and military police who should, in theory, have been protecting them were either nowhere to be seen or turning on them. They were pushed and shoved and spat at, while Mal Evans was punched and kicked by an increasingly frenzied mob. "They were waiting for us to retaliate so that they could finish us off," said Harrison. "I was terrified."[42]

They ran to the plane in genuine fear for their safety. "He had a very, very bad experience in Manila and that remained unforgettable for George," says Boyd. "He was a very slight man, very light in weight, and the fear of being vulnerable to fans, and crazy people, remained with him." The terror never quite seemed to leave him. "It was one of the nastiest times I have had," he said years later.[43]

It scarcely got any better when they arrived in the United States the following month. They landed in Chicago amid a gathering storm over Lennon's remarks during an interview with Maureen Cleave for the *Evening Standard* that The Beatles were "more popular than Jesus." He had made the comment back in March, but when the quote was reprinted in the American teen magazine *DATEbook*, just prior to the tour, it caused a media-hyped flurry of anger in the southern United States. Beatles' records were publicly burned – "they've got to buy them before they can burn them," Harrison noted with a hollow laugh – radio stations imposed bans on their records, press conferences were cancelled and every day seemed to bring a new wave of death threats.

The Ku Klux Klan nailed a Beatles album to a wooden cross and vowed "vengeance". In the end the closest they came was sending the Imperial Wizard of Maryland to picket their show in Washington D.C. Before they played Memphis an anonymous phone call warned that a Beatle would be assassinated during one of the two shows. When a firecracker was set off during the evening performance everyone assumed the worst. "There was this nasty atmosphere," said their press officer Tony Barrow. "It was a very tense and pressured kind of day."[44]

At the LA Dodgers stadium on August 28 the crowd broke through police lines and attempted to rush across the field to the stage. The Beatles froze, before McCartney shrugged and they launched into 'Baby's In Black'. All the way through the song, Harrison was shouting at Joan Baez, who was standing side-stage, "What's *happening*?" Nobody was able to provide an answer. They got out of the stadium first in an ambulance, then an armoured car.

In common with the rest of the tour, that night they had performed for 33 minutes and hadn't played a single song from *Revolver*. Compared to what Bob Dylan and The Hawks were doing on stage by 1966, The Beatles now sounded callow and outdated. The following night, in San Francisco, they played their final ever show.

Touring had become an intolerable accumulation of stress factors. According to Harrison it was in some way their karmic fate. It all "relates to the sort of life we were leading," he said. "We were open to that sort of unhappiness."[45] By the summer of 1966 he was a jangle of exposed nerves, and in danger of being eaten alive by the experience of being a Beatle. The reality gnawed through the smart suits, willing women and fixed grins until it left him feeling utterly empty. His personal evolution had become almost Darwinian – adapt or die.

He was still only 23, just learning how to live, and the narrative of his accelerated early adulthood did not follow a linear path. At the same time as playing Beatle George and singing 'Everybody's Trying To Be My Baby' to a football stadium who couldn't hear him, he discovered the sitar and the music of Ravi Shankar. In the morning he might be eating egg and chips in suburbia, but by nightfall his coffee was being spiked with LSD in a smart London townhouse. Driven to write 'Taxman', he discovered at the same time that the material world was not going to offer him the answer to the questions gathering in his mind. While screwing his way around the world he fell in love, got married, and settled down. Harrison always displayed a knack for travelling parallel lines.

Those listening closely could hear the changes he was facing filtering into The Beatles' recorded music, at first faintly and then more clearly. The ragged sitar that snaked its way through 'Norwegian Wood (This Bird Has Flown)' on *Rubber Soul*, the more authentically Indian sounds of 'Love You To' on *Revolver*, the spiritually searching solo on 'I'm Only Sleeping'. These were the most prominent audible clues, but away from the stage and outside of the studio, much, much more was happening besides.

Be Here Now
Mumbai, September, 1966

It is early morning in the Taj Mahal Palace Hotel, the grand Victorian building which dominates the harbour in Mumbai and overlooks the Gateway of India monument. Recently arrived from London, each day Harrison is receiving instruction in the sitar. Sometimes he is taught by Ravi Shankar, more often by his protégé Shambu Das. He learns about the *taraf* and *chikari* strings, the scales of the raga, how to sit, how to hold, as well as the way the instrument interacts with the complex *taal* rhythms of the tabla and the drone of the tamboura. It is punishing, precise work.

"He told me about learning sitar," says Lon Van Eaton, who as one half of Lon & Derrek worked with Harrison on the duo's two albums for Apple in the early Seventies. "It was outrageous. You show up at seven in the morning and the guy says, 'Okay, today we play this note. I will see you play that note all day and I will see you tonight at seven. In five days we have a raga and then next week we put the raga together.' How deep is that? You play a single note all day. Underlying it was such a discipline. You could see why George loved it."

Struggling with the traditional sitar-playing posture, sitting cross-legged with the gourd resting on the instep of the left foot, Harrison begins to take yoga classes each morning. He discovers that although yoga begins as a physical exercise, its ultimate purpose is to connect to the spirit of the Supreme Being. Later in his trip he meets gurus and reads books by the great Indian swamis and yogis. He learns about karma, levitating saints, 200-year-old holy men and ancient miracle-workers living in caves in the Himalayas.

Each new discovery stretches back to the music he is playing which is, says Shankar, all about "revealing the essence of the universe it reflects."[1] Gradually Harrison's eyes open to an unfolding series of revelations about his life and the world around him. They all seem to lead in one direction: inside. To God.

CHAPTER 6

The Rising Sun

The line is clearly drawn. On August 29, 1966, The Beatles played their last ever live concert at Candlestick Park in San Francisco. The usual drill: 25,000 baying fans, a short and ludicrously uninventive set ending with 'Long Tall Sally', and an accelerated heartbeat dash for the exits. Flying back down the coast to Los Angeles the same night, Harrison said, "Well, that's it, I'm not a Beatle anymore."[1] He was wrong, but he was also right.

Harrison's soul departed The Beatles long before his body. That night he expressed to Epstein his wish to leave the band, but the manager's promise not to book any more tours and to schedule a prolonged break from recording was enough to placate him. In the end he left gradually, in increments, like a train sloughing through the suburbs of a major town, the structure of the city gradually thinning out, the air becoming clearer, cleaner – until finally another destination comes into view. It wasn't quite that simple, of course. Being Fab was a job for life, with an inescapable legacy and numerous assumptions attached, but it became essentially a part-time occupation after Candlestick Park. From the late summer of '66 onward Harrison's passions increasingly lay elsewhere.

On September 14, exactly two weeks after returning to Britain from the final US tour date, he and Boyd flew from Heathrow to Mumbai to embark on their first sustained trip to India. And everything changed forever.

★ ★ ★

The first conscious inkling of the East and all the musical, philosophical and spiritual treasures it harboured came the previous year, during the making of *Help!*. The film was one of The Beatles' least soulful, least committed projects, in which alternative spirituality was mockingly played for the broadest of laughs: "See what you've done with your filthy Eastern ways!" Lennon says to Ahme, played by Eleanor Bron, the high priestess of the fiendish cult.

Filming in the Bahamas during February and March 1965, they were bored, stoned virtually the entire time, and often obviously contemptuous of Richard Lester's brasher follow up to *A Hard Day's Night*. In Nassau, on Harrison's twenty-second birthday, he was approached by Swami Vishnu Devananda, a 37-year-old Indian guru who had started teaching Sivananda Yoga and preaching its wider message throughout north America. Devananda had recently opened one of his yogic ashrams on Paradise Island in the Bahamas, a short hop from Nassau, and he gave each member of the band a copy of his book, *The Complete Illustrated Guide To Yoga*. Harrison later – much later, for he didn't read it for several years – saw this as a sign. Perhaps it was. Either that or a smart piece of opportunism from someone already well practised in the art of converting willing Westerners to the ancient ways of the East. There was no shortage of either type in the Sixties.

Later, in April, filming *Help!* back in England at Twickenham Film Studios, Harrison heard the sitar for the first time, played by the Indian musicians brought in to perform in the movie's Rajahama scene. He picked it up, took a look at it, plucked, twanged, fingered a few shapes, and found himself intrigued. This was essentially the end of his curiosity until he experienced what amounted to a life-changing shift in his perception of the universe and his own consciousness.

Harrison's immersion in eastern spirituality came via an accumulation of experiences – notably music, travel, literature, lecture, yoga and meditation. The initial impetus was his first encounter with LSD, then liquid and legal, in the summer of 1965. Attending a dinner party in London, Harrison, Lennon and their wives were spiked by their host, The Beatles' dentist John Riley. At the end of the meal Riley put acid in their coffee with the intention, they later suspected, of instigating some communal scene of unbridled sexual abandon. Instead, when they learned what had happened, they swiftly left.

By the time they reached the Pickwick Club, another favourite London haunt, Harrison was coming up. He felt "a very concentrated version of the best feeling I'd ever had in my whole life," he recalled. "It was fantastic, I felt in love, not with anything or anybody in particular, but with everything."[2] By the time they had moved on to the Ad Lib club, things had become a little darker and stranger. En route Boyd tried to smash a window. In the club the elevator appeared to be on fire, and hours seemed to pass in seconds. As dawn rose Harrison drove everyone home – very slowly, very carefully – in his Mini. They stopped on the way to play football before falling into Kinfauns, bolting the door, and willing sleep to come.

Amid all the confusion, terror and disorientation of his 12-hour trip Harrison was hit by a life-altering illumination. "It was as if I'd never tasted, talked, seen, thought or heard properly before," he said. "For the first time in my life I wasn't conscious of ego."[3] Unlike alcohol or pot, acid didn't make the edges of existence appealingly fuzzy. Instead, it brought into blinding focus all the questions and doubts already lurking in his consciousness. "It was an awakening, and the realisation that the important thing in life is to ask: 'Who am I?' 'Where am I going?' and 'Where have I been?,'" he said. "All the other bullshit – that *was* just bullshit."[4] He had the hyper-real sense of escaping his body, of becoming pure energy, infinite and omnipresent.

There is, according to Roger McGuinn, "a misunderstanding about what we were doing back in the Sixties with psychedelic drugs. We were really seeking a higher power. We were looking at it like the peyote used by American Indians, as a sacrament to find out what was happening spiritually. It does free you up to see things other than the three dimensions that we're used to. It's not hallucinating so much as seeing into another dimension."

Applied to many other musicians this interpretation would seem fanciful, and certainly not everyone who dropped acid shared such lofty aspirations. But Harrison was spiked. He was not deliberately seeking to alter his perception. He had no expectations and was taken entirely by surprise when he discovered that LSD gave him a temporary glimpse of a higher form of self. Later, he would claim that he only really needed to take it once, that the inaugural experience was enough. In fact his fascination with the drug lasted two years, from the summer of 1965 to the summer of 1967, the year he wrote 'It's All Too Much', not a terribly good song but perhaps his clearest expression of how acid impacted on his wider consciousness. "The more I go inside/The more there is to see," he sang, picturing himself "floating down the stream of time/From life to life." There was also a word of caution: "Take a piece but not too much," advice that he generally heeded even if several of his peers and at least one of his band mates did not.

McGuinn was a happy participant when Harrison took his second trip a few weeks later. The Beatles were on tour in the States, and this time the illumination of transcendence came with a direct connection to the music of India. When they arrived in Los Angeles on August 22 the band holed up for a week in a large rented house belonging to Zsa Zsa Gabor at 2850 Mulholland Drive in Beverly Hills. On the afternoon of August 24 they sent a limousine to pick up McGuinn and David Crosby from The Byrds, who they had met earlier that month at Blaises nightclub in London. The ensemble took LSD soaked in sugar cubes and promptly hid in the bathroom, the designated chill-out zone throughout the peak pressure points of Beatlemania. Harrison thought he had held onto the memory of how extraordinary his first acid trip had been, but as he came up he found that "the concept was nowhere near as big as the reality."[5]

"George, John, Crosby and I, and Peter Fonda, all dropped acid," says McGuinn. "Ringo did, too, I think, but he wasn't hanging out with us. We went into the bathroom to get away from the security guards because they scared us – there were all these armed guards around the house because the little girls were trying to climb in over the fence. It was a wild scene, like *A Hard Day's Night*. So we found solace in this bathroom that had a nine foot-square tub, and we were all sitting on the edge of the tub with a guitar, passing it back and forth and comparing notes. That was when I first learned that the first thing both George and I ever learned was the riff from Gene Vincent's 'Woman Love'.

"Then I played something for him a little like Ravi Shankar, and George immediately said, 'What's that?' I said, 'That's like Ravi.' David Crosby and I had access to Ravi Shankar's records because he recorded for World Pacific and Jim Dickson, our manager, had been the engineer at World Pacific. So we knew about Ravi. David was a big fan, he had seen Ravi in person and got very excited about it. David told George all about Ravi Shankar, and David can be extremely enthusiastic. He kind of jumps up and down, he can sell something to you really easily. The *Help!* movie had been in the can by that time and there was a scene with some Indian music, so obviously it wasn't the first time they had heard Indian music, but I don't think they knew about Ravi Shankar. That was the first time he became aware of him, and George sought him out and became a student."

Ravi Shankar was born in 1920 to one of India's more privileged families. As a child he moved to Paris and toured Europe and America as a dancer and choreographer in his brother Uday's dance troupe; he can be seen, aged 11, in old Pathé newsreel footage dating from 1931. Nothing would ever compare to Beatlemania, but as a young man Shankar had been through his own flirtation with "the sparkle and easy fame of the artist's life."[6] At 18 he renounced it all, returning to India to engage in seven years' intensive tuition in near-ascetic conditions with Ustad Allauddin Khan, one of the towering figures of North Indian classical music. Not for the first time in his life, he followed the path of most resistance.

In that time he became a virtuoso of the sitar, although he always claimed it took 20 years to become competent on the instrument, and at least 40 to really master it. By 1948 he was musical director at All-India Radio, the international branch of the government broadcasting service, and in 1955 he formed the National Orchestra. By the late Fifties he had taken on a roving brief as a cultural ambassador, travelling the world playing concerts and festivals and talking about Indian music and its history.

After being alerted to Shankar by The Byrds, Harrison "went out and bought a record and that was it. It felt very familiar to me to listen to that music."[7] His immediate appreciation of it was vastly heightened by the experience of taking hallucinogens. "Indian music is inspired by transcendence, so it did all fit together," says McGuinn. LSD put him fully in receive mode. "When George heard Indian music that really was the trigger, it was like a bell that went off in his head," said Olivia Harrison. "It not only awakened a desire to hear more music, but also to understand what was going on in Indian philosophy. It was a unique diversion."

At first, at least consciously, it was the sound that fascinated him. Shortly after returning from the 1965 US tour he bought a cheap sitar from India Craft on Oxford Street. The following month he was playing it, crudely if enthusiastically, on 'Norwegian Wood (This Bird Has Flown)', recorded in October and released on *Rubber Soul* in early December. The instrument was already well known in western classical circles – Philip Glass, John Cage and LaMonte Young were all Shankar fans – and also in the world of traditional music: the great folk pioneer Davey Graham created the DADGAD open tuning partly so he could transpose sitar tunes to guitar. It was also beginning to creep into pop music. Earlier in 1965 The Yardbirds and The Kinks had been heavily influenced by sitar in their choice of guitar sounds on 'Heart Full Of Soul' and 'See My Friends' respectively. Indeed the North American release of *Help!* features the instrumental 'Another Hard Day's Night', a medley of three Beatles tunes – 'A Hard Day's Night', 'Can't Buy Me Love' and 'I Should Have Known Better' – rearranged for sitar, tabla, flute and finger cymbals. Included as filler and for comedic effect, this track beats 'Norwegian Wood' by four months to the honour of featuring the first sitar on a Beatles-related recording.

On 'Norwegian Wood' he was effectively playing the sitar like a guitar. "It was lying around," he said. "I hadn't really figured out what to do with it. When we were working on 'Norwegian Wood' it just needed something, and it was quite spontaneous, from what I remember.

I just picked up my sitar, found the notes and just played it. We miked it up and put it on and it just seemed to hit the spot."[8]

He persevered. Always dedicated in his passions to the point of obsession, before long the sitar had "taken over 100 per cent in my musical life."[9] Equally characteristically, his immersion in Indian music came with a reproving dig at those not quite hip enough to keep up. The old us-and-them mantra. "It's very *involved* music," he told the *Detroit Free Press* during a long and terribly earnest interview about his new discovery, which was eventually ended by Beatles press officer Tony Barrow practically dragging him away. "That's why the average listener doesn't understand. They listen to Western music all their lives. Eastern music is a different concept. Indian music is hip, yet 8,000 years old. I find it hard to get much of a kick out of Western music, even out of Western music I used to be interested in a year ago. Most music is still only surface, not very subtle compared to Indian music... Music in general, us included, is still on the surface."[10]

'Love You To' was his first dedicated attempt to delve beneath the surface. It was recorded in April 1966 and released in August on *Revolver*, by which point The Rolling Stones had recorded 'Paint It, Black', featuring Brian Jones' driving sitar riff. 'Love You To' was not, however, an orthodox pop song with its spicy Indian flavour stirred in at the last minute; instead it was "the first song where I consciously tried to use the sitar and tabla on the basic track," said Harrison,[11] and as such is perhaps the earliest notable attempt by a Western pop musician to not simply incorporate Indian sounds within a familiar context but to aspire to create something closer to authentic classical music. Lyrically it mixes the language of sexual permissiveness with a fumbling kind of spiritual slang: "They'll fill you in with all their sins," he sings and, perhaps most tellingly for a man entering a period of rapid personal transformation, "you don't get time to hang a sign on me."

How much of the sitar on 'Love You To' is attributable to Harrison remains open to conjecture. Peter Lavezzoli, author of *The Dawn Of Indian Music In The West*, writes that "his playing throughout the song is an astonishing improvement over 'Norwegian Wood'. In fact 'Love You To' remains the most accomplished performance on sitar by any rock musician."[12] But was he solely responsible for it? Certainly the other Beatles are playing only minor roles; Lennon isn't actually on the track at all. The tabla is played by Anil Bhagwat, who did not recall another sitar player being on the session, but there have since been suggestions that other Indian musicians contributed, adding tamboura and very possibly another sitar.

Bhagwat was recruited for the session by Ayana Deva Angadi, who with his wife Patricia Fell-Clarke founded the Asian Music Circle in 1946, an organisation that did much to introduce Indian music, dance and yoga to the British public, and paved the way for the arrival of musicians such as Shankar and Ali Akbar Khan. "[Angadi] called me and asked if I was free that evening to work with George," Bhagwat later said. "I didn't know who he meant – he didn't say it was Harrison. It was only when a Rolls Royce came to pick me up that I realised I'd be playing on a Beatles session. When I arrived at Abbey Road there were girls everywhere with Thermos flasks, cakes, sandwiches, waiting for The Beatles to come out...[13] George told me what he wanted and I tuned the tabla with him. He suggested I play something in the Ravi Shankar style, 16-beats, though he agreed that I should improvise. Indian music is all improvisation."[14]

Ayana Deva Angadi was also instrumental in Harrison's first meeting with Shankar, which Harrison seemed already to view as potentially auspicious. In the year of the "sitar boom", Shankar had become aware of The Beatles' enthusiasm for him and his instrument, while Harrison recalled that people "kept trying to put us together, and I said 'no', because I knew I'd meet him under the proper circumstances."[15] These occurred in June 1966, while The Beatles were finishing off *Revolver*. The two men met for dinner at Angadi's house, and almost instantly the small, handsome and intensely charismatic Indian became a focal point not only for Harrison's growing interest in Indian music, but for the sense of gathering gloom and disaffection which had been growing over the past two years of being a Beatle. "I realised that nothing was actually giving me a buzz any more," he said. "I wanted something... better. I remember thinking, I'd love to meet someone who would really impress me. And that's when I met Ravi."[16]

Shankar would be his guide through a maze that offered Harrison myriad sources of potential enlightenment. "Our culture and our music is so much attached to our tradition and religion," Shankar told me in 2011, and gradually and generously he teased out the connecting threads for the Beatle. It was like a love affair. "Something about Ravi opened a door in George," says Pattie Boyd. "He became totally fascinated by Ravi and Indian music, and fascinated by the sitar."

In the spaces between those final, hair-raising Beatles tours of the Far East and the United States in the heat of 1966, Shankar and his new protégé managed to meet again in England several times. John Barham, a young English musician studying Indian music at the School of Oriental and African Studies at London University, had recently been introduced to Shankar through mutual friends. "Ravi invited me to accompany him and [tabla player and Shankar's frequent collaborator] Alla Rakha to go to George's house where he had been invited to give a private recital for George and Pattie and Ringo and his wife," says Barham, who recalls that Harrison's bond with Shankar was immediately apparent. Yet although the Indian musician's initial impressions were that the Beatle was "very charming and polite, not at all what I expected,"[17] Shankar was not easily impressed. On first hearing Harrison's recorded efforts on 'Norwegian Wood', he told him, "My goodness, what is this sort of thing you are playing there, George? If you don't mind me saying so, it's the sort of frightful, twangy thing you hear on Radio Bombay advertising soap powders."[18]

He could also be a strict disciplinarian. When Harrison put down the sitar during a lesson at Kinfauns to answer the phone, stepping over it casually, Shankar hit him on the leg and said sternly, "You must have more respect for the instrument." He also requested that nobody smoke during his recitals. Getting artificially high was always a sticky issue. "I was a bit unhappy about one part of the whole scene – and that was drugs," Shankar told me. "All these dear, childlike people, all these young hippies, they were unaware and mixed up the whole thing. That's where I was trying to tell them, not to mix our music and religion along with the drug thing."

Harrison acknowledged his wishes, and yet it was the "drug thing" which had led him to Shankar in the first place. They reached a quiet accommodation. "George became a sitar pupil of Ravi, and he impressed me as being a very respectful and disciplined student," says Barham. "He seemed at ease with the sitar and had a very good sound. I would say he was a natural."

★ ★ ★

Battered by the travails of their final tour, The Beatles agreed to take a three-month hiatus in the autumn of 1966. Lennon went off to star in *How I Won The War*, directed by Richard Lester and to be shot in Spain; McCartney to work on the soundtrack for the Boulting Brothers' film *The Family Way*, and Starr to do whatever it was Starr did away from a drum kit.

Harrison and his wife travelled to India for six weeks. It was his second visit. Fleeing the nightmare in Manila in July, The Beatles and entourage had briefly stopped off in New Delhi. In search of a shop where he could buy a sitar, Harrison was engulfed by crowds and chaos and cries of "Beatles! Beatles!" and instantly thought, Oh no, not again. But later they escaped the tumult of the city and he got a feel for the place. Two weeks after the concert in Candlestick Park he was back again at Shankar's invitation, this time for a more prolonged and intensive trip. To de-Beatle himself he cut his hair short and started growing a moustache. For the first week he looked 15 again. "George could be anonymous in India, nobody really knew who he was, which was an attraction," says Boyd.

They stayed in the Taj Mahal Palace by the harbour, and each day Harrison received instruction in sitar and yoga from Shankar or one of his students. In between there was time to go out and look at temples, do a little shopping and eating out. His anonymity held until one day he was recognised in the hotel lobby and crowds and journalists began to gather. Starting to feel hemmed in, shortly afterwards Harrison and his party headed north on the train. They visited Jaipur, Delhi, Jodhpur, the Taj Mahal in Agra. They watched bodies burning on the banks of the Ganges and attended the religious festival of Ramlila in Benares in Uttar Pradesh, the city in which Shankar had been born, where thousands of itinerant and eccentric holy men flocked from all over India to meet the Maharajah. "Some of them look like Christ, they're really spiritual, and there are also a lot of loonies who look like Allen Ginsberg," said Harrison. "That's where he got his whole trip from – with the frizzy hair, and smoking little pipes called chillums, and smoking hashish. I saw all kinds of groups of people, a lot of them chanting, and it was a mixture of unbelievable things, with the Maharajah coming through the crowd on the back of an elephant, with the dust rising. It gave me a great buzz."[19]

"We had a long trip with Ravi," says Boyd. "He took us to visit ancient caves, and meet holy men. We would go to beautiful houses where Ravi would play sitar in front of very wealthy Indians, and then another time we would go to hear him play to ordinary fans and all his students sitting at the front."

It was a humbling time. Acid, and now India, was about stripping away the ego and the image of Beatle George and opening himself up to new experiences, ideas and interactions on a very human level. They ended up staying on a houseboat on Lake Dal in Srinagar in Kashmir, surrounded by the magnificent Mughal gardens and, in the distance, the towering outline of the north-eastern flank of the Himalayas. "It was incredible," he recalled. "I'd wake up in the morning and a little Kashmiri fellow, Mr Butt, would bring us tea and biscuits and I could hear Ravi in the next room, practising. It was the first feeling I'd ever had of being liberated from being a Beatle or a number. To suddenly find yourself in a place where it feels like 5,000 BC is wonderful."[20]

If Shankar had first had Harrison pegged as a wealthy, well-meaning dilettante, he soon found his singular focus, and humility, rather impressive. "To begin with I think Ravi was rather taken aback, because he was a classical musician, and rock and roll was really out of his sphere," says Boyd. "I think he thought it was rather amusing that George took to him so much, but during that trip he and George really bonded. Ravi realised that it wasn't just a fashion for George, he had dedication. Ravi had such integrity, and was someone to be respected, and at the same time huge fun. George hadn't really met anyone like that, and he really encouraged his interest."

Shankar started guiding his pupil towards the higher impulse that lay behind the music. During the trip he introduced Harrison to Tat Baba, Shankar's spiritual guru, who explained the concept of karma, the cosmic law of action and reaction which posits that the soul is reborn again and again in different physical forms depending on its acts in a previous life. He also gave him the books that would change his life. Harrison had never been much of a reader, but now he was devouring *Autobiography Of A Yogi*, the life story of Paramahansa Yogananda and one of the ur-texts of Indian spiritualism. Yogananda had founded the Self-Realization Fellowship Center in Encinitas, California, and was one of the principal figures in bringing Hinduism to the West. In his book he talked about his meetings with mystics, renunciants and holy magicians. Harrison was entranced. He also read *Raja-Yoga* by the nineteenth-century Swami Vivekananda, and was particularly struck by Vivekananda's discussion of the Sanskrit maxim *Tat tvam asi* (That thou art), and the idea that the Supreme Being responsible for the creation and perpetuation of everything in the cosmos is the same as the divinity lying within every person. "What right has a man to say that he has a soul if he does not feel it, or that there is a God if he does not see Him," he read. "If there is a God we must see Him." This was a key tenet for Harrison. He began to regard religion as a living organism rather than a duty to be observed every Sunday, and God as something to be seen and touched and heard and felt, and which could ultimately only be found within.

He read the *Yoga Sutras*, where he heard echoes of the same revelation he'd had the first time he took acid: the soul was infinite, and though it was the size of "one-thousandth part of the tip of a hair", it had the power of "ten thousand suns." He read the *Bhagavad-Gita*, and stories about ancient ragas that could bring fire, thunder and rainstorms. It was almost too much. "To [follow] the course of that thing was very difficult, but Ravi was my patch chord," he said. "He could plug me into that experience."[21]

He rose each morning in Kashmir in the clear mountain air, with the Himalayas stretching out in the distance, the tranquillity of the lake surrounding him and the scent of saffron on the breeze. He did his yoga exercises, practised the sitar, read, talked, and thought hard about his life. "It was the most fantastic experience, and I know it affected George very deeply," says Boyd. "Ravi was very instrumental in teaching us about India – not just about the music but the culture and the spirituality. It really opened his eyes. Once you get into Eastern philosophy you can't help but start questioning yourself, and once you have an inkling of that you can't deny it. You have to investigate."

He arrived back in London as if from a dream, on October 22, 1966, and began trying to live a meaningful existence in the light of what acid, the sitar, Shankar, yoga and the words of all those swamis and yogis had taught him over the past year. All the physical ties of his life to date, and all the superficial achievements of his music career, seemed to recede to the smallest speck. It is hard to overstate how hard and fast he fell. Harrison was, in many ways, a vulnerable man ripe for conversion. Belittled within the band, pulled apart by Beatlemania, having his component parts laid bare by the blinding illumination of LSD, he was positively thirsting for something that could show him a more nourishing future. "I know that when you believe it's real and nice," he said. "Not believing, it's all confusion and emptiness."[22]

★ ★ ★

The month after he returned from India The Beatles finally reconvened to begin work on their next record. Amid all these great inner changes, the making of *Sgt. Pepper's Lonely Heart's Club Band*, the great lysergic behemoth of The Beatles' post-touring period and an album generally considered to be one of pop music's most remarkable achievements, felt for Harrison little more than a minor distraction. Talking about *Sgt. Pepper* – off-screen – in the Nineties for the *Anthology* series, he said he "couldn't remember going to the studio", telling Geoff Wonfor, "If you roll the cameras I'll say something, odd things will pop into my head, but I really, really can't remember it."

The Beatles now seemed a flimsy, juvenile entity. Choosing not to quote Dylan for once, he instead opted for Shakespeare or Elvis ('Are You Lonesome Tonight?'). "'The world is a stage'? Well, he was right, because we're Beatles, and it's a little scene and we're playing and we're pretending to be Beatles, like Harold Wilson's pretending to be Prime Minister..."[23] Having first publicly announced that "everything we've done so far has been rubbish,"[24] he privately declared himself utterly unimpressed with McCartney's founding concept for the new album, which involved The Beatles adopting the personae of another band and then... well, nobody was quite sure where it went from there. The album's bright, cartoon-psychedelia and the songs' overwhelming interest in abstract imagery and playful narrative seemed to him to be paddling around in the shallows of life and art. It also exposed his unwillingness, or inability, to write what McCartney called "fantasy songs". There are precious few whimsical flights of fancy, shifting perspectives or fictional characters in Harrison's oeuvre. His work tends to be anchored much closer to home. "I remember George once said to me, 'I could never write songs like that'," said McCartney. "'You just make 'em up, they don't mean anything to you'."[25] The irony is that a story-song such as McCartney and Lennon's 'She's Leaving Home' carries a weight of humanity and empathy which is almost entirely absent from Harrison's work.

Smitten with the East, he also did not share the humorous nostalgia for a proud, civic north, and of course Liverpool itself, exhibited in many of the songs. Fitted up in *Sgt. Pepper*'s vibrant satin suits Harrison's face in photographs is frequently a picture; he wears the same look of wounded dignity as a dog forced to wear a dress.

With no tour looming, The Beatles had the time and space to experiment, which meant an instant easing of the unrelenting pressure which had dogged Harrison's life for the past four years. The downside was that, without an enforced structure, the sense of band unity rapidly dissipated. Dave Mason, then a member of Traffic, recalls visiting his friend at Kinfauns and realising that "things weren't what they had been at that point with The Beatles, put it that way. All of us, all those bands, we were all so damn young – we didn't know shit from shinola about life, we were scared and trying to find our place in it all. All that stuff was going on with The Beatles, and though I never really heard him talk about it, you could see what was happening."

They rarely played together in the studio any more, "which was when the rot set in, really," said Harrison.[26] Most of the recording on *Sgt. Pepper* was done piecemeal, each band member devoting the lion's share of their time and energy to their own ideas. "I got known, particularly around that time, as a very melodic bass player," said McCartney. "And that was because I didn't actually have to play on the tracks. It did actually cause a little friction, I know George particularly wasn't too keen at playing a backing track without a bass. It didn't sound like a real band, you had to imagine the bass. It sounded a bit thin. Then, what it enabled me to do, 'cos I lived so near the studio anyway, the other guys would go home and I'd stay a couple of hours and just work."[27]

"It was becoming difficult for me, because I wasn't really that into it," said Harrison. "It became an assembly process – just little parts and then overdubbing – and for me it became a bit tiring and a bit boring. I had a few moments in there that I enjoyed, but generally I didn't really like making that album much. I'd just got back from India, and my heart was still out there."[28] Musically, he drifted in and out. He had become consumed by the sitar, practising three times a day for a minimum of an hour at a time. The boy who had once played the guitar until his fingers bled took to his new instrument with a similarly obsessive dedication. Shankar sent him tape-recorded exercises, he had notebooks full of Indian notation, and he evangelised to his musician friends. "George gave me my first sitar," says Dave Mason. "It was the one he had to kind of fool around on, and then he gave me the address in India to get the really good ones."

By contrast, he barely ever touched his guitar. As a consequence, The Beatles discovered they had a guitarist who no longer wanted to play, and who also didn't have much time for pop music. On *Sgt. Pepper* Harrison was a cameo turn. He contributed only congas on the monumental 'A Day In The Life', harmonica on 'Being For The Benefit Of Mr Kite', comb-and-paper on 'Lovely Rita', and backing vocals on 'When I'm 64'. On the classic pairing of 'Strawberry Fields Forever' and 'Penny Lane', quickly plucked from the album sessions to become a double A-side single in February 1967, he was likewise out on the margins; he doesn't appear at all on the beautiful 'She's Leaving Home'. McCartney played lead guitar on several tracks and was later heard to comment, ungraciously and, as it happens, incorrectly, that "George turned up for his number and a couple of other sessions but not much else."[29]

His initial offering for the album was 'Only A Northern Song', proof that his evolving spiritual awakening didn't preclude sour jokes on the subject of earthly matters. It was the work of a man either not firing on all cylinders creatively, or treating popular music with the contempt he felt it deserved. Lyrically he was once again writing about the act of writing – "You may think the chords are going wrong/But they're not, he just wrote it like that" – and the nefarious mechanics of the publishing industry. Musically, its phased lethargy and dragging ennui induced a kind of mild seasickness. Nobody liked it all that much, with good reason, and George Martin was despatched to have a quiet word. "I had to tell George that, as far as *Pepper* was concerned, I did not think his song would be good enough," said Martin. "I suggested he come up with something a bit better. George was a bit bruised."[30] The song was shelved until they needed material for the *Yellow Submarine* record, at which point it was unenthusiastically resurrected.

He came back fighting with 'Within You Without You', one of his great songs and, not coincidentally, a direct distillation of India both musically and philosophically. Featuring sitar, dilruba, three tamboura, one tabla and a swordmandel, as well as three cellos and eight violins on the string overdub, 'Within You Without You' begins in a shimmering haze which immediately conjures up the heat and dust of the sub-continent. Indeed, its working title was simply 'India'. It is the sound of Harrison putting into practice his determination to seek knowledge through direct experience. Having talked derisorily about people "cashing in on the sitar boom," he wanted "to be able to play Indian music *as* Indian music, instead of using Indian music in pop. It takes years of studying, but I'm willing to do that."[31]

'Within You Without You' was loosely based on a long piece of music Ravi Shankar had previously recorded for All-India Radio. Writing initially on a pedal harmonium, Harrison condensed the music and wrote his own version in three ambitious sections. The lyrics reflect a late night discussion with Klaus Voormann – "we were talking" – on weighty spiritual matters. They express the Vedanta concept of

Maya, the "wall of illusion" which offers a distorted projection of reality and acts as an obstacle to finding divine bliss "within yourself". It is a beautiful, soulful song, and a revolutionary one in The Beatles' catalogue. It also acts as a hefty and rather sombre corrective to the self-absorbed, self-aggrandising optimism of the Summer of Love, with Harrison informing the golden generation that they were really "very small." Meantime, watch out for the people "who gain the world and lose their soul/They don't know, they can't see/Are you one of them?" Harrison, of course, was rich enough not to have to worry any more about directly pursuing materialism. He could turn his consciousness to loftier subjects (though, in reality, money issues were rarely far from his mind). Having glimpsed the answer, his genuine desire to share the message could, partly down to his lack of facility with words, come across as preachy and sanctimonious rather than generous. "Everyone is potentially divine," he said,[32] and couldn't quite understand why no one else could get it, or might not want to. Wasn't it obvious? Wasn't it simple?

'Within You Without You' was among the last tracks completed for *Sgt. Pepper* and featured no other Beatles. It was an impressive assertion of Harrison's growing strength and self-awareness as a person, and also of his independence within the band. Sequenced as the opening track on side two of the album on its release in June 1967, the song had no direct relationship with the rest of the record. It remains distinct and self-sustaining, and can plausibly be viewed as his first ever solo recording.

"I loved 'Within You Without You', I thought that was an amazing track," says Dave Mason. "From the get-go in The Beatles it was John and Paul, it absolutely was, they were the two guys slamming out material all the time, they were such a powerful writing combination. George was so overpowered but he was changing in his head before all of them, and he didn't do anything about it for a while. When he went off on that whole Indian direction everyone else followed. That was his way of stepping out." All his suggestions for the parade of icons adorning Peter Blake's memorable album cover were Indian gurus, among them Paramahansa Yogananda, as well as Sri Yukteswar Giri, Sri Mahauatara Babaji and Sri Lahriri Mahasaya.

With his newfound passions now public knowledge, the general perception of Harrison started to change. The Quiet One suddenly couldn't stop talking. He engaged in serious televised discussions about spirituality on *The Frost Report* – on which he and Lennon, The Beatles' designated spiritual spokesmen, appeared two weeks in a row – and in intense interviews with journalists in the pop papers and the new, very serious rock press. He generally struggled to find the eloquence to put his feelings into words. *Autobiography Of A Yogi* was, he said, "a far-out book, it's a gas."[33] There were generous helpings of stoned ramblings about "vibrations" and getting "buzzed right into the astral plane," as well as bemoaning "ignorance" and jibing at "nasty people" who were "bullshitting themselves."[34] One young journalist, Stephen Ward, who later co-wrote the screenplay for The Beatles Hamburg-era film *Backbeat*, recalls interviewing Harrison in 1967. "All he did was roll the most lethal joint I've ever had in my life, put on Ravi Shankar, and we both went to sleep."[35]

Yet even muddied by the rock star vernacular at its most spacey, and clouded by reefer smoke and haughty disapproval, his sincerity was obvious. "George and I had a lot to talk about as neither of us had any friends with the same deep interest in Indian music," says John Barham. "He invited me over many times to Esher where we played and listened to music and talked, and occasionally he visited me at my parents' flat in Fulham, and then subsequently at the Kensington flat that I shared with my Indian girlfriend at the time. We had many discussions about Indian philosophy and spirituality. Since that time I have been convinced that George was one of the very few people I have ever met who was on a spiritual path."

★ ★ ★

Life at Kinfauns evolved as he did, growing hairier and a little looser. The Harrisons became vegetarians, inspired by a book about the cruelty of veal farming, but also by the Sanskrit codes of *yama*, or self-restraint, which included *Ahimsa*, the pledge of non-violence to all living things. Boyd would shop at the local health food store in Esher for grains, pulses, vegetables and fruit, cooking nut cutlets and stews, but also pakora, samosa, lassi and rasamlai. The scent of hash and joss sticks permeated the house. An ornate hookah pipe sat on a low table in a sitting room which had no chairs, just cushions and rugs.

Life tended to centre around the kitchen. Harrison often wrote at the large pinewood table, or Boyd and her sister would quietly embroider in there while he sat cross-legged in the living room and practised the sitar. He installed a projection room off the garage so they could watch films at home, and he would work up musical ideas on an Ampex four-track reel-to-reel tape recorder he put in one of the spare bedrooms. Music was never far from the centre of the activities. "I'd drop in if I was down that way, just hanging out," says Dave Mason. "He was just a very easygoing guy. The first time I heard *Sgt. Pepper* was with him at his house. 'D'you wanna hear the new record?' 'Of course I do, George!' It was always something to do with music."

At the party for his 24th birthday at Kinfauns he played the sitar and then watched – and recorded – a concert performed in his honour by the great sarod player Ali Akbar Khan, the son of Shankar's mentor Allauddin Khan, and also Shankar's former brother-in-law. No Beatles attended the gathering. Harrison wore a traditional cotton *kurta* and his guests included photographer Henry Grossman and The Byrds' David Crosby and Roger McGuinn, each one arriving with vegetarian dishes for the buffet-style meal. It was, according to McGuinn, a charged occasion. "I remember being at [that] party with him in 1967 and I could feel the room change, there was something happening in the room," he says. "I looked at George and asked what was going on, and he said, 'I'm transcending.' Woah! You could feel something palpable happening there. He was really into it."

As life turned psychedelic so the neat white bungalow erupted into colour, an independent island republic of benign weirdness in a sea of suburban straights. A Dutch couple, Simon Posthuma and Marijke Koger, part of an artistic collective known as The Fool, moved in to paint a Dali-esque mural around the huge circular fireplace. Harrison's instruments were daubed in swirls of yellow, red and blue, his Mini Moke got an acid-friendly paint job, as did his clothes. Eventually even the outer walls of the house itself were covered in graffiti art and psychedelic patterns. Harrison did much of this impromptu redesign while tripping on LSD, and Klaus Voormann also lent a hand. The paintings were loosely inspired by *Tantra Art*, a recently published coffee table book featuring 97 plates of Indian sacred paintings, sculptures and tapestries in a variety of styles, accompanied by text explaining the image and its significance to Indian spirituality.

Tantra Art touched on various traditions in Eastern thought and art: Hindu, Sikh, Buddhist, Jain. Harrison's beliefs were similarly multi-doctrinal, a pick'n'mix selection of eastern religions which illuminated repeated themes and overlapping concepts. These were all different routes to one aim: seeing God, which was the same as seeing the self. For the direct, no-nonsense Liverpool boy the idea was, in essence, very straightforward and simple. He never regarded it as a mystical pursuit. He wrote to reassure his parents that his new path didn't affect his devotion to 'Sacred Heart', or his love for them – and "don't think I've gone off my rocker." It was all about perception: seeing yourself and the world clearly, learning from one life to the next.

It didn't always look or sound like much fun. Indeed, when the Sixties really started swinging Harrison seemed to stop. He came to believe that drugs – apart from marijuana, which was as normal a part of the daily routine as a cup of tea – were now a bum deal. "LSD can help you go from A to B, but when you get to B you see C," he said. "And you see that to get really high you have to do it straight."[36] That this blissful high did not come in a bottle or a blotter was finally confirmed by his trip to the hippie Mecca of Haight-Ashbury in San Francisco in the summer of 1967. It was the height of the Summer Of Love, but the concept meant different things on either side of the Atlantic. In the UK in the mid-Sixties the counterculture was largely the preserve of the intellectual, artistic and social elite – there was nothing remotely egalitarian about it. 'It's All Too Much' is effectively a sound-portrait of the English acid experience, a refined world of cake, country gardens and a genteel, eccentric form of hedonism which plugged into the spirit of Edward Lear and Lewis Carroll. "Show me that I'm everywhere/ And get me home for tea."

In America the context was harder and heavier. When Harrison saw the reality "on the ground" in Haight he was both fearful and horrified. He and his wife, accompanied by Derek Taylor, Neil Aspinall and new Beatle hanger-on and self-appointed technical genius 'Magic' Alexis Mardas, had gone to visit Boyd's sister Jenny in San Francisco. Harrison strolled through the acid-fried hub of the American subculture, sporting heart-shaped sunglasses and strumming his acoustic guitar, and instead of nirvana found "a lotta bums – spotty youths."[37] As they crowded around him, trying to touch him, offering him drugs and in some cases becoming hostile at his attempts to shrug them off, he began to freak out. Having earlier taken some unknown lysergic substance, the whole scene became dark and nightmarish. It was not, he decided, "groovy", and there was nothing spiritual or questing about any of it.

Harrison saw the perils lurking at the edges of the hippie dream sooner than most. "Acid started as a beautiful thing and then army guys and Angels had it and it became darker," says Lon Van Eaton. "Drink and drop acid and shoot people? Oh no!" Everyone he saw in Haight-Ashbury seemed to dropping out from society and relinquishing their personal responsibilities. At that point he turned away from LSD. It had been a blessed access point, but it had become associated in his mind with the kind of "ignorant" people who couldn't see the bigger picture. "Are you one of them?" Not any more. He was already hooked on the hard stuff. "If you really want to get it permanently, you have got to *do* it, you know," he said. "Be healthy, don't eat meat, keep away from those night clubs and *meditate*."[38]

Boyd was a companion, and sometimes a pioneer, in his evolving spiritual journey. She took lessons in the dilruba and in Indian dance, and it was she who had first picked up on transcendental meditation in February 1967, becoming a member of the Spiritual Regeneration Movement and receiving her mantra. According to Tony Bramwell, "Pattie was into the Maharishi before any of them."

Transcendental meditation, or TM, was popularised in the mid-Fifties by the Indian Maharishi Mahesh, a former Physics student at Allahabad University turned yogi, who gave his first lecture in the West in 1958. Bearded, permanently smiling, and with a high-pitched voice which frequently dissolved into giggles, the Maharishi developed the idea of a form of mantra meditation. It was an essentially non-religious doctrine which involved silently repeating the same word or short phrase for 20 minutes twice a day while sitting comfortably with eyes closed, without assuming any special yoga position. The mantra should be kept secret and never said aloud.

Boyd enthused about TM to Harrison, who agreed to come to see the Maharishi on his next trip to London. Lennon, McCartney and their partners came too, to hear his lecture at the Hilton on August 24, just after Harrison had returned from Haight-Ashbury. He bought them all tickets, at a cost of 7/6d each. At the end the Maharishi spoke to them privately for over an hour and invited them to his ten-day conference in Bangor, starting in two days' time. Harrison saw this as the next stage of his journey inward. "I was actually after a mantra," he said. "I had got to the point where I thought I would like to meditate. I'd read about it and I knew I needed a mantra."[39]

The next day they travelled on the 15:50 'Mystic Special', as the *Daily Mirror* named it, from Euston Station to north Wales, amid a media scrum and pandemonium on the train. Mick Jagger and Marianne Faithfull also came along on the five-hour journey which only served to emphasise how detached The Beatles had become from real life. They were so worldly, yet so out of touch with the world. They were scared to leave their first-class compartment in case they got mobbed; no one seemed to have any money or luggage, and Harrison, just like the old days, got angry with autograph hunters. After reaching their destination they were billeted in camp beds in dormitories in Bangor College, like school kids on summer camp.

As for the course itself, they attended an introductory seminar on August 26 at the John Phillips Hall. The following day the news arrived that Brian Epstein had died of an accidental overdose of barbiturates at his house in London. Earlier that Sunday morning Harrison had been given his mantra by the Maharishi, and he saw the timing as auspicious. In the midst of huge changes, on the day that he got his "password to get through into the other world"[40] he was immediately tested by the unexpected death of the man who had, despite his flaws and sometimes questionable business sense, done so much for them both personally and professionally, and whom they genuinely loved.

He took hasty counsel with the Maharishi, along with the rest of The Beatles, and at the press conference in Bangor trotted out a few spaced platitudes. "There's no such thing as death anyway," said Harrison. "I mean, it's death on a physical level, but life goes on everywhere... and you just keep going, really. The thing about the comfort is to know that he's okay."[41] The Beatles were never much given to sentiment, but this was something new: the distancing effects of spiritual elevation. As with money, drugs and fame, there existed the sense that for Harrison religion was just one more way of keeping stark reality at arm's length, a suspicion which lingered right up until his own death. "I feel my course of meditation here has helped me to overcome my grief more easily than before," he said, perhaps forgetting that in his brief time in Bangor he had spent more time in the town's Chinese restaurant than he had communing with God.[42]

* * *

In the wake of Epstein's death The Beatles' lost their rudder, and Paul McCartney became the great chivvier. Harrison wanted them all to go to India straight away to study at length with the Maharishi at his ashram in Rishikesh. He was outvoted, and McCartney persuaded the group to carry on with his idea of making a loosely structured film, *Magical Mystery Tour*, in the autumn of 1967.

Harrison drifted through the experience, which was filmed partly in Devon and Cornwall and also in and around London. His inscrutable expression as he sits in Paul Raymond's Revue Bar watching a striptease act makes his thoughts hard to discern, but it was certainly a long way from levitating yogis. At the sessions for the soundtrack EP, as McCartney worked on the sub-*Pepper* title track Harrison "got a set of crayons out of his painted sheepskin jacket and started to draw a picture."[43]

He contributed 'Blue Jay Way', another queasy, overly literal song, this time about waiting in Los Angeles for Derek Taylor and his wife Joan to show up as the thick fog scrambled their bearings. It was one more example of his difficulties in transcending the specifics of the moment that inspired him to write. 'Blue Jay Way' is about waiting and being bored and, Lord, does it sound like it. It did at least encapsulate accurately his overall feelings about a project he cared little for. "I had no idea what was happening and maybe I didn't pay enough attention because my problem, basically, was that I was in another world," said Harrison. "I didn't really belong; I was just an appendage."[44] On 'Blue Jay Way' he seems to be barely there at all.

Little wonder he jumped at Joe Massot's offer to take charge of his own project. The American film director had worked with Jenny Boyd on a previous film and had become a friend. He was looking for someone to write the music for his new movie *Wonderwall*, starring Jane Birkin. "George told me that he had been working on *Magical Mystery Tour* helping out, but that was Paul's project, that he would like to do something solo," said Massot. "So I told him that he would have a free hand to do anything he liked musically. That was what interested him in particular."[45]

He worked up the music quickly in demo form at home, using ideas he wasn't able to get into The Beatles, and extemporising fragments and themes, mostly using piano as his primary writing instrument. "I was real nervous with the idea, because he [Massot] wanted music running through the whole film, but he kept on with me," Harrison said. "What I'd do was go into [Twickenham] film studio with a stop watch... and I'd just be what they call 'spotting' the scene to see where the music was going to go, doing click-click with the watch. I'd go back into my studio and make 35 seconds, say, of something, mix it, and line it up with the scene."[46]

Wonderwall was Harrison's first independent production as artist-composer-producer. His friend John Barham worked closely with him during the initial recordings, which were made at a late night/early morning session at Abbey Road on November 22 and a long session the following day, and also at De Lane Lea studio. The musicians involved included Colin Hanley, Tony Ashton, Roy Dyke and Philip Rodgers from The Remo Four, old friends from his Liverpool days, as well as harmonica master Tommy Reilly, renowned session man Jim

Sullivan, and various string and woodwind players. A passing Monkee, Peter Tork, was press-ganged into playing banjo, while Eric Clapton contributed backward blues guitar on 'Ski-ing'.

The general approach was loose and free-form. Released in November 1968, *Wonderwall Music* was the first solo album by any Beatle, and it sees Harrison at his most off-the-cuff and experimental. It is indisputably of its time, as is the film itself, with the result that the two fit together rather well. Some of the music is lovely, notably 'Wonderwall To Be Here', a stirring piece in which Ashton's piano melody is framed beautifully by Barham's sweeping strings. Elsewhere there are tender Indian passages, Vedic chants, light-hearted nods to skiffle, ragtime and clip-clopping country, mellow wah-wah outings, mellotron squalls and, in 'Dream Scene', five minutes of music as genuinely out there as anything recorded by a Beatle. The piece moves through backwards treated textures, a pure male/female love call, heavy drums, solo trumpet set against a lowering electronic backdrop, disjointed harmonica wails, atonal piano, an air raid siren weaving between the pealing chimes of a grandfather clock, sampled voices drifting nightmarishly and, finally, the sound of church bells. It's not entirely fanciful to see it as a prototype for Lennon's great experimental piece, 'Revolution 9'.

In London, Barham was there to provide a vital link between the musicians and the often outré ideas. "George had dropped in on one of Ravi Shankar's recording sessions for the BBC/Jonathan Miller production of *Alice In Wonderland* at BBC Television Centre," says Barham. "I had transcribed Ravi's Indian music notations into standard western notation for the western musicians on this project, and I also played piano. I think this may have given George the idea of inviting me to play a similar role in his *Wonderwall* project in which I played piano and flugelhorn and also conducted small ensembles of session musicians.

"At the *Alice In Wonderland* session we were recording a scene where Ravi soloed and I played an accompanying Indian Jhala texture on piano. George was fascinated by the combination of sitar and piano and subsequently asked me to play one of my own compositions which was based on Jhala texture at his house. He looked very closely at how I was playing as well as listening very closely. Later at one of the *Wonderwall* sessions he suddenly and very abruptly sat down at the piano and with great intensity started playing his own Jhala over a chord sequence. I was very impressed how well he had mastered the piano technique, as he wasn't a pianist. At that same session I found a flugelhorn lying around the studio. It turned out to be Paul McCartney's."

Although it is widely believed that Harrison did not play or sing on *Wonderwall Music*, and he is not officially credited as a musician, Barham's memories contradict this. "I told George that I had been a trumpet player, but hadn't played for six years," he says. "He asked if I wanted to play something on any of the tracks, so I went into an empty studio and played long notes for about an hour in order to reactivate my lip embouchure and get my tongue working again. I came back and played flugelhorn over George's Jhala. Later that same day Big Jim Sullivan, who was recording with Tom Jones at Abbey Road, happened to drop in and played bass on the same track: 'On The Bed'. This episode pretty much gives you an idea of the free atmosphere that we were working in on those sessions. They were very creative and very enjoyable."

Harrison's primary interest in taking the job was to advance the western profile of Indian music. At the end of December he wired Shambu Das and asked him to organise musicians for sessions starting in Mumbai early in the New Year, and to sort out a place for him "and one other" to stay. "I was getting so into Indian music then I decided to use the assignment partly as an excuse for a musical anthology to help spread it," he said. "I used all these instruments that at the time weren't as familiar to Western people as they are now, like shanhais, santoor, sarod, surbahars, tablatarangs. I also used tamboura drones."[47]

He spent a week, at his own expense, in India, recording at the EMI/ HMV studio in Mumbai between January 7 and 12. A two-track stereo machine was transported from Kolkata to attend to his needs. On the final day the musicians, whose number included Das on sitar, Ali Akbar Khan's son Ashish on sarod and Mahapurush Misra on tabla and pakavaj, recorded a number of ragas with an eye to future Beatles releases. One of these became 'The Inner Light', its lyrics inspired by the 1958 book *Lamps Of Fire*, a compendium of 300 selected passages from texts on all the world's major religions. The words to 'The Inner Light' were an almost direct lift from a translation of an extract from the *Tao Te Ching* which, again, emphasised the inner search over the physical one: "See all without looking/Do all without doing."

Following Harrison's vocal overdub, recorded on February 6 at Abbey Road, the finished song marked his first appearance on a Beatles single as a composer. A pleasing mix of Indian classical music and English chamber folk, with a passing resemblance to The Rolling Stones' 'Ruby Tuesday', 'The Inner Light' became the B-side to 'Lady Madonna', released in mid-March. By which point the most popular band in the world were trying to find their mojo in north India.

★ ★ ★

Harrison had maintained contact with the Maharishi since the previous summer's trip to Bangor. Despite some reservations within the band about the manner in which the Yogi had immediately begun using The Beatles as an advertising hook – billing himself as The Beatles' Spiritual Teacher and even telling the ABC television network in the US that they would be joining him on his TV special – Harrison was prepared to offer him the benefit of the doubt. "He is not a modern man," he said. "He just doesn't understand such things."[48]

At the beginning of each year the Maharishi held a course at his ashram in Rishikesh, a small town situated spectacularly in the foothills of the Himalayas, where the Ganges poured down from the mountains and created a vast flood plain. Intended to accommodate 60 westerners who wanted to become TM instructors, in 1968 his course was ambushed by The Beatles and their entourage, who had no intention of becoming teachers but did want to find out more about transcendental meditation.

Harrison and Lennon were the first to arrive in India. Of the four Beatles they were the most interested in religion and spiritual matters, and had grown closer since sharing their first acid experience. The fact that McCartney had delayed taking LSD for well over a year afterwards seemed to set him further apart than ever, while he was curious about TM but not hugely committed. Starr simply went along for the ride, armed with one suitcase full of baked beans and another full of reservations.

Accompanied by their wives and Boyd's sister Jenny, as well as the ubiquitous coterie of hangers-on, Harrison and Lennon arrived in Delhi on February 16, 1968. Mal Evans was already there, and arranged for three decrepit taxis to take them to Rishikesh. After five hours they finally crossed the impressive swing suspension bridge over the fast-flowing Ganges – "no camels or elephants," read the sign – which led to the ashram. They were joined four days later by McCartney, Jane Asher, Starr and his wife Maureen. A fleet of journalists and two camera crews also followed, but because the site was private and protected by barbed wire fencing they had little access.

Situated 200 feet up in the hills above the town, the compound comprised the Maharishi's bungalow, six stone cottages providing shared living accommodation, a kitchen, inside and outdoor eating areas, communal tables and benches, and a large lecture hall with a platform where the Yogi would talk. There were monkeys in the trees and spiders, scorpions, peacocks and parrots in the grounds. The views swept over the river and the town on the other side. It was exotic but Harrison wasn't quite roughing it. The ashram had a staff of 40 and was clean, comfortable and boasted most modern facilities. Other notables in attendance included Beach Boy Mike Love, Donovan, Mia Farrow and her sister Prudence, Joe Massot and flute player Paul Horn. This was dropping out, Sixties pop star style.

The days settled into a pleasant routine. Breakfast was communal and simple – cereal, toast, porridge – with the rest of the morning dedicated to meditation. After lunch there was time for reading, sunbathing, or more meditating. At 3.30 p.m. and 8.30 p.m. each day the Maharishi held lectures and question-and-answer sessions. In smaller group sessions he dispensed neat little maxims and homilies about finding peace and overcoming fears.

"Each day we would meditate, and then go and have breakfast, all outside," says Boyd. "Then we would either meditate more or the Maharishi would give us a private talk, or talk with all the people in the retreat. Then we were left very much to ourselves: someone might feel like meditating all day, and you let everybody know. Food would be left outside your door so you wouldn't be disturbed. It was very quiet and gentle." They would take walks down to the river, sometimes into the town, and once they went to see a film at the local travelling cinema, which arrived in town on a lorry. On his 25th birthday Harrison was garlanded with flowers and played sitar for everyone. They brought film cameras and tape machines to record the scenes.

Back home, those closest to The Beatles were amused and bemused. "We were all just laughing in the office," says Tony Bramwell. "It was like, 'Oh, it's another one of those things' – we were used to them coming up with hare-brained ideas by this time, we had gone through *Sgt. Pepper*, which was a long experience. The fact that they weren't working at such a pace, Brian had died, and suddenly people other than our initial circle were getting involved. When Brian was alive no one ever met them without his introduction or okay. The machinery had changed."

It certainly had. Convincing his three band mates to leave their well-feathered nests to camp in the foothills of the Himalayas may well have been Harrison's most miraculous triumph as a Beatle. Finally, his interests were not just being taken seriously, they were driving the narrative of the band, as well as playing a significant part in the popular explosion of western interest, however faddish, in the music and art of the East.

"It was George's idea to go," acknowledged McCartney,[49] while Lennon conceded that "George is a few inches ahead of us," not a sentiment Harrison had heard much anytime in the past decade. Lennon added: "George himself is no mystery, but the mystery inside George is immense. It's watching him uncover it all little by little that's so damn interesting."[50]

"I think he felt a bit more like the leader who had guided everybody into Rishikesh and learning more about meditation," says Boyd. "They kind of had to look up to him because he instigated this."

The results of the band following Harrison's instincts were some of the most pleasantly communal times they had experienced since the very early days, as well as a huge outpouring of creative energy. Removing themselves from the influence of dope and acid, and returning to the brass tacks of songwriting – voice, acoustic guitar, words – had the effect of guiding them away from the rapidly diminishing returns of psychedelia towards more direct forms of expression. They heard Bob

Dylan's *John Wesley Harding* for the first time in Rishikesh and perhaps responded to something of its simplicity, but above all it was a natural reaction to their surroundings. Exactly a decade since Harrison had joined The Quarry Men he, Lennon and McCartney were once again sitting around with acoustic guitars and playing for the sheer love of it. They wrote numerous songs – more than 20 of which would appear on the final three Beatles albums, plus at least another dozen which would show up on solo albums or were recorded by other artists. Little wonder that their next record, *The Beatles*, known as the White Album, was not just their longest, but also their most eclectic.

Harrison, as ever not quite as prolific as his two band mates, wrote 'Long, Long, Long', 'Sour Milk Sea', 'Dehradun', the music to 'While My Guitar Gently Weeps' and contributed a verse to Donovan's 'Hurdy Gurdy Man' while in Rishikesh. "The environment was very inspiring, and Paul and John were in a very mellow mood, which was not always the case when they were songwriting in London," says Boyd. "They were all on the same plane, and it became much easier for George to join in with them and write songs and not be rejected. They got on creatively really, really well in Rishikesh. We were there for a reason and it made everybody really mellow. Plus, I have to say – no drink or drugs. There was no outside stimulating interference, which was a major factor, although George's drug intake before the end of The Beatles was never a major issue. He could really take it or leave it. It was wonderful when they were all writing songs because everybody could enjoy listening to them."

There was, however, the occasional clash over priorities. Harrison wanted to sink deep into the experience. Playing and writing songs for their own sake was a natural and fun part of the process, but he did not want to be hustled into being on Beatle duty. "George actually once got quite annoyed and told me off because I was trying to think of the next album," said McCartney. "He said, 'We're not fucking here to do the next album, we're here to meditate.' It was like, 'Ooh, excuse me for breathing!' You know. George was quite strict about that."[51]

Starr was first to depart, then McCartney, leaving Lennon and Harrison to see out what they started. "At the end I was with George and John and they were doing this duel of who could out-meditate who," said Massot.[52] In April, after two months in Rishikesh, their stay came to an abrupt end when Lennon accused the Maharishi of making sexual advances to at least one of the young female students at the ashram. Pattie Boyd believes it was a rumour started by Magic Alex to get Lennon back under the influence of The Beatles' increasingly erratic circle of advisors, and away from the lure of TM. The Beatle, going through a tumultuous time in his personal life, may also have been looking for an excuse to return to his new muse and prospective lover, Yoko Ono. He quickly wrote a song of bitter disillusionment which began "Maharishi/You fucking cunt..." Harrison demurred, and suggested he change it to 'Sexy Sadie', but even in its moderated form the song lashed out at the giggling yogi who had "made a fool of everyone". Heaven help anyone in whom Lennon invested some degree of trust or faith and was then found wanting.

The next day, Harrison and Boyd left Rishikesh. Aside from the cloud hanging over the Maharishi, the course was relocating to Kashmir and he had already made plans to travel to south India. Harrison was conflicted over the issue at the time but finally decided that the "whole piece of bullshit was invented."[53] While making *Anthology* some 25 years later, Geoff Wonfor recalls having a long discussion with Harrison over how to present their stay in Rishikesh. "To sum up their time with the Maharishi I had used 'Sexy Sadie'," says Wonfor. "And George said, 'All those rumours, Geoff. I know you weren't around, but I know John would have a different view now. There was no substance to those rumours, John was just pissed off.' He would let me have my own head, but he put up the most wonderful argument for about three hours and in the end I changed it from 'Sexy Sadie' to 'Across The Universe'. That was down to George. I believed him, and I still stand by it. That was the right thing to do."

Harrison was the only Beatle who retained his links to the Maharishi after leaving the ashram, ties which remained throughout his life, perhaps not physically, but "spiritually [I] never moved an inch."[54] TM was a good fit for him. It was non-doctrinal, non-denominational, portable and adaptable. Harrison's friend, the percussionist Emil Richards, visited the ashram in Rishikesh not long after The Beatles left. "I'm still a meditator and George was all the way through," says Richards. "Maharishi approached transcendental meditation in a very scientific, practical way. It didn't really have anything to do with religion, so to speak. That's what made it very easy to talk about – and to live, actually. It was easy to grasp and comprehend and practice every day. It just becomes a part of what you do, and you can live a normal life. There are two kinds of meditators: the 'recluse' and the 'householders'. We all fell along with the 'householder' category, where we dipped in to bring it out and use up in our day. It wasn't something where you tried to reach nirvana from a cave like a yogi. Maharishi always stressed: 'Go meditate, and use up what you bring out in your daily life,' and George was the perfect example of that. We talked about it a lot."

After leaving Rishikesh Harrison visited Shambu Das in Mumbai and then went to Chennai, formerly Madras, with the intention of helping Shankar work on a documentary film he was making with director Howard Worth, then provisionally title *East Meets West*. He was deliberately dragging his heels. "George really didn't want to go back to London straight away," says Boyd. "It seemed very extreme after meditating for six weeks to go to London. He wanted to go somewhere else as a sort of in between stage before going back." After catching dysentery, he had to cut short his trip and returned to London at the end of April. He came back to find The Beatles' next madcap enterprise, Apple, about to be launched on the world.

Be Here Now
3 Savile Row, December 4, 1968

Three weeks before Christmas Day, 1968, George Harrison sends a memo to "everyone at Apple", The Beatles' new and reliably gonzo attempt at creating a multi-media business empire. In it, he lets the staff know of an imminent arrival in their midst:

> *Hell's Angels will be in London within the next week, on the way to straighten out Czechoslovakia. There will be twelve in number complete with black leather jackets and motor cycles. They will undoubtedly arrive at Apple and I have heard they may try to make full use of Apple's facilities. They may look as though they are going to do you in but are very straight and do good things, so don't fear them or up-tight them. Try to assist them without neglecting your Apple business and without letting them take control of Savile Row.*

The Angels duly arrive. Their number includes Frisco Pete and "Sweet William" Fritsch, along with *One Flew Over The Cuckoo's Nest* author and acid evangelist Ken Kesey, Grateful Dead manager Rock Scully and various "chicks", freaks and hangers-on. Everyone quickly becomes sick of them hanging around the office, intimidating the staff, leeching off the company and bursting in where they aren't wanted. Harrison resolves to act. Exit the meditative Maharishian, enter the chippy bus driver's son from Liverpool.

"I saw him back-out three Hell's Angels," says Jackie Lomax. "We were in an office together with Alistair [Taylor], and these three Angels just flung open the door and walked straight in. I was looking for the closet, but George walked straight up to the biggest guy in the middle and said, 'What are you doing here? We don't want you here, we're having a meeting.' The guy must have outweighed him by 200lbs, but he just walked back and kept saying, 'I know you, I know you...' He walked out the door and George shut it in his face. Pretty impressive, man! Force of will! Right out the door."

It is a classic demonstration of his Piscean nature, the delicate art of "yin and yang, heads and tails, yes and no."[1] He might invite you in.

He is just as likely to freeze you out. "I didn't see a physically aggressive side to him," says Lomax. "John was aggressive – with George it was all mental. He was the quietly intense one. If he was talking to you he would stare you right in the eye, as if he was boring right through you. Some people could have taken that for aggression, you know."

Shortly afterwards Harrison tells the Angels and their entourage that they have to leave Savile Row. They are gone by the end of the day. Whether they ever managed to "straighten out" Czechoslovakia is not a matter of public record.

CHAPTER 7

White Out

Towards the end of May 1968 Harrison welcomed his three band mates to Kinfauns to make demos of the promising crop of material they had worked up while in India. He had continued writing after leaving Rishikesh, and during the long session in Esher he presented five new compositions: 'While My Guitar Gently Weeps', 'Circles', 'Sour Milk Sea', 'Not Guilty' and 'Piggies'. Those, along with 18 further songs, were recorded on to Harrison's Ampex four-track. The rough-and-ready acoustic versions retained some of the rustic flavour of the ashram, each writer singing his new material while his band mates supplied handclaps, maracas, harmonium and impromptu backing vocals.

Shortly afterwards, on May 30, The Beatles began work on their next album and would continue, on and off, until mid-September – indeed, they would barely take pause from making music until the following summer. The band's final year as a studio entity was almost as heavily compressed as their first: they recorded four albums' worth of material in a little over 12 months, a work rate which hardly suggested a group running out of road.

Harrison missed almost two weeks' work at Abbey Road early on. Sessions continued in his absence while he travelled to the States on

June 7 to fulfil his commitment to appear in Howard Worth's Ravi Shankar documentary. He and his mentor were filmed talking as they walked along the cliffs at Big Sur on the Californian coast, and played sitar together by the sea. It was a farewell of sorts to his intense period of immersion in the instrument. As they chatted for the film, Shankar asked him about his roots. Although Harrison said he now felt that his origins were closer to India than Liverpool, the conversation dredged up an early childhood memory of riding his bike in Speke with Presley's 'Heartbreak Hotel' playing in his head. It was a timely reminder that his love of rock and roll was where this had all begun. It also made him realise that although he might be a serviceable sitar player, by the standards of his teachers he would never be even a good one, let alone a great one. On the way back to London he stopped off in New York and met Jimi Hendrix and Eric Clapton, who had recently given him a Les Paul guitar. He was, he felt, being willed back to his instrument.

One of the many changes that took place in the final year of The Beatles was the re-emergence and evolution of Harrison as a guitar player: on the White Album he and Lennon frequently combined to provide a twin lead-guitar attack on the rockers, notably 'Yer Blues', 'Everybody's Got Something To Hide Except For Me And My Monkey', and 'Happiness Is A Warm Gun'.* Several of his new songs abandoned the eastern drones and spectral atmospherics of his recent material; those that didn't, such as the ponderous 'Circles', were quickly abandoned. He instead moved towards a crunching, riff-heavy, blues-rock idiom which would define his early solo career, early examples including 'Savoy Truffle', 'Sour Milk Sea' and 'While My Guitar Gently Weeps'. This directness was partly attributable to giving up LSD, but was also in tune with prevailing musical trend: pop was becoming rock and "heavy" was the epithet of choice for the likes of Cream, Hendrix, the emerging Led Zeppelin and even the rejuvenated Rolling Stones.

---

* Although it should be said that Lennon often failed to return the favour, and on McCartney's most raucous, upbeat numbers – 'Birthday', 'Helter Skelter', 'Why Don't We Do It In The Road' – Harrison is sidelined, respectively, to bass, rhythm guitar and not appearing at all.

Most significant was the emergence of a more accessible melodic quality in his writing. The period marked Harrison's true coming of age as a songwriter, a manifestation of his increased confidence as a musician in his own right. Lennon and McCartney's indifference was, in many ways, the making of him. It forced him to up his game or else retreat. The irony is that Harrison's refusal to play second fiddle did as much as anything else to hasten the demise of the band.

★ ★ ★

Some of spirit of Rishikesh lingered when they entered Abbey Road. The White Album was not the ill-tempered slog it is often portrayed to be. At least, it was not only that. Engineer Ken Scott, who had worked with The Beatles since 1964, remembers that "the sessions were a blast, we had great fun. Yes, there were a couple of blow-ups, but I worked on numerous two-week projects and at some point someone is going to blow up. Over six months that will happen slightly more, but with regards to them being at each other's throats the entire time, not in the slightest. They became more of the band that I remember in the early days." John Barham, who was working with Harrison on many of his extracurricular projects during the period he was recording *The Beatles*, recalls times when "George's sessions finished and the other three Beatles would come in for an evening session. When this happened George would become re-energised and go into a world apart with the other three that nobody else seemingly could enter. It was obvious that he was still intensely involved in his creative work with The Beatles."

Featuring initially more spontaneity and ensemble playing than on any album since *Revolver*, the sessions began and ended on a note of optimism and general good feeling. In between, however, some serious cracks were beginning to show. Perhaps they were in the studio too long for goodwill to entirely prosper, or for old grievances to be set aside. "I went down to a few of the sessions before I started working with them and it seemed to be a bit of grind," says Chris Thomas, George Martin's 21-year-old assistant at AIR studios who took over production work on the album in early September. "Initially there seemed to be a bit more energy going and then the sessions got slower and slower. I got the impression it became hard work."

The first major bump in the road came over 'Hey Jude', which was carved off to become a single in late August. "I remember sitting down and showing George the song and George did the natural thing for a guitar player to do, which is to answer every vocal line," said McCartney. "And it was like, 'No George.' And he was pretty offended."[1] Having chafed against figures of authority since he was in short trousers, Harrison was getting increasingly annoyed at McCartney's domineering streak and his insistence on treating him like a glorified session-man. "Paul... wasn't open to anybody else's suggestions," he said. "It was taken to the most ridiculous situations, where I'd open my guitar case and go to get my guitar out and he'd say, 'No, no, we're not doing that yet.' It became stifling.... Paul wanted nobody to play on his songs until he had decided how it should go."[2] "George saw Paul as being difficult," says Pattie Boyd. "Of course they would tolerate each other, but I think George basically didn't like Paul's personality. Maybe I shouldn't say that. I don't know. I just think they really didn't love each other, actually."

It was not a one-way street. Harrison could be hard work: stubborn, pernickety and often laborious in the studio. He liked to be meticulously prepared yet he was also indecisive when it came to his own arrangements. Throughout the entire history of The Beatles his songs consistently needed many more takes than those written by Lennon or McCartney, and so it proved again. It was late July, two months into the project, before they began to work on some of his own material. Shortly after the spat over 'Hey Jude' they attempted 'Not Guilty'. Over the course of two mind-melting days The Beatles spent 102 takes wrestling with its shifting time signatures and jazzy stop-start structure ("it would make a great tune for Peggy Lee," Harrison reckoned).[3] In the end it was abandoned, although he re-recorded the song for his 1979 *George Harrison* album, and take 102 of The Beatles' version finally surfaced on *Anthology 3* in 1996, at which point it revealed itself to be at least the equal of many of the songs that made it onto the finished record. Perhaps his colleagues picked up on the not-altogether subtle subtext of lines such as "I won't upset the Apple cart/I only want what I can get," which were, he said, "me getting pissed off at Lennon and McCartney for the grief I was catching during the making of the White Album. I said I wasn't guilty of getting in the way of their careers. I said I wasn't guilty of leading them astray in our all going to Rishikesh to see the Maharishi. I was sticking up for myself."[4]

Giles Martin, son of George and nowadays carrying on his father's work as the custodian of The Beatles' recorded legacy, as well as helping oversee Harrison's audio archive, recalls that "my dad always said that when George was writing a song it was like he was embroidering a very complex tapestry with a very fine needle."[5] It was a procedure not always to everybody's tastes. Lennon later remembered that when he asked Harrison to play spontaneously on his own tracks 'Gimme Some Truth' and 'How Do You Sleep?' in 1971, the guitarist wanted to do his solos again. "That's the best he's ever fucking played in his life, he'd never get that feeling again," Lennon said, adding pointedly, "He'd go on forever if you let him."[6] There is, in that brief statement, a revealing window into how The Beatles' conflicting creative metabolisms could easily, over the course of a decade, lead to tension and frustration on all sides.

Harrison's big song on the record, 'While My Guitar Gently Weeps', went through a typically tortuous evolution. Musically, its minor-key melody had its origins in India, but the lyric was written back in Britain. The title phrase was inspired by a randomly selected passage from the *I Ching*, which Harrison had taken with him on a visit to his parents' house. Scanning the *Chinese Book of Changes* in a bungalow in Cheshire, the words "gently weeps" jumped out. The remainder of the lyric is another pen portrait of Harrison as a strict spiritual headmaster, loftily surveying society's massed ranks of Great Unbelievers – "I look at you all...." – before pointing out their myriad inadequacies with a weary shake of the head. It was intended to be a compassionate song, an attempt to draw out the "love there that's sleeping" in order that everyone could share his new awareness of potential bliss, and indeed the gentle acoustic version he recorded originally for the album, adorned only with organ and one of his most beautiful vocal performances, has a tenderness which complements the underlying sadness and humanity in the lyric. It also contained the best lines in the song: "I look from the wings at the play you are staging/While I'm sitting here doing nothing but ageing," a neat summation of the internal dynamic of the band and his personal sense of frustration and isolation, as well as having a more universal resonance. By contrast, the "diverted/perverted/inverted/alerted" scheme is more than a little contrived.

The "wings" couplet was excised from later versions, which were beefed up and electrified. After more than 20 failed attempts in August to get the song right, Harrison abruptly left Abbey Road again, this time to take a short, unscheduled trip to Greece, leading to the cancellation of some sessions. By this point he was not the only one needing a break. Assistant engineer Geoff Emerick had already quit working on the album, sick of the increased bickering, swearing and bad vibes. Later in August Ringo Starr announced he was leaving the band, feeling undervalued and unsatisfied. He finally returned after a fortnight, but "George was devastated," says Boyd. "That was the beginning of it all breaking up." George Martin took almost a month's holiday in September, handing the keys to the kingdom to the callow Chris Thomas, aided by engineers Ken Scott and Barry Sheffield.

Among the many extenuating circumstances that led to the album hitting some choppy water was Harrison's piety – the other Beatles had taken to calling him His Holiness behind his back. Then there was McCartney's overbearing bossiness, and the stylistic breadth of the material, which meant that almost by necessity the sessions became increasingly fragmented, members pairing off or working independently on different songs at the same time. This was now a motley union of three songwriters who all wanted to do very different things with both their music and their lives, and who were becoming more and more frustrated at having to corral their songs within the remit of The Beatles, Harrison perhaps most of all.

Tensions were further exacerbated by the presence of Yoko Ono. Lennon and his new partner had recently gone public as an item, and the extent of their coupledom was rapidly becoming apparent to the rest of the band. Building on the idea of 'Dream Scene' from *Wonderwall Music,* Harrison may have been the only other Beatle asked to contribute to

'Revolution 9', the eight-minute avant-garde sound collage compiled by Lennon and Ono, but he was less accommodating when it came to his band-mate bringing his girlfriend to work. "He said it was like when you were a kid watching a Western movie and the love interest came in," says Dave Mason. "'Okay, well that's fucked *that* up!'"

Ono penetrated their sacred domain on the studio floor, attending every Beatles recording session, sitting next to Lennon, whispering in his ear, and generally making a deteriorating situation considerably worse. "It was Yoko who was provoking all that," says Bramwell. "George just hated the idea of anybody hanging around the studio. He didn't even like George Martin to be there – his job was to be in the box, not down on the floor – and he didn't disguise the fact at all [that he disliked Ono]. The [*Living In The Material World*] documentary by Martin Scorsese amused me, to have Yoko on it talking about George, because George *could not stand* to be in the same room as her. She was interfering with everything – with John, with The Beatles."

"John and Yoko were out on a limb," said Harrison. "I don't think he wanted much to be hanging out with us, and I think Yoko was pushing him out of the band, inasmuch as she didn't want him hanging out with us."[7] Lennon's attachment to Ono, and their dalliance with heroin, distanced Harrison from the one person in the band he regarded as a true ally. "He was much closer to John than Paul," says Geoff Wonfor. "He said to me later that John sometimes mucked up his head, but the relationship with Yoko and John, and the drugs, that really did fuck up his heart. Yoko became the be all and end all, and things changed."

Chris Thomas, conversely, says that "I wasn't aware that Yoko caused any particular ructions or bad feelings," but The Beatles were never the most emotionally demonstrative of bands. They were practised enough in the art of public performance to generally keep their domestic tiffs firmly in house. The tension was largely a powerful undercurrent; on the surface only ripples appeared. "We didn't really see any of the bad stuff," says Thomas. "They used to have meetings in the studio, if we started at 2.30 in the afternoon, at about seven o'clock they would stop, have a joint, and chat about things. We would not be listening to that, we wouldn't have the mikes on and we would be sitting upstairs, so who knows what was going on in those periods. It was none of our business."

Within The Beatles inner circle, Harrison dealt with his feelings for Ono in a more typically direct fashion. Lennon later recalled: "George, shit, insulted her right to her face in the office at the beginning, just being 'straight-forward.' You know, that game of 'I'm going to be up front, because this is what we've heard and Dylan and a few people said she'd got a lousy name in New York, and gives off bad vibes.' That's what George said to her! And we both sat through it. I didn't hit him, I don't know why."[8]

Perhaps it was little wonder that when Harrison returned once more to 'While My Guitar Gently Weeps', he felt that the band weren't putting in the requisite amount of effort. Chris Thomas insists he never saw any evidence that The Beatles worked on Harrison's songs "under sufferance," but their author felt differently, complaining in this case that "we tried to record it but Paul and John were just so used to cranking out their tunes that it was very difficult at times to get serious and record one of mine. It wasn't happening. They weren't taking it seriously, and I don't think they were even all playing on it."[9] The next day, driving into London from Surrey with Eric Clapton, he asked the Cream guitarist to come in and play lead on the song. "George felt our friendship would give him some support, and that having me there to play might stabilise the situation, and maybe even draw some respect," Clapton said. "We did just one take. John and Paul were fairly non-committal, but I knew George was happy because he listened to it over and over in the control room."[10]

This was the version released on *The Beatles*, featuring Clapton's sinewy guitar solo and fills and McCartney's arresting Morse code piano intro. The heavier, busier arrangement and Harrison's harsher vocal bent the overall tone towards something more sanctimonious and accusatory than was probably intended. There is a furrow-browed, rather hectoring beauty to the verses as they descend down a decidedly chiding A-minor scale, rendering the end result more impressive than genuinely likeable.

Completing the track to his satisfaction seemed to clear a path to getting more of his own material down on tape; it also coincided with an improvement in the mood in the studio. "The atmosphere was fantastic," says Chris Thomas. "I think beforehand [it wasn't great], Ringo had left and whatnot, but I hadn't witnessed any of that. All I know is that by September it seemed good and *jolly*, to be quite honest. They were really fun, there was a lot of laughing and it was really, really productive." Ken Scott agrees. "After Ringo came back into the band they were going gung ho. George Martin was on vacation and he couldn't believe how much we'd done in the time he'd been away. I remember it as a happy and productive time."

During the second night of recording on 'Helter Skelter', Harrison unveiled his "Arthur Brown impersonation," says Thomas.* "The ashtrays were pretty large at Abbey Road, so George set fire to the ashtray and ran around with it on his head, shouting and being silly. They were definitely all out of their heads. Mal and John were making a racket, and he was just having fun." It's easy to forget that he was still only 25, and capable of cutting loose and enjoying himself, but at the back of his mind was the knowledge that this was a pale imitation of something more precious. He was looking for bliss – and he knew he could never find it within The Beatles. "We had happiness at times, but not the kind of bliss I mean, where every atom of your body is just buzzing," he said. "It's beyond the mind."[11]

During the last month of the sessions The Beatles recorded three more Harrison songs, each one utterly distinct from the other. 'Savoy Truffle' is a stuttering rocker with a jokey lyric about Clapton's compulsive consumption of Good News chocolates, driven by a rather thrillingly overloaded in–your–face horn score, some stinging guitar playing and Chris Thomas' almost-funky organ and piano. After a night spent working with him as he pieced together his solo, Harrison impulsively gave the engineer a guitar as a gift. "He tried to give me

---

* Arthur Brown's 'Fire' had recently been released, promoted by live shows and a television clip which featured Brown performing the song in flowing robes and wearing a flaming helmet. This quickly became an integral part of his act.

the Fender Strat from *Magical Mystery Tour* with all the paint on it, but it was too much," says Thomas. "I was really embarrassed, and so I said I didn't have an amp and that it would be a waste. He gave me a Jumbo acoustic instead. He was quite insistent, then he gave me a lift to Shepherd's Bush tube at six o'clock in the morning. He could be very thoughtful and kind." More than ten years later Harrison demanded that the guitar be returned.

'Savoy Truffle' was a relatively rare example of Harrison's brand of quirky leftfield humour finding its way unforced into song. 'Piggies', by contrast, was intended as acerbic "social comment"[12] but the blunt-force trauma inflicted on some cartoon version of the bourgeoisie comes off only as smug and superior. It's not an anti-police song, despite the popular counterculture coinage of "pigs" as a derogatory term; its holier-than-thou misanthropy reaches far wider than that. The jangling harpsichord and bitter scratch of strings give it the edge-of-violence tone of an old nursery rhyme, and the satire is similarly juvenile. The lack of a cutting edge to match its sourness is underlined by the fact that one line – "What they need's a damn good whacking" – was suggested by his mother.

At times listening to Harrison's music, it's a struggle to find much evidence at all of his faith in the redeeming qualities of humanity. And then along comes 'Long, Long, Long', a marvellous, moving song in which all defences are dropped, all grievances and reproving glances set aside, and the warm, loving man recalled by so many of his closest friends shines through just as clearly as his hyper-cynical alter ego. Loosely based on Dylan's 'Sad Eyed Lady Of The Lowlands', it is perhaps the first of his songs to capture the inner struggle and trauma that drove him into the arms of God: "So many tears I was searching/So many tears I was wasting... How I want you/Oh I love you/You know that I need you/Oh I love you." A simple act of bittersweet spiritual surrender, 'Long, Long, Long' also brings out the loveliness of his voice when he isn't straining to be heard or striving to be understood. In every possible sense, he was never at his most alluring when he shouted.

★ ★ ★

Away from the increasingly topsy-turvy atmosphere within the band, Harrison was busy cultivating his own musical allegiances. Clapton in particular was now a close friend and neighbour, and their bond spilled over into the music, not just on 'While My Guitar Gently Weeps' but also on 'Badge', which the pair wrote together for Cream in 1968, Harrison helping Clapton finish the melody and contributing some of the – largely nonsensical – words.

Opportunities to expand his musical frame of reference and work beyond the boundaries of the band were improved by the fact that instead of calmly taking stock after Epstein's death, The Beatles had "impulsively launched their business empire."[13] They had founded Apple Corps after the dissolution of Beatles Ltd and appointed friends, including Neil Aspinall, Mal Evans (who went from roadie/fixer to company President), Magic Alex, Terry Doran, Tony Bramwell and Derek Taylor, to oversee a range of new companies, among them Apple Electronics, Apple Films, Apple Music Publishing, Apple Retailing and Apple Tailoring.

The general aim, McCartney said, was "controlled weirdness",[14] the kind of loftily spurious sentiment which seemed to chime with the mood of the times. Inevitably, in the end there was considerably more weirdness than there was control. An open-door policy on recruiting new talent brought every loon, loser and drop-out in the country and beyond to the doorstep of the Apple offices; some of them even started working there. The 'refreshment' budget was particularly lavish: in one two-week period the press office knocked off eight bottles of whisky, four bottles of brandy, three bottles of vodka and hundreds of bottles of Kronenbourg, coke and mixers. Nearly one thousand cigarettes were consumed. Chris O'Dell, recently arrived from the US and now working for Apple, would buy-in lunch for the office each day from a different Cordon Bleu restaurant. Everyone was smoking dope and taking cabs home at night and putting the cost on The Beatles' tab.

Harrison had made his delayed return from India to find Apple already drifting into madness. "George came back from Rishikesh and reacted with real horror to what was going on in the building, particularly in my office," recalled Derek Taylor.[15] He described the company and its founding impulse as "John and Paul's madness... basically it was chaos. We just gave away huge quantities of money."[16]

He was, however, far from immune to encouraging the craziness – "George's Krishna office was pretty weird," says Bramwell – as his misguided, conflicted tryst with the Hell's Angels illustrated. He had met the bikers while in California that autumn working on Jackie Lomax's new album. One of the more positive aspects of Apple was the opportunity it gave Harrison to stretch his legs musically; he and McCartney were easily the most dominant Beatles when it came to shaping the label's early output.

The outlet it provided undoubtedly bolstered his sense of confidence, and his range. Between 1968 and 1970 Harrison played, produced, wrote for and generally mentored – with typical thoroughness – Doris Troy, Billy Preston and Ronnie Spector, as well as Lomax, The Beatles' old friend from Liverpool band The Undertakers who was, at Harrison's instigation, Apple's first signing. "I sensed that he was honing his skills as a record producer and for the most part enjoying himself," says John Barham, who assisted on many of these sessions. "I didn't feel any strain. To me looking back to those days, I would say he was happier and more outgoing then than in his latter years."

The idea of writing for other people freed him from having to think about fitting into The Beatles or the ever-fraught process of presenting material to his band-mates. Many of his songs during this period – several of which ended up on his later solo records – were instigated with others in mind, either specifically or subconsciously, notably 'What Is Life' for Preston, 'You' for Spector, and 'Something' and 'Sour Milk Sea' for Lomax. The latter was the first non-Beatles Harrison song recorded by another artist, a mark of his growing independence. Inspired by a picture in *Tantra Art*, it was a punchy call to arms: if things are dark, dig around in your subconscious through meditation and get yourself to a better place.

One of the quartet of singles that launched Apple on August 30, 1968, 'Sour Milk Sea' was included on Lomax's 1969 album *Is This What You Want?*, which Harrison also produced, squeezing in sessions in Abbey Road's Studio Three at the same time as The Beatles were working in the building, and also recording at Trident studios. "It was great," says

Lomax. "He was the best musician I've ever worked with. I'd go to his house and we'd sit around jamming on acoustics and discussing ideas. He had the ability to totally absorb the song and then come up with a part that enhances it. Like 'New Day' – that riff all the way through it, I wouldn't have thought of that, and it worked really good. He was incredibly kind and generous with his time and his advice, and he got the best people, of course. He was George! I couldn't have got Eric Clapton on my own."

Already he was starting to assemble the retinue of musicians who would prove so important in the early days of his solo career. In London the musicians who played on *Is This What You Want?* included Clapton, Klaus Voormann, Billy Preston, Leon Russell and Nicky Hopkins. When he flew out to Los Angeles on October 16, right at the end of work on the White Album, to continue the sessions at Sound Recorders in Los Angeles, he called in Larry Knechtel, Joe Osborn and Hal Blaine, part of the crack squad of West Coast session players known as the Wrecking Crew. In Los Angeles he also met for the first time Delaney & Bonnie who, together with their backing band, or 'Friends' as they were billed, were to play a major role in the next few years of his musical life. He was becoming enamoured of the American concept of loosely structured groups with constantly changing musicians, as opposed to rigid groups with fixed personnel exemplified by The Beatles. The overall vibe, to deploy late Sixties parlance, of a Harrison-curated production was focused but inclusive and fun. None of the records he oversaw during this time are particularly groundbreaking, but at the very least everyone involved sounds like they are enjoying the act of making music together.

While in LA he and Lomax rented Zsa Zsa Gabor's house in Beverly Hills. Mama Cass visited one night with a "joint the size of a knockwurst,"[17] while on other evenings the two friends from Liverpool would talk about Harrison's recent spiritual awakening. "It was clear that he was passionate about it," says Lomax. "I thought it was a load of bunk – I'm from Liverpool, I'm cynical to the end, I just thought it was a bit silly. Meditating is fine. I prefer a spliff myself, but George got into it, and stayed with it. He was a very deep guy, and that stuff had thousands of years of *depth* to it. Still waters run deep – you know that one? He was the quietest in the band, but the deepest. He was looking for something beyond the ordinary."

While finishing *Is This What You Want?* Harrison wanted to add Moog to several songs. The latest in electronic musical technology, the Moog was a hefty cabinet-like analogue synthesizer which enabled players to produce a variety of noises and styles, both mimicking real instruments and creating new sounds, all electronically. It had been demonstrated at the Monterey Pop Festival in June 1967 by Paul Beaver and Bernie Krause, after which the two musicians found themselves in constant demand among the West Coast rock elite, not least because getting to grips with the instrument required the kind of patience and technical know-how well beyond most of the artists who fancied giving it a test run.

Harrison was no different, and wanted to see what all the fuss was about. The meeting at Sound Recorders with Beaver & Krause on November 11 led, circuitously and not altogether happily, to his second solo album, *Electronic Sound*. "We did the session, it was very normal, and we finished in the wee hours of the next morning," says Krause. "Harrison asked me to stick around and show him some more things on the synthesizer. Paul and I were just preparing some new material for our second Warner Brothers album, and I was showing Harrison some of the patches and ways in which we were thinking of doing our work. What I didn't realise, because it was late and I was tired and I wasn't paying attention, was that he had asked the engineer to record the session that I was demonstrating. I didn't think anything of it at the time."

Harrison went back to England, and shortly afterwards called Krause to ask how he could get his hands on his own Moog. "There was a kind of urgency in his voice," says Krause. "I said he'd have to get in line with Moog like everybody else, we were just representatives, we didn't have any control over the factory. I asked him for the folks at Apple to write a cheque for a deposit. He said, 'I want one right away,' and I said, 'You're not going to get one right away, you'll have to do what everyone else does.' He got in a huff but then he said okay, he'd do that." Within the lofty metaphysics of Harrison's 'Be Here Now' message lurked a more literal meaning: being a Beatle brought with it a child's sense of entitlement. Me want, me get. None of them were renowned for their patience.

In early February 1969 the Moog finally arrived at Heathrow and Krause was summoned to London to help the impatient Beatle get to grips with it. He travelled first class and was billeted in the Dorchester Hotel, although Harrison had neglected to tell Krause that he was going into hospital to have his tonsils removed. Left twiddling his thumbs for over a week while he recuperated, Krause was eventually taken to Kinfauns to find "a lot of Mercedes and other accoutrements in the drive. He and Pattie met us at the door, offered us something vegetarian to eat. Pattie was very quiet, a blonde chick on the scene. My sense was that she was really in awe of him and stayed in the background. I hardly remember exchanging words with her at all. All the attention was on George – people were coming in and out all the time, he was buying and selling cars, doing stuff, it was very weird.

"The vegetarian then took me into the living room where there was this long leather couch – I thought that was interesting. Across from that was the Moog synthesizer set up on a table. Understand, he had just got it delivered that afternoon. It had just arrived. He said, 'I want to play you something.' After supplying the requisite amount of smoke he put on this tape. Now, one thing I have is a really good memory for sound, and I remembered what we had done back in California in November – and here it was on that tape! Harrison says to me, 'Well, I'm putting it out as an album. If it makes a couple of quid I'll send it to you.' I said, 'Not without my permission you're not, that's Paul and I's stuff.' And then he said, 'Trust me, I'm a Beatle.' *Trust me, I'm a Beatle!* I said, 'Yeah? Call me a cab, I'm going home, and don't use my stuff.' He said, 'When Ravi Shankar comes to my house he's humble,' and something else about Jimi Hendrix. Then he asked me to patch him a bagpipe sound. Perhaps he was more conscientious about his behaviour at other times. Maybe it depended on how much you genuflected."

Harrison's album of Moog music, *Electronic Sound*, was released on Apple's experimental offshoot label Zapple in May 1969. The first side, 'No Time Or Space', consists entirely of the pieces Krause played at the end of the Jackie Lomax session in California. For the second side, titled 'Under The Mersey Wall', "he managed to patch some things together," says Krause. "I have no opinion on it. His cats did it. His cats ran over the keyboard, and that was the album." In the right light on certain copies Krause's name can still be seen, misspelled, on the cover. "I wrote to Apple and said, 'Take my name off it, I don't want to be on it.' I wasn't litigious, I just let it go, but it was my stuff. It's an incredible story, but it's incredible too about [him plagiarising] 'My Sweet Lord' – and Randy Newman has stories too. I had no control over any of it. I didn't know it was being recorded, I didn't want it out, and I felt very badly that he had to do that. I guess spirituality comes to different people in different ways. An expression of his seemed to be, 'Trust me, I'm a Beatle'."

Harrison's opinion of *Electronic Sound* – "a load of rubbish"[18] – scarcely differed from that of Krause, or indeed anyone else who has heard the record. Its ham-fisted space-age indulgences were a rare dilettantish folly (although his new Moog did not go entirely to waste. It was carted into the studio and used frequently on *Abbey Road*). He was, in fact, gravitating towards more organic musical styles. After his first meeting with Krause, at the end of his sessions with Lomax in LA he and Boyd had gone to visit The Band at the invitation of their guitarist and principal songwriter Robbie Robertson.

Having performed as Bob Dylan's backing group throughout 1965 and 1966, the five multi-instrumentalists and singers formerly billed as The Hawks released their debut album, *Music From Big Pink*, in September 1968. Harrison, turned on to it by Clapton, was immediately smitten. Named after the house they shared in West Saugerties, Woodstock, in upstate New York, the record was the absolute antithesis of anything currently happening on the scene: there was nothing heavy, nothing psychedelic, nothing *groovy* about *Music From Big Pink*. Featuring soon-to-be classic originals like 'The Weight' alongside strange, funny and portentous new Dylan songs, this was instead a freshly-minted strain of mythical North American music. Stately, spare and intimate, its warm rusticity seemed to make no distinction between past and present.

Music From Big Pink quickly became a foundation stone of roots rock, and Harrison wanted to know more. "He came to visit with me and met a couple of the other guys," says Robbie Robertson. "He wanted to see what was *real*. Like, 'What do they do up in those mountains?' He wanted to hang out and have some of this rub off on him."

"It was kind of an escape from Beatledom for him, and he was really drawn to what Bob and The Band were doing," says Jonathan Taplin, The Band's road manager at the time, who later worked with Harrison on the Concert For Bangladesh. "It was quite different from what was happening in London or San Francisco. In Woodstock it was much more grounded, very family-orientated, kids all around." During Harrison's visit Robertson was, he says, "really under the weather, so I hooked it up for him to stay at [Dylan manager] Albert Grossman's house. I also called Bob and said, 'George is here, he'd really like to visit with you.' So George then did go and spend some time with Bob, but he didn't know if he was even going to see Bob when he came."

It was an awkward meeting, partly because at the time Dylan and his manager were at loggerheads, and partly because, well, "Bob was an odd person," says Pattie Boyd. "When we went to see him in Woodstock, God, it was absolute agony. He just wouldn't talk. He *would not talk*. He certainly had no social graces whatsoever. I don't know whether it was because he was shy of George or what the story was, but it was agonisingly difficult. And [his wife] Sara wasn't much help, she had the babies to look after."

The Harrisons were invited to Thanksgiving dinner at Dylan's house on November 28, where the guests included author Mason Hoffenberg, who had co-written *Candy* with Terry Southern. It was, says Taplin with admirable understatement, "kind of stiff and formal," until after dinner Hoffenberg suggested that we 'get all the boys over on this side, and all the girls over on *this* side. The first couple to get their clothes off and screw wins.' "It was funny enough, it broke the ice," says Taplin. "It had been such a puritan Thanksgiving, all these children, and the adults wandered into this big room and Mason made everyone laugh, and it got a bit looser."

Dylan later told his neighbour Bruce Dorfman quietly that "it wasn't such a hot visit after all."[19] Harrison begged to differ. He was profoundly influenced by the trip, during which he wrote 'I'd Have You Anytime' with Dylan as an attempt to get his host to open up: the words – "Let me in here/let me into your heart" – are a direct and disarming plea. "We were both shy," he said. "I was nervous in his house and he was nervous as well. We fidgeted about for two days and only relaxed when we starting playing some guitars."[20] He also wrote 'All Things Must Pass' in Woodstock, seeking out the simple, soulful spirit that informed 'The Weight', a song "which had a religious and a country feeling to it, and I wanted that."[21]

According to Boyd, despite the somewhat strained atmosphere, "George loved it. He loved that he was with Dylan because he adored his music and so he was very jolly. He was totally free from the people he thought were holding him back. Writing and playing with Bob definitely gave him an extra sense of validation."

A few days later he returned to a British "winter of discontent"[22] to play out the final act in The Beatles' story.

Be Here Now
London, January 1969

During a break in the deeply demoralising sessions for *Get Back*, George Harrison takes engineer Glyn Johns to one side. He has a new song, he says, that he would like to record. Perhaps mindful of the lacklustre reception they have given his new material in recent days, Harrison has not yet presented it to the band. Instead, he steps alone into the studio and unwraps 'Something' like a precious gift to himself.

"I thought it was astonishing," says Johns. "He asked me if I would stay behind after a session because he wanted to put down a demo on his own with no one else in the room, which made me assume that he was a little insecure about it. I think he had been made to feel that way. I don't think he had lost confidence in his own ability, I just think he had lost confidence in [The Beatles] believing in what he was doing. I don't think he felt that they recognised what he was up to."

Singing with just an electric guitar accompaniment, Harrison offers up his most enduring, accessible and universal song. Even its composer doesn't seem to realise quite how good it is.

"I was in the control room, he was in the studio," says Johns. "And I remember listening to that song and thinking, 'Fucking hell, why isn't he playing this to everyone else? What is going on here?' And then him coming in and asking what did I think. That remains my overriding memory of George: *What did I think?* I said, 'You've got to be fucking joking. It's incredible, what are you talking about?' It's entirely possible, reading between the lines, that he was saving his really good songs for his own stuff. That's the most logical reasoning."

Never a songwriter who could routinely summon lightning to his fingertips, Harrison seems suspicious when it strikes. 'Something' is indisputable proof that his hot streak is well underway. He's just not sure what to do with it, or who it is for.

CHAPTER 8

Beatle: Blue

Scarcely a month after leaving Bob Dylan's dinner table, George Harrison left The Beatles. On January 2, 1969, perilously hot on the heels of the completion of the White Album, they had started work at Twickenham Film Studios on a new project, provisionally and pointedly titled *Get Back*. Aware that they needed a pressing reason to continue, they hatched a somewhat foggily formulated plan: a spectacular return to live performance, to be broadcast worldwide on television from either the Roundhouse in north London or some other, more exotic location – perhaps the Sahara, suggested McCartney, or a Roman amphitheatre in Tunisia? ("You're so full of shit, man," was Harrison's response to the latter suggestion.)[1] McCartney also mooted the idea of playing low-key, spontaneous dates in small clubs, billed as Ricky & The Red Streaks.

Nobody could quite agree on the specifics, but in the meantime they set to work. The rehearsal process and the show itself were to be filmed by director Michael Lindsay-Hogg, and because this was intended to be primarily a live affair rather than a studio enterprise, George Martin's expertise was thought not to be required. In his place came Glyn Johns, billed (and paid) as an engineer rather than a producer, who had worked with The Who, The Rolling Stones, The Small Faces and The Steve Miller Band.

In theory, the notion of The Beatles once again playing together live in a room, without any overdubs or studio trickery, appealed to Harrison, who had just seen first-hand how effective that approach could be in Woodstock. "I think [*Get Back*] was very influenced by The Band, more pared down, much simpler, and that was in part George's influence," says Jon Taplin. "Even though I know those sessions were not comfortable and not fun, that was him saying, 'This is where we should go'." Robbie Robertson adds: "I just recently got a message from Donald Fagen. He was listening to *Let It Be – Naked* and he said, 'Oh my God, were these guys ever influenced by The Band?'"

The parallels in reality were almost non-existent. The Band worked in a comfortable old wooden house in the Catskill Mountains, making music all day, playing American football in the yard and chess and cards in the living room, eating and drinking together. The warm, easy sound they made was a natural extension of their friendships and the lives they were living. The Beatles, by contrast, were recording in a sterile film studio and were finding it increasingly hard to be civil to one another. Not only that, they struggled to function as a band any more.

They just didn't *sound* good. They were rusty, ill-at-ease and either too lazy or uninterested to knuckle down, all of which played against the strengths of a guitarist who was "incredibly professional", says Glyn Johns. "Other guitar players tend not to be as formulaic as George, but that in its own way set him apart, because what he did come up with was pretty astonishing, really precise, and always what was required for the piece of music. I respect the fact that he would have a clear objective as far as a solo, or riff, or sound was concerned. He wouldn't settle for whatever flew out, he'd work on it and get it honed until it was absolutely right. I don't recall him holding anything up, he'd work his part out while we were running the song down at rehearsals, and possibly refine it at home, but it was never laboured."

For Harrison, with his dread of intrusion, the presence of cameras documenting every bum note, cross word and strained silence was particularly unwelcome. It was cold in the vast sound studio, he left Kinfauns at the ungodly hour of eight o'clock each morning, and Ono was an ever-present irritant, perched on amps or sitting inscrutably by Lennon's side.

They jumped back and forth between new material, old Beatles numbers, novelties, current pop hits, Dylan songs and Hamburg-era covers. Few things got their undivided attention. A half-hearted attempt at 'All Things Must Pass' aspired to The Band's sound, with the churchy three-part harmonies and warm pastoral feel, but missed by a mile. How could it work? There was no love in it, not in the performance and not in the room. "It was terrible," Harrison said. "Really tense and nasty."[2] In the cavernous studio he told his band mates bleakly that "we have been in the doldrums for at least a year," and suggested that "maybe we should get a divorce." To Lennon, who had retreated into stoned silence most of the time, he muttered darkly "hear no evil, speak no evil, see no evil." To McCartney, who was forced by the indifference of the others into being even more hectoring than ever, he said, "You're not annoying me. You don't annoy me any more." It was the language of a dead marriage transposed to a dying band.

Not long after *Get Back* McCartney expressed the opinion, in front of both Harrison and Lennon, that "our songs have [always] been better than George's."[3] Few would argue, including Harrison, but he wasn't trying to compete with them. He was only, as he sang in 'Not Guilty', "trying to do my bit," and wanted a little more support in his attempts to express himself. Later in the *Get Back* sessions he brought in the superb, soulful 'Isn't It A Pity', a song which had been kicking around for three years but had been consistently vetoed by Lennon. "It can be any speed you want, really," he said dolefully as he ran through it to general indifference and background chatter. It was never played by The Beatles again. 'Hear Me Lord' and 'Let It Down' were given similarly chilly receptions. Bob Dylan and Eric Clapton seemed to think he was pretty good. They were happy to write and play with him. Why were The Beatles still so resistant? And why should he continue to put up with it?

"I had spent the last few months producing an album by Jackie Lomax and hanging out in Woodstock, having a great time," said Harrison. "For me to come into the winter of discontent with The Beatles in

Twickenham was very unhealthy and unhappy. I think the first couple of days were okay, but it was soon quite apparent that it was just the same as it had been when we were last in the studio, and it was going to be painful again. There was a lot of trivia and games being played."[4]

No longer willing to fulfil a subservient role, by lunchtime on January 10 he had had enough. After another 'Hey Jude'-style episode with McCartney, this time a low volume but bitter row over what to play, or rather what not to play, on 'Two Of Us' – "Whatever it is that will please you, I'll do it," he said acidly – Harrison then clashed with Lennon. During the lunch break in the canteen he told them he was leaving. When? "Now. You can replace me. Put an ad in the *New Musical Express* and get a few people in. See you 'round the clubs."[5] That afternoon in the studio, Ono assumed ownership of Harrison's blue cushion and howled into his microphone as the other three Beatles improvised slabs of dissonant noise. You could cut the symbolism with a knife.

"There was quite a bit of tension between individual members of the band during those rehearsals," says Johns. "From day one there was internal stuff going on between them that wasn't sitting comfortably. Things were not normal. It came to a head that day. I don't remember anybody criticising what George was playing. Well, actually, when it became apparent that there was going to be a bit of an argument those of us who weren't in the band left the room. It was clear that it would be intrusive for us to remain. So what actually was said and what went on I don't know, but I do know that George left the band that day. The whole thing was very uncomfortable, and it was very embarrassing for me and others who were not in the band to be close by while this was going on – to have to watch this begin and be there in the immediate aftermath. It was very unpleasant and I felt really awkward."

That afternoon Harrison left London, went home, and poured all his frustration into 'Wah Wah'. With its violent riff and almost primal vocal hook, it was an unambiguous swipe at the band who made him a star because he was "there at the right time" and "cheaper than a dime," but who never "see my crying."

"He was unhappy," says Boyd. "The Beatles *made* him unhappy, with the constant arguments and rows. This had gone on for over a year, they could be vicious to each other. That was all really upsetting, and even more so for him because he had discovered this new avenue of life. He would come home from recording or seeing them and be just full of anger, and then he would be cross with himself. It was a very bad state that he was in."

After Harrison's exit, the band fully expected him to return the next day after cooling down. When he didn't, Lennon was adamant that he wanted to continue without him, and talked about getting Clapton in as his replacement. He was not, however, insensible to the fact that their treatment of Harrison was "a festering wound. It's only this year that [George] has realised who he is, and all the fucking shit we've done to him."[6]

Eventually, after many meetings and phone calls and second-hand conversations relayed by minions between one Surrey bolthole or another, Harrison showed up to a five-hour meeting at Starr's house on January 15. He was persuaded by Derek Taylor that, in light of Lennon's retreat into a heroin daze and Starr's general diffidence, he had a responsibility to help McCartney see the project through. "I felt that George's sense of decency could be touched," said Taylor, "And it was."[7]

He reluctantly agreed to return as long as the idea of a live extravaganza in some far flung location was immediately dropped. He had no desire to perform with The Beatles in public again, suffering as he was still from the aftershock of 1964–1966, and musically he knew they weren't up to the job: lacking the necessary climax of a grand concert, the raw rehearsal footage would now be edited into a fly-on-the-wall film. He also demanded that they leave Twickenham and move to the new recording studio being assembled by Apple Electronics wizard Magic Alex in the basement of their offices, and that the songs they were playing would go towards a new album. The other Beatles all agreed – here he was, finally, calling the shots – though part of him wished that they hadn't. His feelings about the group had become a complex tangle of familial loyalties meeting head-on with creative and spiritual necessities. On the one hand, says Chris O'Dell, "George got sick of the band, he got sick of being a Beatle. He certainly said it: 'How do I leave the band?' Paul was the one who was most determined to keep it going. They were at opposite ends, at odds." On the other hand, says Boyd, "it wasn't just about walking away from The Beatles, it was walking away from three people he had known for a very long time. In a way, though he was unhappy, he was also hanging on to the security of the group. He would brood a lot on these things, they affected him deeply."

★ ★ ★

Everybody noticed that the extremes of his behaviour, always evident, were growing more pronounced. Starr recalled the clear delineation of these "two incredible separate personalities. He had the love – bag of beads – personality, and the bag of anger. He was very black and white."[8] At home he became more distant and detached. "I couldn't reach him," says Boyd, who attributes the start of the long breakdown of their marriage to her husband's immersion in his own spiritual quest post-Rishikesh. As well as accentuating his ingrained personality traits, the trip seemed to have altered his self-image. O'Dell, who had to parry his occasional amorous advances, remembers her first meeting with Harrison in 1968. As well as noting that "he was better looking than I had thought," she recalls that he arrived for lunch at Club del Aretusa on the King's Road doused in *eau du guru*. "He smelled so good, always," she says. "I could never quite figure out how he did it – he always smelled like sandalwood. Everything, from his hair down." He came back from India "wanting to be some kind of spiritual being surrounded by concubines," says Boyd. "And no woman was out of bounds."[9]

At precisely the same time as *Get Back* was limping into life Harrison became briefly involved with French model Charlotte Martin, who had recently split up with Eric Clapton. The ex-Cream guitarist had already developed feelings – at this point unrequited and undeclared – for Harrison's wife, and in order to "work them out" he broke off his relationship with Martin, who happened to be a good friend of Boyd. To help Martin get over the breakup, she invited the model to come and stay at Kinfauns, where she almost immediately began an affair with

Harrison. Boyd was so distraught that during the first week of January she left to stay with friends in London while Martin and Harrison continued their fling in Esher. This was the fraught domestic backdrop to his first week's work at Twickenham Film Studios. After walking out on the band on January 10 he returned to Kinfauns, asked Martin to leave, and phoned Boyd to tell her the news. He later drove north to Warrington to spend the weekend with his parents, perhaps to ponder whether the stress at home was exacerbating the deterioration of his relationship with The Beatles, or whether the poisonous mood within the group was filtering into his home life? Whichever was the case, his affair with Martin was the first act in a prolonged sexual psychodrama which eventually saw Boyd leave Harrison for Clapton, and which produced several sidebars and sub-plots as it stretched into the Seventies and lingered even into the Nineties.

He was not, generally, one for flaunting his infidelities. "It certainly appeared, and I thought, that George was totally committed to Pattie," says Ken Scott. "If anyone came around [to the studio] it would be her, and he seemed perfectly happy. He certainly didn't bring in women and say, 'This is just between you and I', or anything like that." In this respect the affair with Charlotte Martin was particularly distressing for Boyd, an unwelcome expansion of his policy to dump the truth on everyone's doorstep, however hurtful it might be.

Similarly, his attacks on Lennon over Ono were, in one sense, simply an extension of the person he had always been; this was the same man, after all, who'd had no compunction about telling his band-mate a decade earlier that Cynthia had teeth like a horse. Yet he seemed to have become more intolerant and outspoken. "I was naive and thought we could express our feelings to each other, not suppress them and keep holding them back," he said. "Well, it was what I felt, and why should I be untrue to myself? I came to believe the importance that if you feel something strong enough then you should say it."[10]

If the failings of others became more pronounced to him, so did his own. Much of his anger was self-directed. He longed to be above such petty squabbles and the demands of his ego and the flesh, but couldn't help but get pulled in. The frustration made him quick to lash out. "I hated everything about my ego," he said. "It was a flash of everything false and impermanent which I disliked."[11]

He would snap and snarl in the Apple offices, particularly at people he didn't know or whom he suspected wanted something from him. "The first time I met him, he attacked me," said David Dalton, a founding contributor to *Rolling Stone* who was spending time at Apple writing the official account of the *Get Back* sessions. "He took one look at me and pounced. 'What the fuck have we here, then? Hair down to your arse, beads and bracelets? Oh, you think you're so bloody hip don't you, you guys from the great Haight-Ashbury!'"[12] When Lauren Bacall arrived at Savile Row with her young children, who were understandably excited at seeing a living, breathing Beatle, he ignored them and sped away.

As in his dealings with Bernie Krause, he was accustomed to his bidding being done at the first asking and could be arrogant and unreasonable when reality proved reluctant to bend immediately to his needs. "One night George and Billy Preston were watching a TV show up at Apple," Dalton recalled. "Billy was performing that night on a variety show called *Talk Of The Town*. I was sitting on the floor... when George asked me to turn the sound up. After several more requests to 'turn the fucking thing up,' I told him that that was as loud as it went. George looked at me ferociously and in high imperial mode demanded that I *turn the bloody volume up*."[13] He had been a Beatle long enough for the sense of entitlement to have become ingrained. "George could be very easy to be with and down to earth, but he was well aware of who he was," says Chris O'Dell. "For us it was like, 'Well, he's George. We'll just have to adjust to his mood, he's not going to adjust to ours.'" Then again, he could be kind, considerate and thoughtful. And when his minions scored him a pound of prime hash to keep him going over the Christmas period in 1968, he happily carved off a huge chunk and wished them a happy holiday.

It wasn't just The Beatles and their entourage who caught the brunt of his mood swings. After the White Album had been completed but not yet released, Harrison gave Eric Clapton acetates to listen to while on Cream's farewell tour of the US. When word reached him that Clapton had been playing the album to friends in Los Angeles he was "furious and gave me a huge bollocking. I remember being incredibly hurt. It brought me down to earth with a bang, and after that I was always a little wary of letting my guard down around him."[14]

He never set himself up a saint, but many friends and colleagues were troubled by the whiff of hypocrisy hanging in the air. "It was always a bit of a conflict for me, the fact that the way he operated in his personal life wasn't always in parallel with his beliefs," says Glyn Johns. "He wasn't always the most lovely person on the planet. He did have an unpleasant side, like all of us. He could be quite tricky. He wasn't a pushover, if you said something in the wrong way he could take issue, even if what you said was completely innocent. He kept you in your place, let's put it like that. That chippiness, I don't know where it came from. But then, I know very, very, very few human beings who have firm beliefs of that type who are perfect. I think it's a bit unfair to be too critical."

It was a deeply stressful time, both inside and outside the band. While he was recording with Jackie Lomax on March 12, 1969 Harrison got a call from Boyd telling him the police had just raided Kinfauns and found marijuana on the premises. It was open season on the British pop elite. Following a raid by Sussex Police at Keith Richards' home in West Wittering in February 1967, and the subsequent much-publicised trial on drugs charges of Richards and Mick Jagger, Donovan, Brian Jones, Lennon and Jagger had also been busted by Sergeant Norman Pilcher and his over-officious drug squad, while an attempt to bust Clapton misfired when the guitarist was warned in advance of Pilcher's intentions and had fled to Ireland. On this occasion Pilcher timed the raid to coincide with the day of Paul McCartney's wedding to Linda Eastman, presumably on the assumption that the Harrisons would be attending (they weren't) and that therefore no one would be at home.

In the event, when Boyd opened the door she was greeted by eight policemen and women, a pack of sniffer dogs and a search warrant. They almost immediately found a large lump of black hashish in one of Harrison's shoes. When he returned home, calm but livid, he said: "You needn't have turned the whole bloody place upside down. All you would have had to do is ask and I would have shown you where I keep everything." When a photographer emerged from the bushes as he and his wife were being led out of the house to be taken to the police station he chased him and jumped on his camera, reportedly shouting, "I'm going to fucking kill you, you bastard!"

When he appeared at Esher and Walton Magistrate's Court on March 31, Harrison didn't dispute the charge. He did, however, publicly query the police procedure which found pot in a place where previously there hadn't been any, and yet failed to find the dope that was already in the house. "It just happened that, you know, they seemed to bring it with them that day," he said. "I'm a tidy man. I keep my socks in the sock drawer and [my] stash in the stash box. It's not mine."[15] His instincts proved correct. In September 1973 Pilcher was convicted of "conspiracy to pervert the course of justice" for having planted drugs in several of his cases, and was sentenced to four years in prison. Harrison and Boyd escaped with the lesser punishment of a £250 fine each and ten guineas costs. Nonetheless, he viewed the entire episode as a gross intrusion into his private life.

Meanwhile, The Beatles' finances were in turmoil. At the end of January 1969 Allen Klein had appeared on the scene. An accountant by trade, Klein had been managing the business affairs of The Rolling Stones, Donovan, The Animals and The Kinks during recent years and had gained a reputation for his abrasive, hard-nosed tenacity and bloodlust for a killer deal. Following Lennon's decision to ask the pugnacious New Yorker to take charge of his own financial affairs, in May Harrison and Starr agreed that Klein should also manage The Beatles in an attempt to straighten out the catastrophic financial situation that the mismanagement of Apple had created.

McCartney preferred Lee Eastman, a more urbane New York lawyer who happened to be the father of his new wife. The thinking behind Harrison's choice of Klein wasn't hugely sophisticated. "Because we were all from Liverpool we favoured people who were street people," he said. "Lee Eastman was more like a class-conscious type of person. As John was going with Klein, it was much easier if we went with him too."[16] The Beatles' long term financial future came down, essentially, to a tussle between Klein's polo necks and Eastman's suspiciously expensive suits, and also to the growing schism in the band which placed McCartney on one side and the remaining three on the other.

The dispute over who should be in control of their money hung like a persistent raincloud over 1969 – and for many years afterwards. "There was a combination of things happening that could be dreadful and crushing, and everything George had worked for he felt could be taken away," says Boyd. "It was like this huge five-way, six-way divorce going on," says Tony Bramwell. "John or Paul would ask me to do something but 'don't tell any of the others.' Just horrible." A new song by McCartney summed up the prevailing mood, both financially and emotionally. 'You Never Give Me Your Money' lamented their preoccupation with the "funny papers" of contracts and balance sheets, adding poignantly that "in the middle of negotiations, we break down."

★ ★ ★

It seems astonishing, given the circumstances, that they had one final record in them. In the end *Abbey Road* began almost as an afterthought as the band, perhaps in order to avoid having to face the facts of their plight, just kept on going out of force of habit. "The *Get Back* sessions basically continued and morphed in to what became *Abbey Road*, but without anyone having much of an idea about where it began and ended," says Chris Thomas.

The recording possessed little of the dark drama of *Get Back*, which was concluded initially in much the same careless manner in which it had been started. The state-of-the-art studio in the basement of 3 Savile Row proved to be just one more Apple pipe dream which evaporated as soon as it made contact with the chill air of reality. "I went to see it only to discover that the console that had been built looked like something from a Buck Rogers movie in the Thirties," says Glyn Johns. "It was hopeless. Magic fuckin' Alex? What a twat! What a rip-off merchant! It was extraordinary that anyone could get taken in by him, but there we are. So that console was removed, and George was really pissed off at me when I said it was a piece of shit."

Deploying the same logic that inspired him to ask Clapton to appear on 'While My Guitar Gently Weeps', once installed at Savile Row

Harrison corralled Billy Preston to play keyboards on the sessions, which improved the mood and helped flesh out the often painfully threadbare music. Harrison recalled that when Preston joined "straight away there was 100 per cent improvement in the vibe in the room. Having this fifth person was just enough to cut the ice that we'd created among ourselves."[17]

Filming and recording continued for the rest of January. In order to provide the project with some kind of climactic third act, on the afternoon of January 30 The Beatles performed five songs into a stiff winter breeze on the roof of the Apple building, Harrison playing a rosewood Fender Telecaster and protected from the winter chill by a black fur coat. It was, aptly, a last-minute compromise and a mere apparition of the grandiose concept concert originally planned. Now the question was, what to do with it all? Johns worked throughout 1969 on editing the material and assembling a running order and a final mix for the *Get Back* album. "It was a bit like *The Basement Tapes*," he says. "The idea was to show them as ordinary people with a sense of humour." Twice he presented The Beatles with a completed album, an audio-vérité document of a band with their trousers down. Twice it was rejected. By the time the project had been taken over by Phil Spector – who, in the words of Johns, "vomited all over it" by adding glutinous strings, choral voices, edits, overdubs and splicing of multiple takes – and finally released as *Let It Be* in May 1970, The Beatles were already history.

In the end, Harrison's contributions to *Let It Be* were almost comically slight for a man with 'Something' in his back pocket and otherwise enjoying a rich vein of writing form. 'For You Blue', a chugging, archetypal blues played for laughs, with Lennon's ramshackle slide guitar wheezing away in the background next to McCartney's high, irritatingly jaunty roadhouse piano, was a true featherweight. The sense of fun – "Go Johnny go!" he laughs at Lennon, "Elmore James got nothing on this baby!" – sounds a mite forced. 'I Me Mine', rejected during the initial recording sessions, was added to the record at the last minute because a brief rehearsal version had been included in the film. Another pointed comment on "ego: the eternal problem,"[18] this heavy, Gallicflavoured waltz was so short that, in order for it to reach a respectable length, Spector spliced the first 1:20 onto the end, effectively repeating the entire track.

If the songs recorded for *Get Back* had been Harrison's farewell offering to The Beatles it would have been a meek, desultory ending. As it was, like a poker player waiting until dawn breaks before revealing his winning hand, he unveiled his two most beloved Beatles songs right at the death for *Abbey Road*.

'Here Comes The Sun' was started at Eric Clapton's house, Hurtwood Edge near Ewhurst, about 20 miles down the A3 from Kinfauns, while the pair wandered around the gardens with their guitars on a beautiful spring morning. It was another reaction to Apple and his own "long, cold, lonely winter" in the band. "We had meetings and meetings with all this, you know, banks, bankers and lawyers and all sorts of things," he said. "Contracts and shares. It was really awful, 'cos it's not the sort of thing we enjoy, and one day I didn't come into the office. It was like sagging off school. It was sunny and it was all just the release of that tension that had been building up on me."[19]

Between the lines about the ice finally melting and the years of cloudy skies being swept away, it's not hard to find a heartfelt comment on his own transformation into a strong-willed independent musician, at ease with his own musical identity, and also the awareness that The Beatles were reaching the end of their lifespan. The simple folk-picking structure of the verse gracefully incorporates a complex Indian *tihai* polyrhythm on the "sun, sun, sun, here it comes" segment, one of Harrison's most organic mergings of the west and the east. The whole has a charm and a lack of guile that puts it among his most easy to love compositions. An "awakening, an exaltation of the dawn,"[20] both literal and figurative, it was finished in June during a holiday in Sardinia with Boyd.

His other ace in the hole was 'Something', which provided further irrefutable evidence of the new clarity, confidence and quality in his writing. No single song epitomises Harrison's travails as a songwriter in The Beatles quite as starkly. Its progress from initial composition, to shy, almost reluctant unveiling, to demo, to cover, to Beatles song, to his first ever A-side travels through all the major stages of his battles – as much with his own nature as with his band-mates – to be heard.

If McCartney had written a song so obviously persuasive it would surely have been recorded by The Beatles within the week. As it was, it took Harrison an age to get around to presenting it to the band and even longer to settle on a recording with which he was satisfied. He was never one to be rushed. "George used to sit in Esher and he would run through songs over and over, and hone them before revealing them to anyone," says Tony Bramwell. "He had his little studio at home where he could do that. He took a long time to write songs. The other two were like some kind of machinery, churning one out every ten minutes. George could take six months."

'Something' first appeared, played on piano, during the White Album sessions. Chris Thomas had discovered a harpsichord which they were going to use on 'Piggies'. Finding themselves alone in Studio One, "George sat down and just played it to me," says Thomas. "It was one of those songs you hear straight away and think, God, that's fantastic. I said, 'That's amazing, why don't we do that?' He said, 'Oh, do you think it's all right?' I said, 'Yes! We should do that one instead of "Piggies".' He said, 'Maybe I'll give it to Jackie Lomax instead.' It was odd. He thought, 'I'll give it to Jackie Lomax,' not, 'Oh my God, *we* should obviously do it.' I was really disappointed that we didn't do it that night, and we did 'Piggies' instead. He just pushed it under the carpet. He didn't seem to have faith in the song himself. Sometimes people can't see when one of their songs is really not up to much and one of them is really good."

Harrison later said the song didn't appear on the White Album because they had already completed all the tracks. He first played 'Something' to Thomas on September 19, four weeks before the album sessions ended, but while Thomas recalls that the version he heard was "completely fully-formed, he played the whole thing," Lomax's recollection is that Harrison hadn't quite completed the song when he showed it to him in Los Angeles a little over a month later, while they were recording *Is This What You Want?*. "I said, 'That's great. You finish it off and we can put it on the album,'" says Lomax. "I think when he finished it off he thought, This is a Beatles song." Harrison was certainly still working on the lyrics in January; the tune was already there, but during one *Get Back* session at Apple Lennon could be heard advising him on the right lyrics; at the time, Harrison was singing "attracts me like a pomegranate."

Once finished, he may then have taken stock of the shambolic *Get Back* sessions and – probably correctly – calculated that this was not going to be the right context for 'Something' to shine, particularly as 'All Things Must Pass' and 'Isn't It A Pity' had already been given such short shrift. Instead, he gave it to Joe Cocker, who recorded it early in 1969 for his second album *Joe Cocker!*. After playing it privately for Glyn Johns he recorded it again shortly afterwards on February 25, his twenty-sixth birthday, along with 'Old Brown Shoe' and 'All Things Must Pass'. This very precise and beautiful take, with piano overdubs, was recorded at Abbey Road with engineer Brian Gibson, again without the knowledge of the other Beatles. "Why waste them on [the band] when he could do them on his own?" says Johns in an attempt to explain this cloak-and-dagger behaviour. Ken Scott agrees. "George knew the situation, and I almost feel he was just kind of waiting to do his own thing," says Scott. "He had gone through enough albums, he knew what it was all about. He knew the score. He was stockpiling."

He was possibly working on the assumption that *Get Back* would be The Beatles' swan-song. When it transpired that they would be making another album, the band were finally permitted a crack at 'Something'. A more carefully curated project, and one which better suited Harrison's creative temperament, *Abbey Road* saw George Martin back on board and was certainly a more positive environment in which to attempt the song. Recording through the spring and summer of 1969, in general the band behaved civilly towards each other. The shared knowledge, recognised though not explicitly articulated, that this would be their final work took the pressure off and brought some relief to the proceedings.

'Something' was pieced together during several sessions, cut down from its original eight minutes. Recorded at a time when The Beatles no longer had a defined sound, it is a Harrison song through and through, from its meticulously crafted solo (it took him four months to nail it) to its characteristic slide from C major to A major between the verse and chorus. Although the modus operandi on *Abbey Road* was, like the White Album, generally inclined towards four men dedicating the bulk of their time to their own songs, 'Something' was given the collective commitment it deserved, gilded with Starr's simpatico drums, McCartney's busy but arresting bass, Billy Preston's warm organ and George Martin's lush string arrangement. Yet however wonderful the results, Chris Thomas insists the song lost some almost indefinable quality as it evolved from its original inception to full production number. Harrison's recordings frequently did. There was a beguiling frailty, a vulnerability, to many of his demos which he didn't often allow to be publicly exposed. "On the record it was more like somebody's *done* it, do you know what I mean?" says Thomas. "In the same way that 'Long, Long, Long' had a real atmosphere to it, when he played it to me solo 'Something' had more of that feeling. The recorded version didn't seem to have the emotion I remembered when he sang it to me."

Harrison later claimed that he was thinking about Ray Charles when he wrote 'Something', though presumably not romantically. He was also thinking about new Apple signing James Taylor, from whose song 'Something In The Way She Moves' he shamelessly purloined his opening line. Having originally stated that the "she" in 'Something' was "maybe Pattie – probably,"[21] he later qualified even that tentative statement by denying that the song was written specifically about his wife. It was the video, filmed on August 25, five days after the last ever Beatles recording session attended by all four members of the band, that popularised that perception, depicting as it did the four men at home with their wives, and with Boyd prominently featured.

In fact, one of the reasons 'Something' remains by far Harrison's most popular and frequently covered song is its graceful vagueness – telegraphed immediately in the title – and his refusal to burden the lyric with too much personal baggage. The subject is fluid, and the romantic impulse behind the song can also be interpreted as a spiritual one. "I don't want to lose you now/You know I believe and how," as well as the confusion over which way his love should go, are as applicable to matters of faith as to a more conventional kind of love. He told friends, "Actually, it's about Krishna, but I couldn't say *he*, could I? I had to say *she*, or they'd think I'm a poof."[22] Just occasionally in his writing the manifestations of personal, spiritual and universal love melt into one and the result is pure, easeful joy, a direct communication of glimpsed bliss. This quality can be heard in both 'Here Comes The Sun' and in the gliding, effortless inevitability of 'Something', both of which radiate spiritual well-being far more convincingly than many of his 'God' songs.

Described by Lennon as "a great song,"[23] 'Something' is, along with 'Yesterday', the most adaptable, egalitarian Beatles composition, as comfortable settling into an easy listening lounge environment as adopting a soul or country style. It has been covered at least 200 times, by everyone from Elvis Presley and Frank Sinatra to James Brown and Smokey Robinson. The Beatles' version, however, remains definitive. It was released as a single in October 1969, and eventually reached number four in the UK and US charts, backed by 'Come Together'. Eleven years after joining the band, six years after 'Don't Bother Me', Harrison was finally deemed worthy of equal top billing on a Beatles single, even if it was The Beatles poorest chart showing in the UK since 'Love Me Do' in 1962.

It was too little, too late. "George had just given up [on The Beatles]," says Tony Bramwell. "He was off doing his own thing. He was playing with other musicians who had boosted his ego massively, and he had all those songs he had been writing all that time. Suddenly he had loads of them, and he went in and recorded them all with his new found friends." His true musical allegiances were depicted graphically on the cover of *Abbey Road*. Last in line on the zebra crossing, dressed head to toe in bright blue denim where the other three band members are in suits, the heavily hirsute Harrison looked like a roadie or second guitarist for one of the bands of American roots-rockers whose music now fascinated him, and whose members he counted as friends and allies.

By the time McCartney officially declared that he was leaving The Beatles on April 10, 1970, simply confirming in words what everybody already knew in their hearts, Harrison was long gone in body and soul. He had even been tempted back on to a stage for the first time in over three years. Yet he still found the time to be rankled by the fact that it was McCartney who went public with the announcement. "That was what killed him!" says Chris O'Dell, who was living with the Harrisons at the time. "He was like, 'What, are you kidding me? After *we've* all quit!' I think it kind of pissed him off, to be honest. I woke up and there were newspapers all over the kitchen table and Pattie went, 'Oh my God, you won't believe what's happened...' John came over shortly afterwards and they went off on their own to talk, and my impression was he found out at the same time as everyone else. But it didn't take long for him to start work on his own album. He didn't sit around thinking, 'What am I going to do with my life?'"

Be Here Now
Abbey Road, June 1970

The early stages of George Harrison's solo career are anything but tentative. Recording at Abbey Road, at the genesis of sessions that will stretch into early winter and sometimes look like never stopping, everywhere one looks people are engaged in a kind of frenzy of creative activity.

Phil Spector buzzes about in the control room. Having been "hitting the Courvoisier pretty hard,"[1] he will shortly fall over, break his arm, and go home. For now, he is keeping his distance behind the glass, "a paranoid little dude" missing his revolver, according to Bobby Whitlock, building his wall of sound ever higher and thicker, ensuring every possible component part is phased to the max and drenched in reverb.

Down on the studio floor the atmosphere is one of controlled chaos. Two drum kits are set up on a pair of risers, and everyone – and it really *seems* like everyone – plays live in a circle around Harrison in the centre. Today the ensemble is recording 'Isn't It A Pity'. Chris Thomas, enlisted on Moog, is finding it something of a squeeze. "It was bizarre," he says. "You went in there and all of Badfinger were strumming acoustics, Alan White was on drums, Mal Evans was banging tambourines, there was a session guitarist, Klaus Voormann was on bass. We were all playing and then all of a sudden Billy Preston turned up and sat down at the organ, and then within a couple of minutes Ringo turns up and sits down at the other drum kit. Oh, and there's Eric Clapton. What's going on here! It was like 'Intro/Outro' by the Bonzo Dog Doo-Dah Band. I think there were 18 people on that session."

It looks like madness, but George Harrison knows precisely what he is doing.

CHAPTER 9

How High Will You Leap?

New decade, new home, new playmates, new record. New life.
1970 was a landmark year for Harrison, which began with him
and his wife moving into an eccentric neo-Gothic mansion in south
Oxfordshire, and culminated with the release of six sides of music, two-
thirds of which remain, by some distance, his crowning glory as a solo
recording artist.

It was all forward motion. As if to illustrate the point, he had ended
1969 in an unlikely place: back on the bus, playing guitar for Delaney &
Bonnie and Friends during their short tour of England and Scandinavia.
He may have baulked at spending any road-time at all with The Beatles,
but he was not so reticent when it came to performing with other, more
simpatico musicians with no baggage on board, or at least none that
had anything to do with him. "It was a band of gypsies," recalls Dave
Mason, just one of the numerous players along for the ride. "It was a
very free period, and a great time."

Harrison had first come across the music of Delaney & Bonnie a year
earlier in Los Angeles when working with Jackie Lomax. Their manager
Alan Pariser "was friends with George," says Bobby Keys, future sax
player for The Rolling Stones, and another of the numerous Friends.
"He used to take pot to him." Delaney Bramlett was a 30-year-old

Mississippi singer, songwriter and guitar player who had moved to LA in the early Sixties. Having earned his stripes as a session man, in 1967 he formed a band with his new wife Bonnie and a retinue of musical associates, playing a tight-but-loose blend of R&B, blue-eyed southern soul and gospel. Though sonically poles apart, like The Band Delaney & Bonnie made music which cared little for prevailing pop trends. This was steamy, protracted jam-music, with the emphasis on that elusive "feel", the interaction between voice and instruments, rather than the song. It has not, in all truth, dated terribly well.

When Harrison came across the band they had recently left Stax and had just recorded their second album *Accept No Substitute* for Elektra, although that didn't stop him – in full Beatling, must-have mode – trying to poach them for Apple when he heard the mixes, nor did it stop Delaney & Bonnie signing the contract they were offered despite already being legally beholden to another. A few copies of the album were pressed with the Apple logo on the label before litigation kicked in, but Delaney & Bonnie would not be joining the ranks at Savile Row. It was an auspicious meeting in other ways, however. More than any other group of musicians, Delaney & Bonnie and Friends would dictate the sound, personnel and general ethos of Harrison's earliest solo moves. Seven of the band appear on *All Things Must Pass*.

Clapton had also heard the acetates of *Accept No Substitute* via Pariser, and immediately booked Delaney & Bonnie to support his new band Blind Faith on their 1969 US tour. Realising he preferred the good-time vibe of the support act to the stiff sour grapes of his own stuttering supergroup, he jumped on their bus and, in doing so, effectively left one band and joined another. "There was something infectious about their approach to music," he said. "They would have their guitars on the bus and would play songs all day as we travelled. The band was made up of all these great Southern musicians, who had such a strong sound and performed with absolute confidence."[1]

After the 'insular' world of Blind Faith it looked like heaven to Clapton. And after the uptight, proscriptive dynamic of The Beatles, which remained ongoing long after the music ceased, it looked like nirvana to Harrison. This was, in theory, a return to playing as uncomplicated fun, spontaneous expression shorn of any legal complications, outside expectations and games of one-upmanship or empire building.

He watched Clapton perform with Delaney & Bonnie and Friends at the Royal Albert Hall on December 1, 1969, and joined the throng later at the after-show party at the Speakeasy. There he asked Bramlett, "Would you mind if I joined the band? Would there be too many guitars?" It wasn't an entirely impulsive thought. As early as October *NME* had reported that Clapton and Harrison (as well as Lennon and an unnamed Rolling Stone, most likely Keith Richards) were going to be joining the tour, and during the same month he had provided guitar backing alongside members of the group on Leon Russell's eponymous album.

A few hours after leaving the Speakeasy, Harrison – with his amp, guitar and Mal Evans in tow – was sitting outside Kinfauns awaiting collection, much to the irritation of his wife. "I don't think Pattie was okay with it," said Bramlett. "It sure didn't seem like she liked the idea very much."[2] Undeterred, he hopped on the bus clutching a present for the band leader who, Pariser had already warned him, had an embarrassing habit of asking people for their guitars: in order to circumnavigate any awkwardness Harrison came prepared, offering his custom made one-of-a-kind Rosewood Telecaster, the one he'd played on the Apple roof, as a welcome gift. "The first thing he did was hand it to Delaney," says Bobby Whitlock, another Friend. "He got that out of his way because he had been informed that Delaney would ask everybody for something if he wanted it." This established the mood of his cameo: one of respect, even mild deference, to his new gang.

That night at Bristol Colston Hall he made his first appearance on stage since August 1966, alongside Delaney & Bonnie, Clapton, Rita Coolidge on vocals, Dave Mason on guitar, Bobby Whitlock on keyboards and vocals, Carl Radle on bass, Jim Gordon on drums, Tex Johnson on percussion, Jim Price on trumpet and Bobby Keys on saxophone. "I can remember being on stage and thinking, We've got a Beatle over there, Clapton over there - quite a line up!" says Keys. "But George was just one of the guys, he wasn't eaten up with any 'I'm a Beatle and you're not,' kind of attitude."

The exact opposite, in fact. In Bristol he went on unannounced and was almost invisible, playing at the back of the stage behind Clapton, tight left of the drums, sticking to rhythm guitar and steering clear of the microphone. By the time the tour hit Liverpool four nights later, after calling at Birmingham, Sheffield and Newcastle, he was finally persuaded to sing, dusting off 'Everybody's Trying To Be My Baby' for what would be his final ever performance in his home city.

It was in Liverpool that "George first introduced me to Newcastle Brown Ale," says Keys. "He said, 'Here's something that ought to appeal to you, Texas cowboy', and I was like, 'I can drink a bucket of whisky, this is just some beer.' But it was a little more than I'd bargained for, which was rather amusing to George. The tour was typical young rock and roll – there was an excessive amount of drinking, particularly." After one gig Harrison organised an illicit lock-in at a local pub, during which the entourage embarked in food fights and a heavy session to the soundtrack of Tony Ashton – whose new band, Ashton, Gardner & Dyke, were support act on the tour – playing piano. As Mal Evans shepherded them out into the early morning light, Harrison, perhaps reminded of the innocently wired days of Hamburg, pulled down Bramlett's trousers and made a run for it. It was that kind of tour. "We were travelling in a bus together and it didn't take long before bonds were made and friendships established," says Keys. "It was all a rollicking good time."

But he was older now, and more than a little wiser, and hyper-sensitive to the dynamic of several musicians coexisting in a small space and on an even smaller stage. He slipped into the role that Clapton and Billy Preston had previously adopted when they had joined The Beatles in the studio, becoming a unifying presence among a complex mix of temperaments and agendas.

"Him coming along was the best thing that happened to that group, it was the only time that egos were quelled and there was peace," says Whitlock. "Having him with us was good for the soul, man. George pretty much glowed. He carried this sense of well-being and quietude with him wherever he went. There was this aura about him – like walking into a monastery, a sense of peace. Don't get me wrong, it wasn't all holier than thou – that's not what I'm talking about, but he had an air about him, and that was a constant for the whole time I knew George. He took his time to talk to everybody, he's laughing and having a good time, playing and singing and doing his thing. He became another one of the Friends, it wasn't like having a Beatle in the band. It was a helluva tour, a lot of fun, and just what George needed after all that hoopla with The Beatles; to get involved with a bunch of redneck rock and rollers and just have a good time."

He continued guesting with the band as the tour travelled to Scandinavia between December 8 and 12, and returned to play John Lennon's Peace For Christmas benefit for UNICEF at the Lyceum on December 15, the last time he and Lennon would ever share a stage. It was not one for the annals. Harrison was part of a bloated incarnation of the Plastic Ono Band churning out bleakly attritional noise, the kind of 'challenging' music he would routinely file under "avant-garde a clue". "What key is the first one in?" asked Delaney, a proficient Southern boy unaccustomed to such indulgent free-form excesses being inflicted on a paying audience. "It doesn't matter," came Harrison's sniggering reply. For the avoidance of any doubt, to their left Yoko Ono emerged from a sack shrieking like a lit banshee.

If the culmination of the tour was a capering dalliance with advanced forms of art-torture, the rest of it had been a vibrant palette cleanser; more than that, it was a definitive fork in the road. By the time he landed back in Esher after his two week busman's holiday, Harrison had undergone an essential regeneration as a guitarist. In their lifetime The Beatles had never been much acclaimed for their instrumental virtuosity, and certainly Harrison was no standard issue guitar hero – his aim was to serve the song with economy and care; not until he went solo did a clear stylistic imprimatur start to emerge.

Dave Mason recalls the last date of the English leg of the tour, at Fairfield Halls in Croydon on December 7. "We were getting on stage to jam and there was a song they did called 'Comin' Home'. On the record I'm playing that slide guitar part in the background. So before George went on he said, 'What can I play?' I showed him this simple slide part, we fucked around with it a little bit and he got that down and came up and played it. Later, he credited me for him starting to play all that slide guitar stuff after I taught him to play that part on the song."

The sweet, sad sigh of his slide guitar playing quickly became Harrison's signature sound – unmistakeable to the point where at times it came close to self-parody. Slide suited him: it was unflashy, soulful and melodic, and seemed to capture the very essence of that "weeping" sound. Never a blues aficionado like so many of his contemporaries, it was a place he felt he could call home. "I started thinking... maybe this is how I can come up with something that's half-decent," he said, with typical self-deprecation.[3] As usual, he wanted to apply what he had learned immediately. In Scandinavia he wrote a new song, 'Woman Don't You Cry For Me', an acoustic blues which in its original form was based around zinging bottleneck slide but which wasn't released until 1976 on *Thirty Three And 1/3*, by which time it had regenerated into a disco-funk tune, not entirely to its benefit.

His new playing style was heard to perhaps greatest effect on the instantly recognisable hook to 'My Sweet Lord', another new song written towards the end of the tour which fused his enduring spiritual journey with his two most recent musical passions: slide guitar and gospel music. His attraction to the latter was hardly a surprise. Gospel was the most obvious trysting point between God and the populist soul music Harrison loved. It was also one of the bedrock sounds of Delaney & Bonnie's music, and on tour they talked long into the night about its origins, how Bramlett wrote his own devotional songs and where he got the inspiration from. Gospel was in the air and on the charts. The Edwin Hawkins Singers' classic 'Oh Happy Day' was a huge hit in the summer of 1969, and its uncomplicated message of spiritual uplift directly inspired 'My Sweet Lord'. "I remember Eric and Delaney & Bonnie were doing interviews with somebody in either Copenhagen or Gothenburg, and I was so thrilled with 'Oh Happy Day'," said Harrison. "It really just knocked me out, the idea of that song and I just felt a great feeling of the Lord. So I thought, I'll write another 'Oh Happy Day', which became 'My Sweet Lord'."[4]

The fact that God had come back into his music in abundance was largely thanks to his immersion in the Hare Krishna movement, the Hindu sect which advocated chanting as a means of being at one with the Lord. Devotees of the Hindu avatar Krishna believe that He is the complete supreme ruler, of which other religious deities – God, Allah, Jehovah, Vishnu – are manifestations. They also believe that He is not different from His name: when you chant Krishna, you are automatically associating directly with Him, a belief which appealed to Harrison's need for an immediate connection with God. In 1965, aged 69, Swami A. C. Bhaktivedanta Srila Prabhupada had left India to spread the word of Krishna devotion in the west. In New York he set up the International Society for Krishna Consciousness (ISKCON) at 26 Second Avenue in the East Village and slowly gathered a following of hip margin-hangers and East Coast oddballs. A 1966 record, *The Happening Album: Krishna Consciousness*, featured Prabhupada leading ISKCON disciples in chants celebrating Krishna. Allen Ginsberg had written the sleeve notes.

Harrison knew about Krishna. He had visited Vrindavan, where Krishna spent his childhood days, on his 1966 trip to India with Ravi Shankar. The sacred town was full of temples and devotees, and while there he had joined in the chanting. He got hold of a copy of *The Happening Album: Krishna Consciousness*, and when The Beatles went on holiday to Greece in the summer of 1967 – to buy an island where they all could live; another acid-fried escapade which naturally came to naught – he played the album constantly. He and Lennon took acid and sang the 'Hare Krishna Mantra' "for hours and hours"[5] as they sailed around the islands. It made them feel good. He later ordered 30 copies of the album for the Apple offices.

At home he would chant for an hour in the morning in a yoga position. As ever, he was looking for direct access. "It's the same if you were just to go around chanting 'Christ, Christ, Christ, Christ'," he explained in 1969. "If you say it long enough then you build up this identification. Whatever you identify with, you become one with it. So it's really a method of becoming one with God. It's just another process. It's really the same sort of thing as meditation, but this is the thing – it has more effect, I think. Or quicker effect, because music is such a powerful force. The more you do it, the more you don't wanna stop it, because it feels so nice. Peaceful. I believe in the saying, 'If there's a God, we must see Him.' It's a process of actually having that realization and direct God perception, which is the thing you can attain through chanting and through meditation."[6]

At the height of the madness at the Apple offices Harrison's devotion to Krishna provided a prime part of the intrigue. He would chant up on the roof at Savile Row, or walk through the building fingering his two-foot loop of wooden prayer beads; a visiting journalist from *Disc & Music Echo* noted the presence in his office of a "weird American woman gibbering incessantly" and members of a "cult",[7] with their robes and shaved heads. These included American Krishna devotees Shyamasundar Das and Mukunda Das and other disciples of Prabhupada who had recently arrived in London to set up a British branch of ISKCON called the Radha Krishna Temple. They courted Harrison by sending him clockwork apples and apple pies with the Krishna mantra on them, and eventually came to see him at Savile Row. Soon they were well known faces at Kinfauns, where they would sit, talk, eat vegetarian food and sing *bhakti* kirtans accompanied by harmonium and tabla.

Harrison resolved to take these informal gatherings into the studio, recording the Radha Krishna's version of 'Hare Krishna Mantra' during one long session at the beginning of The Beatles' work on *Abbey Road*. It was the sound of the temple given a tentative hippie-rock makeover. Harrison played harmonium, as he would at Kinfauns, and overdubbed guitar and bass around the chanting devotees. The sound of Alan White's rock drums blended with hand cymbals as the chant escalated to a furious climax. Released as a single on Apple in August 1969, 'Hare Krishna Mantra' reached number 12 in the UK charts, and earned Radha Krishna Temple an incongruous appearance on *Top Of The Pops*. It was a number one in Germany and Czechoslovakia. Hare Krishna – regarded by most observers as part joke, part novelty trend, and partly just another thread in the Sixties' colourful fabric of spiritual digressions – was suddenly implanted in the general consciousness. The follow-up, 'Govinda', less of a commercial success but much more of a song, is still played every morning at all ISKCON temples around the world.

Shortly after the first Radha Krishna Temple single was released, on September 11 Srila Prabhupada, the pioneer of Hare Krishna in the west, arrived in London. He slipped into a waiting Apple limousine and was taken to Lennon's home at Tittenhurst Park near Ascot. Harrison arrived later in a black Porsche, speed no doubt being of the essence when it came to convening with yet another potential guru. They talked for over two hours, about the *Bhagavad Gita*, about how Prabhupada was merely "the servant of the servant of the servant," and perhaps most pertinently, about the importance of spreading the word through music. Wisely, the Swami gave Harrison a free pass as far as devoting himself to the strict tenets of the Krishna lifestyle – vegetarianism he could handle, but no drink, drugs, or 'illicit' sex was never going to fly, nor the robes or bald head. "That is a little awkward for him," agreed the worldly Bhakta Yogi. "I have told him there is no need to change name or shave head. Just carrying on serving Krishna."[8]

Harrison instead became a kind of honorary member, an affiliate, "a closet Krishna"[9] who was alchemised by a mission to spread the word of the Lord through song. What had been more vaguely philosophical in tracks such as 'Within You Without You' and 'The Inner Light' now became explicit and evangelical. The success of 'Hare Krishna Mantra' seemed to him to prove the point. Several of the songs he was writing – 'Hear Me Lord', 'The Art Of Dying', 'Beware Of Darkness', 'Run Of The Mill' – were explicitly derived either from the thoughts and words of Prabhupada or from his own contemplations of them. He wrote in one new song, 'Awaiting On You All', that "by chanting the names of the Lord you'll be free."

It was this direct expression of Krishna consciousness which provided the final component to 'My Sweet Lord'. It had begun as a team effort on the Delaney & Bonnie tour. "I first heard the beginnings of 'My Sweet Lord' on that bus ride," says Keys. "Everyone had their guitars out, pickin' and grinnin', and I can remember the germ of the idea for that song came about then." Harrison had asked everyone to think of a kick-start for a gospel tune. Delaney Bramlett started singing "Oh My Lord" while Bonnie and Rita Coolidge added an improvised call-and-response of "Hallelujah". It became a kind of tour sing-along.

He came home and finished it in the kitchen of Kinfauns. Directly influenced by Prabhupada's encouragement to sing out what was in his heart, it was the ultimate expression not just of Swami Vivekananda's teachings from the *Raja-Yoga* – "[the message] ought to be preached in the public streets in broad daylight" – but also of his own personal commitment; he was, he realised, "sticking my neck out on the chopping block."[10] 'My Sweet Lord' fused eastern spirituality to the Christian gospel, moving seamlessly from the traditional Judaeo-Christian "Hallelujah" to Hare Krishna and Hare Rama, and finally to the Vedic Sanskrit prayer of "Gurur Brahmaa, Gurur Vishnu, Gurur Deva Maheshwara, Gurur Sakshat, Parabrahma, Tasmai Shri Gurave Namah", which broadly translates as: "The teacher is Brahma, the teacher is Vishnu, the teacher is the Lord Mahesvarah. Verily the teacher is the supreme Brahman, to that respected teacher I bow down." For those tuned in to such matters he could hardly have been any clearer, although not everyone's Sanskrit was quite up to speed. "When we were doing 'My Sweet Lord' with all those names at the end, I said, 'What the hell are all these guys?'," says Bobby Whitlock. "He said, 'They're all Gods.' And I said, '*Way* too many Gods, George!'"

★ ★ ★

'My Sweet Lord' was one of the last songs he wrote in Esher. Not long after seeing in the New Year and the new decade Harrison and his wife moved to Friar Park on the outskirts of Henley-On-Thames, a well-heeled town on the river 40 miles west of London. A 120-room late Victorian oddity, Friar Park would be home for the remainder of his life. More than bricks and mortar, it was part sanctuary, part folly, part cosmic joke, and a life-long passion which he restored and nurtured and which became so closely associated with the man who lived there it is now almost impossible to imagine one without the other. Like the music he was about to make, Friar Park reflected the complexities of his inner character on a monumental scale.

Kinfauns was too small, too conventional, too exposed. "I am seeking the absolute peace of complete privacy," he said during his hunt for a new home. "I am also insisting on a private lake, because water is very peaceful for the mind."[11] "George said to me, 'I don't care what the house is like as long as it's not on the road and there is room to put in a recording studio'," says Pattie Boyd. "At Esher, girls managed to get into the garden, even into the house, and it was a bit of a nightmare. And he really wanted a studio where he could work on stuff himself, that was the real reason for having a big house." Boyd spent much of 1969 looking for a suitable location. She found one: Plumpton Place, near Lewes in East Sussex, at the end of a sweeping drive surrounded by moats and gardens. But the elderly owner refused Harrison's offer on the grounds that "she didn't want rock and roll musicians buying her lovely house."[12] The lady must have either experienced a swift change of heart or an offer she couldn't refuse: shortly afterwards Jimmy Page bought the property.

Boyd finally spotted a small advert in the *Sunday Times* placed by the Salesian Sisters of St. John Bosco. The nuns had been running a school in Friar Park in Henley-On-Thames which had recently closed, and the remarkable building was now facing demolition unless a buyer could be found. Its vast husk was inhabited by six nuns and a monk, which must have appealed to Harrison's sense of humour. Boyd went to view it and instantly fell in love; Harrison came the next day and fell equally hard. Built by Sir Frank Crisp in 1898 on the site of an old monastery, the redbrick neo-Gothic pile was an essay in English eccentricity writ large. Harrison's £140,000 bought him a gatehouse, two lodges, 12 acres of formal gardens, another 20 acres of land, a three-storey mansion with 25 bedrooms and numerous public rooms, including a ballroom and a library. There were turrets, towers and parapets with glowering gargoyles.

But that was the least of it. As well as being an eminent lawyer and keen amateur horticulturalist, Crisp was also a microscopist, and the home he built rewarded those with an eye for detail and a taste for the playfully absurd. "He was clearly a wonderful man with a great sense of humour, he travelled extensively and brought back all sorts of things he discovered in other countries," says Boyd. "His attention to detail was exquisite and just what George understood. He loved it for many reasons."

The parkland, open to the public during Crisp's lifetime and long after his death in 1919, was a cross between Botanical garden, fairground attraction and Lewis Carroll's Wonderland. The centrepiece of the Alpine garden was a replica of the Matterhorn made from 20,000 tons of Yorkshire granite. There was a series of man-made underground caves and grottos through which one could travel by boat from one lake to another, the journey enlivened by distorting circus mirrors, gnomes, fairies, toadstools and shimmering blue glass. Above ground there were Elizabethan and Japanese gardens, topiary, a maze. Signs on the lawn read, to the delight of the future hippie interlopers, 'Don't keep off the grass.'

Inside, the double doors led to a marble vestibule and then a huge hall with a grand staircase and a minstrel's gallery above. The fireplace was vast, flanked on each side by a panel showing the Tree of Life and the Tree of Destiny. The dining room had stained glass windows and the ballroom ceiling was dotted with cherubs. There were Swastikas all over the house: the sacred Hindu symbols were removed when World War Two began but there was still evidence of them in the Seventies. A closer look revealed the true art of the microscopist: all the light switches were monk's faces, activated by clicking the nose; the walls were adorned with puns, aphorisms, maxims and proverbs, several of which found their way into Harrison's conversation and eventually his songs. Every new corner seemed to reveal some new whimsical delight, but there was a dark, shadowy intrigue to the place as well. Friar Park was, in many ways, the ultimate expression of Harrison's worldview. How could he not love it?

Unfortunately, on his arrival in March 1970 he found only the ghost of Friar Park's past splendour: the gardens had been used as a local dump, brambles and ivy covered everything, the lakes had been filled in, and internally the house was in a state of extreme disrepair, with grass growing through the floors, whole walls crumbling, and many parts of the building closed off. In the early months they lived like gold-class squatters. There was no heating, no furniture and no beds, so they slept in the hall in sleeping bags, wrapped in coats and scarves and with a fire burning constantly in the huge grate. Even then they almost froze. The only other inhabitable space was the original kitchen, a huge tiled room with flagstone floors, industrial-sized sinks and a walk-in pantry. Slowly, with the guiding hand of architect David Platt, they began to restore parts of the property. For a period they lived in one of the lodges. Back in the house they would sleep on a mattress on the floor in a different room every other night. It was a game. "We were like children – we were playing," says Boyd. "We could decorate, we embarked on a huge garden programme, it was so exciting. It was huge fun."

Friar Park soon began filling up with people: first to land was Terry Doran, the "man from the motor trade" of 'She's Leaving Home' fame who had graduated from flogging cars to running Apple Publishing. Now, post-Beatles, he became Harrison's personal fixer. Chris O'Dell moved in after falling foul of Allen Klein's cull of Apple staff, and was quick to form a lasting friendship with Pattie Boyd. "I think Friar Park was a folly for them as much as for the man who built it," says O'Dell. "There were no boundaries – George's main goal was to get it back to how it was before the nuns had it and closed everything up. He read everything he could and got all this information from people in the village who knew the house, and it became his passion. Pattie had her mind inside the house and he had his outside the house. He loved the gardens."

Lennon popped around – he called it Henley-on-Toast and thought Friar Park a little gloomy – and musicians gravitated there, especially when, shortly after moving in, Harrison began working on his album. Every new visitor got the tour and a sleeping bag. The first person up in the morning brought everyone else tea. "I was there when George was just exploring it himself," says Bobby Whitlock. "We put the wellies and jackets on, got a couple of torches and went down this hole in his yard and suddenly we're in a tunnel with a creek going down the middle of it. It was real interesting! Came out on another pond, and another tunnel, a cave. One bathroom had 12 wooden holes going around the walls, and all the light switches had little friars. It was very cold. I stayed right up at the very top, the tallest room in the tower, Room 101 Pattie called it. There was supposed to be a ghost but I never saw it."

They would mess around on the replica of the Matterhorn, or ride around the property on go-karts. In the morning it was tea, eggs or porridge and newspapers at the kitchen table, and then into London to record or setting to work on the house and gardens. At night there would be Indian cooking, and they would sit in the kitchen to eat, drink and talk. Harrison might play them his new songs, or else disappear to meditate. They would listen to music, or watch a movie in the makeshift screening room in the office next to the kitchen. "He loved *The Producers*," says O'Dell. "I can't tell you how many times we watched that in a very short space of time." His favourite new TV show was *Monty Python's Flying Circus*. He saw something of The Beatles' iconoclastic appeal in their irreverent though essentially benign anarchy. He would explain the humour to the bemused American contingent and memorise lines, much as he had Dylan lyrics. "He had that obsessive compulsive part of him, definitely," says O'Dell.

The house teased out the prankster in Harrison, the same strain which prompted him to tear off Delaney Bramlett's trousers, put a flaming ashtray on his head and, years earlier, to play 'gear' practical jokes with Gerry Marsden. "This shows the playful side of George," says Bobby Keys, recalling the first time he arrived at Friar Park. "He said to Mal, 'Okay Mal, take the guys to their rooms.' Mal said, 'Follow me, boys.' This place had a subterranean cave network underneath, so we followed Mal down into this cave, thinking 'The guy's a Beatle, but this is still a little weird.' Eventually in the middle of this labyrinth of caves George jumped out and tried to scare us: 'Woohooohoo.' Well, it didn't really scare us much. So that was his introduction."

Moving to Friar Park was, in part, all one huge joke – on life, on his friends, on the more austere part of his nature. "At times it seemed that George was amused by the grandiosity of the situation that he created by moving into such an enormous Victorian mansion," says John Barham. "I think initially his approach to the purchase of Friar Park was partly whimsical and humorous. At this stage George wasn't aware to what extent he would be drawn into the material aspects of improving and maintaining an enormous property."

Like all good jokes, there was an uncomfortable truth lurking below the punch line. Friar Park was symbolism of the most crude kind – if he was unable to dedicate himself entirely to a truly spiritual vocation and turn away from the lure of the material world, then why hide the fact? Why not make the dichotomy the entire point, and illustrate it with turrets and towers and a mini Alp? "The style of living was totally in contradiction to the path that he was taking, let's put it that way," says Dave Mason. "But we're human beings and we're full of contradictions." Barham felt he was "caught in the net of his great wealth and possessions. I certainly felt that there was a conflict between on the one hand, the purchase of a 120-room mansion for just two people to live in and, on the other hand, a spiritual path, particularly an Indian one."

In his darker moments Harrison, too, was troubled by the excesses of his new home. Even before he moved in he almost backed out of buying it, and afterwards he toyed with the idea of turning it into a communal spiritual retreat. Instead, as a kind of karmic compromise, he invited several families of Hare Krishna devotees to stay at Friar Park. The men helped out in the grounds and created a vegetable garden; the women cooked. They proved an acquired taste. "All these people," Boyd sighs. "I loved it initially, but the Hare Krishnas really got to me in the end. They started cooking really pungent food at six o'clock in the morning, and we didn't really get up till about nine, so you would wake up to this really strong food. I don't know, it seemed to me that they were overstaying their welcome. George was slightly a soft touch for people in the Hare Krishna movement."

Many of his more grounded friends also felt he was being exploited. When the ISKCON disciples first arrived in England John Lennon had let them stay in part of his Tittenhurst Park estate in exchange for doing some repairs. Shortly afterwards, Harrison co-signed the lease on accommodation at 7 Bury Place, close to the British Museum in Bloomsbury, enabling them to set up their first temple. But it was too small, so he told them to find a suitable building and he would buy it for them. They settled on Piggott's Manor, a former nursing home in Hertfordshire with 17 acres of land, which he bought for the Radha Krishna Temple, sight unseen, for £230,000. He was also asked to provide $19,000 to help Prabhupada publish *KRSNA Book*, a lavishly illustrated series of short stories forming a biography of Krishna. He stumped up and then wrote the foreword.

He was not above gentle recruitment drives. Phone numbers and pamphlets would be pressed into palms, judicious quotes offered. "He gave me a Hare Krishna book and *The Prophet* by Kahlil Gibran," says Whitlock, while O'Dell recalls that he bought "cartons" of copies of *Autobiography Of A Yogi* to give away to people. "My first marriage was at Kensington registry office and George and Pattie came to the reception," says John Barham. "Some weeks before this he had tried to gently persuade me to have the ceremony at the Radna Krishna Temple headquarters. Maybe he wanted me to get involved with the Krishna people in a spiritual way, but he didn't push." "He taught me how to chant," says Keys, "But he never forced anything or said, 'Quit your evil, naughty ways and find the true light!'"

For those who shared his beliefs he was, says Whitlock, "an easy touch. He wanted to do good and well for everyone, especially people that he assumed were of like mind and who would not use and abuse him – but they did, hand over fist, every time he turned around, at least in my estimation. They were just a bunch of moochers as far as I was concerned. One guy had a bagful of rubies. They were a lot of fun banging their drums, ringing their bells, but they were poor in spirit as far as I was concerned. George didn't need all of that. They weren't contributing anything, all they were doing was sleeping all over the place and eating his food. I wasn't buying it for a second!"

There was also something disquieting about their willingness to hand over responsibility for every part of their lives to a higher power. Three times at Friar Park young children belonging to the Krishnas almost drowned in the fountain – each time their fate was left to the Lord's will. "When the baby was in the fountain at Friar Park no one would pull it out, they said God would do it," says Whitlock. "Terry Doran dived in and came out with the kid. I was in the kitchen with Pattie and Terry came and freaked out. They were going to let that baby die in George Harrison's fountain." After it happened a third time Boyd told them, "You've got to look after your children." "Krishna looks after them," she was told.

Harrison was unmoved. He wanted them to stay, and his loyalty to Krishna, and the time he spent chanting in his makeshift prayer room, meditating, or simply walking around with his prayer beads, set him apart from others. His prime concern was for the betterment of his own soul. "Like Christ said, 'Put your own house in order'," he said, "Maharishi said, 'For a forest to be green, each tree must be green.' So the same for the world to have peace, each individual must have peace. And you don't get it through society's normal channels. That's why each individual must tend to himself and get his own peace, and that way the whole society will have peace."[13]

Such an ideology left his wife, in particular, feeling excluded. "I know his meditation got in the way of he and Pattie's relationship," says Whitlock, who had started dating Boyd's sister Paula. Unlike with TM and the Maharishi, Boyd hadn't joined him in his obsession with Krishna, and now felt increasingly outside the circle of his interests and his affections. Soon she would start encouraging the romantic entreaties of another. "He was a soft touch for [the Krishnas] but not for other people, because spirituality was very dear to his heart," she says. "He was really open to their needs – perhaps much more than other people's. It did distance him." To Whitlock "he seemed to be pretty much focused on an inner world, zeroing in on the inner kingdom."

Boyd had hoped that Friar Park would be a place where the Harrisons regularly entertained, held lavish parties, met the neighbours and lived it up a little. Harrison saw it more as an opportunity to create a self-contained universe which few outsiders could penetrate. That, it transpired, was the whole point. "He did ensconce himself out there," says Tony Bramwell. "We used to go motor racing occasionally, or we would meet in town for a drink, but..." Trusted friends, spirit guides and musicians – always musicians – would be welcome, but largely he wanted to be left alone and unseen. "He resented what The Beatles did to him, that he couldn't have his privacy, that people could assume that they could just approach him," says Chris O'Dell. "That's why Friar Park was perfect. It was so away from everything, he could just be himself there. There was a gate on the driveway and a gate all around the place. Pattie and I would want to go to a club in town or go out to dinner and he just did not want to go through all that, people looking at him, wanting something from him."

★ ★ ★

Such was the chaotic, conflicted, exciting and grandiose backdrop to the making of a conflicted, chaotic, exciting and equally grandiose musical masterwork. At his new home he took stock of his new songs, some of which dated back to 1966, but most of which had been written in a recent spurt. Chris O'Dell typed out all the lyrics and, when he was in the right frame of mind, Harrison would run through them at the kitchen table to anyone who cared to listen. "The first time I heard any of the songs on *All Things Must Pass* was after I had dinner with George and Pattie at Friar Park one Saturday evening," says John Barham. "After eating, George picked up an acoustic guitar and without a word began playing a lot of the songs. At the time I had no idea that he was planning a solo album." Bobby Whitlock similarly recalls that "he played me all of them. God, 'Run Of The Mill' had a chord change that was really unique, the original intro was different [Whitlock plays it for me]. He never did that in the studio. It was great, a real George Harrison thing, but he never used it." It remains Olivia Harrison's favourite song by her late husband. "I'd always ask him to play it, and he would," she told me. "I think it's got a great message, and if you listen to the lyrics it's a good little reminder: 'How high will you leap?'"

He had momentum in his songwriting. "He hit his stride shortly before *All Things Must Pass*, and that was perfect timing for him," says Ken Scott. "The success of his songs on *Abbey Road*, and how they were picked up on, definitely gave him more confidence."

In many ways it was a seamless transition from Beatle to solo artist. The drama of the split was happening in Savile Row, in their lawyer's offices, and in the papers, where each member was having their say and often slating the other's comments in interviews or casually deriding their solo work. But in terms of making music, Harrison continued much as he had done for the past two years – writing songs, playing with his friends, and still retaining personal and musical contact with two-thirds of The Beatles, recording with Lennon and writing with Starr on their own projects.

Among his new circle, The Beatles was rarely a topic of conversation. "There was a lot in the press about them," says Ken Scott. "I was with each of them individually, and I didn't hear about it or see the rancour that was going on. They didn't vent." Says Bobby Keys, "He never mentioned The Beatles, and I didn't want to being it up." In any case, his feelings were clearly expressed in the music, all the sadness ('Isn't It A Pity'), anger ('Wah Wah') and weary acceptance ('All Things Must Pass'). The cheeky snatch of 'Hey Jude' at the end of 'Isn't It A Pity'; the dig at Ono and Lennon – with their "love-ins" and "bed-pans" – at the start of 'Awaiting On You All'. It was all codified comment on what had happened and was still happening.

On 'Apple Scruffs', an appropriately dishevelled folk strum, he even paid tribute to the girls who had spent the past few years hanging around outside Abbey Road morning, noon and night. Even now, "there was always a little knot of them," says Bobby Keys. "They weren't fashion model types, they were just little girls – just kids. He always took time to have a word with them, and I seem to remember him going out with tea for them sometimes when it was cold. I was impressed with how caring he was about these girls. I've been around a lot of other folks who have quite a different way of dealing with people, let's put it that way."

Right up until he went into Abbey Road at the end of May to begin work on *All Things Must Pass* Harrison was working, and learning. He had recently finished Doris Troy's album for Apple, and on April 23 he had flown to New York to complete Billy Preston's *Encouraging Words*, for which they recorded the fully-fledged gospel version of 'My Sweet Lord' as well as 'Sing One For The Lord', his first attempt at an out-and-out church song. Smitten with 'Oh Happy Day', he recorded both with the Edwin Hawkins Singers. Harrison and Preston also cut a rather saccharine arrangement of 'All Things Must Pass', drenched in strings, all dressed up for the supper club.

While in New York he spent two days making music with Bob Dylan. After their tentative meeting in Woodstock at the end of 1968 they had become closer. When Dylan and The Band played the Isle of Wight festival in August 1969 "we all went down there together," says Boyd. "This is where George and Bob really became friends. They were very fond of each other, and they had great fun together." While there, between seven-a-side games of tennis and checking out the festival, Harrison wrote the simple country song 'Behind That Locked Door', another attempt to draw Dylan out from his reticence and into friendship. It worked.

In New York a little under a year later they taped some songs in Dylan's new townhouse at 94 MacDougall Street in the West Village. The following day, May 1, they went into Columbia's Studio B to run through many more. The repertoire ranged from a solemn stab at 'Yesterday' to numerous Dylan compositions, from old classics ('Don't Think Twice It's All Right') to songs intended for *New Morning*, the album he was currently working on. They also attempted several oldies and oddities, among them 'Ghost Riders In The Sky', 'All I Have To Do Is Dream', 'Matchbox' and 'Cupid'. Many of the recordings were jokes or brief snippets, but three of the songs played – 'I'd Have You Anytime', 'If Not For You', and 'I Don't Want To Do It' – were recorded for *All Things Must Pass*. The first two – Harrison and Dylan co-writes – made the final cut. Harrison would return to the latter in the Eighties.

He was spoilt for choice. There were songs everywhere he looked. When Phil Spector came to discuss his production role on the new album Harrison played virtually everything he had, in simple solo acoustic versions and in stark arrangements backed by Ringo Starr and Klaus Voormann. "It was endless," said Spector, "And each one was better than the [last]."[14] Spector had suddenly appeared in The Beatles' orbit. In January, at Harrison's insistence, he had produced Lennon's do-it-in-a-day single 'Instant Karma', on which Harrison played guitar and piano. The song had turned out so well that Spector had been asked to work on turning *Get Back* into *Let It Be*. With that job finally completed – The Beatles' ragged swan-song was released on May 8, 1970 – Harrison decided he wanted Spector to produce *All Things Must Pass*.

On May 26 they went into Abbey Road. More than simply making an album, the aim was to clear through the backlog of songs that had built up over the past three or four years. "I didn't really want to chuck anything away," Harrison said. "I wanted to get shot of them so I could catch up on myself."[15] Among the pieces attempted but not released on the album were 'Dehradun', retrieved from Rishikesh, 'Beautiful Girl', which later appeared on *Thirty Three And 1/3*, and at least a dozen other songs, most of which were never heard of again after his initial run through for Spector. These included 'Window, Window', 'Everybody, Nobody' – the melody of which he adapted for 'Ballad Of Sir Frankie Crisp' – 'Nowhere To Go', another Dylan co-write, and 'Cosmic Empire', 'Mother Divine' and 'Tell Me What Has Happened To You'.

There was, perhaps for the only time in his solo career, a real sense of creative urgency driving him on. "He was obviously out to make his mark with this record, no question about it," says Chris Thomas, who played on two tracks. "I didn't get the impression that it was make or break," says Ken Scott, who engineered the album. "But he had just come out of the biggest band in the world, so it was definitely a big deal." He also had a point to prove – to himself as much as anyone, but also to his old band. "All that material that George had amassed over a few years, stuff that was rejected, all those great songs," says Bobby Whitlock. "It was like he wanted to stick it to 'em!"

Much of his confidence derived from the cumulative experience of the past two years of making music independently. *All Things Must Pass* was the destination of his journeys – spiritually, personally, musically. It pulled together all those sources of inspiration, drawing on gospel, Southern rock, country, soul, heavy rock, early Dylan. The love and knowledge of Indian music was in there, too, just below the surface, while lyrically the album distilled every meaningful revelation he had had since his awakening in 1966.

Never a natural front man, he surrounded himself with as many friends as possible. The core band was Clapton, Carl Radle, Jim Gordon and Bobby Whitlock, who were in the process of becoming Derek & The Dominos. Around that nucleus a busload of guests filed in and out of Abbey Road. The musicians who appeared on the album, credited or very often otherwise, included all of Badfinger, Billy Preston, Ringo

201

Starr, Peter Frampton, Klaus Voormann, Alan White, Ginger Baker, Tony Ashton, Dave Mason, Bobby Keys and Jim Price, Gary Wright, Gary Brooker, Chris Thomas and Pete Drake, the latter shipped over at a day's notice from Nashville to provide his distinctive pedal steel playing.

If life was increasingly complex, at least making music had never seemed so easy. "It was the most fantastic time," says Boyd. "He now was free and he realised that that freedom was bringing him so much happiness and joy. He could choose which musicians he would like to play on the album. He was like a child with all these great players, and they were thrilled to be invited. It was wonderful. He hated being in the spotlight, he was very inclusive."

He knew exactly what he wanted but he was trusting enough in his players to let them find it. After his frustrations with The Beatles and taking into account his own precise nature, it might have been expected for him to be very deliberate in his approach to recording. Instead, "he was always laid back, nothing demonstrative," says Peter Frampton, who played (uncredited) acoustic on *All Things Must Pass*. "Everyone was there because they were great players, and when you get a bunch of great players you don't say, 'I want you to play it like this.' You just say, 'Here's the song, what can you bring to it?' He hired people for their inspiration, and the only thing George ever said was, 'That was a good one,' or 'Let's try it again.' No one was left out, it was like we were a band. No one was treated as a session musician. George was not wrapped up in a me-me-me thing, he knew what he could do and what he couldn't do. He was sort of egoless, which was strange because he was a Beatle – or maybe that's why! Good players are usually insecure, that's how you get better, and he blossomed – as a player, and as a writer."

The contrast with McCartney's auteur-like approach was pointed. "I just remember there being a lot of people in the studio, and George would say, 'Here's a song, let's start playing it and see what happens'," says Dave Mason. "He was willing to let things evolve rather than ask for specific parts." "He had the finest, the crème de la crème at his disposal, and he wasn't telling anybody what to play," says Whitlock.

"He just let it roll. It didn't get any tighter than Carl Radle, Jim Gordon and me – we had been playing for years prior to that. We were tight as bark on a tree."

The *modus operandi* recalled by Chris Thomas for the recording of 'Isn't It A Pity' was typical. Multiple musicians playing the same simple parts in unison was a key component in Phil Spector's wall of sound, and on *All Things Must Pass* he went further out there than ever before. After running through 'Wah Wah', the first track they recorded for the album, Harrison was truly aghast at the effects Spector had added when he played it back in the control room. He quickly came to enjoy, however, the sheer over-the-top power and eccentricity of the sound. It was the producer's trademark, but it was also an aural safety net for a man making his first record and not quite sure where to start – or stop. "He was making a transition," says Whitlock. "Can you imagine being him? Trying to make a record with all those musicians, with Phil Spector, and really not knowing how this thing is going to play out, just knowing you have the best on the planet in that room at your disposal." If in doubt, keep piling it on.

On every level the combination of Harrison and Spector was "kind of an odd pairing," says Bobby Keys. "They were complete polar opposites as far as personality went: Phil was energetic and nervous, and George was laid-back and let-it-come-easy. I can remember them overdubbing strings on one track, and at a certain time during the hour, no matter what is going on, the leader taps his baton and everyone has a tea break. In the States that doesn't happen. Phil apparently had not seen this before, and his eyes get bigger and he starts running on the spot and he screams, 'Where are they going, where are they going? George, get them back!' And George just says, 'Don't worry about it, Phil, it's an English thing'. George never got excited or overwrought about anything."

Harrison's instinct was to create the sessions in his own image: democratic, laid-back, business-like but fun. "I never saw him concerned about anything, he had a smile on his face when he arrived, during it and after," says Whitlock. Spector, by contrast, was aloof, dictatorial and possessed of an alienating bedside manner. He had a bodyguard and was "pissed off because they wouldn't let him bring his gun into the studio," says Whitlock. "Phil didn't have a grip on any spiritual aspect of the world or the universe. I could not see how George landed on him to co-produce it. I think it had to do with the old rock and roll, the 'Da Doo Ron Ron Ron'. That was George, he grew up with all that stuff."

In the end it was a case of the producer's vision and pedigree trumping his myriad personality quirks. According to Frampton "Phil was a little out of his element" among the low-key Englishmen and horizontal southerners, so it was left to Harrison to interact with the musicians on the floor, allowing Spector to communicate from the control room, which he rarely left. In July, however, he abruptly departed for Los Angeles. "He was going through a bad time with drinking and it made him ill," said Harrison. "He did half the backing tracks. Then, because of the condition he was in, he had to leave and I completed the rest of the backing without him – and did maybe 50 per cent of the overdubbing, all the backing vocals and all the guitar parts. Then he came back when I was mixing it."[16]

Spector was around long enough to supervise the recording of 'My Sweet Lord', perhaps the high-water mark of the wave of late Sixties pop music with a genuinely spiritual dimension – either expressed explicitly, such as 'Oh Happy Day', Judy Collins' 'Amazing Grace' and Norman Greenbaum's 'Spirit In The Sky', or more holistically, as in Simon & Garfunkel's 'Bridge Over Troubled Water', Marvin Gaye's 'Abraham, Martin And John' and Blue Mink's 'Melting Pot'. Everyone involved in the song was at the top of their game. The triumph of 'My Sweet Lord' is delivered through a combination of Spector's mastery of studio dynamics, Harrison's clarity of vision for the song, and the fact that neither element was allowed to overshadow the raw emotion of his naked prayer. It was a wonder created in real time. The multitudinous backing vocals and slide guitar were overdubbed. Everything else is live.

"The sound of that record, it sounds like one huge guitar," said Harrison. "The way Phil Spector and I put that down was we had two drummers, a bass player, two pianos and about five acoustic guitars, a tambourine player and we sequenced it in order. Everybody plays live in the studio. I spent a lot of time with the other rhythm guitar players to get them all to play exactly the same rhythm so it just sounded perfectly in synch. The way we spread the stereo in the recording, the spread of five guitars across the stereo, made it sound like one big record."[17]

Dark clouds would soon roll across its open-hearted premise. For now, the song was simply further evidence that "something special was being created," says John Barham, who arranged all the string parts for the album, and attended almost all the sessions. "The combination of two music giants and the large ensemble of musicians certainly made me feel that, and I could see that other musicians were also intrigued and enthusiastic about what was developing."

After Spector went AWOL Harrison shouldered greater responsibility. His focus and dedication was all the more impressive in the light of the distractions surrounding him. Apart from its artistic achievements, *All Things Must Pass* was a supreme expression of grace under pressure. It was a trying time. "He had a 100-odd-room house and about 50 Hare Krishna nutcases running loose out there, he had all the handlers and gardeners, then he had Spector and the roomful of musicians, and he still had Allen Klein to deal with and the breakup of The Beatles," says Whitlock.

He also had to contend with his mother dying and his father falling ill. In September 1969, following a cursory misdiagnosis which cited 'psychological problems', and which had left Harrison fuming at the doctor, Louise Harrison had been diagnosed with a brain tumour. She would at times be unable to recognise her youngest son. After he insisted she see a specialist his mother was operated on and her condition stabilised for a few months, during which time his father was admitted to the same hospital with severe ulcers. "So I was pretending to both of them that the other was okay, then running back and forth to do the record," he recalled.[18] Harold would recover but Louise would not. Sitting with her one morning shortly before she died, "filled with frustration and the gloom of going into these hospitals,"[19] he wrote 'Deep Blue'. It was a lament for the loss of the woman who had done so much to nurture, love, and encourage him; a cry of anger at his helplessness in the face of her pain; and a prayer to God to help him understand why he must go through life after life experiencing such sorrow. His faith could only take him so far. He was bereft. Lennon sent a postcard from Los Angeles: "Sorry about your Ma."

Shortly after her death on July 7, 1970, Harrison brought his brothers down to live in Henley-On-Thames. Harry was installed in the gatehouse as estate manager, while Peter became one of an increasingly large team whose job was to look after the gardens. Their fraternal bond was unbreakable, but the distancing effects of fame and their divergent interests and paths had only grown wider through the years. "I wouldn't say they were affectionate with each other," says Chris O'Dell. "He had this huge house he lived in and his brother [Harry] lived in the front lodge, and Peter lived just outside, but I don't even remember them seeing each other that much. What they had in common was Friar Park. They were close by proximity, and history. Like how they'd say, 'our Peter', or 'our George', but I didn't see anything to suggest that this was a really close family. I don't remember Harry and his wife even coming up and having dinner."

Their lifestyles were almost impossible to reconcile. Up at Friar Park it was an off-the-wall mix of music, musicians, eye-wateringly expensive antiquity, Krishna and dope, although Harrison was "very well behaved" during the making of *All Things Must Pass*, according to Ken Scott. "I think there was too much riding on it. When The Beatles were smoking joints in the studio it was okay because there was always someone to fall back on – if you got too out of it someone else could take it on. Whereas now it was just George. He was carrying the can, so he couldn't get too out of it." According to Bobby Keys, who was a house guest during the recording of the album, "he occasionally indulged, but at this time he was pretty exclusively focused on his music and his record – he didn't really need many distractions." The domestic routine was unremarkable. "He got his guitar out and we sat around the table and he played the songs he wanted to have the horns play on. He made us so comfortable. Lots of vegetables, a lot of lovely Indian food. Everyday we would drive into the studio, he drove us himself, and then back to the house and listen to the tapes."

Once the basic tracks were recorded and roughly mixed the sessions moved to Trident for overdubs of horns, strings, guitars and backing vocals. Spector was still absent, but by now Harrison almost seemed to want to out-Spector him. Technically superior to Abbey Road, Trident had a 16-track machine which was used to its full capability. Almost all of the backing vocals were sung by Harrison, with Whitlock also contributing. On 'My Sweet Lord' he layered and layered and layered again, constructing a symphony of multi-part voices credited as The George O'Hara-Smith Singers.

"The overdubbing was amazing," says Ken Scott. "Almost all of the backing vocals being George, that took a tremendous amount of time. We would record four tracks of his vocals, then I would bounce them across to another track at the same time, adding a live vocal. We just kept doing that all the time until we got as big a sound as we wanted. And *lots* of guitars."

Spector was pushing the faders from a distance. He sent a long, detailed letter advising that Harrison's voice, always regarded by its owner as a weak point, should not be buried apologetically in the mix. "I really think your voice has got to be heard throughout the album so that the greatness of the songs can really come through," he wrote. He also said that he wanted more guitars, even after having four or five acoustics playing live simultaneously in the studio. "More?" laughs Peter Frampton. "There was already George, me and all of Badfinger on acoustics! But you understand, Phil has to have 94 of everything – twice. But we admired his production, we were all in awe of the legendary sound he got. So we went back in, just me and George, adding two acoustics as many times as he wanted on the songs. Most of them I hadn't played on, so George would show me quickly what it was. In the old days you had to change a reel, which could take 15 minutes, so we had time between songs to chat and jam, joking around. You don't forget things like that."

Spector returned to London for a short time during the mixing process, "but even then he wasn't around much," says Scott. "He'd come in in the evenings. Once George and I had got it to where we thought it should be, then Phil would come and pass comment – some we'd agree with and change, some we wouldn't. We would finish the mix and then George would go away and set up for the next day. The tapes were so damn good, there was a very clear sense that this was going to make him."

Included alongside the four loose band blow-outs, recorded early in the proceedings at the Savile Row studio and included on 'disc three as "Apple Jams", in August Harrison had taped a short, humorously warped bastardisation of Cliff Richards' 'Congratulations', retitled 'It's Johnny's Birthday', to mark his old friend's thirtieth birthday on October 9, 1970. On the day itself Lennon and Ono were at Abbey Road working on Lennon's post primal therapy statement *John Lennon/ Plastic Ono Band*. A session tape conveys the sheer joy when Lennon exclaims 'GEO--R-G-E!!'' as Harrison stepped into the studio to play him his birthday tape. When Lennon visited Harrison's session, he was played selected highlights of everything that had been worked on over the past few months. "When [John] heard the stuff we were doing he was completely blown away," says Whitlock. "When he walked out I saw George – man, he was beaming from ear to ear and he was smiling on the inside too. I could tell. It was like Tiger Woods after he had sunk a great putt – like, 'Try that one on for size!'" That Lennon was later characteristically derogatory in print about the music was, perhaps, an even greater compliment. He tended only to strike out when he felt threatened.

Still the sessions stretched on. Harrison betrayed classic signs of completion anxiety; he loved making the music, but releasing and promoting it was another matter, especially at such a crucial time. In the end EMI intervened and told him to wrap it up, having already bumped back the release date from October to November. He bristled at the intrusion but they were doing him a favour.

★ ★ ★

All Things Must Pass was released in the UK on November 30, 1970, with 'My Sweet Lord' issued as a single in America a week beforehand. He was unsure about that, too, worried that such a bold statement of faith would alienate listeners. He gave notice of its imminent release on October 24, then three days later announced that it wouldn't be coming out after all. Eventually, Spector correctly identified the fact that its simplicity and repetition, the drive and sheer *power* of its sound would trump any lyrical concerns. And he was right. In the end the medium *was* the message. This inclusive pop-mantra worked: people felt better just by hearing it, and it sold in its millions.

The album did likewise. Released in an elaborately hinged cardboard box, with a huge colour poster of Harrison inside, it was the first ever triple box-set released by a rock artist. Barry Feinstein's monochrome cover image depicted him in Friar Park, an eccentric, rather mournful country squire in Wellington boots and battered hat. He is surrounded by four gnomes reclining on the lawn – 'Do not keep off the grass' – the composition slyly and symbolically illustrating his emancipation from the tyranny of The Beatles' collective identity. Precisely the same meaning can be derived from one of the many possible interpretations of the album title itself.

Both the lavish package and the music inside provided a striking assertion of self-confidence and irrefutable evidence of how far Harrison had come in such a short time, yet the connective tissue that holds the record together thematically is not vindication, but instead the conflict of opposites. It is there for all to hear in the 18 songs, and may never have been expressed more honestly or with more emotional, if not always literary, eloquence. Beatles Good and Beatles Bad, Frankie Crisp and Swami Vivekananda, life and death, love and anger, doubt and faith, *Maya* and bliss, struggle and reward, Hare Krishna and base humanity. Above all, it lays bare the intrinsic confusions of a superstar who can have whatever material or bodily satisfaction he craves yet above all desires some kind of spiritual succour from his life. "The whole album is about God and rock and roll," says Bobby Whitlock. "All of it. The whole album is one big cryptic message – the two tides hit together on that record."

In this sense, *All Things Must Pass* is a question which supplies its own answer. It is far from perfect, but how could it be? Its ragged lack of resolution is part of the deal and accounts for much of its charm. Certainly the third disc of "Apple Jams" illustrates how perilously close the enterprise came to continually slipping into matey indulgence, an unfettered demonstration of proficiency and prime-cut chops. It also indicated how Harrison's innate inclusiveness could be his undoing; a more ruthless hand at the rudder would have left these work-outs in the can. Few reviewers lingered long on their limited charms, and even fewer listeners.

On the double-album proper, there are also appealing flaws. The absence of 'Let It Down' or the five minute-throwaway 'I Dig Love' would hardly diminish the work as a whole, nor the second version of 'Isn't It A Pity', nor the oddly unformed 'I'd Have You Anytime', which seemed to demand inclusion simply by virtue of its Dylan credit rather than any other obvious merits. But to unstitch the tapestry is to miss the point. It had to be all or nothing.

The songs are generally robust enough to survive Spector's sonic onslaught. The strikingly personal concerns are projected onto a vast canvas, ensuring the best tracks deliver first and foremost on the strength of their dynamism, melody and numerous hooks. 'What Is Life', for one, was proof positive that no amount of hanging out with "feel" musicians or berobed American drop-outs was going to stop Harrison writing a joyously mindless pop song when the urge arose. It was also a reminder that he was one of the great riff writers.

The wildly eccentric production time-stamped the album badly, however, and was something Harrison would come to regret. Thirty years later, working on the reissue of *All Things Must Pass*, he and Ken Scott listened to "all the reverb and wondered how we could possibly have ever have liked it like that. It was just so overboard. Both of us would have loved to have remixed it but EMI didn't want that at that point. They just wanted a straight re-release. I wonder how many mistakes you might hear if you pulled off all the effects? How much got covered up?" Hearing the solo acoustic demos of many of the tracks, not least 'Run Of The Mill' and 'Beware Of Darkness', comfortably two of his most beautiful songs, suggests that in sacrificing intimacy for grandeur something precious was lost. Hindsight also provides persuasive evidence that he may have been wise to keep a few of the songs in his back pocket to stiffen the resolve of his future solo albums.

But no one was thinking such thoughts at the time. There was already considerable anticipation leading up to the release. His close association with Dylan and with The Band, his star turns on *Abbey Road*, his ability to add something to the music of Eric Clapton, or Delaney & Bonnie, or Billy Preston, suggested depths which were no longer content to be hidden. He was both tasteful and a tastemaker, and even before the album came out his credibility had never been higher. On top of all that, the sheer scale of *All Things Must Pass* when it finally did arrive simply demanded attention. Ben Gerson of *Rolling Stone* called it the "*War And Peace* of rock and roll," describing Spector's production as "Wagnerian, Brucknerian, the music of mountain tops and vast horizons." In *NME*, Alan Smith – an old Beatle confidante – praised Harrison's "music of the mind" set to "words which are often both profound and profoundly beautiful." Richard Williams, reviewing in both *Melody Maker* and *The Times*, made the timely iteration that, no matter what Harrison had achieved in previous months and years, nobody quite expected riches on *this* scale. It was, he said, "the rock equivalent of the shock felt by pre-war moviegoers when Garbo first opened her mouth in a talkie: Garbo talks! – Harrison is free!" Measured up against the output of the other ex-Beatles, he claimed *All Things Must Pass* "makes far and away the best listening, perhaps because it is the one which most nearly continues the tradition they began eight years ago."

The latter observation was a pertinent one, and not quite the garland of out-and-out positivity it initially seemed. Although *All Things Must Pass* was Harrison's first 'proper' solo album of songs it was, in hindsight, a destination, or perhaps a culmination, rather than a new start. It was hard to divine as much at the time, at the end of The Beatles and the beginning of a new decade, as the six-sided beast bestrode the latter part of 1970 and swaggered into 1971, spending eight weeks at number one in the UK, and seven weeks at the top of the *Billboard* 200 in the US. With 'My Sweet Lord' replicating this transatlantic double number one in the singles charts, it seemed obvious that Harrison had finally stolen a march on his band mates and had become The Beatle Most Likely To for a new decade.

In truth he would never have the benefit of that kind of creative tail wind again, nor the drive to fulfil it. *All Things Must Pass* may well have been the only time Harrison was genuinely powered by ambition:

to get these songs out of his system, to show his band mates what they had missed all these years, to clear some space around him so that The Beatles wouldn't hang so heavy. Nor would the context ever again be so perfectly attuned to him making the maximum impact. The culture of cynicism had not quite yet hardened over the soft, fruitful promise of the Sixties; rock and roll and religion still had something to say to one another, but by the time Harrison released his next record, the world had spun several degrees and he increasingly seemed a man out of time, bereft of his bearings.

Looking back down the telescope some 40 years, in early 1971 Harrison was not so much in the throes of a long, triumphant ascent as already very near the top of the mountain. "He raised the bar so high that he couldn't reach it again," says Bobby Whitlock. "He didn't have to make another record – period. Even though he did. He did it all with *All Things Must Pass*."

Be Here Now
New York City, July 31, 1971

A matter of hours before one of the most feverishly anticipated rock concerts in recent memory is due to start, the musicians taking part are sharing a room for the first time. That room happens to be Madison Square Garden, which tomorrow afternoon and evening will be filled, twice, with 20,000 people. Eric Clapton has just arrived from London looking like a wraith; somebody has scurried off to try to find him some uncut heroin. Bob Dylan, meanwhile, is so terrified he is ready to run for the hills.

As the instigator and organiser, Harrison is in charge of crisis management. "The night before the show was a bit tricky," he later recalled. "We went down where they were setting it up. Eric was in a bad way... and [Dylan] stood on the stage and it suddenly was a whole frightening scenario. Bob turned to me and said, 'Hey man, I don't think I can make this. I've got a lot of things to do in New Jersey.' I was so stressed, I said, 'Look, don't tell me about that. I've always been in a band, I've never stood out front, so I don't want to know about that.' I always just tried to be straight with him, and he responded. But right up until he came on stage I didn't know if he was going to come."[1]

The lecture comes from the heart. Harrison has never regarded himself as a solo performer, nor has he ever wanted to be one. Far less has he ever seen himself as Master of Ceremonies, charged with carrying an entire show. It is a role to which he believes he is almost wholly ill-suited. "Just thinking about it," he said at the press conference on July 27, "makes me shake."

"He had to really steel himself and be very brave to do this, and he knew that," says Pattie Boyd. "Apart from the stress of putting it all together he was actually going to have to front it. He was excited and he was extremely nervous."

The Concert For Bangladesh is rock music's first, chaotic attempt to be socially useful on a global scale. There is no blueprint, and no safety net.

213

CHAPTER 10

Bread For Bangladesh

The changes in The Beatles' post-split power base and public profiles were not just a matter of shifting units and topping charts. There was no tour to consolidate the success of *All Things Must Pass*, otherwise the change in Harrison's status would have been reflected back at him every night in a manner he would undoubtedly have found rather uncomfortable; but he was now a songwriter and producer much in demand. In February 1971 he began working on a mooted solo album for Ronnie Spector, formerly of The Ronettes and long-suffering spouse of his current producer. Not an unmitigated success musically, and hampered by Phil Spector's increasing insistence on "falling over"[1], as Harrison put it, the best that could be said about the only single released from the sessions, 'Try Some, Buy Some', is that it would later provide the backing track for his own version of the song on his next album; but as a vehicle for Spector it was a poor choice. The uptempo soul stomper 'You', also tried at the sessions, was later retrieved for *Extra Texture (Read All About It)*.

He was, perhaps, spreading himself a little thin. In the early summer came a dalliance with Badfinger on their album *Straight Up*. Having been unimpressed with the work the band had done with producer Al Kooper, in June Harrison hired himself as a typically hands-on producer and player. In particular he added instantly recognisable slide overdubs to 'Day After Day', which became a Top 10 hit in both the UK and US, but it was left to Todd Rundgren to complete the final mixes after Harrison called a meeting at Savile Row on July 12 to tell them he was going to America to organise the Concert For Bangladesh. Badfinger would play a part in that adventure, too.

A new realm of success was also signalled by the fact that Harrison's songs were being sung by the kind of mainstream pop artists who tended not to trifle with small fry. Matt Monro and Dana covered 'Isn't It A Pity', while Shirley Bassey's version of 'Something' gave the Welsh diva her biggest hit for years, and has rarely left her live repertoire since. Olivia Newton-John recorded perky pop versions of both 'If Not For You' and 'What Is Life', while Johnny Mathis was responsible for one of numerous cover versions of 'My Sweet Lord'. Many of these might not have been to Harrison's personal taste, but they were proof positive that the notion of God Consciousness was catching.

Another single inspired by the original proved more ominous. In 1971 country singer Jody Miller released a version of The Chiffons' 'He's So Fine' arranged with a bank of acoustic guitars and a tell-tale slide riff. It was specifically designed to highlight the remarkable similarities between the 1962 hit, written by Ronnie Mack, and Harrison's 'My Sweet Lord'. Miller wasn't the only one to spot the connection. On February 10, 1971, while 'My Sweet Lord' was still on the singles chart, the publishers of 'He's So Fine', Bright Tunes, launched a lawsuit for plagiarism against Harrison, Harrisongs Music Ltd and Harrisongs Music Inc (his UK and US publishing companies), Apple Records, BMI and Hansen Publications. To add insult to injury, Miller's version featured *All Things Must Pass* steel player Pete Drake.

Harrison later claimed that it wasn't until 'My Sweet Lord' had been released and – many – people started mentioning the similarities that he thought, "Why didn't I realise?"[2] Chances are he was being more than a little disingenuous. Delaney Bramlett, who was there at the song's communal conception in Scandinavia at the end of 1969, was clear that The Chiffons' hit provided a direct and conscious template for 'My Sweet Lord' from the very beginning. In Copenhagen, when Harrison had asked for guidance on writing a gospel song, Bramlett had "grabbed my guitar and started playing The Chiffons' melody from 'He's So Fine' and then sang the words 'My sweet Lord/Oh my Lord/Oh my Lord/ I just wanna be with you...'"[3] When 'My Sweet Lord' was released as the single Bramlett "immediately called George up and told him that I didn't mean for him to use the melody of 'He's So Fine'. He said, 'Well it's not *exactly* the same,' and I guess it really wasn't. I could tell by listening to the song that he did put some curves on it."[4] Bramlett also insisted that he had originally been promised a writing credit on the song. "When I saw that I was not credited I called George and said, 'George, I didn't see my name on the song.' He promised me that it would be on the next printing of the record. So I let it slide, thinking he would make good on that. George admitted to me that the song, to a large extent, was mine. But I was never given credit for the song and I never saw any money from it."[5] They never spoke again. When Bramlett was asked by Harrison's lawyers to testify on his behalf during the 1976 trial he "couldn't come", while his ex-wife's evidence was dismissed by the judge as "hearsay".

Regardless of the exact veracity of Bramlett's account of the song's origins, the matter of its similarity to Mack's song was raised during the recording sessions for *All Things Must Pass*. Bobby Keys' recollection is that, at least while he was present, "The Chiffons song... wasn't even mentioned. Nobody said, 'Hell, that sounds like 'He's So Fine''." Other accounts contradict this. In the studio, Bobby Whitlock – who played keyboards on the song and was the only person other than Harrison to contribute backing vocals – recalls that "when we did it, I was standing in the control room afterwards and I started singing along: 'He's so fine/ Wish he was mine.' I said, 'That's 'He's So Fine' and you [Spector], you produced that! It just fell out of me because it was the truth, the absolute truth. And George said, 'Well, we'll work that out.' He didn't mean to copy that, it just happened." John Barham adds that "years later Tony Ashton told me that when he was working on a Plastic Ono [Band] session that George had also attended, he had brought up the subject of the similarity of 'My Sweet Lord' to 'He's So Fine'." Could it have been that, as a Beatle, Harrison simply thought he could get away with it?

Never an unequivocal fan of Harrison's music, George Martin weighed in to the debate with the opinion – rather sweeping, and not easily backed up – that "an awful lot of George's songs do sound like something else."[6] It's true, however, that 'My Sweet Lord' was not the only case of him flying too close to the wind. If Bernie Krause was near the top of the scale and James Taylor towards the bottom, another song he wrote in 1971, the pleasingly whimsical 'Miss O'Dell', was somewhere near the middle. This time the 'inspiration' was 'Without The Lord' by new Apple signings Lon & Derrek. "When I first met George it was in New York right before the Concert For Bangladesh," says Lon Van Eaton. "We were in Allen Klein's office and he said, 'Oh, I nicked part of your song and put it in one of my songs'. I was like, 'Okay!' I was way beyond the idea of owning anything, but it was my melody he put on 'Miss O'Dell'." A cursory listen to both leaves little room for doubt.

The 'My Sweet Lord' plagiarism suit was delayed by a series of torturous complications. Klein, despite often giving the impression that litigation was his most beloved hobby, at first tried to keep it all out of court. He arranged a meeting with Bright Tunes' president Seymour Barash at which he suggested that Harrison could buy the entire Bright Tunes catalogue as a means of settlement. Barash duly suggested that the copyright for 'My Sweet Lord' be signed over to Bright Tunes, although Harrison would still receive half of the revenue. With Klein aware of just how much money he would be surrendering by giving away even 50 per cent of the song (as well as lengthy spells at the top in the US and UK, it spent nine and ten weeks at number one in France and Germany respectively, and was also a number one in Australia, Austria, Ireland, the Netherlands, New Zealand, Norway and Switzerland) he refused to sign up to the deal.

With an out-of-court settlement stalled, lawyers and musicologists prepared for their day in court. Before they got there, however, Bright Tunes went into receivership and then, in 1973, Harrison severed his business relationship with Klein, causing further delays. The case would not be resolved until 1976. The initial – very public – accusation and the ensuing five years of legal limbo threw a long shadow. It marked the end of Harrison's friendship with Delaney Bramlett and cast a pall over his greatest success as a solo artist. It made him feel even more embittered towards an industry for which he already harboured little love. Perhaps most importantly, it made him second guess his own instincts as a writer. "It's difficult to just start writing again after you've been through that," he said at the end of the decade. "Even now when I put the radio on, every tune I hear sounds like something else."[7]

1971 proved to be a year in which the warm glow of colossal success was consistently dulled by the gloom of the courtroom. Early in the year Harrison found himself up at Wells Street Magistrates Court on a charge of "driving without reasonable consideration" which dated back to September 1969, when he drove his Mercedes against the legs of a policeman in the West End after he was signalled to stop. He was fined £35 and banned for driving for a month.

More significantly, the bilious aftershock of The Beatles' breakup began to escalate. Lennon's huge, candid, and coruscating *Rolling Stone* interview, published in late January and early February, laid waste to every shred of sentiment anyone might have felt about the band, and Harrison – though far from the primary target – was not spared the wrath of his old friend. Lennon dismissed *All Things Must Pass* ("I wouldn't play that kind of music at home") and had a dig at his guitar style ("I prefer myself, I have to be honest... George produced some beautiful guitar playing, but I think he's too hung up to really let go"). He made clear their emotional estrangement ("I can't imagine what George thinks") and above all his anger at the way he treated Yoko Ono. "Ringo was all right, so was Maureen, but the other two really gave it to us," said Lennon. "I'll never forgive them, I don't care what fuckin' shit about Hare Krishna and God, and Paul with his 'Well, I've changed me mind.' I can't forgive 'em for that, really. Although I can't help still loving them either."[8]

This was painful catharsis enacted in a global goldfish bowl, but on January 19, 1971, in the High Court, the matter of The Beatles' past, present and future became a legal matter. The nub of the horrendously tangled case was McCartney's desire to dissolve their four-way business partnership in order that they could each have complete financial and artistic freedom: as it stood, the proceeds from all their solo albums was still treated as 'Beatle money'. In late 1970 Harrison and McCartney had met in New York, for the first time since the split had become official. It started cordially but did not go well, turning, as McCartney later remembered, into "a classic conversation. I said, 'Look George, I want to get off the label,' and George ended the conversation, and as I say it now I almost feel like I'm lying with the devil's tongue, but I swear George said to me, 'You're staying on the fucking label. Hare Krishna.' That's how it was, that's how the times were."[9]

Convinced that common sense was not going to prevail, McCartney felt forced to tackle the issue in court. He instructed Eastman to issue a writ for the dissolution of The Beatles' partnership, a restriction on Allen Klein's powers, and the appointment of a receiver to handle their finances. It induced a new wave of Beatlemania in the media. They all had solo singles out or about to come out, and as the case rolled on through early spring there was a fever of speculation about secret recording sessions, their imminent reformation, or that Klaus Voormann was going to take McCartney's place in the band. Though Harrison, along with Starr and Lennon, did not appear in court, like each Beatle he submitted a written affidavit that was read out. His focused in particular on the bad feeling at the beginning of 1969 and "the superior attitude which, for years past, Paul has shown towards me musically." The judge, unswayed, eventually ruled in favour of McCartney on March 12, though it would be years before the Gordian knot tying them together could be even partially untangled.

It was a strangely schizoid time. The ex-Beatles would niggle at each other in the press, pass judgement on each other's music, and flaunt the scars of old wounds. Lennon would agree with Ono's assertion that Harrison was "not sophisticated, intellectually," adding, "He's very narrow-minded and he doesn't really have a broader view."[10] Then they would jump into the studio with each other as though nothing had happened. Harrison was firmly in Team Lennon, though he was far less outspoken; his digs at McCartney were registered primarily by proximity. In the process of adding – often superb – guitar parts to Lennon's *Imagine* album, he recorded a searing, improvised slide solo for Lennon's vitriolic jab at McCartney, 'How Do You Sleep?'. In its own way it was as eloquent a statement of his long-standing anger as Lennon's rather childish lyric.

Harrison was always happy to play with Starr and Lennon – though it's notable that the latter never once returned the favour. His attitude to McCartney's music was less generous. "I was at Friar Park when George received 'Another Day' as a demo from Paul," says Bobby Whitlock. "We were sitting in the gatehouse, sitting in the dining room having a Scotch and green ginger, and the post came. George opened it up and put on the acetate, didn't tell me who it was or anything. I went, 'What the hell is that?' And he said, 'It's Paul', and kinda laughed."

How did he really feel about The Beatles? Who can say? It was complicated. "George took me over to Eric Clapton's house one day and on the way he played me what sounded like a series of Beatles songs," says Leon Russell. "He had taken one song out of all their solo records and put them together, and it sounded just like a Beatles record. He thought that was amazing and I did too."

"Every one of them was trying to get an identity, to become themselves," says Whitlock. "Everyone was growing rapidly in different directions."

★ ★ ★

The borders of modern Bangladesh were drawn during the partition of the British Indian Empire in 1947. Despite its lack of physical proximity, eastern Bengal became part of the newly formed state of Pakistan, separated from West Pakistan by almost 1,000 miles of India. It was an ill-conceived plan, and East Pakistan very quickly fell prey to political, economic, cultural and ethnic discrimination by the centralised Pakistani state. By 1971, the tensions had led to the Bangladesh Liberation War.

One of the immediate triggers was the Bhola cyclone of November 1970, which had ravaged East Pakistan and West Bengal, killing an estimated 500,000 people and displacing hundreds of thousands more who spilled over the borders. The lacklustre response of the Pakistani government to the disaster and its catastrophic aftermath brought matters to a head. On March 26, 1971, a declaration of Bangladeshi independence was broadcast. In response, Pakistan ordered the killing of insurgency leaders and intellectuals. The violence of the war resulted in many civilian deaths, particularly among the country's minority Hindu population. Estimates of those massacred range from 30,000 to three million, while in the region of one million refugees fled to India.

Back in the material world, the crisis barely registered with the western media. "I was in Los Angeles, I was staying there then, when all this happened," Ravi Shankar told me in 2011. His father had been born in eastern Bengal. "I was reading and getting news on television about the terrible tragedy, the hundreds of thousands of refugees coming to Calcutta, and their plight. The whole thing was so horrible yet almost nobody knew about it. I was in this terrible state of mind when George came to LA for a few days."

Harrison had gone to Los Angeles in June 1971 to produce the soundtrack album for Howard Worth's long-gestating film of Ravi Shankar, which had finally been completed and was now called simply *Raga*. While staying in a rented house overlooking the ocean in Malibu he wrote 'Miss O'Dell', a friendly come-hither to his "good friend"[11] and old Apple employee, currently based in California after a romance with Leon Russell. It was a breezy, knockabout confection which had plenty of the zip and zest his next album would lack.

Buried among the in-jokes and local references was mention of "the war" and "the rice that keeps going astray on its way to Bombay." "I don't really think the song is for me, it's more about Bangladesh," says Chris O'Dell, who was summoned to Malibu just after the song was written to hear it. "I remember him telling me all about it and I didn't really understand, but he had a love for India and the people and of course for Ravi, and he felt a real connection."

Harrison's empathy for Bangladesh was indeed largely down to his personal connection with Shankar, many of whose friends and their families were directly affected by the tragedy. "He saw I was looking so sad, he was really concerned, and so I asked him if he could help me," says Shankar. "I said I felt that I had to do something, and I had decided to do my own concert to raise money. Immediately he called his friends."

Almost overnight Bangladesh became Harrison's number one priority. He would spend the second half of the year living in Nichols Canyon in Los Angeles, shuttling between there and hotels in New York. His wife was with him much of the time, and his father also came out to stay; it was still only a year since Louise had died. There was much to be done. As the first major fundraising concert, there was no blueprint to fall back on. Had there been, it probably would not have included consulting with an Indian astrologer to check whether there was any cosmically auspicious dates on which to hold the show. Harrison left nothing to chance, however, and was told the first two days of August looked good. His preference was for New York, and August 1 was the only day for months on which Madison Square Garden was free. It allowed for a period of around six weeks to put together the entire project from scratch.

Thus began "weeks on the phone, 12 hours a day",[12] organising all the various aspects of the show while cajoling his friends into performing. Aside from the concert itself, an album and a movie would be released to maximise the money raised. He had, he later admitted, become emboldened by virtue of being a Beatle, and he was also learning from Lennon's bolshie chutzpah: "Let's film it and make a million dollars!"[13] Much of the heavy lifting was delegated to Klein, but Harrison was typically hands on. He personally hired Jon Taplin as production manager. Taplin had a crew available from touring with The Band; it was their personnel and sound system which Harrison used for the concert. Taplin recalls that "the basic group of Leon Russell, Klaus Voormann, Starr and Jim Keltner came together pretty quickly. The rest only really came together just before the concert."

There was also a song to write and record, at Record Plant West in Los Angeles on July 4 and 5. With Russell as his right hand man Harrison cut the hastily assembled track designed to raise awareness of the situation in eastern Bengal, and also to promote the show. 'Bangla Desh' – literally "Bengal nation" in Bengali – was raw and direct, songwriting as activism, which made up in urgency and energy what it lacked in sophistication. The heartfelt lyric moves between an effective summary of the situation and an uncomplicated plea for help, with a neat pun on giving "some bread" to feed the starving.

The hard, swinging minor-key track, driven by Starr and Keltner's double-drum attack, is otherwise dominated by Voormann's bass, Jim Horn's saxophone and Russell's piano. It was Russell, too, who suggested the slow introductory verse, a framing device which states unambiguously Harrison's motives for getting involved: "My friend came to me with sadness in his eyes..." It was this sense of kinship between friends which was a key component all the way down the line. The single of 'Bangla Desh' was backed by 'Deep Blue', the warm and rather wonderful folk-blues Harrison had written as a cathartic response to his mother's death.

He spent much of the rest of the week in the studio finishing the soundtrack for *Raga*, before returning briefly to the UK to continue working with Badfinger and to record with Lennon on *Imagine*. Harrison was back in the States by mid July for the final push. He moved into the Park Lane Hotel in New York, and on July 27 held a press conference with Shankar. Harrison looked extraordinary: sporting a long, narrow beard, not dissimilar to Billy Connolly in his pomp, his thick weave of hair accentuated his dark eyes, lending him an undeniable aura of spiritual charisma. The inference of the joint press call – that the concert should be regarded as a joint endeavour – was not only hopelessly naive but inevitably unsuccessful. Quickly he was asked about being the "number one star" of the show. He replied that he felt "nervous, personally I prefer to be part of a band, but this was something we had to do quick so I just had to put myself out there and hope that I could get a few friends to come and support me."

Allen Klein, also in attendance, wasn't slow to advertise that his organisation was paying everybody's expenses so that "every dime" raised would go to the charity, a statement which would soon ring hollow enough for it to echo onto the pages of many prominent publications. Harrison was mildly tetchy about the inevitable Beatles questions – "Shouldn't we talk about the concert?" – but he knew that there had been much speculation in the media about the Concert For Bangladesh providing the perfect arena for a reunion. The ever-willing Starr was cutting short his filming commitments on *Blindman* in Spain to come on board, but McCartney had flatly refused to participate, unsurprisingly given the bad blood and Klein's involvement. Lennon at first agreed and then said he wanted to bring Ono on stage with him, which was a condition too far as far as Harrison was concerned. He was probably relieved. "At the time people were offering large sums of money for them to get back together and play," says Boyd. "I think it was kind of tempting but things had gone too far between them." He also recognised that having four Beatles in the same room and sharing the same stage, even separately, would have overshadowed the entire event and obscured its very reason for existing. Harrison later claimed to have turned down several artists who arrived in New York at the eleventh hour wanting to participate; all the tickets were sold and it was too much of a headache.

The Concert For Bangladesh did not have an overt political or ideological agenda. Its purpose was overwhelmingly humanitarian, but the origins of the crisis were not lost on Harrison. Later he talked about the "Pakistani Hitlers."[14] At the press conference he was not nearly so outspoken; he made clear his awareness of the political context while insisting "I don't want to get into the cause of it." He also knew that his very presence in the room, along with half of the world's media, in itself hastened the act of nation-building. Bangladesh suddenly became a tangible entity, culturally and intellectually if not yet in physical reality. Every press article about the concert had to give at least a thumbnail sketch of what was happening in eastern Bengal. And although the single, released on July 28, only reached 23 in the US charts and number 10 in the UK, it was all over the radio and for many marked the very first time they had heard the phrase "Bangla Desh". Shankar claims it changed perceptions and awareness "overnight".

In New York, rehearsals had begun at Nola Studios, just down the block from the Carnegie Hall on West 57th Street. The Concert For Bangladesh was in many ways a triumph of hope over logic. "That whole show was a stroke of luck," said Harrison. "It was all happening so fast it's amazing we managed to get anything [done]... We did it in dribs and drabs and under difficulties."[15] On the first day of rehearsals only Harrison, Voormann, Badfinger and the six-piece horn section, led by Jim Horn, were present. A skeleton crew, to put it mildly. Of the songs Harrison considered during these early stages but eventually didn't perform were 'All Things Must Pass', 'Art Of Dying' and 'Deep Blue'. By the Thursday before the Sunday shows Starr had arrived, and the next day Leon Russell hit town. Billy Preston also joined the ranks, as well as a squadron of backing singers, headed by Claudia Lennear, bolstering the numbers.

Harrison was in charge, with his usual mix of good vibes and strong work ethic. Shankar recalls that "in the beginning everyone involved was quite ignorant" of the cause, but "they all became very much involved and they had a lot of feeling and support and the spirit was good." Nonetheless, good intentions can only take you so far. Even late in the day at Nola there were a couple of notable absences. Harrison had earmarked Eric Clapton to be his lead guitar player. Holed up in Surrey going through the latest variation on his seemingly constant agonies with heroin addiction and romantic gloom, in the days prior to the concert Slowhand looked increasingly like a no show. "No Eric," says Taplin. "George was concerned. He needed a lead guitar player. I was sending telex from Klein's office to Terry Doran in Apple, who went out to Hurtwood Edge to try to pour Clapton on the plane. Terry was told he was too sick to travel. George said, 'Give him one more day,' and started looking for substitutes."

One of them was Peter Frampton, in town mixing the Humble Pie live album *Performance Rockin' The Fillmore*. "George asked me over," says Frampton. "He had a couple of Champ amps and a couple of guitars in the corner, and he asked if I wanted to jam. All of a sudden we weren't jamming, we were playing George Harrison songs and Beatles songs – and I thought, Wow, wait a minute! He said, 'Yeah, these are some of the numbers we're going to do at Bangladesh.' I didn't realise it at the time but I was being routined as a back up; an understudy for Eric." In the end they brought in Taj Mahal guitarist, Jesse Ed Davis, a friend of Russell who had also recently recorded with Clapton.

The other wild card was Dylan. Harrison thought he had managed to convince his friend to make his first public performance since the Isle of Wight festival two years earlier, but Dylan did not attend rehearsals

225

and nobody was quite sure whether he was going to pull through. "Bob always liked to hedge his bets," says Taplin.

Eventually both Dylan and Clapton showed up the night before the show at the full technical rehearsal at Madison Square Garden, an occasion which turned into a musical dress rehearsal by virtue of the simple fact that it was the first time everyone involved had been in the same place. Harrison gave Dylan a stern talking to. Clapton, meanwhile, had arrived from London looking like death only slightly reheated. "He was in a really bad way, still strung out, and he brought baggage with him," says Boyd. "He still wasn't well, he needed his medication, so that was a big problem to be solved."

Harrison stayed calm on the outside, but inside he was a bundle of anxiety. "He was definitely nervous about it," says Chris O'Dell. "That was George really going out on a limb. It could have failed miserably, he had to push his own boundaries really far, to be the key person in a concert, and to believe that people like Bob Dylan, who he really respected, would be willing to do it and go on stage for free. That was his sacrifice for Ravi."

On the weekend of the concert there was a palpable fizz of anticipation even in super cool New York. The show was billed as George Harrison & Friends – no other artists were advertised, and although rumours were rife, nobody was really sure what to expect. Boyd recalls that "all sorts of people crawled out of the woodwork, it was a big deal, very exciting. The whole area was buzzing, it was a momentous occasion. Nobody thought that they would see The Beatles perform again, so you could feel the electricity in the air." Dylan and (half of) The Beatles – their presence alone ensured that the concert was more than just a worthy cause, in accordance with what we might call Bob Geldof's First Law of the Charity Gig: "The only responsibility the artist has is to create good art," says Geldof, the man behind Live Aid. "They only fail when they create bad art."

The Concert For Bangladesh scored high on those terms. There were two shows: a matinee starting at 2 p.m., and an evening performance at 8 pm. There was little material difference between the two, save for some minor readjustments to the running order, but in terms of atmosphere and performance the late show was deemed by most to have shaded it.

Rather than the standard rock star habit of delaying gratification to build anticipation, Harrison came on immediately to introduce the proceedings, outline the reason they were all there, and explain that the concert would start with a performance featuring Ravi Shankar, Ali Akbar Khan on sarod and Alla Rakha on tabla. Unlike Live Aid, the natural heir to Concert For Bangladesh held in 1985 to alleviate famine of Ethiopia, Harrison wanted the musical content to reflect in some way on the cause: the subtext made clear that this was not a poor relation coming to America with its begging bowl, but rather a culturally rich region being torn to shreds. "We planned it together," says Shankar. "He thought it would be best if it started with me and my colleagues performing."

"George's notion was to present the three greatest Indian musicians in the history of the world, and make these kids sit and watch a whole raga at the start of the concert," says Taplin. "It was outrageous! Pretty bold."

"George wanted to bring Ravi's music to a lot of people who hadn't heard it before," says Boyd. "So he also saw this as a splendid opportunity. He was excited about that." In the event, it would be fair to say that the Indian set was tolerated by most of the crowd rather than actively enjoyed. The general level of the audience's understanding of Indian music could be measured by the fact that a sizeable percentage applauded Shankar tuning up.

After their set came an intermission, during which several minutes of graphic footage from a Dutch television station was shown, depicting images of the war atrocities and the effect of natural disasters in the area. Again the parallel with Live Aid, where famously harrowing footage of the famine was projected over 'Drive' by The Cars, is striking.

Then it was the turn of Harrison's mildly chaotic but undeniably exciting set, his overloaded rock-soul-gospel revue hammering into 'Wah Wah' and all but overwhelming his vocals. His voice settled, though his nerves were never far from the surface, and he tended to look more solemn than he probably felt. Boyd and Chris O'Dell watched from the wings, full of pride and excitement at what he had, somehow, succeeded in pulling off. "It was this amazing feeling of watching something start from scratch for a cause," says O'Dell. "It was exciting on a personal level to see George start with the idea and see it manifest itself, and to watch how much people loved it." And loved him. The ovation he received at the start of Concert For Bangladesh lasted several minutes, an outpouring of genuine and spontaneous affection. A "gracious, low-keyed host," according to *The Village Voice* reviewer Don Heckman, in extremis he fell back on the hokey patter learned from the early days playing the clubs. Dylan was memorably introduced as "a friend of us all," while Clapton was "your friend and mine". It was the kind of spiel that might have heralded the arrival of a local comedian at the British Legion in Speke in the late Fifties.

The structure of his own set was a study in democracy, as well as an astute piece of limelight dodging. There was a turn, raucously received, for Ringo Starr on 'It Don't Come Easy', a song largely written by Harrison. Leon Russell was a bit of a bore with his glassy rock star pose and accentuated histrionics on a never-ending medley of 'Jumping Jack Flash/Youngblood', but Billy Preston brought some good-natured showbiz pizzazz with 'That's The Way God Planned It'.

Clapton, by contrast, was a somewhat ghostly presence, obviously under both the weather and the influence. After half of New York had been scoured in vain in search of the correct composition of uncut heroin, he was eventually dosed with methadone. "He got himself together enough to show up onstage but he wasn't totally there," says Taplin. "He wasn't on top of his game." He played the wrong guitar on 'While My Guitar Gently Weeps', and while he performed more than adequately, many of Harrison's friends and fellow musicians regarded his decision to use Clapton as a misjudgement, putting personal loyalties above basic musical matters.

After a beautifully downscaled 'Here Comes The Sun', performed on two acoustics by Harrison and Badfinger's Pete Ham, it was time for Dylan. To Bob or not to Bob? Even despite his assurances the previous night, at the matinee no one was sure if he was going to show up. Harrison glanced around gingerly in the gloom, only to see that Dylan had already materialised, so nervous he shot onto the stage like a bullet from a gun. In Harrison's estimation his appearance "gave it that extra bit of clout".[16] He also delivered musically. His pared down set (just Dylan, Harrison, Russell on bass and Starr on tambourine) was spellbinding stuff, Harrison once again nailing his colours to the mast with a selfless supporting performance which spoke of real love and empathy. "I think their performances together are some of the best live stuff Bob ever did," says Taplin. Dylan seemed to be of a similar mind, and was ecstatic after the first show, travelling back with Harrison to the Park Lane Hotel to mull over the evening performance. "He said to me, 'Do you think the second audience will be like the first one?'" says Russell, who recalls Dylan happily accepting requests from other musicians, trotting out 'It's All Over Now, Baby Blue' and other classics backstage as they prepared for the 8 p.m. show.

After Dylan's set came the big finale. In the afternoon this consisted of Harrison and band tearing through 'Hear Me Lord', 'My Sweet Lord' and 'Bangla Desh'. For the second show, an exquisite 'Something' and rollicking 'My Sweet Lord' were swapped in the running order, and 'Hear My Lord' dropped altogether. The final version of 'Bangla Desh' raged to its conclusion – and then curtain, relief, and justifiable pride at a job well done. "Boy, George stepped up," says Taplin. "He was so cool throughout the whole thing, and it turned out to be one of the best concerts I ever had anything to do with." The scene backstage was one of triumph. "Afterward the feeling was that it had been a huge success, a real sense of elation," says Boyd. "We all got into the black limos to go back to the hotel and everybody had thoroughly enjoyed it."

Later, the ensemble headed to Ungano's, a nightclub in Manhattan, to play some more. Dylan embraced Harrison and said he wished they had scheduled three concerts. Boyd recalls the musicians being "quite well behaved. The buzz from the gig was the real high." Some conformed to this description more closely than others. Taplin remembers Shankar tearing a strip off Clapton for being "a chickenshit junkie, because he was just snorting heroin." A paralytic Phil Spector showed up, having nominally spent a hard day at work recording the music for the album, although according to Harrison he had not been overly taxed. "Phil was

229

at the concert dancing in the front when it was being recorded!" he said. "There was a guy, Gary Kellgren, who did the key work in the live recording."[17] At Ungano's Spector performed a fantastically inebriated version of 'Da Doo Ron Ron Ron', while Keith Moon smashed up a drum kit. Rock wasn't ready for its sainthood just yet.

In the following days the reviews of the event were almost universally euphoric, a mix of keenly felt nostalgia for the waning spirit of the Sixties and genuine musical appreciation. Bangladesh was widely regarded as a balm for cultural disillusionment in the post-Woodstock era, evidence, according to the *Rolling Stone* review, that "the utopian spirit of the Sixties was still flickering." Musically, *NME* declared the concert 'The Greatest Rock Spectacle of the Decade!', while there was widespread and genuine delight that the hype had been matched by the reality. "Somehow, incredibly, George Harrison's hastily organized benefit show for the starving and dying millions in East Pakistan *did* meet expectations," said *The Village Voice*. "It began as an Event, and hit every point anyone could have asked for."[18]

★ ★ ★

If the concert itself was a clear triumph, the aftermath was all muddy water – providing a far from simple lesson that charity and music might be natural bedfellows, but factor in two governments, the taxman, the recording industry and a shady manager and you have the makings of a very different kind of catastrophe. There were two major strands to Harrison's post-concert duties: preparing the album and film for release, and ensuring the structures were in place to enable the money raised to filter through to those who needed it as quickly as possible.

Having declared at the press conference that he was hoping the triple live album of the Concert For Bangladesh might be out on Apple within ten days of the show, Harrison found the reality endlessly more complex. The two performances had been recorded on Record Plant's 16-track mobile unit, and the day after the show mixing work began in the same New York studio. Again, Spector was suffering from alcohol problems and was "in and out of hospital,"[19] leaving Harrison to carry most of the burden.

Capturing so many musicians on stage was a complex job, and some overdubbing was required, notably on Leon Russell's medley and 'While My Guitar Gently Weeps', while 'Wah Wah' was a composite pieced together from both performances. Harrison let every one of the artists have the power of veto if they were unhappy with the way they sounded, but nobody took it. Having worked for a little over a week in Record Plant, final mixes were done at Sunset Sound in Los Angeles in September, at which point Harrison and Boyd returned briefly to the UK aboard the *QE2*.

Achieving satisfactory results against a poor quality live recording and Spector's erratic behaviour was one thing. More troubling than the audio issues were the problems he encountered within the industry. Dylan's record company, Columbia, claimed that they should have the right to release the album and fought their corner; eventually they were placated after being given significant distribution rights and 25 cents on every album sold, the only company to make money from the music. Then Bhaskar Menon, head of Capitol and Harrison's chief of command in the US, wanted his company to be compensated to the tune of up to $500,000 as recognition of their part in getting the album on the shelves. Harrison was equally clear in expressing his view that, since all the musicians had provided their services free and Apple was supplying the album packaging at no charge, the record company should not be exempt from making some sacrifices too.

These tussles went on long after a mix of the album had been completed. Harrison was soon back in New York, this time leaving the UK on October 2 on the *SS France*. Staying in the Plaza on Fifth Avenue, he grappled with the detail as well as the big picture. The cover image was to be a powerful still taken from news footage of a naked, malnourished child sitting behind a huge, empty food bowl. The executives at Capitol felt it was too depressing and suggested instead using the image from the back cover of the album's lavish 64-page booklet, which showed a guitar case filled with food and medical supplies below a copy of the cheque for the Madison Square Garden box-office takings. Harrison was having none of it. The original proof of the guitar "was awful," he wrote to Boyd from the Plaza, "so I had to jump on that and change it and shout at them and now it will be okay with the original idea of the kid. It's such a pain, all that messing around just because they didn't like the truth."

He also began to examine the extremely ragged film footage, starting by cutting Shankar's 45-minute opening section down to nearer 15 minutes for the film. It would be the first of several months of work trying to negotiate a decent 55-minute edit from badly compromised raw footage. All the while he was still trying to get the album out. When he appeared on *The Dick Cavett Show* on November 23, ostensibly to promote *Raga*, which had opened in New York that day, he publicly called out Menon, calling him a "bastard" and saying he would take the entire package to Columbia and you can "Sue me, Bhaskar!", before muttering, just about audibly, "It's none of your business to fucking be in... Bleep!" Having been publicly vilified, Menon responded a few days later, saying that "Harrison is clearly not in possession of all the facts." As it was Capitol eventually backed down, presenting Apple in December with a cheque for $3,750,000 for advance album sales, but by that time much goodwill had been lost, while bootlegs of the concert had been doing a roaring trade, forcing Harrison to place adverts saying: 'Save A Starving Child! Don't Buy A Bootleg!' Everywhere he looked someone seemed to be profiting from his good faith, while after almost four months none of the money was going where it was supposed to. The experience had a profound effect on his mood over the next two or three years.

The *Concert For Bangladesh* was finally released as a beautifully packaged three-album box-set in the United States on December 20, 1971, and in Britain on January 10, 1972. It retailed at $12.98 in the US and £5.50 in the UK, far exceeding the standard cost of an album, particularly in Britain, where its exorbitant price attracted considerable criticism. Partly, it was to offset the surcharges and percentages that were been chipped away from the core sum earmarked for the refugees. In October, Harrison had met with Patrick Jenkin of the British Treasury in an attempt to have the government waive the "purchase tax" being levied on the album, which was one factor in the decision to hike up the price of the album. He failed.

Having hosted the concert with entirely honourable intentions, he had stumbled into what would become a perennial problem for the fundraising rock star: getting the cash to the intended destination without too much spillage. As a pioneer, inevitably he took a few hard knocks. "It was very sad," says Boyd. "At the end of the day I don't know how much money did actually reach where it should have gone. I think in this case money did go walkabout."

The implication lurking behind Bhaskar Menon's rebuttal of Harrison's outburst on *The Dick Cavett Show* was that somewhere in the background Klein was stirring the pot, and was not averse to using the Bangladesh album as a bargaining tool with Capitol – and perhaps, subsequently, doing far worse. An in-depth and highly informed *New York* magazine article published in February 1972 reported that $1.14 per album remained unaccounted for, and suggested that Klein, not Capitol, had been responsible for the delay in getting the album out by driving up the price in order to line his own pockets. It was not a notion entirely lacking in credibility.

It was, however, tax which proved the real killer. "It was not straightforward," Jonathan Clyde told me in 2011; Clyde worked with Harrison at his Dark Horse label in the Seventies and went on to join Apple, where he oversees the Concert For Bangladesh's legacy in tandem with Olivia Harrison. "The concert was put together very quickly, and the mistake that was made was that the charity was not chosen upfront of the concert. All George could think about was, 'I've got to get this concert done, raise some money,' and it was only after the concert that he thought about who could distribute the aid. He met with Red Cross, he met with UNICEF, and a couple of others, and he decided that UNICEF would be the agency. The IRS took the view that because the charity were not involved in the staging of the concert, that they would take their cut. As you can imagine, this distressed him hugely. More than distressed – it really angered him. There was an ongoing tussle for years, and I'm afraid that the IRS still take their cut even now. But everyone learns. Bob Geldof called George when he was starting to mount Live Aid asking for advice, and one thing George said was, 'Do your homework.' In 1971 it was uncharted territory. Just the scale of it."

The oversight on securing the concert's tax-exempt status was a grave dereliction of duty on the part of Klein who was, after all, an accountant. It ensured that most of the money generated in the Seventies through film and album sales was held in an Internal Revenue Service escrow account for years. In 1978, Harrison put this figure at somewhere between $8 million and $10 million. "Once the tussles with the IRS were done it did reach Bangladesh," says Clyde. "The majority of that [money] didn't reach there in time to help the refugees at that point, but they needed a huge amount of support once the war was over and they had to rebuild the country."

What tangible results did the concert achieve? It raised $243,418.50 overnight, a sum presented to UNICEF 11 days after the concert, and the record and film enjoyed immediate success and a long afterlife. Despite the prohibitive cost, the triple album was an immediate best-seller, spending six weeks at number two on the *Billboard* chart and becoming Harrison's second number one album (another triple) in the UK. Reviews arrived suffused with the glow of goodwill. Everyone found something to love, whether it was the opening Indian set, Preston's infectious *joie de vivre*, Harrison's solo on 'Something', Dylan's moving return to the stage, or Clapton and Harrison duelling on 'While My Guitar Gently Weeps'. "If you buy only one LP in 1972, for God's sake make it this one," said Richard Williams in *Melody Maker*, adding that "Harrison and Phil Spector have managed to transfer all the astonishing emotion of the event onto vinyl. It's hard, in places, to keep a dry eye." *NME* lauded a document of "probably the greatest indoor rock 'n' roll event ever held."

Although it was not conceived with such a goal in mind, it only added to Harrison's status as a new kind of rock superstar: compassionate, democratic, with diverse and interesting musical tastes and real integrity. Jon Landau in *Rolling Stone*, an organ for which the concert had already assumed almost mythic status, noted the man at the centre of it all, whose sense of calm benevolence seemed to radiate from his centre and wash over the entire project. "The spirit he creates through his own demeanour is inspirational. From the personal point of view, *Concert For Bangladesh* was George's moment."

In March 1973, the album won a Grammy for Album of the Year, and although Khan and Shankar's set may have been met with indifference on the day, the success of the album and the film fulfilled another one of Harrison's aims: to bring Indian classical music to a large, populist Western audience.

Before Harrison died in 2001 he had expressed a desire to personally restore the *Concert For Bangladesh*. Sadly his wish was overtaken by events, but in 2005 the film and the album were released on DVD and on remastered CD. At the same time the George Harrison Fund for UNICEF was created at the personal suggestion of Kofi Annan, then the UN Secretary General. Proceeds from the album, and Saul Swimmer's concert documentary had, by the summer of 2011, raked in some $17 million for UNICEF, funding projects not only in Bangladesh but in global troublespots from Angola to Romania.

Not everything it achieved can be so easily measured. In paving the way for popular music to explore what Americans like to call its 'better self', 40 years on it still encapsulates much of what is perceived to be best about rock fundraising – a pile of money, heightened awareness for a clear cause, and a rich cultural and musical legacy – while managing to avoid some of the less palatable aspects: ego, half-baked sermonising, hypocrisy. The wider response to Concert For Bangladesh began only a month afterwards, on September 18, 1971, when the UK version was held before 30,000 fans at The Oval in south London, with a bill featuring The Who, The Faces, Mott The Hoople, America and Lindisfarne. Since then it has inspired, whether directly or indirectly, not only Live Aid but hundreds of other major charity concerts.

Most important of all, it gave an emerging nation mired in violence and poverty a global identity stamp. By the end of 1971 the liberation war was won, and Bangladesh officially born. Harrison never made it to the country, but Shankar did, and he discovered that the concert made a tangible impact. "I have been three times to Bangladesh, they invited me, and I can't tell you the love and respect and the wonderful feeling they have for me," he says. "They really love me, and they really love George."

Jonathan Clyde and Olivia Harrison visited in February 2011, spending several days in Dhaka. "It was actually very moving," said Clyde. "George's name means a lot in Bangladesh – very much so. Even at the press conference George realised that the awareness was going to be more valuable than the money raised at the concert. For people who were young then and involved in the war of liberation against Pakistan it meant a huge amount, and it really helped their independence get recognised. For that generation, that concert put the name Bangladesh on the map."

Forty years later, it shines like a beacon of practical, clear-headed, empathetic activism amid the bed-ins, bagism and myriad woolly gestures of the age which generated lots of heat but very little light. Or, indeed, money. It was *The Village Voice* that noted, astutely, "how surprising [it was] that the most introspective of The Beatles should be the one who, in the long run, takes the most effective actions."[20] Bangladesh was a team effort but also a measure of the man. Few, if any, of his peers could have pulled it off with such grace and style. As Jon Taplin suggests, "Jimmy Page or Mick Jagger could not have organised the Concert For Bangladesh." Nor, he might have added, could John Lennon.

Be Here Now
Friar Park, early 1972

When the American musicians Lon & Derrek Van Eaton arrive at Friar Park during sessions for their first Apple album, *Brother*, they find a malevolent weirdness starting to creep into life at Henley-On-Thames. Cocaine, hints of cruelty, secrets, silence, relationships breaking apart. It leads to pranks and mind games which sometimes seem to have lost their previously playful edge.

"We all had some substances and then we went underneath [to the caves]," recalls Lon Van Eaton of his introduction to Harrison's home. "The drug is kicking in and people were blowing out candles and hiding from us, and then George whispered in my ear: '*Just playing.*' It was kind of fun but a real fright, too."

The following day Harrison asks to see the band's lyrics, before passing them silently over to Klaus Voormann. "Klaus took this big stamp – like one of those stamps that says PAID – and he put it in the ink and went BAAM on every sheet of my lyrics. I looked, and it said 'Fuck Off'. In retrospect it was, like, 'Get rid of your ego and any vestiges of who you thought you were, and once you've come back then we can deal with you so you won't be full of shit'."

This is, perhaps, a generous explanation of the extremes of behaviour Harrison is undergoing. Caught hard between spiritual pursuits and earthly pleasure, "he was angry a lot, and because of who he was it hurt people more," says Chris O'Dell. "He definitely had an acidic tongue, and an attitude of 'I can say what I want' – we all have that feeling, it's just most of us don't get away with it! It's very hard to live with people who are famous."

A fact that everyone, including George Harrison, was beginning to find out.

CHAPTER 11

Deep Blue

Nicky Hopkins, the great session piano player, recalled reconnecting with Harrison in New York at the end of October 1971 during the recording of Lennon and Ono's 'Happy Xmas (War Is Over)'. "He played some new songs for us for about two or three hours," said Hopkins in an interview a month or two later. "They were really incredible. So he has plenty of material for an album."[1]

The plan was to begin work on the follow-up to *All Things Must Pass* early in the New Year, with a view to a release later in 1972. One of the less positive legacies of Bangladesh, however, was that its demands took Harrison away from his own music-making and stalled much of his early career momentum. "He did say it took up a few years of his life, organising the concert, doing the music and the film," Olivia Harrison told me. "It was a big undertaking for a young man."

The film, in particular, was a hard slog. He even had to drag in a reluctant Bob Dylan to help, and to make sure that he was happy with the results. "It didn't 'come out', really," he said of the film. "The one camera right at the back of Madison Square Garden produced film that was all black, with just a little pin of light at the centre. Couldn't see a thing. Another camera, half-way down the right of the building, was out of focus all the way through; there was a fault on the camera. Over on the left of the building, half-way down, there was another camera; this one had huge cables hanging in front of it all the way through, so we were left with the camera that was just in the pit in the front of the stage and another one hand-held...The film that you see is the result of a lot of juggling."[2]

Director Saul Swimmer would later reveal the tortuous process of audio syncing and making the frame-by-frame conversion to 70mm format from the original 16mm. David Acomba, who filmed Harrison's 1974 tour, claims that Harrison told him then that he had "to almost entirely redub the *Concert For Bangladesh* – at least 80 per cent, he said."

The film ate up the final months of 1971 and stretched into 1972. He had planned to produce Lon & Derrek's debut, *Brother*, but sidetracked by Bangladesh he handed that duty over to Klaus Voormann. He did produce their single, 'Sweet Music', for which he had high hopes. Its disappointing commercial performance resulted in a terse telegram to Apple marketing staff: "What the !!!!! is the matter out there? 'Sweet Music' is a No. 1 Hit!" Lon & Derrek almost immediately found themselves in a meeting with Klein, recalls Lon Van Eaton. "He was like, 'George is really upset with this. Whaddyawant? Anything!'" Whatever they were given, it didn't amount to a hit single.

The *Concert For Bangladesh* film received its premiere in New York on March 22, 1972, and in the UK at the end of July. The generally positive reception was counterbalanced by continuing rumours about where all the money was going, and persistent headaches with the finances. Despite the fact that Harrison was giving all the proceeds away to UNICEF, the project's lack of tax-exempt status meant the revenue was being treated as his personal income, with the result that he was being pursued by the authorities for tax from British earnings from the film and movie. Peter Doggett, in his excellent account of The Beatles' financial affairs, *You Never Give Me Your Money*, claims that eventually this loophole personally cost Harrison £1 million. "It's sure enough to make you go crazy and commit suicide," he said in 1977.[3]

There were some benefits. In June UNICEF awarded Harrison and Shankar (and, ironically, Klein), its 'Child Is The Father Of The Man' award in recognition of their efforts. The following month he was in rather less exalted surroundings, up in court after yet another car accident which almost had serious consequences. In February, just before midnight on the M4 between Henley and London, Harrison's Mercedes had collided with a lamppost in the central barrier. He and Boyd were taken to Maidenhead hospital and treated for head injuries; photographs showed Harrison with blood pouring down his face and a bandage tied roughly around his head. He needed only stitches, but Boyd was transferred to a hospital in Slough and treated for concussion. In court five months later he was found guilty of careless driving, fined £20, and had his licence endorsed for the second year in a row.

This was the fractured, slightly fraught prelude to starting work on the much delayed follow-up to *All Things Must Pass*. Harrison took a very different approach to the record than he had on his first. Some of what became *Living In The Material World* was recorded at Savile Row, but most of the sessions took place at Friar Park, where he had installed Altec speakers and an old 16-track EMI console in the ballroom, calling the home studio FPSHOT (Friar Park Studios, Henley-On-Thames). The sleeve notes on *Living In The Material World* make no mention of FPSHOT, very possibly because Harrison was keen to promote the Savile Row studio as a commercial enterprise; he had been the only Beatle to attend the opening of Apple's new £500,000 facility the previous September. "On the record it says it was done at Apple, but it was cut at his house," said Klaus Voormann, who played bass.[4] Every solo record Harrison subsequently made, apart from *Extra Texture (Read All About It)*, would be recorded at home.

He had, once again, brought in Phil Spector as his co-producer, but "Phil was never there. I literally used to have to go and break in to the hotel to get him. I'd go along the roof of The Inn On The Park in London and climb in his window yelling, 'Come on, we're supposed to be making a record'. He'd say, 'Oh okay,' and then he used to have 18 cherry brandies before he could get himself down to the studio... I was ending up with more work than if I'd just been doing it on my own."[5] The producer's participation quickly fell by the wayside, which had a significant and not displeasing impact on the end result. "For me, the first impression when hearing the backing tracks of

Living In The Material World and comparing it to *All Things Must Pass*, is the sound," says John Barham, who was again handling all the string arrangements. "I immediately heard that Phil Spector wasn't involved in the production, which surprised me. Most people would have tried to repeat a great success. George's decision to produce it without Phil was a gamble. George was an accomplished producer but certainly not in Phil's league."

Spector did appear on one song on the record. The backing track of 'Try Some, Buy Some' had been taken from the Ronnie Spector sessions of 1971 and was now given a new vocal. It was pitched a little high for comfort, and in all seemed an odd choice of filler given the volume of material Harrison had left over from the *All Things Must Pass* demo sessions (most of which still remain in the vaults).* There are other moments on the record – most obviously the dramatic double-drum and timpani fanfare on 'Don't Let Me Wait Too Long' – which pay homage to Spector, but in general this was to be a much more intimate affair than *All Things Must Pass*.

No longer hiding behind the Wall of Sound, Harrison rounded up a basic five-piece band, consisting of Nicky Hopkins and Gary Wright on pianos and keyboards, Voormann on bass, and Ringo Starr and Jim Keltner on drums, augmented by Jim Horn's saxophone and flute, Zakir Hussein's tabla and Barham's orchestrations. There was to be no recourse to the kitchen sink this time, nor to eight guitarists. Instead, there was just one: Harrison. Relying primarily on acoustic guitars, and often unusual open tunings, he created some of the finest work of his career. More so than on *All Things Must Pass*, the versatility, warmth and unique sonic quality of his playing shines through on his second album, which, says Peter Frampton, is where "he made a style out of his slide playing that a lot of people copied but couldn't master. That was his own thing. I always felt he was terribly underrated." The solo demo of 'Sue Me, Sue You Blues', cut in December 1972 at Friar Park, shows what a terrific bottleneck player he had become.

---

* David Bowie recorded 'Try Some, Buy Some' on his 2003 album *Reality* as a tribute to Harrison following his death in 2001.

He had started recording in October, and continued until March, after the New Year working primarily on overdubs in Savile Row. At Friar Park "he created an atmosphere in the studio," says Voormann. "He put up joss sticks, made a nice smell, turned the lights down, a really nice surrounding. He would sit down, with a guitar most of the time, play the song and then slowly we would start picking up the feel of the song. We could take our time, do what we wanted, make suggestions."[6]

Recorded in the shadow of Krishna images and Eastern ornaments, the sessions were largely lacking in drama, although there was a little colour here and there: Voormann's stand-up bass on 'Be Here Now' was recorded in the toilets at Friar Park to get the best sound, but after the chaotic, kaleidoscopic, come-all-ye sessions for *All Things Must Pass*, *Living In The Material World* was a more subdued affair. It was not just that the music was gentler, or that fewer people were participating, or that he was at home. There was a cloud hanging over Harrison at the time, both spiritual and personal.

"It was obvious to anyone who knew George that he was seriously stressed," says Barham. "I think it was most likely the daunting task of attempting to match the extraordinary artistic and commercial success of *All Things Must Pass*. Added to that was the stress of litigation in connection with 'My Sweet Lord', and I believe George and Pattie were having problems in their relationship. They are not amongst my happiest memories of working with him. His stress, the causes of which I think I understand much better now than I did then, sometimes made him short tempered and irritable. As orchestral arranger and music director working with session musicians at the time, I felt that George's stress was negatively affecting the working atmosphere in the studio."

This impending sense of what Barham describes as "a crisis" came through loud and clear in the sometimes austere music and the recurring preoccupations in his lyrics. He returned again to the legacy of being a Beatle in 'Living In The Material World', 'Who Can See It' and 'Sue Me, Sue You Blues'. There seemed no way of breaking free. "Apple and The Beatles, the whole trip we've been through, has been like throwing boulders in the lake," he said. "Because everything comes

's the normal age for people to get married. That's when a petrol pump attendant gets married, though he hasn't got all these people looking at him." Aged 22 and 21 respectively, Harrison and Boyd at Epsom Registry Office on their wedding day, January 21, 1966. AUBREY HART/EVENING STANDARD/GETTY IMAGES

"He had a very conservative, traditional view of marriage." – Pattie Boyd. Harrison and his new wife with his parents and Boyd's mother on their wedding day. KEYSTONE PICTURES USA/ALAMY

"They realised that they were living in a different world." – Bill Harry. Harrison and the other Beatles display their MBEs at the Saville Theatre following their investiture at Buckingham Palace, October 26, 1965. MIRRORPIX

"Be healthy, don't eat meat, keep away from those night clubs and meditate." Harrison and Lennon appear on David Frost's TV show on October 4, 1967, to discuss spirituality and LSD. BETTMANN/CORBIS

"George was my brother, my friend and my son, all together." – Ravi Shankar. Harrison with his musical and spiritual mentor in Los Angeles, August 1967. AP FILE PHOTO

think he felt a bit more like the leader who had guided everybody into Rishikesh. They had to look up to him because he instigated is." – Pattie Boyd. In Rishikesh, 1968. From left to right, front two rows: John Lennon, Paul McCartney, the Maharishi Mahesh ogi, Harrison, Mia Farrow and Donovan. KEYSTONE-FRANCE/GAMMA-KEYSTONE VIA GETTY IMAGES

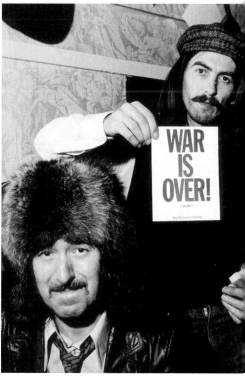

"I'm a tidy man. I keep my socks in the sock drawer and my stash in the stash box." Harrison and Boyd leave Walton Magistrate's Court on March 31, 1969, after being fined £250 for possession of cannabis. CUMMINGS ARCHIVES/REDFERNS

"He was such an upbeat guy to be around, he was always laughin telling stories and goofing." – Robben Ford. Harrison and 'Legs' Larry Smith at John and Yoko's Peace For Christmas Concert at the London Lyceum, December 15, 1969.
MICHAEL PUTLAND/PHOTOSHOT/RETNA

"I can remember being on stage and thinking, 'We've got a Beatle over there, Clapton over there: quite a line up!'" – Bobby Keys. Harrison and Eric Clapton, left, with Delaney & Bonnie, backstage at Birmingham Town Hall, December 4, 1969. MIRRORPIX

...ertainly felt that there was a conflict between the purchase of a 120-room mansion and a spiritual path." – John Barham. Harrison's ...ne from 1970 until his death: the neo-Gothic splendour of Friar Park in Henley-On-Thames. AMORET TANNER/ALAMY

...eorge was slightly a soft touch for people in the Hare Krishna movement." – Pattie Boyd. Harrison with members of the Radha ...ishna Temple on the roof of Apple, March 1970. MIRRORPIX

"Writing and playing with Bob definitely gave him an extra sense of validation." – Pattie Boyd. Harrison and Bob Dylan perform together at the Concert For Bangladesh, August 1, 1971. MICHAEL OCHS ARCHIVES/GETTY IMAGES

"That was George really going out on a limb. It could have failed miserably, he had to push his own boundaries really far." – Chris O'Dell. The Concert For Bangladesh, August 1, 1971. THOMAS MONASTER/NY DAILY NEWS VIA GETTY IMAGES

was frustrated. He was trying to reconstruct the entire nature of the rock and roll tour, he wanted to move things forward." – David
omba. A contemplative Harrison, left, and with Billy Preston, right, at Madison Square Garden at the end of the controversial Dark
rse tour in 1974. THOMAS MONASTER/NY DAILY NEWS ARCHIVE VIA GETTY IMAGES/ FRED W. MCDARRAH/GETTY IMAGES

e used to call the White House the Black and White House." – Olivia Harrison. Harrison and Billy Preston meet President Ford in
Oval Office, December 13, 1974. BETTMANN/CORBIS

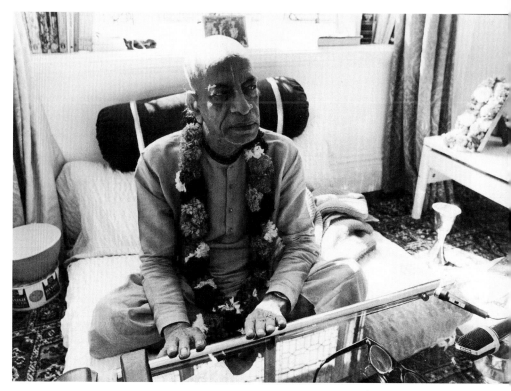

"The servant of the servant of the servant." Harrison's guru A.C. Bhaktivedanta Swami Prabhupada, in the Hertfordshire mansion Harrison bought for the Hare Krishna movement, August 9, 1973. EXPRESS NEWSPAPERS/GETTY IMAGES

"Sometimes I feel like I'm actually on the wrong planet. It's great when I'm in my garden, but the minute I go out the gate I think, 'What the hell am I doing here?'" Harrison by the lake at Friar Park, 1975. TERRY O'NEILL/GETTY IMAGES

"I only ever saw the person – George. I don't think we'd have been together so long if it had been any other way." – Olivia Harrison. With his future wife, Olivia Arias, November 1976. MIRRORPIX

bouncing back and ties you up forever, or for as long as it takes to untie it."[7]

He lingered longest on spiritual matters, frequently and uncompromisingly telling the world that it had better mend its ways (and in doing so, apparently, it could do worse than follow his own example). Beyond what many listeners subsequently regarded as the dour dogma of enlightenment espoused on 'The Light That Has Lighted The World', 'The Day The World Gets 'Round' and 'The Lord Loves The One (That Loves The Lord)', however, lay some of his most overtly exposed writing. 'Who Can See It' was, in its own way, as naked an expression of hurt and need as anything Lennon wrote in the late Sixties and early Seventies. 'Be Here Now', the most intimate performance on the album, encapsulated his sense of personal isolation, his longing to be free from the past and to live entirely in the moment – a universal aim, perhaps, but a particularly pointed one for a man who had escaped The Beatles physically but was still tangled in their web, and who had subsequently contrived to become a solo superstar almost without trying. Snared in the perceptions, illusions and presumptions of others, Harrison informs both the world at large and those closest to him that "it's not like it was before."

This dedication to living in the Eternal Now inevitably caused casualties. Life at Friar Park was increasingly odd, conflicted and heading towards some final reckoning. One new song that didn't make it onto *Living In The Material World* was 'So Sad', which he had started writing in New York in 1972. It was a bereft but absolutely clear-eyed reflection on the calcified state of his marriage, which was over in all but name. Boyd had been frozen out of his obsessions, whether they were restoring the gardens, pursuing spirituality, or making music. They had also found, to their mutual distress, that she was unable to have children. His studio was at home, he didn't tour, and as they grew further apart they found themselves, conversely, more and more in each other's company. "There was a little bit of that feeling when a couple retire and you have to be with each other every single day: 'Oh my God, who are you?'," says Chris O'Dell. "People were changing, and everyone was looking for their own direction. Spirituality was a major piece of their relationship breaking up. George had become so spiritual, so focused, and the passion that he might have had at one time for Pattie went more to his spirituality."

He had become, said Voormann, a "very extreme character."[8] He would retreat into his own world, rising with the sun and meditating all day in a special room, or chanting alone for days and sometimes weeks on end. He grew his hair down his back and his beard gave way to a thick moustache. In August 1972 he headed off to Europe on his own, driving down to the south of France and later visiting Gary Wright and his wife in Portugal. Boyd wasn't invited; the passenger seat was reserved for Krishna. "I drove for about 23 hours and chanted all the way," he later said. "It gets you feeling a bit invincible. The funny thing was that I didn't even know where I was going. I mean I had brought a map, and I knew basically which way I was aiming, but I couldn't speak French, Spanish, or Portuguese. But none of that seemed to matter. You know, once you get chanting, then things start to happen transcendentally."[9]

He told Wright that he still loved his wife, but that love was no longer enough. "He was extreme, always extreme," sighs Boyd. "He could be hugely generous and kind, and then he just wouldn't want to talk to people sometimes, he would just close off. I guess it was exhausting to be philanthropic all the time. Artists need their own time, to listen to the music in their head. It's what they do."

When he emerged from these intense periods of spiritual contemplation he would be on the lookout for some more traditional forms of release: cocaine had become more common in the wider drug culture and an increasingly integral part of the music industry, and Harrison had starting using it, sporadically but at times heavily. Voormann was saddened to learn that he felt the need to hide the drug when he was around, while those closest to him agree that it changed him, making him, in the words of Boyd, "a bit harder and a bit tougher. I do think a lot of it was down to cocaine."

Some of his other earthly pursuits took a familiar shape. Although opportunities were fewer after he stopped touring, even in the Seventies Mal Evans or another trusted go-between was still charged with selecting willing young females from hotel lobbies and spiriting them upstairs to hotel suites. He seduced one young woman days before the Concert For Bangladesh, and even made overtures to another in the wings during the concert itself. "He was not the most monogamous man in the world," says O'Dell. "He was a flirt, and if you flirted back it was game on, for at least a few days."

Throughout the early Seventies he would ping-pong back and forth between the sacred and the profane, going slightly further in either direction each time. The inhabitants at Friar Park would tiptoe around asking, "Has he got his hands in the bean bag or the coke bag?" says O'Dell. "He'd do all these crazy things then get really spiritual again. No matter what your spiritual drive is, you still fall back into your humanness." Harrison's very vocal dedication to religious pursuits made his drug use and sexual promiscuity seem more extreme than they really were; in truth, such behaviour was par for the course for the time, and O'Dell insists that "I never saw him as an abuser of drugs and alcohol. He was an occasional imbiber."

Between these polar incarnations the boy from Wavertree who liked music, a laugh, a few drinks, and the company of his friends would sometimes magically appear, but less and less frequently. He rarely went out, preferring instead to stay at home with the same small group of familiar faces. "George stayed pretty isolated," says O'Dell. "I'm not sure that he didn't do that his entire life. I would always see the same people at the house, I would never see different people. And there was no more going to the studio, he had one at home, so he didn't have to leave."

He was far from oblivious to these conflicts – and at times they troubled him greatly. He consulted with his Krishna guru, Swami Prabhupada, at the Hertfordshire mansion he had recently bought as their headquarters, now renamed Bhaktivedanta Manor. During a long and very forthright meeting in 1973 he confessed, "I seem to be going around in circles. I have periods when I just can't stop chanting, and then other periods where, you know, I turn into a demon again."[10]

Friends would call him 'His Lectureship' behind his back. Reading about the Concert For Bangladesh, The Rolling Stones could barely stifle their scornful hilarity at the idea of Harrison as the leader of a new wave of righteous, responsible rock stars. He was not unaware of how he was perceived. He was convinced of the need to sing his beliefs, but in doing so, he told Prabhupada, "I find that now I'm getting people angry. I'm provoking a bad reaction. The stronger the commitment on my part, the stronger the animosity becomes. And I'm not sure if it all balances out in the end, whether reaching that one person is worth the ten or 20 who get annoyed with you."[11] Had he done the right thing, putting his head "on the chopping block"?

And finally, there was a recognition that he was growing apart from those closest to him. "Most of the other people in my life, my friends – even my wife – I suddenly find myself on such a different level that it's hard to relate to them," he said.[12]

He wanted more than anything to experience pure consciousness, to rise above the physical. But at what cost? He seemed in danger of dumping everything in his life into the realm of the transitory: not merely wealth and possessions, but people, too. If none of it really mattered, if it was all illusion, then what was left? Just his own consciousness and its relationship with God. "It doesn't matter what happens, the plan can't be affected, even having wars or dropping the H-bomb," he had said. "None of it matters."[13] It was a view of enlightenment that seemed to leave compassion and the joy of basic human interaction in short supply.

His wife looked on with a mixture of sadness, anger and helplessness. "He had demons, he had battles," says Boyd. "He found life difficult. To have absolutely anything and anybody you want, in every area, for a sensitive person there has to come a time when you question it. He felt he had to make choices then, and everything did become a bit more polarised. The temptation, the temptation.... it's the Oscar Wilde thing. He found the extremes of experience very difficult, very frustrating. *Very*. He wanted to pursue both paths. He wanted to pursue spirituality, but he also loved and really enjoyed being a wealthy, famous and beautiful human being, and everything that that offered as well. It is unresolvable."

He had grown used to living a conflicted life on a material level, but it still brought unique contradictions. One letter to Boyd during this period found him talking in one sentence about the starving in

Bangladesh and in the next asking, like a character from Evelyn Waugh, "Has Quinnell done the stairs and rails in 203/4, 109 yet?" "He liked to live a nice life," says Jon Taplin. "He liked good things, he liked to smoke reefer and have a drink, and I don't think he had contradictions about that. He was not an ascetic but he did have a spiritual centre that was truly genuine."

However, the vast amounts of money he was spending on the grand folly of Friar Park – on the grounds, on the studio, on buying and importing desirable objects from all over the world – occasionally raised a few eyebrows, and caused Harrison at least a few internalised arguments. He could console himself with the knowledge that he put a lot of his money where his mouth was. As well as having to personally shell out huge sums to cover the Bangladesh mess, in 1973 he set up The Material World Charitable Foundation, which received royalties from all his future publishing and was used to fund various philanthropic causes.

Money matters were rarely far from his mind. In early April 1973, along with Starr and Lennon, Harrison chose not to renew his contract with Allen Klein, effectively sacking him as his business manager. Klein, predictably, did not take it lying down. He quickly calculated that Harrison had personally borrowed around $270,000 from his company ABCKO in the past four years, and in June sued Harrison in the Supreme Court in New York for the sum owed. The suit was finally settled in 1975. Klein also tried to claim ownership of Harrisongs, Harrison's publishing company. All in all, extricating himself from the hands of the New Yorker became yet another headache which dragged on for a number of years.

In July he took on a new business manager, Denis O'Brien, a tall, thin, bespectacled, besuited American who had studied law and accountancy, served his professional apprenticeship with Rothschild's bank, and had previously looked after the affairs of Harrison's friend Peter Sellers. He seemed, at least at first, more than just a reliable pair of hands. "In 20 minutes he gets more from a budget sheet than most people do in 20 hours," said Harrison.[14] O'Brien similarly appreciated Harrison's lack of rock star bullshit, making it his priority to sort out Harrison's personal tax bill, which had been neglected by Klein. They became good friends.

At the same time as Klein was being ousted, perhaps not coincidentally, The Beatles became a more tangible entity than they had for years. Relations settled into something more cordial, meetings became more frequent, and in March in Los Angeles, Harrison, Starr and Lennon even played together in the studio, spontaneously, on 'I'm The Greatest', written by Lennon for Starr's latest album *Ringo*. Harrison contributed one song and two co-writes to the same record, including the effortlessly catchy 'Photograph', which later became a US number one. Buoyed by the experience of 'I'm The Greatest' and always on the lookout for a band to disappear into, Harrison misread the signals, suggesting that the three former Beatles, as well as Preston and Voormann, form a group. Like a man on a second date suddenly confronted with a marriage proposal, Lennon recoiled, instantly rejecting the idea. They wouldn't see each other again for 18 months.

Instead, the focus fell on past glories. The following month two compilation albums, *The Beatles 1962–1966* and *The Beatles 1967–1970*, were released, primarily to combat the sales of a bootleg compilation, *Alpha Omega*. Forever after known as the 'Red' and 'Blue' albums respectively, they were instant hits and in the 40 years since have remained the gateway for generations of fans starting their investigations into the music of The Beatles.

★ ★ ★

Living In The Material World was released on May 30, 1973 in the United States and June 22 in the UK. It was a hugely successful record at the time – it could hardly have been otherwise given Harrison's profile and the successes that had come before. Once again he had a single and an album at the top of the US charts, although he couldn't repeat the feat in the UK, where the album reached number two and 'Give Me Love (Give Me Peace On Earth)' went to number eight.

It somehow contrived to be a triumph and a disappointment at the same time, its impact being immediate but relatively short-lived. A record that has been largely overlooked by posterity, *Living In The Material World* certainly marks a turning point in Harrison's career, yet in many ways it is a more coherent and confident work than *All Things Must Pass*.

248

For those of us who feel that Harrison loses something precious when he is buried in the centre of a maelstrom of sound, the quieter textures, the more thoughtful arrangements, the very clear glimpses of his soul, were welcome progressions. But it is not an easy listen. *All Things Must Pass* fused the quest for spiritual understanding with a crackling mix of gospel, rock and soul which transmitted its own joyous charge, while *Concert For Bangladesh* successfully took that self-same spirit on to the stage. *Living In The Material World* is a different kind of beast altogether.

Musically low-key, only three songs feature electric guitar, although there are moments of humour and touches of rock and roll raucousness. The title track is the album's big production number, perhaps created already with live performance in mind, and punctuated with musical puns: following a light-hearted reference to "John and Paul", there is a heavily-signalled drum roll by Starr when his name is mentioned; Hussein's tabla, added late on as an overdub, harks back to Harrison's Indian-flavoured Beatles' songs and soundtracks his talk of the "Spiritual Sky". The rhythm chugs rather than motors at full throttle, but the combination of Hopkins' rolling piano, Horn's full-blown sax interacting with Harrison's slide, Starr and Keltner's combined might and an amusingly cheesy 'showbiz' finale keeps things interesting.

There are other moments of relatively light relief. The breezy 'Don't Let Me Wait Too Long' is Harrison's great lost single, and yet another iteration of the basic message of 'My Sweet Lord': God, please reveal yourself. The happily banal lyric, in which the singer could be falling before a woman or The Lord, is lifted by the Spector-esque double-drums, comically dramatic timpani, and an all-round feeling of good-hearted regeneration. 'Give Me Love (Give Me Peace On Earth)', the lead single, is a gentler reflection on the need to "touch and reach you". Essentially one long chorus, the track provides another showcase for Harrison's now-trademark dual slide guitars.

After Lennon's confrontational 'How Do You Sleep?', Harrison's take on The Beatles' post-1970 affairs, 'Sue Me, Sue You Blues' is far less contentious, preferring dark humour over playground name-calling. Taking a raw bottleneck blues and welding it forcefully to the sing-song rhythms of a square dance, it draws the inevitable conclusion that the only people getting rich are the lawyers. He even manages to shoehorn "escrow" in there.

But even in these, the album's most carefree songs, there are tears, heavy burdens, frustrations, drownings, people getting screwed and senses being left eternally ungratified. There is ultimately no escape from the conclusion that *Living In The Material World* is a record ingrained with an almost suffocating sense of sadness. The dichotomy of Harrison's existence was made clear before anybody heard a note. The sleeve's denotations of a spiritual life – the Om symbol, the message 'All Glory to Sri Krishna' and the Hindu medallion on the cover – contrasted with photographs of a *Monty Python*-esque Last Supper held at the mock-Tudor Los Angeles home of showbiz lawyer Abe Somers. This was a scene of sheer indulgence: a palatial spread of food and wine laid before Harrison, who is depicted as some absurdist, gun-toting emperor-priest in rock star shades; behind him the alluring leg of a young lady dangles from an upper window. Literally and metaphorically it was an all-you-can-eat buffet laid before a man who was trying to starve himself of life's more basic temptations, and failing miserably.

How did it feel to be George Harrison in 1973? Take a seat. Ken Marcus' cornea-burning photos juxtaposed with the vivid painting of Krishna from a Prabhupada-published edition of the *Bhagavad Gita* went some way towards providing an explanation, but anybody wishing to get a full reading of where Harrison's head was at needed only to listen to the music. 'Who Can See It' lays down all the fear and longing of a past spent "towing the line," and aches with the hope that history will not repeat itself. "I only ask/That what I feel/Should not be denied me now," might be the single most heartbreaking line Harrison ever wrote, and encapsulates the sense of both transformation and crisis which hung over him at this time. Vocally, he wrings every inch out of the song with an astonishing performance; he was thinking of Roy Orbison at the time he wrote it, and the comparison does not entirely embarrass him. On 'Be Here Now' Voormann's stand-up bass and Harrison's beautiful acoustic guitar weave a magical spell around a simple melody based on a minimum of notes and vaguely Eastern vocal ululations.

But it is not beauty which has proven to be the lasting legacy of *Living In The Material World*. In the public and critical perception it is generally defined in terms of its apparent piousness and desire to preach. Reviewers at the time and ever since have bewailed its "transcendent dogma".[15] For every writer lauding its "exquisite musical underpinnings"[16] or "profoundly seductive"[17] nature there is another deeming it "so damn holy I could scream".[18]

It's not hard to hear why. On 'The Light That Has Lighted The World', the prettiness of the music, the perfect symmetry of its structure, and the quavering vocals can't quite distract from an astonishingly sour attack on all the "people" who are "hateful" of Harrison's changes and who sit in judgement upon him, a sentiment emitting more than a whiff of hypocrisy. If only he had been able to find the words and feelings to match Hopkins' beautiful piano, one of the most glorious musical passages in any Harrison song, particularly when it connects to the gentle sob of his own slide solo.

Similarly 'The Day The World Gets 'Round', started the day after the Concert For Bangladesh, considers why poor old pop stars should have to step into the breach to solve the ills of the world. "It seemed to me a poor state of affairs," said Harrison. "If everyone would wake up and do even a little, there could be no misery in the world."[19] It's a valid opinion, if naive and somewhat self-absorbed, but one that the song fails to sell due to its ponderous melody and alienating phrases like "I don't want to be like you".

The chugging 'The Lord Loves The One (That Loves The Lord)' was welded to an equally uncompromising lyric which can be boiled down to: *Karma's gonna get ya*. It was widely read as the crowing of a privileged superstar who professed to have seen the emptiness of the rock 'lifestyle' from his 120-room mansion, or perhaps while driving one of his very fast cars, while everyone else was stumbling stupidly in the dark. In fact, it was written after a meeting with Prabhupada, and makes much more sense if regarded as a stern note-to-self rather than an instruction for everyone else to mend their ways. "I do not exclude myself," he said about this song and others on the album, "and write a lot of things to make *myself* remember."[20]

Given the fault lines running through his private life, it is indeed instructive to view much of the moralising evident on *Living In The Material World* as being addressed to the man in the mirror. Part of the problem was that his limited skills as a lyricist hampered his ability to communicate; there's a lot of "you" and a lot of "I" in these songs, the curse of Harrison's lyric writing. The lovely 'That Is All', which echoes 'Yesterday' in its opening seconds and hints at the grandeur of 'Something' in its elegant structure and sweeping strings, returned to a perennial theme: the inability to say what needs to be said, and the superiority of silence. It became a self-fulfilling prophecy. On *Living In The Material World* Harrison was largely unable to alchemise his palpable sincerity into something that everyone could embrace. He was incapable of telling a story, or forming a narrative, or framing his experiences in the poetry of the everyday. Instead of building a bridge across the depth of his feelings he instead created a chasm – and in doing so often appeared to be a man who had seen a glimpse of heaven and was pulling up the ladder behind him. "Lord, there are just a few of us who bow before you," he sang on 'The Day The World Gets 'Round'. It sounded suspiciously like a rather exclusive form of enlightenment. It also didn't sound like much fun. From the outside Harrison seemed to many – both critics and those closer to him – self-involved and monomaniacal, his worldview laced with cynicism and moral reproval; a humanitarian with a jaundiced view of humanity itself, detached and distrustful of the world. The tour he embarked upon the following year would only enhance this perspective.

The other problem with *Living In The Material World* was one of context. In the days when it was still normal to release at least one and often two records every 12 months, in the two years since *Concert For Bangladesh*, and near three since *All Things Must Pass*, the ground beneath his feet had shifted. That the gap between the Concert For Bangladesh and Live Aid, the next live charity event of comparable stature, was 14 years – almost a generation – is no coincidence. The show at Madison Square Garden was the sound of an era ending. The new age which welcomed Harrison's next record in the summer of 1973 had different ideas and ideals, and its own icons. In Britain David Bowie, Marc Bolan,

Slade and Roxy Music were the new pop stars, and they offered colour, theatre and escapism. Spiritual soul-searching was passé; artists strived for otherness rather than Godliness. Glam looked back to the Fifties but it also nodded towards punk, reconfiguring rock and roll's settings for the coming decade, sweeping away the tyranny of double denim and the lingering legacy of the Great British Blues Boom. Progressive rock, meanwhile, met the demand for triple albums and textured proficiency with heightened drama and a keen sense of the absurd.

In a way that couldn't yet be measured by record sales, Harrison had been culturally cut adrift, as out of touch to the mood of the times as Cliff Richard had seemed when The Beatles first arrived. Between Bangladesh and *Living In The Material World* the Seventies had truly begun and increasingly he resembled a relic of a bygone age. He liked Bob Marley, but admitted that he "never read the pop papers now and never listen to Radio Luxembourg."[21] His big tip for the top was Peter Skellern.

In this light *Living In The Material World* marked the beginning of an alarmingly swift descent into fogeyism. Not only was he out of touch with the world of music, he also seemed disconnected from the reality of life in 1973. He had come a long, long way in ten years. He never took public transport, never went to the pub, rarely engaged with anyone outside his own sanctum, had retained no strong roots in Liverpool. Asked about the meaning of The Material World he replied, "I'm living in it. But people interpret it to mean money, cars, that sort of thing – although those are part of the material world, the material world is like the physical world, as opposed to the spiritual. For me, living in the material world just meant being in this physical body with all the things that go along with it."[22]

One man's 'struggles' in this material world looked like luxury compared to what most of the rest of the population were having to negotiate. In Britain it was a year of strikes, wage freezes, creeping dole queues, rising inflation and IRA bombs. There was a global fuel crisis. Americans were dealing with the devaluing of the dollar, Vietnam, Watergate and the Cold War. A secluded millionaire's cry to "help me cope with my heavy load" was not to everyone's taste. Harrison's only major public appearance around the time of the album's release came on July 8, when he joined Prabhupada in a religious procession from Marble Arch to Piccadilly. Had he popped up on *Top Of The Pops* wearing his Krishna hat, a smile and a pair of bright trousers he might have scored a few more brownie points.

★ ★ ★

At home, domestic matters were coming to a head. In October Harrison was one of an all-star cast roped in to work on Ronnie Wood's first solo record, *I've Got My Own Album To Do*. Most of it was recorded at Wood's house in Richmond Wick, but work was also done at Friar Park, where Harrison invited Wood and his wife Krissy to come and stay. Things quickly fell apart. Harrison embarked on an affair with Krissy; the pair even went on holiday together. "There were things he wasn't very discreet about," says O'Dell. "Like with Ronnie Wood's wife, he was very blatant about that, he would flirt with her right in front of Pattie." To complicate matters further, Boyd embarked on a brief fling with Wood.

The former Beatles engineer Chris Thomas, now a successful producer, had started going out with Chris O'Dell, and came to stay at Friar Park in 1973. He found some "very weird things going on at that time. It was like a magic roundabout, people jumping on and off and swapping around. I turned a blind eye to it, because some of it was really not what you expected and quite surprising. It was very, very weird. 'Oh blimey, what are this lot on?' No one got up before six in the evening. Very weird. And it was quite obvious that George and Pattie weren't getting on."

The final, unrecoverable move in this endgame was Harrison's affair with Ringo Starr's wife Maureen, whom he had known since the early Sixties and who was a central figure in The Beatles' family. Boyd had discovered photographs which revealed that Maureen had been at Friar Park on a weekend when she had been away. Undaunted, Starr's wife would start arriving late at night and disappear into the studio with Harrison, then stay overnight. If guests were there, the pair would huddle together in a corner. On one occasion Boyd discovered them locked in a room. When O'Dell arrived to visit over Christmas and New Year she was picked up at Heathrow by a welcoming party of Harrison, Maureen Starkey, Boyd and Ronnie Wood, and was immediately struck by the strangeness of the atmosphere. On New Year's Eve Harrison said to his wife, "Let's have a divorce this year." Early in January 1974 he told Starr, in front of both Maureen and Pattie Boyd, "I'm in love with your wife." Starr was distraught, muttering "nothing is real, nothing is real." Lennon later described it as "incest".

Harrison and Maureen Starkey always denied that they were sleeping together. "I don't know if anything ever happened physically between them, or whether it was an emotional affair," says O'Dell. "She would never admit it. Pattie believes that it was [physical]. I don't know. But it certainly ruined two marriages that were already on the brink. There is a question of whether George was [deliberately] trying to destroy the marriage, or to find out if Pattie really cared – 'Is she going to fight for me or not?' Who knows what was going on behind it all, but it was the last straw. It was nuts, and very complicated. Within the strong walls of The Beatles' complex there weren't many rules."

Meanwhile Eric Clapton was sensing the chance to fill a vacuum, making "amateur inroads into finding out what was going on in their relationship."[23] Clapton had been pursuing Pattie Boyd for years. Since Harrison had had an affair with his girlfriend Charlotte Martin back in 1968 the pair seemed to be engaged in a high-stakes game of sexual and emotional brinksmanship. "There were a few funny things," said Harrison. "I pulled his chick once. That's happened, and now you'd think he was trying to get his own back on me."[24] It was as though two of the great guitar icons of the Sixties had to assert their potency by sleeping with each other's current or former partners. On the Delaney & Bonnie and Friends tour in late 1969, during that drunken revelry in Liverpool, Clapton recalled that "George had taken me aside and suggested that I should spend the night with Pattie so that he could sleep with [her sister] Paula... At the last moment he lost his nerve and nothing happened."[25]

Clapton spent the night with Paula Boyd instead, and began dating her, but his real infatuation was with Pattie. He started sending her notes and poems, and in the spring and summer of 1970 they began having secret assignations. He wrote 'Layla' for her, based on the ancient poem 'Layla and Majnun' by the 12th-century Persian poet Nizami Ganjavi of the Ganja. Nizami's tale told of a princess who was married off by her father to someone other than the man who was in love with her, resulting in Majnun's madness; the theme was adopted by Clapton to address his unrequited feelings for Boyd. At a party held by Robert Stigwood, Harrison confronted the pair after he found them together in the garden. "I have to tell you, man," responded Clapton, "that I'm in love with your wife." Still Boyd wouldn't countenance leaving Harrison, and Clapton took refuge in heroin. "He had made overtures to me and then sunk into a druggie depression," says Boyd.

Everything cooled for a while. Now, three years later, Clapton continued his pursuit and Boyd's resolve weakened in light of her husband's growing distance and indifference. Each time Clapton came around to Friar Park or entreated her to leave she came a little closer to acquiescing. Harrison, well aware of what was going on, adopted what Clapton called a "cavalier"[26] attitude: 'If you want her, take her. She's yours.' There was, after all, a lot of partner swapping going on, and it seemed to go against the spirit of the times to care too much. And in any case, the game was already up. "Pattie and [Eric] got together after we'd really split," he said. "Actually we'd been splitting up for years."[27]

Clapton, the more volatile and openly emotional of the pair, was desperate for some kind of reaction to clear the air. Boyd, too. Instead, Harrison remained maddeningly sanguine. "I didn't get annoyed at him and I think that has always annoyed him," he said much later. "I think that deep down inside he wishes that it really pissed me off, but it didn't, because I was happy that she went off, because we'd finished together, and it made things easier for me, you see, because otherwise we'd have had to go through all these big rows and divorces. And you know, she went off to live in the same style she became accustomed to and it was really very convenient for me."[28]

Everyone was free. Everything was transitory. Meanwhile, underneath it all, everybody was feeling terrible. Life at Friar Park, says Boyd, had become "madness. Complete madness. Helped of course by copious amounts of drink and drugs, which gives one a very disjointed view of life. Now I wonder, 'Where did that come from? Why did that happen?' On reflection, I think, What happened? It's not as if we were addicts, that's a different thing altogether, but just playing around with it, and too much alcohol, and it became insane really, from 1973 and into 1974. It was everybody we knew, as well, who seemed to be in the same mad state. That was the real end of the Sixties, and everything seemed to get a bit colder, a bit harder."

Everyone dutifully played out their final moves. By the summer of 1974 Boyd had left Harrison and Friar Park and had taken up with Clapton. They married in 1979, after Harrison and Boyd had finally divorced in 1977. Somehow, all parties remained friends, which reflects admirably on them all, although the relationship between Clapton and Harrison was always febrile, and could easily flare up from time to time. "Eric had the problem," says Harrison. "Every time I'd go and see him, he'd be really hung up about it, and I was saying, 'Fuck it, man. Don't be apologising,' and he didn't believe me. I was saying, 'I don't care.'"[29]

Did he really not care? Harrison's actions around this time, and at certain points in the future, certainly suggest that the end of his ten-year relationship with Boyd cut deeper than he would ever let on. At the beginning of 1974 he went to India for the first time in six years, to visit Ravi Shankar and to stay in an ashram in the Krishna centre of Vrindavan. He wrote, meditated, and tried to shake himself free of the entanglements of the Material World. He wasn't entirely successful. He returned to Britain in March and buried himself in an insane workload, embarked on an extended bender, and steeled himself for his first ever tour – where he immediately met the woman who would become his second wife.

Be Here Now
Vancouver, November 2, 1974

It is a night of firsts. Awaiting the first song of the first show on the first solo tour of the US by a former Beatle, the 17,500-capacity Pacific Coliseum is full and buzzing. The barkers selling the concert programmes are calling the main attraction 'George ex-Beatle Harrison', the music press are out in force, and it is not fanciful to detect the resurgent scent of Beatlemania in the air.

What occurs in the ensuing two hours, however, might be expressly designed to puncture every last bright balloon of nostalgic reverie. "Sorry we're late," says Harrison, dressed down in denim dungarees and sensible shoes, sporting a droopy moustache and a ragged, shoulder-length shag cut. The stage is similarly casually attired, draped with a simple Dark Horse banner and the Om symbol, illuminated and written in Sanskrit. Harrison, sinking anonymously into his eight-piece band, chooses to open with an unreleased instrumental, as though wishing to underline his deep-rooted distaste for the spotlight, and indeed the past. He might also be delaying the revelation that his voice is already completely shot.

The following show includes some remarkable Indian music, entertaining turns from Billy Preston and Tom Scott, even an airing of the beloved 'Something', but nothing that displays an urgent inclination to meet, or indeed even to acknowledge, the excitement and sense of expectation that filled the arena earlier in the evening.

"He drove [promoter] Bill Graham crazy," says director David Acomba, who was filming the tour. "The way he started the show, the band would play a tune and George would kind of drift out into a guitar solo. Bill wanted it like: 'Okay, the band does a number, then the house goes dark, and all of a sudden you hear the opening strains to 'Here Comes The Sun'. *Please* George, do it.' 'No, no, I don't want to do that.' That was George, you know. He never wanted to be up front – he just wanted to play music. He didn't want to be the star. He never was the kind of person who sought the limelight in that way."

And so begins one of George Harrison's strangest ever trips.

CHAPTER 12

Dark Horse Rides Out

Had he pulled it off, George Harrison's tour of North America in late 1974 might still be talked about in hushed tones. It would have been widely recognised as a groundbreaking fusion of Western rock and Eastern classical music, it would have spawned an unusual and irreverent film and very probably a double live album. On the heels of two number one records, either side of the Concert For Bangladesh, it would have sealed Harrison's status as one of the elite solo rock stars of the Seventies.

In reality, it is the major fault line dividing his solo career. It provided an opportunity for those alienated by the pious finger-pointing of *Living In The Material World* to vent their spleen, and it offered Harrison an arena in which to display just how little the legacy of The Beatles meant to him, and indeed to show borderline contempt for the routine expectations of a rock and roll audience.

In the end nobody quite got what they wanted. At the beginning of the tour he said "this is really a test. I'll either finish this tour ecstatically happy or end up going back to my cave for another five years."[1] He *did* have a cave, of course – several, in fact – which made the statement false in only one major respect. Following the tour it would be much longer than five years before he again became an active participant in the music industry. Many would argue that he never fully did.

★ ★ ★

The idea for a tour had been circulating since the Concert For Bangladesh. "That band would have gone on the road with him in a heartbeat," says Jon Taplin, and Billy Preston noted that "he was definitely inspired after Bangladesh, he wanted to [perform live] again right away."[2] His euphoria was, however, tempered by the lingering memories of Beatlemania, and the Catch 22 that found him enjoying playing live yet hating touring, and lacking any desire to be the main attraction.

As it was, the notion only really took shape in India in February 1974, his first visit since going to Rishikesh with The Beatles.* He had gone to India to take part in a ceremony to bless the new home of Ravi Shankar, and to seek some spiritual sustenance in the gardens and temples of Vrindavan. It was also a chance to liaise on the prospects for their shared project, *Shankar Family & Friends*. The bulk of that album had been recorded in April and May 1973 at A&M Studios in Los Angeles, produced by Harrison, with Ringo Starr, Tom Scott, Emil Richards, Jim Keltner, Klaus Voormann and Billy Preston augmenting the large cast of Indian musicians, which included Alla Rakha and Shankar's sister-in-law Lakshmi Shankar. *Shankar Family & Friends* was intended to fuse East and West: the 14 tracks blend, often intriguingly but not altogether successfully, traditional Indian music with jazz, funk, rock and pop.

There was another musical item on the agenda during his Indian visit. The stated intention of Harrison's Material World Charitable Foundation was to "sponsor diverse forms of artistic expression and to encourage the exploration of alternative life views and philosophies." He had decided that the first practical application of this aim would be The Music Festival From India, an ambitious classical revue headed

* Gary Wright has stated that he went with Harrison to India in 1972, but in his autobiography, *I Me Mine*, Harrison says that his trip in 1974 was his first since 1968; one of them is clearly mistaken.

by Shankar which would open at the Royal Albert Hall in London in the autumn, before touring Europe. Then, the two men decided, why not bring the show to the United States, with Harrison joining the bill as co-headliner? The tour was intended from the very start to be a co-production.

The first inkling that an ex-Beatle was finally going to hit the road in the US came when Harrison returned to Britain the following month, via a statement from Apple issued on March 4. It was front page news in *Melody Maker* a few days later (ironically, in an issue with a picture of McCartney on the cover; he had also been touring, most recently in May 1973 with Wings). Immediately, Harrison started prevaricating, scotching rumours that Starr would be appearing – "there will be no link up!" – and also insisting that "no final decisions have been taken" about the tour itself.[3]

It wouldn't officially be announced until late September, but plans were already well underway. The powerful American promoter Bill Graham – whose professional obsession had become to reunite The Beatles – came to see Harrison at Friar Park to discuss the details, where he caught a flavour of what lay in store. "They were having dinner at this enormously long table, with Bill at one end and George at the other," recalls Jerry Pompili, who worked with Graham in the early Seventies. "There's no silverware, and Bill doesn't know what to do. It's all this Indian cuisine and George starts shovelling food into his mouth with his hand. So Bill thinks, 'Okay, when in Rome...' Bill's left-handed, and so he starts shovelling food into his mouth with his left hand. George looked horrified and explained that you eat with your right hand and wipe your ass with your left." The scene provided an apt metaphor for the cross purposes at which the pair would later find themselves.

Instead of clearing his schedule to focus on such a vast undertaking, Harrison attempted to do several things at once. As well as starting work on his next album, *Dark Horse*, he was putting the finishing touches to *Shankar Family & Friends*; setting up his own record label; overseeing The Music Festival From India; and continuing the seemingly endless sessions for the first album by Bob Purvis and Bill Elliott, a pair of singer-songwriters from the north-east of England who performed as Splinter. On top of all that, he had a new girlfriend, the 24-year-old model Kathy Simmonds, who had previously dated Harry Nilsson and Rod Stewart. He was also consuming cocaine and alcohol with a rather desperate relish. "I would class those as the dark days," says Bill Elliott. "They were the dark days, the days of Courvoisier. He was hammering that down, I witnessed all of that. A failure in any marriage is a dark period, it's the end of a chapter, and it was quite upsetting for him." Harrison told Houston radio station KLOL later that year that he would need to sell five million copies of the Splinter album just to cover the expense of all the brandy that been consumed during its production.

He had been working with Splinter since the previous year. Managed by Mal Evans, they had originally entered Harrison's orbit via the Apple film, *Little Malcolm And His Struggle Against The Eunuchs*, for which they provided a song, 'Lonely Man', for the nightclub scene. Impressed, Harrison smelled a hit, which in turn he hoped would help sell the movie. Their music was a superior example of voguish soft-rock, built on acoustic guitars, harmonies and strong melody, and distinctly Beatlesesque in places. After hearing more of their songs he decided he wanted to produce an entire album, which became *The Place I Love*.

It proved a protracted affair. Novices in the studio, Harrison drilled them in the art of harmony and song arrangement. Some recording was done at Savile Row but primarily they worked at FPSHOT, where periodically the pair came to stay. Harrison nicknamed Elliott 'Kentucky Fried Billy' due to his preference for dining at the local takeaway chicken outlet rather than eating curried sea bass at Friar Park. All the main protagonists in the unfolding domestic soap opera put in appearances. "Eric Clapton might be in the corner, Ronnie Wood was around," says Elliott. "I've got a great picture in the studio – Bob [Purvis] has got his arm around Pattie and she's got his arm round him. They've got a drink, and Ronnie is looking down and checking out Pattie's backside. You never knew who was going to be there. You'd turn up and Peter Sellers would be walking around the garden with him. Alvin Lee would turn up on his big motorbike."

Basic tracking was completed by January 1974, but after Harrison's return from India overdubbing continued, almost obsessively. As well as producing the entire record, he played guitars, Moog, dobro, mandolin, bass and percussion under the guise of Hari Georgeson, Jai Raj Harisein and P. Roducer. "He was very hands-on, and it had to be perfect," says Elliott. "He would keep you there all night just to get one harmony right. He was very, very meticulous when it came to the finished product. The ultimate perfectionist. He was a good taskmaster and he taught me an awful lot about singing. If it was a difficult harmony he would sit and work it all out at the piano and give everybody their part."

The Place I Love was eventually finished in August 1974. At times working 24 hours straight, fuelled by whatever was at hand, Harrison ended up lavishing more care on Splinter's record than he did on his own. "His own album did suffer a little bit," says Elliott. Indeed it did. Sessions for *Dark Horse* had begun at FPSHOT in November 1973 using the same core line-up which had worked on *Living In The Material World*, recording 'Ding Dong, Ding Dong', the apposite 'So Sad' and an early stab at the lively title track. He had high hopes for 'Ding Dong, Ding Dong' in particular, a deliberately mindless almost-glam stomper inspired by carvings on the wall at Friar Park, which he clearly envisaged becoming the next big seasonal hit after Wizzard and Slade had cleaned up in the winter of 1973 with 'I Wish It Could Be Christmas Everyday' and 'Merry Christmas Everybody'. He sent an early mix of the song to David Geffen, whom he was sounding out about potential distribution deals for the Splinter and Shankar albums. He wrote: "It's one of them [sic] repetitious numbers which is gonna have 20 million people, with the Phil Spector nymphomaniacs, all doing backing vocals by the end of the day, and it's gonna be wonderful. But I'd appreciate it if you don't let anyone steal it, 'cos I want the hit myself." In the event, a year later it barely scraped into the Top 40.

After returning from India, in April he cut two further tracks with saxophonist Tom Scott, who had played on *Shankar Family & Friends*, and guitarist Robben Ford. Both were members of L.A. Express, which was in London backing Joni Mitchell at her shows at the New Victoria Theatre. "We all went back to the hotel and the next day, the band and Joni went out to Henley-On-Thames to hang out," says Ford. "That night Joni went back to London and the band stayed and recorded with George until all hours of the morning. We cut those two tracks on *Dark Horse*: 'Hari's On Tour (Express)' and 'Simply Shady'."

'Simply Shady' had been written in Bombay at the start of his trip, but its heart (and other parts) belonged to Henley-On-Thames. It marked a 180-degree turn from the themes of his last record. This was a glimpse beneath the public veneer of sanctity, a warts-and-all account of life at Friar Park over the past year: the women, the booze, and all the rest. "Came off the rails so crazy," he sings, "My senses took a dip." Only at the end, perhaps in deference to the surroundings in which it was composed, is there an acknowledgement that at some point he'll have to face up to the consequences of all this recklessness.

"After I split up from Pattie I went on a bit of a bender to make up for all the years I'd been married," he said, perhaps a little disingenuously, for he was hardly overly constrained by his marriage vows. "If you listen to 'Simply Shady' it's all in there... I wasn't ready to join Alcoholics Anonymous or anything – I don't think I was that far gone – but I could put back a bottle of brandy occasionally, plus all the other naughty things that fly around. I just went on a binge."[4]

The words of the song are framed by a sluggish country-rock sound, as loose as the times it described. The sensitive soul of the previous year seemed to have been consigned to the back-burner. Now he was back in a rock and roll band, with Tom Scott's horns foregrounding the soul and R&B influences. Further emphasising the rhythm track, for the final *Dark Horse* sessions at FPSHOT in August and September, Harrison drafted in drummer Andy Newmark and bassist Willie Weeks, both of whom he had met while recording the Harrison-Wood composition 'Far East Man' for Ronnie Wood's solo album. With them he cut 'Maya Love' and 'It Is 'He' (Jai Sri Krishna)', a nimble bhajan inspired by his meeting with the ascetic Sripad Maharaj in Vrindavan. The song saw him grappling with such exotic instruments as the *khrmack*, an inverted drum with two gut strings on the inside traditionally played by the Bauls of Bengal.

During these sessions the line-up also recut the long, languid 'Far East Man', an unusually relaxed and conversational expression of Harrison's spiritual search, and one which looked forward to David Bowie's *Young Americans* with its easy Philly soul groove. It was one of the highlights of a mismatched and rather ragged collection of songs. There was already an inescapable feeling that the album they were working on was more of a hurried stop-gap than something groundbreaking. "I didn't have the sense at the time that I was part of anything Biblical," says Andy Newmark. "I knew he was coming off big records with *All Things Must Pass* and *Living In The Material World*, and I don't think *Dark Horse* came anywhere near that. It didn't reach those heights. They were nice tunes, he was a good songwriter, he had a great style as a player, but I didn't think that record was going to bring down the heavens."

In August he took a much-needed break, heading to St George's Bay in Grenada with Kathy Simmonds. He returned to announce that Splinter would be the first signing on his new Dark Horse Records imprint. As it became clear that Apple was heading for the buffers, the company was gradually wound down and the remaining artists released from their contracts. Harrison duly set about forming his own label. It was partly a public assertion of artistic independence, and partly a place for him to champion the musicians he liked. It was also a reaction to Capitol's hardball stance over the Concert For Bangladesh: he intended for Dark Horse to become a home for his own music once his contract with EMI lapsed in 1976.

He signed a partnership agreement with Jerry Moss and Herb Alpert's A&M Records on May 15, 1974, creating a five-year deal that included the right to Harrison's first four solo albums as well as his personal services as a producer for Dark Horse artists. The label set up offices at 40 Royal Avenue in Chelsea, and in June Jonathan Clyde was named the director, responsible for marketing, promotion and A&R in Britain and Europe. The US operation opened in August, with offices at A&M in Los Angeles. "George was more or less a figurehead," says Bill Elliott. "The manager was Jonathan Clyde, he ran the label, but ultimately George had the final say on artists, album covers, final mixes. It was his baby."

Dark Horse was launched on September 13 with the simultaneous release, Apple-style, of two singles: Ravi Shankar's 'I Am Missing

You', a love song to Krishna sung by Lakshmi Shankar, and Splinter's 'Costafine Town'. These were followed a week later by their parent albums, *Shankar Family & Friends* and *The Place I Love*. The logo was inspired by the seven-headed flying horse Uchchaihshravas, which Krishna can be seen riding in the painting inside *Living In The Material World*. Far from 'dark', it is traditionally pictured as snow–white.

The launch of the label coincided with The Music Festival Of India, held at the Royal Albert Hall on September 23. As well as Shankar and Alla Rakha the 20-piece ensemble included some of the greatest Indian musicians of the age: flautist Hariprasad Chaurasia, T.V. Gopalkrishnan on mridangam and vocals, South Indian violin virtuoso L. Subramaniam, sarangi master Sultan Khan and santoor player Shivkumar Sharma. Arranging the show (which was also filmed) and overseeing the related album made further pressing claims on Harrison's time. Shankar and the musicians had been in Britain for the past month, recording and rehearsing in the grand hall at Friar Park. From the outside it looked like chaos. "It was amazing," Harrison recalled, "because [Ravi] would sit there and say to one person, 'This is where you play,' and the next one, 'And you do this,' and 'You do that,' and they're all going, 'What?' 'Okay, one, two, three...' And you'd think, 'This is going to be a catastrophe' – and it would be the most amazing thing."[5] Even so, when he took to the stage to introduce the show he looked nervous and admitted "we're behind schedule".

Everything was behind schedule. By this point it had become clear that *Dark Horse* was rapidly running out of track. The US dates were booked from November 2. Had there been no tour there is certainly no doubt that the album would have been delayed and a little more care and attention lavished on it. As it was, that wasn't an option: to tour without a new record in 1974 went against every basic tenet of the industry. As a result, Harrison was still working on overdubs, mixing and even basic tracking after he arrived in Los Angeles in October to start rehearsals. The title track was recorded from scratch with the live band on the A&M soundstage, and Harrison's badly strained bark, on one of his better songs, gives some indication of how he sounded throughout the tour. He also padded out the record with a truly terrible cover of The

Everly Brothers' 'Bye Bye, Love'. Making mention of "our Lady" and "old Clapper", it was a loose-tongued, misfiring mix of ill-humour and unpleasant sarcasm, taped solo on acoustic guitar before Harrison added all the other music. Changing the words and decimating the melody, he sounded like a man teetering on the brink of reason itself. He also recorded the spoofy but mildly disturbing 'I Don't Care Anymore', released as the B-side of 'Ding Dong, Ding Dong'. It was another drunken, disheartening snapshot of where he found himself vocally and emotionally just as he was about to head off on the biggest challenge of his solo career.

He came into the tour ill, harassed and exhausted. He looked awful: always thin, he was now truly gaunt, his cheeks hollow and his skin pale and stretched. He had also lost his voice, a combination of overwork and too much "naughtiness"[6] triggering a historic weakness in his throat. He had been plagued by tonsillitis as a child, and aged 12 the infection spread to his kidneys and he spent six weeks in Alder Hey hospital suffering from nephritis. He finally had his tonsils removed in 1969. When he sang over a band he tended to shout, further straining his throat, and now he was completely hoarse. He was given the option to cancel, but at such a late stage the fall-out would have been enormous. Also, says David Acomba, who filmed the tour, "he was into making money too, that was a big part of it, that was important to him. He was a business guy, he wasn't into wasting money."

★ ★ ★

At the same time as trying to make the best of a bad job on his new album, he started three weeks of rehearsals at the soundstage at A&M. The band he had assembled consisted of Harrison on vocals and guitar, Robben Ford on second guitar, Willie Weeks on bass, Andy Newmark on drums, Billy Preston on keyboards, Emil Richards on percussion, and Tom Scott, Chuck Findley and Jim Horn as the three-piece horn section. Later in the tour Jim Keltner arrived and he and Newmark performed together, again indulging Harrison's questionable taste for playing with twin drummers.

Both Scott and Richards had appeared on *Shankar Family & Friends* and had studied Indian music at UCLA with a Shankar protégé, Harihar Rao. Robben Ford was picked over perhaps more high profile guitarists because of his unflashy versatility. Newmark and Weeks were the funkiest rhythm section in town. Horn and Findley had played at the Concert For Bangladesh and understood the revue-style nature of the tour, which would feature slots by Billy Preston, Tom Scott and collaborations with the slightly reduced 15-piece Indian orchestra from The Music Festival Of India, led by Shankar on sitar.

Scott recalled that far from hogging the spotlight, "George wanted to give the impression of a band, with him as host, soloist, singer and guitarist."[7] Harrison's press conference for the tour at the Beverley Wilshire Hotel on October 23 provided further evidence of his reticence. A droll masterclass in puncturing expectations, it was Harrison at his plain-speaking best/worst. At times it made one wonder what he was doing there in the first place. *Is your guitar playing sharper?* ("Not particularly, no.") *Any all-star jams planned?* ("I hardly know the tunes myself. The wrong people always seem to want to jump up and jam.") *Are you going to be doing any solo acoustic tunes?* ("I hope not.") *Do you have any anxieties?* ("The main one is that I've lost my voice.") *What are you feeling about the upcoming tour?* ("I think if I had more time I'd be panic-stricken, but I don't even have time to worry about it.") His blunt answers to the inevitable Beatles questions provided a clue to where the tour was heading: "The problem comes when [people] want to live in the past, when they want to hold on to something. People are afraid of change." To which he might have added: don't say you haven't been warned.

Quizzed about the end of his marriage, he said: "Eric Clapton's been a close friend for years. I'm very happy about it. I'm still very friendly with him. I'd rather she was with him than with some dope... If you get my album, it's like *Peyton Place*. I mean, it will tell you exactly what I've been doing."

His romantic life had taken a new twist almost as soon as he had touched down in Los Angeles. Olivia Arias, a 25-year-old Californian of Mexican descent, was working as a secretary for Dark Horse. Harrison had spoken to her a few times on the phone and felt they had a rapport. Like him, she came from working-class roots – her mother was a seamstress; her father a dry-cleaner – and she had a taste for the spiritual while keeping her feet firmly on the ground. "I met Olivia before he did, while I was delivering some stuff to A&M," says Chris O'Dell, who was working on the tour. "He had told me about her. He had talked to her on the phone and he asked me to check her out and send him a Polaroid of her. To which I replied, 'Yeah, *right!*'" It was percussionist Emil Richards who made the first introduction. "I used to go in her office all the time," he says. "She would give me stickers for my trunks from all the great groups who had played at A&M. I went in one day and she said, 'You know I always do you favours, I always give you stickers, are you going to do something for me?' I said, 'What do you want?' She said, 'You've got to introduce me to George.' I said, 'Olivia, turn around and say hello to George, he's standing right behind you!' That's how they met. It's all my fault."

The connection was immediate. "I think I was a little surprised that it happened so quickly and so intensely," says O'Dell. "On the other hand, George had had his [astrological] chart done a couple of years before in California, and he was told he would meet a dark woman who would become an important woman in his life. I think at the time he thought that it would be an Indian woman. He told me that while he was still married to Pattie, and when he met Olivia I thought, Ah, he's met her!" Says Andy Newmark, "They went out that night, and never parted."

The new relationship inevitably drew some of his focus away from the tour. "George would stay up all night," says Robben Ford. "He had just fallen in love with Olivia, and they were just over the moon over each other. We would all show up for rehearsal at noon and he would show up around four! There was a lot of hanging out on the A&M lot. Then rehearsals would begin, and we would work into the evening. He was catering the whole thing with incredible Indian food, which we all loved, and after two weeks of that we basically hit the road."

★ ★ ★

The tour consisted of 45 dates in 26 cities, often with two concerts in one day. It involved an entourage of 71 people, a private plane, top class hotels and a travelling kitchen dispensing vegetarian and Indian food. At concerts Harrison had his own private dressing room with Indian rugs and bedspreads covering the walls and incense burning. The band shared another room.

It was a significant year on the concert circuit in North America. In the theatres David Bowie's *Diamond Dogs* tour was redefining the boundaries of what a dramatic rock show could achieve. Crosby, Stills, Nash & Young had just returned from a hugely lucrative stadium tour, and most significantly Bob Dylan had emerged from his bunker with The Band in tow, touring for the first time since 1966. Dylan was behaving himself, serving up an expertly programmed set which touched on all the significant bases of his career, heavy on the Sixties anthems, while still emitting a sense of danger and evolution. He was aware that there was a degree of contrivance to this. "I think I was just playing a role on that tour, I was playing Bob Dylan, and The Band were playing The Band," Dylan later said.[8]

Even an artist as wilful and unpredictable as Dylan was prepared to cut his cloth to fit the times after such a long lay-off. Harrison refused to do likewise. He wanted the show to be billed as "George Harrison and Ravi Shankar". Bill Graham talked him out of that, but the handsome programme, full of Krishna scripture and imagery and lavish biographies of all the musicians, made clear that this was a meeting of equals. "I even wanted the ads to read, 'Don't come if you don't like Indian music'," Harrison said. "I thought it would give people another kind of experience other than watching Led Zeppelin all their lives."[9]

An admirable sentiment, in many ways, but impossibly wilful in its refusal to consider the hard facts. This was the first solo tour of America by an ex-Beatle, and as such the narrative was bound to be dictated by the legacy of that band, as well as Harrison's own status as a star in his own right.

No doubt aware of this, his inclination was to subvert the notion of what The Beatles supposedly represented, and expose the pretensions of the entire rock and roll circus while he was at it. Intending to release a movie of the tour, he met with filmmaker David Acomba in Los Angeles. A director with a grounding in music television who had just won two gongs at the Canadian Film Awards, Acomba was recommended to Harrison by Bill Graham. He was looking to get out of rock and roll. Harrison could sympathise. Together they came up with an idea.

"I had decided no more music for me, I want to concentrate on drama, when a Beatle calls," says Acomba. "I flew down and he put me up at a hotel in LA, and I go over there in the morning and sit out by the pool. George comes out with his coffee and his white robe and he's coming around the pool at me, and it's like, 'Oh shit, it's a Beatle!' He was charming, a great sense of humour all the time. I did say, 'I'm not interested in regular music documentary films any more, I want to do something different.' I proposed filming one concert in this new, high definition video, where you could shoot and transfer to 35mm right away – and then do a satire of the music industry in between those numbers. He was good friends with Peter Sellers at the time, and the idea was to do a satire of the tour afterwards with comic actors. Spinal Tap before Spinal Tap. *Way* before. He just lit up. He said, 'Absolutely, let's do this!' It all made sense to him, the idea of breaking new ground both musically and filmically. 'It's not sacred, come on, it's not that important.' The first order of business was to shoot one concert, and we set everything up for The Forum in Los Angeles."

The Forum date fell nine days after the opening concert at the Pacific Coliseum in Vancouver, on Saturday November 2. "He was really nervous about it," says Robben Ford. "He was such an upbeat guy to be around, he was always laughing and telling stories and goofing, he liked to have a good time, so most of the time you wouldn't have known. We were on our way to the very first show, on the bus driving over to the gig, and at one point George says, 'So, do you think there's an audience for this sort of music?' It was so funny. That's when I realised he actually had some nerves about this."

With good cause. It was a difficult concept for many people to grasp. The Concert For Bangladesh had been one thing, but it was extraordinary to see a superstar – nay, a *Beatle* – cede so much time and space on stage to his supporting cast over the stretch of a two-month tour. Chris O'Dell recalls that "*Monty Python*'s 'The Lumberjack Song' was his theme throughout the tour. His booking-in name in the hotels was Jack Lumber, he kept singing that song and he played it on the PA before every show." He seemed to identify personally with the humble wood-chopper. "I'm the servant of the servant of the servant of the servant of the servant of Krishna," he said. "I'm just a grovelling lumberjack lucky to be a grain of dirt in creation. That's how I feel. Never been so humble in all my life."[10]

That attitude carried on to the stage. Billy Preston took the spotlight for three songs, Tom Scott held the reins for 'Tom Cat', and there were two instrumentals. Meanwhile, the Indian musicians had six songs, and Harrison made a huge fuss of Shankar, greeting him with a *pranum*, prostrating himself before the musician when he came on stage, and practically begging the crowd to "show a little patience."

It all amounted to a seemingly fatal lack of star quality. On that first night in Vancouver he followed the underwhelming opening instrumental, 'Hari's On Tour (Express)', with 'The Lord Loves The One (Who Loves The Lord)' and 'Who Can See It' from *Living In The Material World*. It wasn't until the fourth song that he threw the audience a bone with 'Something' and then 'While My Guitar Gently Weeps', but just as some momentum was building Billy Preston took a song, 'Will It Go Round In Circles', before Harrison sang 'Sue Me, Sue You Blues'.

Shankar and his ensemble then performed three songs: 'Zoon, Zoon, Zoon', played with the rock musicians, and 'Na Na Dahni' and 'Cheparte' without. Harrison returned to play 'For You Blue', 'Give Me Love (Give Me Peace On Earth)', 'Sound Stage Of Mind', a jam originated on the A&M lot, and 'In My Life', the John Lennon song from *Rubber Soul*, before Tom Scott was handed the spotlight for 'Tom Cat'. Then it was 'Maya Love', then Billy Preston on 'Outta Space', then 'Dark Horse', then Preston again on 'Nothing From Nothing', then 'What Is Life', then another Indian interlude for 'Anurag', 'I Am Missing You' and 'Dispute And Violence', the last two again accompanied by the rock and roll musicians. The show closed with an encore of 'My Sweet Lord', in an up-tempo arrangement which was more like an extended vamp, far closer to the gospel version on Billy Preston's *Encouraging Words* than the one familiar to the most of the crowd.

The band were tight and some of the Indian music was remarkable, but Harrison's voice was dead in the water, and remained so throughout the tour. "It was the winter, cold, and his voice was just a mess, even during rehearsals," says Robben Ford. "I don't think he quite knew how to take care of himself in that way. He was constantly hoarse and could barely sing most of the time. That was a little difficult for everyone. He had not being doing it, man, that was the only tour. He was obviously capable of it, but he wasn't ready for it. And he was obviously in an excessive phase, which didn't help his performance."

Indeed, a steady diet of the super-strength French cigarettes Disque Bleu, punctuated by regular doses of reefer and cocaine, was not the best way to mend a ragged throat. Then again, he had a lot on his plate. "He had recently split up with Pattie, he met Olivia, The Beatles were trying to sign their separation papers, Allen Klein was trying to sue him," says Acomba. "He had this incredible pressure. It was the first [US] tour by a Beatle and he had to rehearse the band, bring over the Indian musicians, he had just started Dark Horse record label and he had to attend to that, plus he was putting out an album to go with the tour. No wonder he didn't have a voice! His energy level was just drained every which way."

Aside from his vocal problems, it was immediately clear that the show as performed in Vancouver simply didn't work: the flow was all wrong. No sooner had one musician created some kind of forward motion than he would hand over to someone else. The second half in particular was a nightmare of momentum-burning jump-cuts. Half-way through the Vancouver concert "the continuity has gone," said *Melody Maker* reviewer Rob Geldof, better known these days as Sir Bob. "There's total disruption in its place." He also noted that "George's voice is shot" and found the band "limp".

And yet the crowd – and the critics – would have cut Harrison more slack had he not shown a stubborn refusal to honour past glories, or to at least pay lip service to some essentially benign, albeit fanciful, notion of who they wanted him to be. The show featured only three of his Beatles songs: 'Something', 'While My Guitar Gently Weeps' and 'For You Blue', as well as Lennon's 'In My Life'. No 'Here Comes The Sun', no

'Taxman', nor any sign of tracks which might have fitted in with the spirit of the show, such as 'Love You To', 'The Inner Light' or 'Within You Without You'.

Even these relatively meagre rations were only included after his friends and band members – including Shankar – urged him to consider the fact that people were paying money to see him and would arrive with certain expectations. At first, during rehearsals, "George didn't want to do 'Something' at all," Billy Preston said. "I knew he was gonna have to do it, and he started rebelling against it by doing it a different way, rewriting the lyrics."[11]

As Preston intimates, the sentiment of 'Something' was all but destroyed on the 1974 tour thanks to Harrison's lyrical reconstruction. "If there's something in the way, we move it," he rasped, adding, "Find yourself another lover – well, I did!" An oddly souped-up 'In My Life', now bordering on the funky, concluded "In my life, I love God more". 'While My Guitar Gently Weeps' became 'While My Guitar Gently Smiles', with various other disorientating lyrical augmentations. On the one hand, what else is live performance for if not to allow songs to continue evolving? Then again, it's a brave man who tinkers with the sacred text of The Beatles' back catalogue in order to have an awkward dig at his estranged wife and praise Krishna. Harrison didn't seem to care. He was either unable or unwilling to create a dramatic construct to use as an onstage persona. Instead, what you saw was what you got. "The image of my choice is not Beatle George," he said. "If they want to do that they can go and see Wings, then. Why live in the past? Be here now – and now, whether you like me or not, this is what I am."[12]

The Vancouver show led to a crisis meeting between the publicists, some of the musicians, and Bill Graham. "To Bill, the main reason people came was because George was a quarter of The Beatles, and he thought George should play more Beatle tunes," said Tom Scott. "But George would rather have less people come and have them be interested in what he wants to present to them. That's a dangerous, or risky attitude. It's not the most commercial approach you can take."[13]

By the second night in Seattle on November 4 (the matinee show was cancelled due to poor sales) both 'The Lord Loves The One (Who

Loves The Lord)' and 'Who Can See It' had been unceremoniously dumped, never to reappear. The Indian interlude was also unified into one half-hour mini-set nearer the beginning of the show, and 'What Is Life' joined 'My Sweet Lord' for the big finish. But these were relatively minor adjustments, albeit improvements, the kind which might take place at the start of any major tour as it finds it feet. Once the running order settled, there were still only four Beatles songs in the set; there were just four Harrison songs in the opening hour and only ten in the entire show, three of which were from *Dark Horse*, which would not be released until a week before the tour ended. The mighty *All Things Must Pass* was represented by just two tracks.

Ben Fong-Torres' damning *Rolling Stone* article on the tour, 'Lumbering In The Material World', has becomes the primary source for the historical view of the entire seven-week run. However, the piece did not come out until mid-December, when the tour was already heading down the home stretch. Although on November 12 Fong-Torres had filed a radio report for the Rolling Stone News Service, syndicated throughout the United States, in which he had critiqued the show, there was plenty of criticism from other reviewers. Many used Bob Dylan's recent outing as a point of comparison. "All I could think about was Dylan a few months ago, singing all his songs wrong for all the people who wanted to hear them the way they were used to hearing them," wrote Jeani Read in the *Vancouver Province*. "Because Harrison sang most of his songs wrong, too. Except the painful difference was that Dylan was in complete control of what he was doing. It was an extraordinary experience in image breaking, of personal integrity. And George – well, George didn't seem as if he knew what he was doing at all." Wrote Don Stanley in the *Vancouver Sun*, "He attempted to storm through the material, *a la* Dylan's recent magnificent tour, and ended up agonisingly hoarse."

As the tour moved south down the coast to California, only one of the eight concerts sold out. Reviewing the show at the Cow Palace in San Francisco, Phil Elwood of the *Examiner* wrote: "Never a strong singer, but a moving one, Harrison found that he had virtually no voice left and he had to croak his way through even the delicate 'Something'." That night Bill Graham, having failed to persuade his artist to relent even a little, sat up into the small hours and pondered what he, and a sizeable part of the crowds, were missing. The audience, he said, "would definitely have wanted more of George Harrison. I think what the public leaves with is a continuing respect and reverence for what he has done, and perhaps a feeling of bittersweetness about not having gotten just a bit closer to what their expectations were. I don't know. They didn't get to go back in the time machine enough."[14]

When the tour reached Los Angeles for three dates at the Forum on November 11 and 12, Robert Kemitz of the *Los Angeles Herald* lamented yet another desecration of 'Something': "Shouting the lyrics of a most tender ballad like a possessed Bob Dylan on an off night, you realized the voice was almost gone." Between shows at the Forum, Harrison finally relaxed his no-interview policy and spoke to Fong-Torres, who was embedded, like a thorn, in the early part of the tour. He responded directly to the specific question of whether he was reneging on some kind of contract with his fans by playing such a seemingly obtuse set. "You know, I didn't force you or anybody at gunpoint to come to see me," he said. "And I don't care if nobody comes to see me, [if] nobody ever buys another record of me. I don't give a shit, it doesn't matter to me, but I'm going to do what I feel within myself."[15]

Says Fong-Torres today: "He was very focused backstage, wanting to get across the points he did: that he had spiritual over showbiz priorities, and that he was answering only to one force. And it wasn't the audience, the media, or Bill Graham."

His mood onstage was sometimes no less abrasive. His attitude could swing between amusement and real contempt of the spectacle in which he was participating. At the Forum he told the crowd: "I don't know how it feels down there, but from up here you seem pretty dead." A little later in the set he responded to a shout for him to play 'Bangla Desh'. "Don't just *shout* Bangladesh, give them something to help," he said. "You can chant 'Krishna, Krishna, Krishna' and maybe you'll feel better. But if you just shout 'Bangladesh, Bangladesh, Bangladesh', it's not going to help anybody."

There were some parallels with Dylan's post-Christian conversion shows of the late Seventies, in which the harsh, unrelenting nature of the message tended to obscure everything else. He was also unashamedly evangelical about Indian music: "I'd die for it," he told the audience, and then gestured to his electric guitar, "but not for this." Many in the crowd responded positively to Shankar and his colleagues, but many more couldn't care less about Harrison's private passions. They had come to see a rock and roll show by a Beatle. "He underestimated [the reaction]," says Emil Richards. "Ravi was such a strong influence on him musically that he insisted that the Indian factions be there and be heard. It was a little touch and go on most of the tour because of that. People kept yelling 'rock and roll, rock and roll!' when Ravi came out."

Perhaps mercifully, the plan to film the Forum show was scrapped at the last moment, when it became apparent that his voice still wasn't going to be up to it. "He was taking tea and honey after every song, but he really needed rest, and he didn't have a chance to do that," says Richards. The extent of the problem would vary, with his vocals sounding better on some days than on others. At times it lent him a not unpleasant weathered blues edge, like a gruffer Eric Clapton; at others it recalled Dylan at his most belligerent; at his worst he was the human equivalent of a barking seal. And yet he wasn't going through the motions – each night he turned in a committed vocal performance, with Preston gamely covering for him on the high notes (and many of the others), essentially becoming a co-vocalist on 'What Is Life'.

Filming was rescheduled for Toronto on December 6. In the meantime, "George wanted to get the cameras out," says Acomba. "It may not be going the way we want it to, he said, but let's do it. I hired this great cinema-vérité guy, Rick Robertson, and we just followed him around as much as we could as all this was unfolding. It suddenly became a real life *A Hard Day's Night* for George. This really was not very much fun to watch. He was frustrated, he was trying to reconstruct the entire nature of the rock and roll tour, he wanted to change things and move things forward."

In this respect, the shorthand consensus that the tour was an unmitigated catastrophe is an inaccurate and an unfair one. The musical, if not the vocal, performances were generally superb – a "great band," says Richards, "all top players, everybody giving their all" – and the

Indian part of the show was often dazzling. Shankar recalls it as being "wonderful, very successful, it was a fantastic thing." At its best the combination of the music and the spectacle was indeed extraordinary. On 'Zoon Zoon Zoon' and 'Dispute And Violence' the stage flooded with sound and colour as more than 20 musicians from all over the world mixed funk, soul, R&B and Indian classical music. "When you see that now you realise what a groundbreaking musical event it was," says Acomba. "World music! It was ahead of its time, and I know there were fans who kept saying, 'It's not that bad! It's really pretty good.'"

Hundreds of thousands of people went away happy with what their $9.50 ticket had bought them, often content to simply be in the same room as a Beatle. There were times when Harrison was clearly enjoying himself too, taking out all the pressure of the day and releasing it in a joyous outpouring on stage. He was generally playful on a swinging 'For You Blue', opening the song with the name of the city they were in ("Here in Fort Worth, Texas, I love you..."). He would wink jokily at some of the screaming girls in the crowd, laugh and smile at their excitement. During Preston's set, he would join the organist on some comic formation high kicks. At the second show in Detroit the audience reaction was so strong that he had to come back out to say a second goodbye. Philadelphia was another memorable concert, with a ten-minute version of 'While My Guitar Gently Weeps' providing one of the musical highlights of the entire tour.

Harrison seemed in fine spirits on November 25, when he dropped in unannounced at KLOL–FM in Houston, talking unguardedly about Splinter, *Monty Python* and The Beatles' legal woes, and previewing 'Maya Love' from the as yet unreleased *Dark Horse* album. He carried around his beloved copy of *The Producers* on videocassette, watching it over and over again, quoting lines and making converts, and there was also the occasional opportunity for some light-hearted hi-jinks. "We would make each guy pay their dues," says Richards. "Willie Weeks was afraid of crabs and lobsters, and one night he got in his room and his bath tub was full of crabs and lobsters – live ones, crawling around. Everybody caught it. With George we filled his hotel room with Christmas trees. He couldn't even get into it."

Harrison would hang out with the band at dinner and on the plane after the show, but away from the concert halls he tended to hole up with Olivia, and perhaps Tom Scott or Billy Preston might join him. Now and again he would take part in some relaxed after-hours music-making. "One thing that was really cool was his guitar playing," says Robben Ford. "There was one evening when it was just George and I in his hotel room after the show, and he pulled out his guitar and his slide to play a song for me, and it was, like, wow! I got it way more than I did even out on the bandstand. There was this strength in this thing that he did that was powerful and really musical. That really made an impression on me."

On November 27, Jim Keltner joined the tour. Initially he had declined the offer, but he was finally persuaded by Harrison's promise of a Mercedes 450SL for his trouble. He already had a drummer, of course, in Andy Newmark, but Keltner's presence was as much about friendship as music, and his arrival coincided almost exactly with the blow of Shankar having to leave the tour for two weeks due to illness.

"I think George just needed moral support," says Newmark, who was nonetheless surprised by Keltner's arrival. "I didn't know anything about it. Ravi's nephew, Kumar [Shankar], just came up to me on the tour bus and told me, 'Jim will be joining us for the rest of the tour.' I said, 'Oh, right.' Jim was an important part of George's musical life [but] it came as a little bit of a knock to me when I heard. I certainly would have appreciated George talking to me. I would have preferred that and respected that more than the way the news came to me, from Ravi's nephew. I always prefer that a bandleader looks his players in the eyes and says, 'I'm not happy with this,' or whatever. And George *was* the bandleader: it was his show, he picked the players and called the shots. [Apart from that] he was pretty easy to read. What you saw was who he was. He was very straightforward. He seemed very open and honest with everyone. I didn't see any distance or disguise put on for the public. No star bullshit going on."

In Tulsa, another old friend, Leon Russell, joined him on stage for 'My Sweet Lord', and there were various cameos off stage to relieve the tedium of touring. Bob Dylan came to rehearsals – Harrison played him

'Dark Horse' – and also caught the show in Los Angeles, though the much rumoured collaboration on stage never happened. Peter Sellers jumped on the plane for a couple of days. At the Memphis show Steve Cropper and David Bowie came backstage.

He even met the President. Gerry Ford's son Jack was attending the Maryland show on December 13 and invited them to the White House for lunch beforehand. Harrison – wearing a garish hound's-tooth sports jacket festooned in badges – started telling the President about the time Muhammed Ali had carried The Beatles under his arms. "Somehow they got straight into that conversation," said Olivia Harrison. "Gerry Ford asked him what all the badges were, and he explained that one was Krishna, one was [Indian saint] Babaji, and another was the Om sign. Then Ford went to his desk and pulled out a badge that said WIN, which meant 'Whip Inflation Now'. So funny! George wore red handmade Tibetan boots, probably the first hint of any protest about Tibet. A sly political statement! He used to call the White House the Black and White House. He had Billy Preston and Willie Weeks on tour with him, and Ravi, and so of course he took them all with him." Harrison later said he felt "good vibes" emanating from Capitol Hill.

There was fun to be had, and some release, and more than a few fine, fiery gigs. Yet the pall of disappointment hung over the tour as it progressed and could not be shaken off, affecting everyone's mood. "Good reviews were very few and far between," says Ford, and while Chris O'Dell echoes the view of several of the musicians when she says "I don't think the reviews matched what we felt about the show," she adds, "I know they upset George tremendously and his confidence waned as it went on."

"We all read the reviews every morning, at breakfast, or on the plane," says Andy Newmark. "We were not shielded or in any kind of bubble. It was pulling him down. He would mention that he was really getting killed by the press. It was a difficult time for him, that tour. The press slammed him, he lost his voice, his wife had left him, and the shit was really hitting the fan. It seemed like the strain of all that was getting to him."

The spiritual life called for solitude and quiet, but touring is an essentially communal and very public enterprise. He disliked the noise, the crowds, the travel – although his regular gripe in later interviews about staying in "crummy hotels"[16] seemed to be plucked either from his imagination or from 1963; the 1974 tour was a thoroughly five-star affair. Yet the sense of physical frailty and mental dislocation he felt was very real, as was the memory of the nerve-shredding final days of touring as a Beatle. "George was *constantly* worried about being shot," says Acomba. "It was after Watergate, the Kennedys, Martin Luther King, and security wasn't great at these places. It could have happened at any time. That was another thing about touring and going out on stage." "I don't think he really wanted to do it in the first place and I don't think he enjoyed it," says O'Dell. "I think it cemented his thinking that being out there was too risky."

After the show at Long Beach he stayed behind and stared out at the "mountains of empty bottles of gin and bourbon and tequila and the brassieres and shoes and coats and trash," and wondered exactly what good he was contributing by being on the road.[17] He also felt the strain of being the man carrying the whole tour. "Very rarely did he just seem relaxed," says Ford. "He was completely likeable but, if anything, a little overwhelming. He was kind of always 'on' – like on 'ten' at all times. It was like he was talking to you rather than you were having a conversation. I think he might have felt that he had to perform in some way, because he was George Harrison."

He took refuge in the traditional pursuits available to any rock star on the road. "I remember him coming up to me one night and saying, 'I'm only going to get to heaven on Ravi's coattails, with this rock and roll life...'" says Acomba. "There were drugs around, the usual stuff. Spirituality helped him, but a lot of other self-medicating substances helped him too. Whatever gets you through the night. He was totally drained. He was a thin guy anyway, and when he lost his voice I don't know if he had the physical wherewithal to surmount that."

Robben Ford says Jim Keltner later told him that "George used to drink everybody under the table," while Newmark recalls that "we were all doing coke. That was what everyone was doing at that time, smoking weed and doing coke. George would do that with us sometimes, but it's not like the whole fuel of the tour was substances – it was just normal, that's what everyone was doing in that period. He never seemed excessive to me, and it would alternate between a few days when he would partake and then a period when he would be more on the spiritual thing. He meditated and had all the incense going, this prayer and that prayer, speaking Indian words. The whole shtick. He was seeking peace of mind and something to balance all that hysteria and Beatles stuff. His spiritual thing was real – he wanted to help people, he had a conscience. It wasn't clearly defined what his trip was, but he was just seeking the highest person within himself, his best self. He was totally serious about it. He would talk about it, and would sometimes expand on how it was affecting his life and his decisions. He was just trying to live his life and find some truth and reality. Within that, I don't think he had any conflict in his mind over whether getting high was against any kind of rule."

★ ★ ★

The tour ended in New York with three shows at Madison Square Garden, one on December 19 and two on December 20. Reaching the end of his period of estrangement from Yoko Ono, John Lennon, with his girlfriend May Pang, had joined Harrison and Olivia for dinner at the Plaza Hotel on December 14. "George was pretty weird" – in Lennon's estimation[18] – and came to the concert at Nassau Coliseum on nearby Long Island the following night. It gave Lennon the chance to form some conclusions about the show. They weren't markedly different from almost everybody else's. "I think he made a mistake on the tour," he said shortly afterwards. "One of the basic mistakes seemed to be that people wanted to hear the old stuff. George wasn't prepared to do that."[19]

At dinner the pair also agreed that Lennon would – reluctantly – join Harrison for a cameo during the first of his Madison Square Garden dates. Having appeared at the same venue with Elton John three weeks previously, he felt it would be "mean of me not to go on with George."[20] It was an auspicious time for them all. Four-and-a-half years after McCartney had belatedly confirmed their split, The Beatles had finally agreed on the terms of a separation document which would dissolve their partnership. Since Harrison, McCartney and Lennon were all in New York, the morning of December 19 was designated as the day they would put pen to paper. Documents had been flown over for Starr to sign in London.

At the last minute, however, May Pang called to say Lennon wouldn't be coming to the meeting because his astrologer had told him the date was ill-starred. Harrison screamed abuse down the phone. "George was absolutely livid," says Acomba. "I have footage of him on the phone but I didn't put it in the film." Having spent the preceding seven weeks doing his utmost to kill off any lingering misconceptions about Beatle George, he now wanted his demise confirmed in writing. As it was, Lennon finally signed on December 27, in Disneyworld, and on January 9, 1975, The Beatles partnership was officially dissolved in the High Court in London. Everything they had earned or would earn from their solo recordings after October 1974 was now entirely their own.

The uproar over the signing put paid to Lennon's appearance at Madison Square Garden. A disgruntled Harrison told him not to bother, informing May Pang: "I started the tour without him and I'll finish it without him."[21] At least McCartney attended the first New York show, disguised in an afro wig, aviator shades and a comedy moustache. The next day, at the final concert on the night of December 20, after 'In My Life', Harrison said, "Thank you! God bless John, Paul and Ringo, and all the other ex, ex, ex exes!" As the set reached its conclusion he settled a few more recent scores. Before 'What Is Life' he said, "for the last 50 gigs there have been those who've put us down. Some liked us, some didn't, some had too much ink in their pens. Well for everyone, this is it. It all comes out in the wash."

He prefaced 'My Sweet Lord' by saying, "I'm here to tell you the Lord is in your heart. After all, somebody's gotta tell you!" The song ended with the musicians, crew members, and even Denis O'Brien gathered together on stage. "I remember doing a line kick behind the band," says Ford. "Afterwards George gave gifts to everybody. To me he handed a drawing of a guitar, and he said, 'This is your Christmas present, Robben. It's being custom made by Gibson right now and it will be with you in a couple of months.' It was a beautiful big-bodied blonde Gibson with a single cutaway."

The end of tour party was held at the chic Hippopotamus Club. The band, entourage, friends and even a swiftly reconciled Lennon all attended. A reporter noted tartly that "a bottle of pharmaceutical cocaine travelled around the table. Harrison, who earlier that evening had lectured his Madison Square Garden crowd about the evils of drugs, did not seem to notice."[22]

★ ★ ★

The tour was a colourful tangle of contradictions which fascinated and baffled and frustrated even those who were involved in it. There was something heroically single-minded about Harrison's refusal to play safe, and parts of the show were innovative and genuinely progressive. To a greater extent he was simply following his heart. He loved these musicians, and the sounds they made, and he enjoyed performing with them. Conversely, he had no feel for songs that belonged to what he felt was another band and another lifetime. Yet his attempts to push the boundaries would surely have been more successful had he relented a little, and not been so maddeningly entrenched in his desire not to give the audience at least a little of what they came for.

On a personal level, he seemed to have undertaken the tour partly as a kind of test. Perhaps aware that it was easy to be pious in seclusion, going on the road required Harrison to throw himself out there among the sharks of temptation and all these "heavy duty people,"[23] pushing him to the extremes of his own comfort zone. After all, faith never tested isn't really faith at all. He confessed the experience often left him "wasted... sometimes I feel physically very frail".[24]

"On so many of these shows I've just about been able to stand up onstage, but the weaker I am the more I have to own up that personally as a human I just could not make it," he said at the end of the tour. "That's where my belief, my spiritual belief has become stronger and stronger, because the more I realise I can't do it, the more I get this surge of energy which upholds me. It's magic."[25] Was the tour a kind of prolonged spiritual firewalk? "I never met a more tortured person in my life," says David Acomba. "Never. Between the material world and this other quest, this was the whole dichotomy of the tour, back and forth, back and forth."

Above all it was an opportunity to at last face down the musical and personal legacy of The Beatles as their legal partnership finally ceased. Sidestepping nostalgia, doggedly focusing on the present, and playing his best loved songs under sufferance and seemingly purposely turning them into disappointments was the most direct means of ridding himself of all those perceptions and expectations held over from the Sixties – and to a degree it worked. For the next decade the press and particularly the public were increasingly content to all but ignore him and his music.

It was an extraordinary episode, a perfect storm of highs and lows which settled something in his mind. An account of it all still lies, mostly unseen, in the vaults. Acomba did, in the end, film the Toronto show, and later spliced it together with the off-stage documentary footage. He presented an edit of his tour movie to Harrison the following year, but "he didn't want to go ahead with anything," says Acomba. "He said the tour was such a drag for him and his voice was so bad he just couldn't face it. Dylan saw the rough cut of the film later on and apparently told George that it should never see the light of day. That was how down the whole period was. He wanted to move on."

In 2007 Acomba recut his director's copy, and screened it for Olivia Harrison. Brief excerpts surfaced in the 2011 Martin Scorsese documentary *Living In The Material World*, and he hopes the entire film may one day be available. "It's not really a piece of entertainment, it's a time capsule," he says. "It's a story of George and his music and George and the times he lived through. It was a pretty important period in his life, an amazing focus of different energies and crises coming at him. The film has a lot to say about all of that."

It is a valuable document of a moment that marked Harrison's retreat from the grand stage. He would never again throw himself into the fray with such abandon or conviction; his only other tour would be a carefully curated zip around Japan in 1991. It also seemed to crystallise his contempt for the whole childish charade of playing at being a rock star. "I'd rather be silly jumping up and down chanting Krishna than be silly jumping up and down with high-heeled mirrored boots on and eye make-up," he said in defence of the tour. "But there comes a time when you have to realise what life is all about."[26]

"He wanted a life," says Robben Ford. "And touring is not a life."

Be Here Now
Los Angeles, 1977

Every day of his life he is reminded that he is still a Beatle.

Late in 1976 Harrison ties his Dark Horse imprint to the Warner Brothers' wagon, stationed in the Hollywood Hills. Ever since he signed he has been "around the office a lot," says Ted Templeman, at the time senior vice-president of the label. "When he first came to Warner Brothers everyone was really flash, and wanted to see him, wanted to be in pictures with him. It was really intrusive. Being a Beatle still had a huge impact."

One day Templeman and Harrison walk into a Marie Callander's restaurant in Los Angeles. The entire room immediately falls silent. "I've been with a lot of celebrities, from Frank Sinatra on, and I'd never seen that effect before," says Templeman. "Good Lord, here was a Beatle! He could never be allowed to forget it. He told me often how fucking afraid he was in The Beatles, how he thought he was going to die. He had a terror of it, and that did affect him a bit over all."

Even at his lowest commercial and critical ebb, whatever else he is or is not, he is still a Beatle. Sometimes it seems like the worst of all possible worlds.

CHAPTER 13

Blow Away

After all the excitement, controversy, attention and acclaim, not to mention the unimagined success, Harrison's career in the mid-to-late Seventies can sometimes seem like *The Wizard Of Oz* in rewind; 1975 marks the moment when the story goes from vivid Technicolor to stark monochrome.

He released only three patchy albums of new material in the second half of the decade, played no shows, was the figurehead for no cause, wound back his spiritual pronouncements and scaled down his public appearances. Musically, there is a tendency to write off the entire period. Martin Scorsese's 210-minute documentary, *Living In The Material World*, makes no mention whatsoever of the records he made between 1975 and 1979. But while it is tempting to dismiss the albums as inconsequential – they are, unquestionably, largely insubstantial – certain tracks stand out: some for positive reasons, many others for the opposite. Much of it blends into an amorphous whole, a room full of bland aural wallpaper, but whatever else Harrison's songs lacked during this period – and they often lacked plenty: variety, vitality, *choruses* – as ever they did not shirk on honesty, and each one provides a window into a life that was changing slowly but significantly.

The more subdued second act of his solo music career was a backdrop to a time when he expanded his interests and plotted new paths. "He did films, he did books, he made records, he landscaped in three continents, he went to Formula One," Olivia Harrison later commented.[1] Money and lawyers, to almost steal a Warren Zevon song title, once again loomed large, but he also became a father, lost his own father, and married again. Life started to revolve around family and a fiercely protected sense of home. Those permitted past the gates at Friar Park became fewer, but once through the door they found a man essentially unchanged: amused, amusing, forthright, stubborn, increasingly cynical at the ways of the world but gradually developing a more comfortable sense of himself within it. It was a time where the musical possibilities narrowed, but life opened out.

★ ★ ★

After leaving New York for Hawaii to undergo post-tour decompression, one of the first things Harrison did was to write 'This Guitar (Can't Keep From Crying)'. Deliberately conceived as the sequel to 'While My Guitar Gently Weeps', a song which, after playing it live every night, he had come to realise was not just popular but beloved, it was also a direct response to "ignorant" criticism of the tour. It begins, however, with an assertion that he is happier now than he has ever been. He had very quickly fallen in love with Olivia Arias, a woman with her own spiritual agenda, although their methodology sometimes differed: she had an interest in the Indian teenage guru Prem Rawat, better known as Maharaj Ji, leader of the briefly popular Divine Light Mission in the early Seventies.

She shared Harrison's sense of humour and curiosity, and he felt immediately able to declare himself to her openly and honestly, without the need to hide his more disagreeable traits. "We just seemed like partners from the very beginning,"[2] said Olivia Harrison, telling me in 2009 that "I never even thought about the fact he was a Beatle. George was such a natural, warm and kind person, and so humble, that honestly when I met him it was just meeting A Person. He wasn't a Beatle at that time, and so I never saw that. I only ever saw the person, George. I don't think we'd have been together so long if it had been any other way."

Having started 'This Guitar (Can't Keep From Crying)' from a point of positivity, he spends the next four minutes battling with its opposite emotion. On the one hand, informing hardened hacks that he "responds much better to love" than hate displayed a rather touching willingness to reveal his thin skin; it was also somewhat bizarre, and only opened him up to further ridicule. His particular bugbear was with *Rolling Stone*, mentioned specifically in the song and in interviews at the time. The paper which lauded the Concert For Bangladesh with almost religious fervour had performed a brutal volte face. "This is what kills me now, is when I see the people... who supposedly loved me, and as I'm supposed to love them, and I see them – they're just dropping apart at the seams with hate," he said. "I'm talking about *Rolling Stone* actually."[3] He could understand criticism, but he simply couldn't understand the vitriol, much of which was indeed woundingly personal and out of proportion to the reality of the tour, and which spilled over into reviews of his new album.

He had headed straight to Hawaii with Olivia at the end of the tour, accompanied by Emil Richards and his wife. He may have been trying to get as far away as possible from the *Dark Horse* notices – they were by no means all unkind or negative, but the bad ones were downright vicious. Even a stronger album would have struggled to stand a chance given the context; as it was, *Dark Horse* was a middling contender, further fettered by the very enterprise intended to promote it. His new nemesis, *Rolling Stone*, called it "a disastrous album".[4] Bob Woffinden in an *NME* review which described the album – incorrectly – as "totally colourless," began by stating that "there's nothing more disappointing than finding one's teenage heroes crumbling ineluctably into middle-aged mediocrity. Hari Georgeson (as he often refers to himself) is on a more determined course than most. It is now beginning to seem as though everything he had to offer as a solo artist was crammed into the triple album *All Things Must Pass*."[5]

In fact any enduring interest in his third post-Beatles solo album, released in the US and UK in December, is attributable to its "colour", those moments of illicit drama which feel like pages torn from a diary. At other times the performances have a certain scuffed charm, but as a unified body of work it fails badly. Compare the utter mess that is 'Bye Bye Love', or the insipid orthodoxies of 'Maya Love' and 'Hari's On Tour (Express)' to the carefully constructed – if sombre – beauty of *Living In The Material World* and the decline is clear. Pit them against most of *All Things Must Pass* and it's almost shocking. There are some highlights: of the fleshbound tracks, 'So Sad' and 'Simply Shady' are lyrically candid and musically appealing. Of the despatches from the spiritual world, 'It Is 'He' (Jai Sri Krishna)' is too long but otherwise charming, and 'Far East Man' has a pleasing after-hours atmosphere.

Beneath the hoarse holler and over-busy arrangement of the title track there also lies a potential winner; it's a neat slice of personal myth-making. Who could fail to raise a smile at the image of Harrison "stepping out of the womb" and into the world? It's also one of the most nuanced self-portraits of a man generally getting away with much more mischief than he was letting on. "He wasn't wild," says Ted Templeman, who as a musician, producer and senior vice-president at Warner Brothers became close to Harrison in the late Seventies. "But he was kind of a sly guy, and he *loved* women. The whole thing about the quiet ones being the dangerous ones? That's true! But he was always careful, and careful of his privacy. He could be quite wary."

Overall, however, *Dark Horse* was sloppy and disjointed. Once again Bob Dylan loomed large, and again not to Harrison's benefit. Released a month after *Dark Horse*, *Blood On The Tracks* alchemised the emotional upheaval in Dylan's domestic life into a multi-layered allusive masterpiece; Harrison's recounting of Hard Times at Friar Park was, characteristically, far more blunt but also considerably less inspired. The hand-scrawled liner notes accentuated the sense of a private scrapbook made public. He mischievously credited Boyd and Clapton on 'Bye Bye Love', though in reality they were naturally nowhere to be heard, and next to the song title scribbled the words "Hello Los Angeles" and OHLIVHERE, references to his new girlfriend. The label on the record itself depicted close-ups of Harrison on Side A and Olivia on Side B. Things in that regard were moving fast, and he seemed keen to make the point that he had moved on.

Inside were pictures of Harrison looking like a raggedly dandified gentleman of the road, slouched on a bench and walking around Friar Park with Peter Sellers. The pair were nearing the end of the closest part of their friendship, which had begun in the Sixties, bonding over shared interests in Ravi Shankar, spiritualism and *The Producers*. The speech bubble in the picture – "Well Leo, what say we promenade through the park?" – is taken from the film. "Peter was a devoted hippie, a free soul," said Harrison. "When Peter was up, he was the funniest person you could ever imagine; so many voices and characters. But that was his problem: when he wasn't up he didn't know who he was supposed to be."[6]

The front cover was a *Monty Python*-esque distortion of an old class photo from the Liverpool Institute, with Harrison elevated to the top and his headmaster – "who never liked me anyway"[7] – in the centre with a target on his chest. All the other teachers sported colourful jumpers with spiritual signs on them; in the background were the Himalayas, and Babaji hovered over them all. The dark horse clearly hadn't forgotten his even darker schooldays.

Not merely the beginning of an artistic slide, *Dark Horse* marked the start of a rapid commercial decline. For once public and critical tastes concurred. It flopped spectacularly in the UK, failing to reach even the Top 60, a quite astonishing fall from favour. In the US advance orders made it a number four record, although sales quickly faded. The two singles, 'Ding Dong, Ding Dong' and 'Dark Horse' suffered a similar fate: number 38 and nowhere, respectively, in Britain; number 36 and 15 in America. This was to be the general pattern for his next few albums: at best mid-chart respectability in the States; near oblivion in his own country.

In the almost imperceptible way that these things often happen, by some common unspoken agreement it seemed simply to be his turn; it wasn't just the tour, the adverse reaction to which had been primarily confined to North America. Even in his own country Harrison was yesterday's news, a bit of an old bore who seemed incapable of saying anything meaningful about the world at large and the changes impacting upon it. The common view was that he was "someone whose universe is confined to himself."[8] And it's true that, increasingly through the Seventies, unless one harboured an urgent fascination with the soul of George Harrison (and plenty still did, particularly in the US, where the legacy of The Beatles retained greater cachet), there was little emotional or intellectual sustenance to be had from his records.

He returned to Friar Park in January still shaken. "When I got off the plane and back home, I went into the garden and I was so relieved," he said. "That was the nearest I got to a nervous breakdown. I couldn't even go into the house. I was a bit wound up."[9] Although in theory he was supposed to be beyond the need for outside affirmation and above swinging around in the rock and roll circus, he was deeply affected. He felt misunderstood, undervalued and personally attacked. "The flak about the tour was terrible," he said. "There are always people who don't like something, but on the average it wasn't a disaster. But the press clippings were unbelievable. By the time I got back to England people were saying, 'That's it, you're finished, man.' It was the worst thing I'd ever done in my life according to the papers. But really, there were moments of that show that were fantastic. So all the negativity about that was a bit depressing."[10]

As ever, the music directly reflected the mood of the man, which once more seemed to be in direct conflict. He was writing "four o'clock in the morning sorts of songs,"[11] naked pleas for compassion and understanding, alongside his most direct and unabashed love songs. On top of 'This Guitar (Can't Keep From Crying)' came 'World Of Stone', a track which sounded like the work of a very weary Elton John and on which he seemed, literally, lost. 'The Answer's At The End', another Harrison song which took its opening lines from the wisdom scrawled into the fabric of Friar Park – "a lot of my songs are off the wall," he joked[12] – reached out for tolerance and kindness. "You know my faults," he wrote. "Now let my foibles pass." 'Grey Cloudy Lies' had the weary roll of a funeral march and a lyric which spoke of utter depression – there was no attempt here at transcending to the astral plane; this was the sound of a man stuck in the psychic mire. "If people keep on at you long enough," he said, "chances are you will become depressed."[13]

The solution was to keep going. Within five months of releasing *Dark Horse* he was back in the studio. It might have seemed foolhardy to embark on the follow-up to a rushed album in similar haste, but there were some pressing reasons for doing so – although, tellingly, none of them were creative. Splinter, preparing to make their second album, *Harder To Live*, at A&M in Los Angeles following the moderate success of *The Place I Love*, had postponed their session at short notice due to illness. With the studio time booked and paid for, Harrison decided to step in. He was looking to write a new chapter quickly to erase the memory of the last, while also being acutely aware that this would be his final album for EMI and Capitol, and the sooner he got it out of the way the better.

He started recording *Extra Texture (Read All About It)* in late April and cut the basic tracks in a little over two weeks, with overdubbing continuing into the early summer. The musicians included Jim Keltner, Gary Wright, Klaus Voormann, Leon Russell, Carl Radle, Jesse Ed Davis, David Foster and Paul Stallworth. The result is Harrison's one and only LA studio record: slick, smooth, bereft of much in the way of personality, the kind of album where one can practically smell the white powder lined up along the amps. It is at heart a vanilla-flavoured soft-soul album, topped and tailed by two old songs. 'You' was another track retrieved from the 1971 Ronnie Spector sessions, and by far the most lively thing on the record. A barnstorming soul stomp which transmits some of the euphoria of new love, as the first single it at least gave some suggestion that Harrison was returning to the fray re-energised. Its tight, snappy guitar lick was also a timely reminder that he had, once upon a time, been one of the greatest and most economical riff writers.

The more revealing truth lay in the fact that the recording, his new vocal aside, was over four years old. 'His Name Is Legs (Ladies & Gentlemen)' was more recent, a hangover from the *Dark Horse* sessions, and a six-minute punchline in search of a gag. It was written in honour of 'Legs' Larry Smith, the playfully camp drummer with the Bonzo Dog Doo-Dah Band who had become a friend and amused Harrison with his "dinky doos" and "la-di-dahs". "I'm very partial to eccentrics," said

Harrison, adding, "It's the craziest song, both musically and lyrically."[14] Naturally, given this description, it could hardly fail to be a tedious in-joke. "He loved *Monty Python* and *Fawlty Towers*, he wanted to incorporate a bit of humour into his songs," says Ted Templeman. "He liked puns and double meanings, or double entendres." In person his penchant for silly word games seemed to delight those around him; on record the tortuous puns and dread wackiness almost always fell flat. The working title of *Extra Texture* was OHNOTHIMAGEN, a phrase which ended up captioning the inner sleeve photo of Harrison. Rather than giving the intended impression that he was one self-deprecating step ahead of the critics, it simply underlined his inability not to respond directly to slights.

Apart from 'You', an entirely misleading curtain raiser, there was scant evidence of Harrison as a lead guitarist on *Extra Texture*; instead he played a lot of Moog and Arp synth, inspired by Stevie Wonder's recent records. He seemed intent on making the blandest, most cravenly inoffensive record he possibly could. 'Ooh Baby (You Know That I Love You)' aimed for the universal simplicities of Smokey Robinson but was little more than a string of somnambulant vocal clichés laced along smooth, jazzy chords and mellow horns; 'Can't Stop Thinking About You' was similarly vaporous, written with Joe Cocker in mind and striving for that perfect storm of banality which sometimes brings a hit single. And on it went. Reining in the harsh bray of the previous year, he sang softly, close in to the microphone. It was so effective he was forced to insert a brief instrumental reprise of 'You' half-way through just to jolt the listener back into consciousness.

One of the better tracks was the bluesy 'Tired Of Midnight Blue', which told of participating in "naughtiness" in the back room of a Los Angeles club and suddenly being overcome by a wave of depression and self-disgust which made him wish he had stayed at home. There was a lot of excess, and it didn't help either his mood or the music. "I can get high like the rest of them, but it's actually low," he said. "The more dope you take, the lower you get, really."[15]

"It was a terrible time because I think there was a lot of cocaine going around, and that's when I got out of the picture," said Klaus Voormann, who was saddened to see the changes in someone he had known for 15 years. "I realised that it was the whole Hollywood thing – the problem was that if you wanted to stay in that scene, you had to hang out with those people, and go and do the clubs... George was in it too far at the time."[16]

It was noticeably a record on which any overt signs of spirituality had been removed, almost certainly consciously. The misgivings he had articulated to Prabhupada in 1973 – "I find that I'm getting people angry... I'm provoking a bad reaction" – had duly come to pass. *Extra Texture* wound down the proselytising in the music, as well as the symbolism in the packaging which surrounded it. 'World Of Stone' was far removed from the strident certainties of 'The Lord Loves The One (That Loves The Lord)' and its ilk, its underlying message being: "Don't follow me if you want to be a wise man".[17] It left a vacuum which he filled only with grey despair and mid-paced smooch. Harrison described it as an album with "a lot of spaces, deliberately."[18] He meant sonically, but there was something else missing too. Much of the heart and fire had left his music.

While in Los Angeles, he caught The Rolling Stones' residency at the LA Forum in July and saw Bob Marley & The Wailers three times during their five-night run at the Roxy Club. Back in Britain he publicised *Extra Texture*, released in early October, with a substantial interview in *Melody Maker* – optimistically titled 'George Bounces Back!' – and a long track-by-track conversation with Paul Gambaccini on Radio One's *Rockweek*.

He gamely talked it up but within a year he had dismissed *Extra Texture* as "a bit depressing, actually."[19] Few disagreed. He might have been wiser sitting out his blue period and biding his time. As it was, releasing *Dark Horse* and *Extra Texture* within ten months of each other knocked Harrison's career into the long grass for the next decade. For all the self-deprecation and heart-on-sleeve humility, the only thing that would have really changed people's perceptions in 1975 would have been an absolutely killer record – and this was very far from being one of those. "People who were never really keen on me just really hate my guts right now," he said. "It has become complete opposites, completely black and white."[20]

★ ★ ★

On January 26, 1976, The Beatles' contract with EMI, dating from the beginning of 1967, finally expired. Harrison opted not to re-sign, despite being offered "a great deal which was of more value, from a money point of view, and guarantees, than the one I took."[21] Instead he chose to move to Dark Horse, his own label, recording under the auspices of A&M. He announced these changes in January at the Midem music fair in Cannes, where he and his girlfriend were staying at the Carlton hotel. "We met up with Ringo there, and some friends," said Olivia Harrison. "It was a good time and a new time. He'd just left EMI and moved to A&M, and he was looking forward to feeling a little freer. It felt like a turning point."

It was a year which started with the promise of a clean break but gradually saw him ensnared in the problems of the past and beset by ill health. Shortly after leaving Cannes, Harrison sought to bring an end to the saga of 'My Sweet Lord', which had rumbled on for the past few years to no discernible conclusion. While he was in the south of France his legal team had made his best and final offer to Bright Tunes, offering a settlement of $148,000, which represented 40 per cent of the composer's and publisher's royalties for the song in the United States. For that sum, Harrison would retain copyright. Bright Tunes refused, demanding 75 per cent of worldwide earnings from the song *and* the surrender of its copyright.

The publishers might well have accepted Harrison's offer had Allen Klein not been making waves in the background. Already involved in litigation with The Beatles over commissions he claimed had not been paid while he was acting as their manager between 1969 and 1973, behind the scenes he was also now negotiating to buy Bright Tunes outright for his company, ABCKO, and in the meantime was feeding them invaluable inside information on the details of 'My Sweet Lord' royalties.

Assured of a more substantial payout, Bright Tunes resisted any offer of settlement from Harrison and the plagiarism case finally came to court in New York on February 23, 1976, some six years after it had first been filed. It was a thoroughly demeaning and demoralising affair for Harrison, observing his biggest solo hit, a song written in the spirit of love and intended only to praise, being stripped down to its prosaic nuts and bolts by lawyers and ethnomusicologists. The case centred on the construction of 'Motif A' and 'Motif B': the former constituted the notes that underpinned the "oh my lord" line, while the latter was the second melodic hook, comprising the "I really want to see you" section. How closely did these resemble parts of 'He's So Fine'?

Both sides called in expert witnesses. Harrison himself testified about his prior knowledge of The Chiffons' song, and was obliged to illustrate the writing process on his guitar. "It was the worst experience of my life," he said, "taking my guitar to court, trying to explain how I write a song."[22] Court staff from elsewhere in the building would come to gawp during their cigarette breaks.

At the end of three days' testimony Judge Richard Owen ruled that 'My Sweet Lord' did indeed infringe the copyright of 'He's So Fine'. He acknowledged certain modifications but concluded that "it was perfectly obvious... the two songs are virtually identical." In partial mitigation, he recognised that there was no deliberate intent to steal the song, and that the plagiarism had been "subconsciously accomplished," something which Harrison's legal team pointed out on appeal hardly sounded like plagiarism at all. This argument was dismissed and a date set for November 8 to determine damages. These were calculated using a tortuously complex formula which took into account such absolutes as performance royalties and sales of sheet music and folios, as well as more nebulous figures derived from mechanical royalties and the profits of Apple Records. There was also a truly subjective piece of accounting, used to determine to what extent the success of 'My Sweet Lord' had contributed to the sales of *All Things Must Pass*. In this respect in particular Harrison was hard done by: dismissing some of the "less-than-memorable" songs from the album, Judge Owen concluded that 50 per cent of the mechanical royalties earned by the album were solely down to the inclusion of one song, a remarkably high figure. In total, he adjudged that $1,599,987 of the revenue accrued from 'My Sweet Lord' was attributable to the music of 'He's So Fine', and was therefore owed to Bright Tunes.

At this point Klein's earlier intrusions backfired. With ABCKO finally buying Bright Tunes in 1978, Harrison's team successfully delayed the settlement by arguing that Klein had acted improperly in the case, changing horses in midstream and passing on private information, and that his intervention behind the scenes had prevented an amicable out of court settlement early in 1976. Once again, everything was put on hold. On February 19, 1981, the district court agreed with the main thrust of Harrison's appeal, and ruled that he would only have to give ABKCO $587,000 – the amount Klein had paid to purchase Bright Tunes – instead of the $1.6 million originally awarded. He would also, in an ironic twist, receive the rights to 'He's So Fine'. The debate over the finer details of this settlement crawled into the Nineties, and it was not finally concluded until March 1998, ending one of the most long-winded publishing legal cases in American history and one of the most debilitating experiences of Harrison's life.

At the time he tried to cling to the positives – "I know the motive behind writing the song in the first place and its effect far exceeded the legal hassle,"[23] he said – but its impact on his creative process cannot be discounted. "It's difficult to just start writing again after you've been through that," he told *Rolling Stone* in 1979. "Even now when I put the radio on, every tune I hear sounds like something else." He fantasised about inventing a computer that "I can just play any new song into... and [it] will say, 'Sorry' or, 'Yes, okay.' The last thing I want to do is keep spending my life in court."[24]

It took its toll. When *Monty Python*'s Michael Palin met Harrison in New York shortly after the case he noted that he looked tired and ill. After taking a holiday in the Virgin Islands to recuperate, Harrison returned to Friar Park to begin work on another new album, with Tom Scott assisting the production and familiar faces like Willie Weeks, Billy Preston and Emil Richards playing. The only new recruit was Alvin Taylor, the drummer in Billy Preston's band who was now playing with new Dark Horse signings, Chicago soul band Stairsteps. According to

Taylor, Harrison declared their album *Second Resurrection* "the greatest album of all time" and earmarked the drummer for the album sessions. "It was like no other experience," says Taylor. "We lived at the house and he was a perfect host, really concerned about your well-being, very considerate and extremely kind. He knew how to treat people and make them feel special, he did that with all the players. Most of the tracks were done in one, two or at most three takes. We worked from about 11 in the morning until four or five, recording the basic keyboards, guitar and bass parts."

The sessions started well. They were, recalls Emil Richards, "very informal, but we definitely went in there to work each day, and we did. He was very organised." Shortly after laying down the basic tracks work ground to a halt as Harrison fell sick. Initially he thought he had food poisoning, but as he lost even more weight, his skin became jaundiced and his energy levels depleted. He was diagnosed with the liver disease hepatitis B, a "culmination of all the monkey business I'd been doing. I think it was just the accumulation of those years when there was drugs in my life and those years of staying up all night and partying."[25]

Consulting Paramahansa Yogananda's book *Scientific Healing Affirmations*, Harrison at first tried to cure himself through the power of prayer. Mercifully he saw sense as his condition deteriorated – a conventional doctor ordered a course of vitamins and bed rest, and eventually Olivia persuaded him to visit Dr Yion Zu, an acupuncturist in Los Angeles. Given herbs to boil and eat each morning, he was gradually restored to health. No matter how he had contracted the virus, he acknowledged that "I needed the hepatitis to quit drinking."[26] He didn't quite embrace abstinence, but he did begin to take better care of himself: he cut out the more extreme lifestyle choices, started reading *KRSNA Book* and *Bhagavad Gita* more intently, and chanted with renewed vigour. In the summer he visited Prabhupada at Bhakivedanta Manor, the first time they had seen each other since 1974. He also reaffirmed his belief in the general goodness of TM. "[The Maharishi] was fantastic," he said, adding pointedly that "I admire him for being able, in spite of all the ridicule, to just keep on going."[27] At the end of

1976 he proclaimed he was feeling better than he had for nearly three years.

The illness delayed the completion of his new album, now titled *Thirty Three & 1/3* in reference to his age and the product itself. Contracted to deliver the master tapes to his new label no later than July 25, the deadline proved impossible: work hadn't begun at FPSHOT until late May, then he had fallen ill for nearly two months. When he travelled to Los Angeles with the album in September, he found himself being sued for $10 million by A&M for breach of contract. The late arrival of the new record was merely a pretext; the crux was A&M's desire to terminate its entire agreement with the Dark Horse label, which had not been the success everyone had hoped in the two years it had been running.

As well as records by Splinter and Ravi Shankar, Harrison had added to the roster Eastern-influenced Californian soft-rockers Jiva, ex-Wings guitarist Henry McCullough, Attitudes (a collection of LA session types which included David Foster, Danny Kortchmar and Jim Keltner) and Stairsteps and their bass player and singer, Keni Burke. Some of them made good records but none of them set the world alight. His signing policy for the label underlined a tendency to let his enthusiasm for the music of his friends run away with him. "He would do anything for Jimmy [Keltner]," says Danny Kortchmar. "Jimmy was his best friend and George was a very generous fellow." With A&M paying sizeable advances and liable for Dark Horse losses, and unable to offset these against substantial outgoings for Harrison's new solo deal, they were keen to get out of an agreement which still had three years left to run. Harrison's technical breach of contract, which under any other circumstances they would have been happy to accommodate, provided the perfect opportunity to try to force his hand to renegotiate more preferable terms. But he had signed with A&M at the start of the year "because of the relationship we were supposedly going to have, which it turned out we never did. And that was it. I couldn't live with that sort of situation, so I left. We backed the truck up to the office and filled it with our stuff and we were off."[28]

The two parties settled their differences without recourse to the courts this time, and Harrison immediately took Dark Horse, and his new record, across the Hollywood Hills to Warner Brothers. The album he delivered to his new label was a stronger, more focused piece of work from a stronger, more focused man. He gave it a committed promotional push, making videos for the two best songs. 'Crackerbox Palace' was a jaunty pop-reggae tune inspired by a story about the house of hipster comic Lord Buckley, which in Harrison's hands became symbolic of the absurdity of life itself. It had a sly Hamburg reference and, for once, a real chorus. The equally upbeat 'This Song' took a good-natured, tongue-in-cheek swipe at the 'My Sweet Lord' debacle, the references to copyright, experts and a 'Bright' tune underpinned by a bass line which sounded suspiciously like 'Rescue Me' by Fontella Bass (or was it, asked Eric Idle in a comedy interlude half-way through, 'Sugar Pie Honey Bunch'?).

It was, Harrison said, written to "exorcise the paranoia about songwriting that had started to build up in me."[29] "With each song he would give you a concept of what he was trying to convey," says Alvin Taylor. "He would sit in front of the fireplace with a 12-string guitar and sing the song, and share where the lyrics were coming from and why he was saying certain things. For 'This Song' he explained the whole court case. He was perturbed at the legal system and how ignorant and stupid judges and people in general could be, and that he had been sued for singing about his sweet lord."

Elsewhere, 'Woman Don't You Cry For Me', his 1969 bottleneck blues in open E, was turned into a funky disco strut, David Foster's clavinet driving it along. The cover of Cole Porter's 'True Love' was dead air, straying into the kind of schlocky territory more readily associated with Ringo Starr, although on the plus side it occasioned the return of Harrison's willowy slide guitar. There was also another anaemic Smokey Robinson tribute ('Pure Smokey') and two tracks dedicated to Yogananda: 'Dear One', another devotional song which left some ambiguity over whether the subject was a God or a girl, and the slight 'See Yourself', a strict instruction to greater self-awareness which he had begun in 1967.

Thirty Three & 1/3 was released in the last week of November. To promote it in the States, now by far his biggest market, Harrison undertook a five-city blitz and made a taped appearance on *Saturday Night Live* with Paul Simon which once again made one yearn for a little more simplicity in the presentation of his own music. In later years Tom Petty would tell Harrison as he strummed a guitar around the house, "I wish you would just put a mike up and let's tape you just like that."[30] His performance of 'Homeward Bound' and 'Here Comes The Sun' with Simon, each singing and playing acoustic guitars, made the same case: it was pure and true and easily trumped anything on his new record. Off camera, in front of the audience, the pair messed around with 'Rock Island Line', 'That's All Right', 'Yesterday', 'Bridge Over Troubled Water', and 'Bye Bye Love'. Paul Simon later remembered it as an "effortless collaboration. The mesh of his guitar and voice with my playing and singing gave our duet an ease and musicality that made me realise how intrinsic and subtle his contribution was to The Beatles' brilliant creative weave. He made musicians sound good without drawing attention to himself."[31]

Warner Brothers welcomed Harrison with a dinner at Chasen's on Hollywood Boulevard on November 17, and initially proved a nurturing environment for him. Bonded in friendship with president Mo Ostin and his partner Lenny Waronker, alongside Ted Templeman and staff producer Russ Titelman, Harrison "was around a lot," says Templeman. "He was a shy guy, very self-deprecating, very funny, but he loved to tell Beatle stories with people he trusted. There are things I wouldn't even repeat now, but he told me the day The Beatles was over for him was the day Lennon brought Yoko into the studio."

At the same time as Warner's was pushing *Thirty Three & 1/3* his former label EMI assembled a *Best Of George Harrison* album calculated not only to distract from his first release for his new label, but also to bluntly undermine his entire solo career. It was some ignominy, after having three number one albums between 1970 and 1973, to have to share space with his old band on what was billed as a solo *Best Of*. Harrison's songs for The Beatles made up side one, while his solo material was on the flip side, the former outnumbering the latter seven to six. With EMI ignoring his suggestions for a title and track listing, there was no 'Isn't It A Pity' or 'Deep Blue', no interesting album cuts or superior B-sides.

However aggravating, the evidence of *Best Of George Harrison* combined with *Thirty Three & 1/3* provided a timely reminder of Harrison's talents, both past and present, and resulted in some good reviews and a certain amount of critical kudos being clawed back. It made little difference commercially; the two *Thirty Three & 1/3* singles performed moderately well in the States, but the album was his first not to reach the Top 10. In Britain, the singles vanished and the album only just nudged into the Top 40. *Best Of George Harrison* fared even worse.

A generous interpretation of the failure of both albums would be to conclude that they each queered the pitch for the other; closer to the truth would be to say that few people were terribly interested in his music any more, regardless of its quality. At times he even seemed to share the opinion. "Is it a priority to go 'round the world being a rock and roll star?" Harrison asked rhetorically at the end of 1976. "That's what I'm saying. There's no time to lose, really, and there's gonna have to be a point where I've got to drag myself away and try and fulfil whatever I can."[32]

★ ★ ★

He was as good as his word. In 1977 he "never picked up a guitar, never even thought about it. And I didn't miss it."[33] This was true in spirit if not entirely accurate in reality; it was a year which saw the beginnings of Harrison becoming a part-time professional musician, a man with more pressing calls on his time.

The year began with a trip to India for the wedding of Ravi Shankar's nephew Kumar – Friar Park resident, close friend and sometime recording engineer. The Harrison-Shankar bond remained as tight as ever, and was now shared with his new partner. "I met Ravi not long after I met George... and they already had a history. Our family and their family were very close, and still are. It was a very important relationship for George, Ravi was a bit of a father to him.

304

Sometimes they were like brothers, sometimes father and son. They always played music together and were always discussing ideas about things they could do together. He always said, 'When I was with Ravi I met the best people, ate the best food, read the best books and heard the best music.' Ravi taught him so much, took him to temples and to visit Swamis, and they continued that relationship right up till the end. But it was an exchange – George protected Ravi, too, and looked after him. Ravi also wanted to know about things that George knew about: Cab Calloway, cars, anything."

From India, Harrison embarked on a quick promotional tour of Europe – making a brief visit to his old stamping ground, the Grosse Freiheit in Hamburg – during which he backtracked on previous announcements that he might tour in the summer. He and Olivia then travelled to Mexico. For all the far flung excursions, much of his life now centred on spending time in the garden at Friar Park, working alone, out of the reach of "phone calls, letters, accountants and lawyers," according to Olivia Harrison.[34] From its initial days of grand disrepair, the house and grounds had been transformed into a magnificent home with stunningly ornate gardens. Harrison's eldest brother Harry still manned the gatehouse, while Peter was part of an outdoor team headed by Maurice Milbourne, Harrison's gardener from Kinfauns. "I like gardens," Harrison said. "I like the pleasure they give you. It's like a meditation in a way – you can get everything out of your mind grovelling in the soil."[35]

Behind the gates, when inclined he entertained a diverse social mix: musician friends such as Ron Wood and Alvin Lee might rub shoulders with racing drivers, actors, comedians, Krishna devotees, while the occasional fan was still able to penetrate the sanctum to pose for photos – prior to John Lennon's death in 1980, security was not always particularly tight. "I once showed up at Friar Park and the gates were all open," says guitarist Chris Spedding. "I just barged in – George being George, he had all the gates and all the doors open. Anyone could have come in. I walked straight into the studio and set up my guitar and my amp, and I wasn't even supposed to be there, I was supposed to be playing with Ringo!" Other visitors included members of the *Monty*

Python team; his growing friendship with the troupe would shortly lead to an entirely new diversion in his life. For the time being, he enjoyed being on the fringes of a new gang.

Anyone who came to Friar Park was encouraged to contribute to the upkeep of the house, an almost Sisyphean task. "Everyone who went and stayed there worked on the garden, we'd go and weed the Matterhorn area, or clear up somewhere else," says Russ Titelman, producer of the *George Harrison* album. "It was all a reflection of who he was. It was a beautiful creation that he restored to what it was, and beyond."

There was a jukebox stuffed with early rock and roll and soul, a full-sized snooker table, his recording studio, a rehearsal space and a screening room. Occasionally he would venture through the gates and down the hill into Henley to drop into the local pub, the Row Barge; at the end of 1977 he even played a few tunes there for the regulars. Or he would order vast vegetarian meals from the local Chinese and Indian takeaways. But primarily Friar Park was a self-contained world which increasingly he could shape to his own specifications without having to leave. But at what cost? When *Monty Python*'s Michael Palin visited for the first time he encountered a genial host dispensing wine and "mind-bending delights", yet who seemed "cut off from everyday life by the wealth that's come his way."[36]

He was becoming equally detached from the recording industry. "There were certain types of music that were popular that puzzled him," says Ted Templeman. "They didn't compute, and I think he got a little intimidated. He liked the Doobie Brothers. He liked the idea, smoking a doobie, and he liked their records. He liked Little Feat."

Harrison had already struggled with the decade's taste for heavy rock and overtly theatrical artists: people who were hiding, or shouting, or dressing up on stage made no sense to him. When he met an enigmatic David Bowie backstage after his Memphis show on the 1974 tour Harrison had "pulled his hat off of his eyes and said, 'Let's have a look at you, then.' I think he looked dopey."[37] Now there was punk to contend with. He didn't relate on any level to its furious energy, although in essence it was not dissimilar to the spirit that drove The Beatles towards greatness in Hamburg 20 years earlier.

A "little curmudgeonly about what was going on," in the understated phrase of Russ Titelman, Harrison had become a parody of an out-of-touch, intolerant oldie. "I listen to Clapton, Elton John, Bob Dylan, those sort of people," he said. "I never liked those monotone kinds of yelling records. As far as musicianship goes, the punk bands were just rubbish – no finesse in the drumming, just a lot of noise and nothing." As for punk's righteous rage at social injustice, economic inequality and political complacency, he was unmoved, proclaiming that "you don't fight negativity with negativity. You have to overpower hatred with love, not more hatred. The only way you make more money is to work harder. Now that may be all right for me to say because I don't have to work in a factory, but it's true."[38]

His hair was now styled in a long, shaggy perm which made him look a little like the footballer Kevin Keegan – sporting a moustache and wearing casual flared trousers and sensible shoes, he appeared in his mid-thirties a walking embodiment of the generation gap. As if to confirm that he was living in a bubble, at the end of 1977 he wrote a song about racing drivers. Dedicated to Jackie Stewart and Niki Lauda, 'Faster' was ostensibly about the courage and skill of his Formula One friends, although it could also be read as a fable on fame, "about the Fab Four... jealousies and things like that."[39]

Cars had always been a passion, and one he now indulged more and more, at greater and greater speeds. "I had a lot of collectible Ferraris, and we talked a lot about those," says Ted Templeman. 1978 was the year of Grand Prix hopping, from the Monte Carlo rally to Long Beach to the British Formula One showpiece at Silverstone. Harrison was good friends with several of the drivers, inviting them to post-race get-togethers at Friar Park and spending time with the Scottish F1 champion Jackie Stewart and his family in Switzerland. He even persuaded Stewart to chauffeur him around Monaco racetrack in the video for 'Faster'. "Our closeness seemed to confirm the old saying that opposites attract," said Stewart. "While I like to organise my life with military precision, George took a more laid-back approach. There were times when we could have been living on different planets, when George was procrastinating and I would be all action, when he was wearing way-out clothes and I was traditionally dressed. But we were alike in paying fanatical attention to detail... He could be amazingly fastidious, keeping his cars immaculately clean, working on a song until it was so precisely right that it would sound as if it had evolved out of nothing, dreamily and effortlessly."[40]

Among a garage full of vehicles of all shapes, sizes and colours, some eye-wateringly expensive, some more modest, his current favourite run-around was a yellow Porsche, in which Russ Titelman had the dubious pleasure of being a passenger. "He liked driving *very* fast," says Titelman. "He scared the pants off me. He picked me up at the airport in his yellow Porsche, and he high-tailed it back to Friar Park, little country lanes, and I thought, I'm going to die. White knuckles. Then I finally thought to myself, This is a Beatle. I'm not going to die! He was a bit of a wild man, he had that other side. But he was also drawn to things, like F1, that required a high level of excellence."

'Faster' was a statement of renewed creative engagement, partly written out of embarrassment after "going to all these motor races, and everybody was... asking me if I was making a record... and yet musical thoughts were just a million miles away from my mind."[41] Alongside 'Blow Away', the other new song that arrived around the same time, it jump-started his creative juices. He spent much of the winter of 1977/78 in Hawaii, relaxing and writing. The islands, and in particular Hana, the most isolated part of Maui, became a regular retreat. "He loved Hawaii," said Templeman. "He said you get the feeling that you're high all the time." Within a couple of years he would have his own place there.

In January 1978 he arrived in Los Angeles to present demos of his new songs to Warner Brothers. Uncertain about where he fitted into the current musical landscape, he had decided to work with a co-producer on his next record. Ostin recommended Russ Titelman, who had produced or co-produced records by Ry Cooder, James Taylor and Randy Newman. "I guess he hadn't worked with someone whose job it was to be a producer since Phil [Spector]," says Titelman. "Yes, he did need a push sometimes. He lived in his own world [at Friar Park], and I think he knew that, too. He had the demos and he invited me over to his house in Benedict Canyon to listen. 'Blow Away' was on there and it sounded like a hit, and 'Love Comes To Everyone', which seemed like a pop record, 'Faster', and 'Not Guilty'. He had just the guitar part to 'Your Love Is Forever', no vocal, no lyric, but I was floored by it. I just thought it was the most beautiful thing, and I said, 'Look, you have to finish this song, we need this song for the record, so please write a lyric.' And he did."

He was willing to take advice about what his colleagues wanted to hear from a George Harrison record. At a meeting with Waronker, Titelman and Templeman, he asked a pointed question: 'Tell me what songs you've liked in the past, and what songs you didn't like. Give me a few ideas.' Templeman said he had a soft spot for 'Deep Blue', but had been put off by the downbeat subject matter. "I was plain matter-of-fact about stuff, because everybody else sucked up to the guy," says Templeman. "I used to tell him how great he was, but if he would just think about melody. I'd liked 'Deep Blue', but it was a depressing lyric for me, it was an awkward juxtaposition of happy chords and sad lyric – why not just have happy chords and a happy lyric? And he said, 'You always tell me what you really think, huh!' One time I told him that I thought Paul McCartney was one of the most talented musicians I had ever seen. I don't know if that rankled him, but he liked honesty. I would also say to him, 'You've written some great songs, and it's all about the songs.' Even the most famous people in the world sometimes need to be reminded that they are good."

Returning to Hawaii for two months, he dutifully wrote words to 'Love Comes To Everyone' and attempted to recapture the feel of 'Deep Blue' on 'Soft Hearted Hana', a play on the old Tin Pan Alley tune 'Hard Hearted Hannah'. Its mood was inspired by taking magic mushrooms on a hike with his friend, local restaurateur Bob Longhi. During his stay Stevie Nicks dropped in and helped out on 'Here Comes The Moon'. "We were writing a sort of parody of 'Here Comes The Sun'," she recalled. "Longhi was saying, 'You guys are writing about the moon instead of the sun,' and I said, 'That's because by then we were all such night birds.' We just hung out and wrote and sang and talked. I had been famous for not even quite three years and we were talking with George about being famous and what it meant and what you had to give up."[42]

He returned to Los Angeles with another new song, 'Dark Sweet Lady', written for Olivia, and recorded it with Titelman at Amigo studios as a test run for the album. With everyone happy with the results, work moved to Friar Park in the spring and summer of 1978. The core band was keyboard player Neil Larsen and old friends Willie Weeks and Andy Newmark, veterans of the 1974 tour, who were billeted down the hill at the Red Lion Hotel in Henley. "He was settled, much more into his gardening, and he seemed much more relaxed and peaceful than he had in 1974," says Newmark. "By comparison he seemed quite stressed then. I think he just wanted a simple life and to be happy. It was a little more businesslike, there wasn't much going on in [the drug] department." Titelman recalls that Harrison "was still into it a little bit, but not when we were working. He still smoked a bit, probably, and everybody was drinking. He was hysterical, very funny, little quips and puns."

They worked every day for a fortnight, mostly recording live, Harrison running through the songs until everyone picked them up. "We'd go in in a very workmanlike fashion," says Titelman. "It was methodical, and I would wait for those moments where he would say, 'Okay, I'll do a solo now,' and all of a sudden there would be this beautiful slide sound on something that before was just a *track*. He was very good at arranging and constructing his records. He played that down, but he had all his parts laid out, his guitar parts were constructions, completely."

After a break in the sessions they completed the overdubs. Steve Winwood contributed Moogs and harmonium and backing vocals, adding significant texture to the finished record, while string and horn parts were recorded at AIR Studios. Eric Clapton played on 'Love Comes To Everyone', and "came up to Friar Park with Pattie," says Titelman. "He [Clapton] was still drinking then, he was hitting it pretty hard. He came in and we were sitting in the kitchen drinking tea, Eric was having a cognac, but it was all perfectly fine. No tension."

Harrison's divorce from Boyd had gone through on June 9, 1977, and with Olivia becoming pregnant at the end of that year, they had planned to marry in May, several weeks before the birth. The date was rearranged, however, when Harold, Harrison's father, died of cancer the same month. In the end they were married on September 2, privately, at Henley-On-Thames Registry Office.*

Their son, Dhani – named after the sixth and seventh notes, Dha and Ni, in the Indian music scale – had been born a month before the wedding, on August 1. This tightly-drawn circle of new life, death and romantic union made more sense to Harrison than most, but within the context of a period of profound personal change the new album, called simply *George Harrison* and released in February 1979, was hardly destined to be a major event in anybody's life. A pleasant, well-crafted, highly melodic collection of songs about which it was hard to get excited one way or the other, its dreamy atmosphere was defined by the Roland chorus effect which Harrison applied to his guitar on several tracks. *George Harrison* was not only far removed from *Thirty Three And 1/3*; its polished sheen was light years away from rock music *per se*. As if to consciously confirm how far against the tide Harrison was swimming in a year which saw the release of Elvis Costello's *Armed Forces*, Talking Heads' *Fear Of Music*, The Clash's *London Calling*, AC/DC's *Highway To Hell*, Michael Jackson's *Off The Wall*, PIL's *Metal Box* and The Jam's *Setting Sons*, the liner notes contained credits for 'Hair' and 'Porsches'.

Titelman recalls that Harrison rarely mentioned The Beatles, although when the producer was absent-mindedly singing 'Getting Better' in the studio one day Harrison crept up behind him and said, "I sang *that* bit." Relations between the former members were now cordial but generally distant, and he was not averse to referencing the band in his music. *George Harrison* included not only 'Here Comes The Moon' but 'Not Guilty', resurrected from *The Beatles* sessions ten years earlier, and now mussed by soft-focus lighting and shorn of its rougher edges. "It was on the first demo reel I heard, and there was no discussion about The Beatles' version," says Titelman. "I'm glad we did it. It's kind of

---

* Earlier in the summer they had been the sole witnesses when Russ Titelman married his wife Carol at the same venue after a whirlwind romance.

quiet, there's no bombast to it, it's introspective sounding." The timing of the song's return may have been deliberate. There had been a rash of unsanctioned Beatles-related activity in recent years, including the Broadway musical *Beatlemania*, Robert Stigwood's awful film of *Sgt Pepper*, and Willy Russell's musical *John, Paul, George, Ringo...& Bert*. Harrison had seen the latter in 1975 and loathed it, while he was minded towards litigation when it came to the rest. The lyrically pointed 'Not Guilty' was a low-key protest against the nostalgia market which he felt made money from their past endeavours, fed the myth, and kept them all, to varying degrees, in their Beatle boxes.

The stand-out track was 'Blow Away', another Harrison song employing the weather as a metaphor for emotional change: this time the "clouds dispersed" and "rainbows appeared". It was partly about the burden of maintaining Friar Park, and partly a recognition that, left unchecked, his default setting often lent towards melancholy. In this regard 'Blow Away' expressed similar sentiments to 'Sour Milk Sea', a note-to-self about having to "fight for the right to be happy."[43] It is also, as Titelman says, a "great pop song, constructed in a perfect way. He'd say, 'Hmm, it's kind of a catchy little tune,' maybe a bit dismissively, but it got him back on the radio."

Indeed it did. 'Blow Away' remains one of Harrison's most fondly regarded later period songs, and reached number 16 in the US, although the UK again seemed stubbornly resistant to its charms. He made a video for 'Blow Away' and between a visit to the Brazilian Grand Prix undertook some light media duties for the album, but his heart wasn't in it. He declared himself "sick of the whole thing... the novelty's worn off. If I write a tune and people think it's nice then that's fine by me; but I hate having to compete and promote the thing."[44] Apart from continuing as a shop front for his own records, Dark Horse was now all but dormant, with all his signings released. "It was just too much bullshit," he said. "They think a record company is like a bank that they can go and draw money out of whenever they want... It was just too much of a problem."[45] "We had no conversation with George," says Splinter's Bill Elliott. "He was pretty elusive, and it just fizzled out."

The bitching and battles over his next record would only confirm Harrison's suspicions that he would rather be "turned off from the music business altogether."[46] He was not yet "turned off", but he was already turning away. His next major release was not a record at all, but a comedy film about a very naughty boy called Brian.

Be Here Now
Friar Park, December 9, 1980

As the news breaks worldwide of John Lennon's murder, the gates of Friar Park are chained tight and police summoned to keep the small crowd gathering outside in order. Inside, having already released a public statement to say that he is "shocked and stunned," George Harrison has decided to press ahead with the day's planned recording session for his new album *Somewhere In England*.

"It nearly got cancelled," says Dave Mattacks, who was drumming that day. "[Percussionist] Ray Cooper called and said, 'Have you heard? George isn't sure whether he wants to work or not, I'll give you a call in an hour or two.' Then he called again and said, 'He thinks it's the best thing to do under the circumstances', and off we went. He wanted to work to distract him."

Everyone is subdued and a little unfocused. Not much gets done. In the evening, after the session is finished, the musicians gather in the dining room. Olivia Harrison has cooked a meal; two-year-old Dhani is running around. As they eat and drink the talk finally turns to John Lennon. Old stories are dusted down, memories shared. Ray Cooper says that when you reach that level of fame you start to attract the real crazies. Harrison nods, then speaks.

"The thing I will never forget was George," says Mattacks. "He shrugged his shoulders and said, 'I just wanted to be in a band.' That was the phrase that got me. He said, 'Here we are, 20 years later, and some whack job has shot my mate. I just wanted to play guitar in a band'."

CHAPTER 14

Rough Cuts

It was, as Eric Idle is often fond of saying, "the most anyone has ever paid for a cinema ticket." Harrison's $4 million investment in *Monty Python's Life Of Brian* was one of his riskiest manoeuvres in the material world. In the medium term it paid off, not just financially but creatively, initiating a lively adventure which rejuvenated British movie-making in the Eighties. In the long term, however, the consequences of bankrolling a film company had severe personal and financial ramifications.

During his earliest film work, on *A Hard Day's Night, Help!, Magical Mystery Tour, Wonderwall* and the soul-freezing experience of *Let It Be,* it was not necessary for Harrison to get involved in the production process, although he was more hands-on when it came to the sometimes fraught business of overseeing the transfer of the *Concert For Bangladesh* from stage to screen. He loved films – one of his indulgences was to hire private copies of movies, often at great expense – and was close to several actors, including Peter Sellers and John Hurt. His eventual involvement at the sharp end of the industry stemmed not from any great desire to be a mogul, or an actor, or a director, but from a fan's wish to see the projects of his friends come to fruition.

Long before he stepped in to finance *Monty Python's Life Of Brian,*

Harrison had made philanthropic interventions in two smaller projects. He helped facilitate the limited release, in the United States, of *Raga*, Howard Worth's 1971 documentary of Ravi Shankar, after it ran into financial trouble. At his wit's end, Worth asked Harrison to view the rough footage when he was visiting New York. Harrison left the screening without a word but called the next morning. "He said, 'I have to apologise, I was so moved I couldn't talk to you'," Worth later recalled. He then offered to "finance the rest of the film, put out the album, and distribute it worldwide. He hugged me and that was it. We made the deal with a hug. It's never happened to me since."[1]

In 1974 Harrison was credited as producer on Stuart Cooper's cinematic adaptation of David Halliwell's 1966 play *Little Malcolm And His Struggle Against The Eunuchs*, released through Apple Films. "I definitely got the feeling that *Little Malcolm* may have been the first and last time George ever went to a play," said Cooper. "But he was a big, big fan of it and also a big fan of [its star] John Hurt, so he was in our corner already... He financed *Little Malcolm* through a company called Suba Films. It wasn't a big budget, somewhere around a million, million and a half pounds – not expensive. He financed it top to bottom. He stepped up, wrote the cheque, and we made the movie."[2] In 1974, *Little Malcolm* won the Silver Bear at the Berlin Film Festival.

Much the same course of events led to *Life Of Brian*, only on a larger scale and without the Apple safety net.

A fan of the *Goon Show*, Harrison gravitated towards a very English kind of humorous eccentricity designed to undercut the pomp and prattle of authority figures. He loved *Monty Python's Flying Circus* as soon as it first appeared on British television at the end of 1969. With its depictions of men of rank and education behaving ridiculously, its surreal visual jokes, cross-dressing, silly voices and heartfelt dedication to the art of the absurd, Python had an iconoclastic energy he instinctively embraced. He called it the only sane thing on television. He also recognised, said Olivia Harrison, that "there seemed to be parallels between *Python* and The Beatles, just different means of expression."

He became first a fan and then later friends with the comedy team in the mid-Seventies. Having played it over the PA every night on his

316

1974 tour, the following year he offered to produce a single of 'The Lumberjack Song', recorded at Workhouse Studios in London and mixed the next day at FPSHOT. *Monty Python* fired his imagination in a way that tending solely to his own creative life did not. "He was such an interesting man," says Russ Titelman. "If you think about his post-Beatles career, he was someone who loved making things happen. It [came from] him, it was his energy to get people to do things. He loved being part of a gang." Harrison was an endless source of crazy schemes, often wholly impractical – simply voicing them was usually sufficient sport in itself. When he began bombarding the Pythons with plans about what he and they could do together Michael Palin confessed to being "a little wary, especially when he told me he envisaged a Harrison-Python road show, with us doing really extraordinary things throughout the show, such as swinging out over the audience on wires... He's clearly an idealist."[3] Undeterred, on April 20, 1976, he joined their stage show in New York during its Broadway run, slipping into the Mountie chorus to sing 'The Lumberjack Song'. He did so anonymously, with short hair and his hat pulled down, and did not join the rest of the cast on the curtain call.

He grew closest to Palin and in particular Eric Idle. "He loved comedians, poor sick sad deranged lovable puppies that we are, because they, like him, had the ability to say the wrong thing at the right time," said Idle.[4] A musician, songwriter, sometime spiritual seeker and part-time hedonist, Idle was the member who most closely resembled a rock star. He had a nose for bullshit which sometimes seemed as overdeveloped and mildly paranoiac as Harrison's and, like him, was the odd one out in his group, in that he too wrote alone. The pair collaborated on 'The Pirate Song' for Idle's Python offshoot, *Rutland Weekend Television*, in which Harrison made a brief appearance as Pirate Bob, parodying his dour image by breaking off from 'My Sweet Lord' to sing the lusty sea shanty. "We both got shit-faced afterwards,"[5] said Idle, who a few months later directed two of the three videos for songs from *Thirty Three And 1/3*, both set in Friar Park: 'Crackerbox Palace' was a decidedly Python-friendly mix of cross-dressing, scantily-clad ladies, and Harrison's gurning attempt at screwball comedy. The less interesting 'True Love' was a soft-focus parody of Edwardian romance, all boaters and parasols.*

Harrison returned the favour by appearing in *All You Need Is Cash*, the 1978 mock-documentary featuring The Rutles, a pitch-perfect parody of The Beatles, co-directed and co-written by Idle. It was, in spirit, precisely the kind of irreverent romp he had originally planned to make with David Acomba on the 1974 tour; he became, characteristically, mildly obsessed with it. In the Warner Brothers offices in Hollywood in the late Seventies he "would come down and play *The Rutles* all the time," says Ted Templeman. "George loved it. He loved that part about the tight trousers – he'd play it over and over again and laugh."

He particularly appreciated the manner in which it deflated The Beatles myth and cut through the stifling air of veneration which still surrounded the band. "The Rutles sort of liberated me from The Beatles in a way," he said. "It was the only thing I saw of those Beatles television shows they made. It was actually the best, funniest and most scathing, but at the same time, it was done with the most love."[6] Harrison aided and abetted the caricature: he slipped Idle and his co-writer Neil Innes footage from the unreleased official documentary of the band, *The Long And Winding Road*, which Neil Aspinall had assembled in 1970, and appeared in a cameo role as a grey-haired TV reporter conducting an interview with The Rutles' press agent Eric Manchester (based entirely on the louche charm of Derek Taylor) outside the headquarters of Rootle Corps as the building is plundered behind him. Eventually even his microphone is stolen.

By 1978 the six members of the *Monty Python* team had regrouped to work on their second film, a satirical caper set at the time of Christ in which Brian Cohen, born in a stable a few doors along from the principal action, lives a parallel life to Jesus and ends up as a reluctant Messiah figure. At the eleventh hour of pre-production EMI Films withdrew all

---

* The last video, for 'This Song', Harrison directed himself. A courtroom farce satirising Harrison's recent travails, it featured cameos from Jim Keltner as the judge, Ron Wood as one of the female jurors and Tom Scott and the other musicians camouflaged among the public gallery.

their funding after their chief executive, Bernard Delfont, took fright at the script's potential to cause religious offense. Within a week Idle had approached Harrison to ask whether he could help. Within a month his manager Denis O'Brien had pulled together financing for the film through his company EuroAtlantic, borrowing £400,000 privately and a further £2 million from the bank, telling Harrison that they were both required to put forward their immediate assets as collateral. "We put our [EuroAtlantic] office building, my house, and all our bank accounts – like a pawn shop – into the hands of the bank that was going to loan us the money," Harrison said.[7]

It was a colossally risky move which contravened every basic rule of movie production, and also a tremendous act of faith. It was down to a mixture of sound creative instincts and sheer beginner's luck that the gamble paid off handsomely. *Life Of Brian*'s total US gross in 1979 was $19,398,164, and it was the fourth highest grossing film in Britain that year. Artistically, it was that rare thing: an instant classic. Harrison dropped in to the set in Tunisia for a 24-hour visit and ended up with a tiny cameo as Mr Papadopoulos in what could be described as the Biblical equivalent of the crowd scenes in *A Hard Day's Night*, where Brian is mobbed after being mistaken for the Messiah. He played, Palin recalled, "314th Jewish man in Kitchen."[8]

HandMade Films grew organically out of the film's triumph. "We paid back the loan," said Harrison. "And put anything left over into the next one."[9] Though the company was set up initially solely to keep the revenue of the film distinct from Harrison's other income streams, success writes its own narrative – one thing led to another. After *Life Of Brian* the company quickly picked up *The Long Good Friday*, a tough and terrific British gangster movie starring Bob Hoskins and Helen Mirren which was destined to be screened on television with numerous imposed cuts until HandMade stepped in to release it in its original form. They then gave the green light to their second production, Terry Gilliam's *Time Bandits*, which became a huge box office hit and helped put the company on a more even keel financially.

"The Pythons as individuals were all writing scripts," Harrison explained. "Terry Gilliam presented us with this brilliant idea, which turned into *Time Bandits*. Michael Palin had done a BBC-TV series, *Ripping Yarns*, a series of 30-minute films, and I once mentioned it to him that if he ever wanted to write a big *Ripping Yarn* it would be just great. So he did."[10] This was *The Missionary*, filmed in 1981 and directed by Richard Loncraine. "George said he wasn't really interested in movies, but it happened anyway," Olivia Harrison said. "It had a life of its own, it grew out of his friendships with various creative people."

In addition, and perhaps more significantly, "Denis got a bug for it."[11] It was Harrison's manager who actively pursued the idea of forming an independent film company: he saw various financial advantages and he undoubtedly liked the power and status it afforded. Officially registered in August 1980, HandMade squeezed into the EuroAtlantic offices at 26 Cadogan Square in London, where most of Harrison's business affairs were conducted. At its formation some observers noted that, despite his bruising run-ins with The Beatles and Allen Klein, he seemed willing to sign paperwork without bothering to drill down into the detail or assess the potential consequences. Then again nobody – the Pythons included – could follow O'Brien's head-spinningly complex tapestry of shelters, tax-loss schemes and off-shore companies based in Panama, Luxembourg, the Caymans, Switzerland and the Dutch Antilles. Harrison liked money but he didn't want to be bogged down in the minutiae. He put himself entirely in the hands of the lawyer who had straightened out his chaotic financial affairs following his split from Klein in 1973, and whom he now regarded as a good and trusted friend; O'Brien and his family were frequent visitors to Friar Park throughout the Seventies and Eighties. "George was part of my life for 20 years," recalls Kristen O'Brien, Denis O'Brien's daughter. "Just a nice guy who gave us birthday presents or let us listen to his latest songs in his studio."

As the name implied, at HandMade everything was taken care of in-house, from artwork to advertising, and everybody pitched in. Harrison asked Ray Cooper to be head of production, or as he put it, to "be me in the office."[12] Cooper was a dramatic rock percussionist by trade who had played on *George Harrison* and had become known in particular for his concert work with Elton John. He was also an intelligent, engaging and urbane polymath with fingers in lots of pies and connections in the theatre. Cooper became the living link between Cadogan Square and Friar Park: he would read scripts, take meetings, start the development ball rolling and alert Harrison to any great ideas or potential problems.

Cooper and O'Brien were the two pole stars of HandMade Films, one handling the artistic side, the other doing the deals, but Harrison's commitment to the vision of the artists he worked with, and good taste, did much to define its spirit. It is easy to overstate or romanticise his involvement. He was clear that he did not want it to become a job, and that he did want to be involved in the day-to-day hassles of making deals, fine-tuning dialogue, watching the budget and dealing with suicidal directors. He wanted it to be a creative diversion that would be rewarding and collaborative and bring interesting people into his orbit.

He visited sets, watched the rushes, and was not shy of voicing opinions. He "hated" [13] Alan Bennett's script for *A Private Function*, for example, and Bennett subsequently felt Harrison "was totally a united front with Denis O'Brien. There was no sense of fellow artists about it."[14] Harrison also clashed with Terry Gilliam over *Time Bandits*, in particular regarding the use of two of his songs, 'That Which I Have Lost' and 'Dream Away', in the opening and closing credits. He was wounded when Gilliam insisted on changing some words in the verses to 'Dream Away', and subsequently withdrew a little. Like The Beatles, the Python gang were one thing in public and quite another in private. Gilliam – who has sent many producers grey, and worse, over the years – was a bullish, proprietary director, and his absolute refusal to compromise made Harrison wary of getting overly involved again. Richard Loncraine, who directed *The Missionary*, scripted by and starring Michael Palin, recalls him mostly as a genial absentee landlord who "looked at the script, and the film, and made comments to Michael, who would certainly have listened to them."

"George was more like the friend, even though he had all the money," says Neil Jordan, the Oscar-winning Irish director who made *Mona Lisa* with HandMade. "He was such a terribly sweet man, incredibly supportive. Denis O'Brien was a different type – he was very anxious to play the Hollywood game. I had some arguments with him, but none with George, or Ray. I think Ray was George's voice in the movie. He was a musician, he understood the aesthetic business."

Dick Clement, who directed two HandMade films, *Bullshot* and *Water*, remembers Harrison as "a very, very nice guy. I dealt much more with Denis O'Brien. George did not emerge all the time, then occasionally he would come down from Olympus and enthuse. Denis also had a great enthusiasm which was very infectious, but other people had terrible battles with him and were very unhappy. Other directors have told me that they had quite a bit of trouble with him. I never had any trouble with him at all, actually – there was no interference and a lot of support, and George was part of that. I talked to Ray Cooper a lot and he saw an awful lot of George and he was right in the thick of HandMade."

Harrison loved Clement's 1983 comedy *Bullshot*, says the director, because it was "desperately silly." He wasn't so keen, personally, on Jordan's hard-hitting *Mona Lisa*, with its liberal use of extreme violence and exposed flesh. In both life and art, he had no stomach for the harsher aspects of social realism. "He would look at rushes at the start and he would look at several cuts of the finished film," says Jordan. "He came up several times. On the first day of shooting we were in a steam bath in London and Bob [Hoskins] walks through the pool, takes off his towel and jumps in. There are all these naked men and dangling bits, and George did ask that there wouldn't be too much nudity in the film. He was a very spiritual man, and he didn't want it to be too sleazy. That was the only thing he mentioned. He lived in this strange world, but he was quite an ordinary person. He wasn't like this billionaire type surrounded by minders, he was just a regular guy. Smoked like a trouper, and very funny. He got very excited one day about Bert Weedon. His absolute insistence was that to make great, great, *great* rock and roll you didn't need anything that wasn't in that *Play In A Day* book, which I thought was hilarious."

HandMade rapidly became a fully functioning film production company, and one of the best. They had a tremendous early run: *Life Of Brian*, *The Long Good Friday*, *Time Bandits*, *Mona Lisa* and the cult classic *Withnail And I* are all landmark British films; they worked with Nicolas

Roeg, Sean Connery, Michael Caine, Billy Connolly, John Turturro, Jodie Foster, Maggie Smith, Sean Penn and dozens more fine directors and actors. Harrison started to develop a niggling sense, however, that it had become something other than what he had originally intended it to be, which was simply an artist-friendly environment where his friends could make films. He saw the relationship between HandMade and *Monty Python* as essentially symbiotic; HandMade also produced the Python's 1982 film *Live At The Hollywood Bowl*. When the group left the company in 1983 to make *The Meaning Of Life* he was deeply saddened.

Into the mid–Eighties the sums grew, the schedules expanded, until there might be four or five films in production at once. Success brought greater stability, but the financial stakes became higher each time. "It's sort of frightening when you start a movie and you see all the people you're employing," Harrison said. "It's quite a big responsibility. If I was to think about that, I'd panic. I wouldn't want to be involved. I have a sort of kamikaze side to me that is optimistic, and in some ways I have to trust Denis' business sense and hope he's not going to bankrupt me... I just hope that Denis doesn't turn out to be a madman."[15]

★ ★ ★

HandMade was hardly a full-time job, but it's no coincidence that it was born and flourished during a period when his involvement with the music industry was becoming more distant and sporadic. The mixed blessing of being able to record at home meant that his records no longer had defined start and end points. "He had built his beautiful studio at Friar Park," says his friend, the bass player Herbie Flowers. "And I sometimes felt the act of building it was more fun than going in there to do some work."

The genesis of his next album, *Somewhere In England*, dated back to the autumn of 1979, but he was still working on it over a year later. He had delivered what he regarded as the finished version to Warner Brothers in September 1980, only for Mo Ostin to raise serious misgivings over four tracks: 'Tears Of The World', 'Sat Singing', 'Lay His Head', and 'Flying Hour'. Derek Taylor, then working for the company, was tasked with explaining to Harrison that the songs made the album too downbeat overall, and that furthermore, in a classic reading from the executive's hymn book, they couldn't smell a hit. After the modest success of 'Blow Away', expectations had clearly been artificially inflated. They also rejected the cover art, a black and white profile photograph of the artist with an aerial view of Great Britain – rather than England – attached to the back of his head.

Harrison was less than thrilled. "There was all this stuff they were telling me: 'Well, we like it, but we don't really hear a single'," he recalled. "And then other people were saying, 'Now, look, radio stations are having all these polls done in the street to find out what constitutes a hit single and they've decided a hit single is a song of love gained or lost directed at 14-to-20-year-olds.' And I said, 'Shit, what chance does that give me?'"[16]

His attempt to follow their advice resulted in 'Teardrops', one of the few songs in his catalogue which sounds like it was written to order through gritted teeth; the self-loathing is practically audible as he tries to adhere to the diktats of a musical age he neither liked nor understood.

He recorded 'Teardrops' after regrouping at FPSHOT in November 1980 with a new cast of musicians, including Herbie Flowers, keyboard player Mike Moran and drummer Dave Mattacks, with Ray Cooper now co-producing. To replace the tracks rejected by Warner's, he pulled in 'That Which I Have Lost', a breezy busk which, musically, called to mind 'Miss O'Dell', and 'Blood From A Clone', which deployed yet another of Harrison's blunt-force puns to attack the mindset which had insisted he should record these new songs in the first place. 'Blood From A Clone' lashed out against record company corporatism and the vapid state of music in general. "I think he felt sidelined by everything that was going on," says Dave Mattacks. "It was the rise of the machine, and there was a real sea change in popular music. Soft Cell, Depeche Mode, he felt that was all at the opposite end of the spectrum and he was railing against it. I don't think he was disillusioned, I just think he was sad about what he was going on around him. 'What am I doing? I don't feel a part of contemporary music.' The lyric was basically anti-machine, anti-manufactured pop star song."

'Blood From A Clone' confirmed that there are few things less appetising than a rock star complaining about his record company, especially when the song in question only reinforces their belief that the artist has indeed lost his way. "I remember around that time him grumbling about the records that were being made nowadays," says Chris Thomas. "It was really quite a negative side to him, and I'd never really seen that before. I don't know what it was, but he was obviously a bit unhappy. He didn't like the sort of stuff that was out at the time."

Changes notwithstanding (the rejected 'Tears Of The World' was, in fact, one of the stronger songs Harrison had available), *Somewhere In England* was a weak, rather ugly-sounding record. Aside from the asinine 'Teardrops', 'Life Itself' could have been a Cliff Richard song, while 'Save The World', a blackly comic catalogue of the world's many ills set incongruously to a jaunty cod-reggae beat, posited the solution that "God in your heart lives."

There were two songs by Hoagy Carmichael, whom he had loved since the days living at Arnold Grove, and about whom he still enthused with a passion he simply could not muster for any new artists. "He rang me up once and said, 'I've got this record on the way, I got you a copy as well, you gotta hear this record, it's great'," his friend and neighbour Joe Brown told me. "He didn't say what it was, but eventually I got it in the post and it was Hoagy Carmichael! He loved all that old stuff. It was George who sent me the original record with 'I'll See You In My Dreams' on it. Cliff Edwards his name was, he was known as Ukulele Ike, and he was the voice of Jiminy Cricket in *Pinocchio*."

He had never seemed quite so out of time.

★ ★ ★

It is a cruel irony that *Somewhere In England* was saved from the fate it probably deserved, and indeed gave him his biggest hit single in a decade, due to the murder of John Lennon on December 8, 1980.

Harrison first got word of Lennon's shooting in New York at the hands of Mark Chapman in the early hours of Tuesday, December 9. The news was conveyed at around 5 a.m. in a phone call from his sister, Louise, to Olivia, who immediately spoke to her husband. Half-awake, the situation seemed hazy and unclear, and he went back to sleep. "Maybe it was just a way of getting away from it," he later said.[17]

In the morning he fully absorbed the news that Lennon had been shot four times and killed instantly. One of The Beatles' oldest friends, Pete Shotton, arrived at Friar Park. Harrison talked on the phone to Ringo Starr, who was en route from the Bahamas to New York. Though he wasn't inclined to say anything at all, reluctantly, at Derek Taylor's gentle insistence, Harrison quickly released a statement to the press: "After all we went through together, I had and still have great love and respect for him. I am shocked and stunned. To rob life is the ultimate robbery in life. The perpetual encroachment on other people's space is taken to the limit with the use of a gun. It is an outrage that people can take other people's lives when they obviously haven't got their own lives in order."

It was, understandably, a slightly uncomfortable mix of words and sentiments. "Shocked and stunned" was a cliché which, consciously or otherwise, mimicked a phrase used to comedic effect in The Rutles. It also may not have been the most appropriate occasion to vent against the invasion of privacy, one of his recurring personal bugbears.

But it was what he felt. The death saddened him as much for its horrific violence and utter senselessness as for any deep feeling of personal loss. He and Lennon were estranged in their final years, both by distance and circumstance. On the handful of occasions when they saw each other after 1974, "I always got an overpowering feeling from him," Harrison said. "Almost a feeling that he wanted to say much more than he could, or than he did. You could see it in his eyes, but it was difficult... There was a lot of alienation between us... and then, after the years, when I saw John in New York, it was almost like he was crying out to tell me certain things or to renew things, relationships, but he wasn't able to, because of the situation he was in."[18]

In general, relations between the other ex-Beatles were good. At the occasion of Eric Clapton's marriage to Pattie Boyd in May 1979, Harrison, Starr and McCartney, joined by the groom, Mick Jagger, Denny Laine and Ginger Baker, had jammed drunkenly in an English country garden, just three friends making music again; although, according to Laine "it's lucky nobody made a tape. The music was rubbish, absolutely terrible."[19] But when Harrison made a series of trips to New York in 1979 to deal with the lawsuit Apple was filing against *Beatlemania*, he and Lennon had no contact. They hadn't seen or talked to each other for at least two years before his death. Publicly Harrison wondered, like everyone else, whether he was making any music. "I myself would be interested to know whether John still writes tunes and puts them on a cassette, or does he just forget all about music and not touch the guitar?"[20]

A further rift came when Harrison published his book, *I Me Mine*, in the summer of 1980. It comprised a brief, casual and often typically caustic autobiography, knocked into shape by Derek Taylor and enlivened by memorabilia and handwritten lyrics to most of Harrison's songs, with explanatory text on each and memories of their composition. Published by Genesis Publications, a British company that specialised in expensive, leather-bound limited editions, initially only 2,000 copies of *I Me Mine* were made available, selling for a little under £150. It was intended to be a work of art, something truly beautiful rather than a mass market money-spinner, but its price and exclusivity attracted some raised eyebrows. It was published in a more conventional format as a mainstream paperback in 1982 and again in 2002.

Lennon wasn't put off by the price but he was hurt by the contents. "My glaring omission in the book, my influence on his life is absolutely zilch and nil," he said in an interview with *Playboy* conducted a few months before his death. "Not mentioned. He remembers every two-bit sax player or guitarist he met in subsequent years, yet I'm not in the book."[21] This wasn't true. Lennon is mentioned several times in what is a generally erratic narrative, but the spat did underline the fact that everyone had moved on. *I Me Mine* was an account of Harrison's life and music, not a book about The Beatles – the two things were, he was keen to make clear, very different things. "He misread me," he said of Lennon. "He didn't realise how I was, and this was one of the main faults with John and Paul. They were so busy being John and Paul they failed to realise who else was around at the time."[22]

These were familiar fraternal skirmishes, hardly cataclysmic, and would no doubt have been patched up had time allowed. Andy Newmark, who was working with Lennon on his comeback album *Double Fantasy* just before he was shot, recalls that he was generally upbeat about The Beatles. "John loved the band and what they did, he had been apart from it long enough by then to separate himself from any petty bullshit. He reflected on it and you could tell he was proud of the music he made. His memories were very loving, and he liked George. He'd laugh and say, 'You know, George is just a frightened Catholic. God one day, coke the next.'"

The sense of real closeness, however, had been lost years ago and was irretrievable. Following Lennon's death, Harrison took solace in the fact that they had shared an understanding which transcended the trivialities of flesh and blood; he viewed their first acid trip together in 1965 as the start of an eternal connection, a time when "we saw beyond each other's physical bodies, you know? That's there permanently, whether he's in a physical body or not."[23] His death was just another state of transition – from Manhattan to who-knows-where – but the deeper bond would remain. *Somewhere In England* contained a dedication to "J.O.L" via the words of Krishna: "There was never a time when I did not exist, nor you. Nor will there be any future when we cease to be."

After a rather desultory session at FPSHOT on December 9 the musicians gathered around the dinner table. Harrison was angry and confused, but composed. "I'm sure he did his crying in private, but he wasn't breaking down or in tears or anything," says Dave Mattacks. "One could sense a deeper, grown-up acceptance of what had happened. One could feel a philosophical thing – the body is gone but the heart and the soul remain, I did pick up on that. We got talking about his own mortality and he said, 'Just give me a quiet burial and make sure I'm facing east.'" Interestingly, there was little material difference between Harrison's response to Lennon's death and the way he reacted when Brian Epstein had died over 13 years earlier, just as he was starting to formulate his spiritual beliefs: Lennon was only gone in the strictest physical sense, he believed. It's fine, it's okay.

As Lennon's songs filled the charts and Beatles music filled the air, Harrison considered his own response. He had originally written 'All Those Years Ago' for Ringo Starr to record. They had worked on the song in November at FPSHOT during the later sessions for *Somewhere In England*, but Starr didn't feel comfortable singing it. Harrison took it back and reworked the lyrics as a tribute to Lennon, referencing 'Imagine' and 'All You Need Is Love' and portraying his friend as a complex, misunderstood prophet ridiculed by an inhospitable world. Now he was in a better place, a "world of light". He asked Paul and Linda McCartney to sing backing vocals on the song, and in July 1981 'All Those Years Ago' reached number 13 in the UK charts and became a huge hit in the States, climbing to number two, his highest position since 'Give Me Love (Give Me Peace On Earth)' in 1973.

Having a global hit with a pleasant but mediocre song from a poor album was not indicative of a deep-rooted change in either his commercial or creative fortunes; it was a mere blip in a graph which had been on a steady downward descent since 1974. The irony that Harrison needed a Beatle, even a dead one, to get back into the Top 10 would not have escaped him. The follow up single, the dreaded 'Teardrops', failed to do any business at all, and his next album, *Gone Troppo*, released towards the end of 1982, was a commercial catastrophe. A record cut adrift from any reference point remotely relevant to 1982, it is the sound of a man making music with his friends entirely for his own amusement. Of historical interest at least is 'Circles', the song first heard on the Esher demos of 1968. He had tried recording it for *George Harrison*, but failed to get a version he liked. This time its rather wearying concentric structure and glum reflection on reincarnation concluded a record which failed to crack the Top 100 in America and in Britain disappeared without the faintest trace. The public ignored *Gone Troppo*, and so did Warner Brothers. Harrison duly followed suit. He chose not to do any promotion for the record at all.

★ ★ ★

Lennon's death inevitably altered his mindset. In the immediate aftermath he was almost impossible to reach. Says Ted Templeman, "After John died he just disappeared. Gone. And who the fuck wouldn't, right?"

"There's no doubt that the assassination of John made a huge difference to his morale and his whole attitude to the world," says Dick Clement.

"He became much more cautious after that." And not without cause. A matter of months after the murder, Harrison received a "credible" death threat from an American who phoned to say he had a gun and an air ticket and was on his way to kill him. A man was later arrested in Baltimore. For weeks Friar Park was crawling with policemen. When they left, there were private security men, and a personal bodyguard. "After John was shot, that's when things changed," said Michael Palin. "George became quite paranoid. He put barbed wire up around his house and retreated."[24] Friar Park gardener Colin Davis said that "he was always worried that somebody would try to kill him. He kept himself hidden and was even afraid to go for a walk in the garden."[25]

He began constructing his defences. The gates stayed locked; visits to the local pub, rare enough before, stopped; phone calls were screened by staff and then, beyond that first buffer, by his wife. If he went to the bathroom in a public place he might ask a friend to come and stand guard. For a substantial period there were no interviews, no official appearances, no promotion, and within a year he had taken on two new homes which seemed to perch on the very edge of the world itself. "George was always on a quest to get as far away as he could," Olivia Harrison said. "We found Hawaii and built a house there, but he wanted to keep going. We went to Tasmania, New Zealand, Australia. I had the feeling that he maxed the planet out, looking for solitude. It was about 'How far away can I get?'"[26]

The house in Hawaii was built on a 63-acre site in Nahiku along the steep, winding Hana Highway, overlooking the sea on a cliff top in the remotest part of Maui. "His place was really hard to get to," says Emil Richards, who was a frequent guest. "Especially if it rained – forget it. The one road was washed out. We were there two or three times a year with him, he was suddenly in Hawaii a lot. I had a place there on the other side [of Maui], and he would call me and say, 'What are you doing? Are you free right now? Okay, I'll have the helicopter pick you up in 20 minutes.'" The gardens which stretched down to the Pacific Ocean became a tropical twin to the grounds at Friar Park. "He brought trees in from all over the world, and flowers, and he wanted to plant a lot of the native trees on his land," says Richards. "He did all the work.

He had help but he laboured on that property like crazy." Says Neil Jordan: "He would plant things in his house in Henley and they would grow three inches, and then he would plant them in Hawaii and they would grow seven foot tall!"

His other bolthole was a six-acre lot on Hamilton Island in Australia's Whitsunday Islands, off the coast of Queensland, 1,000 miles due north of Sydney. The area was off the trail and underdeveloped, and had been recommended by Jackie Stewart. Harrison built a main house and three guest huts and called it Letsbeavenue. It was all wood, water and bamboo, surrounded by exotic animal life. He wrote the South Seas trifle 'Gone Troppo' there, a song born to be sung from a hammock, and which described the highlight of the local night life as "counting de fruit bat."

Increasingly throughout the Eighties, especially during the British winter, when he wasn't at Friar Park Harrison would be beyond easy reach at one of these properties. The veneer of reclusiveness, and the hints at retirement that grew as *Gone Troppo* drifted into the distance and no new music arrived in its wake, allowed him room to get on with his life. Often it was mundane. He would garden whenever and wherever he could, sometimes by moonlight so the imperfections blended into the shadows. He was a big fan of the American TV soap *Dallas* and would become a little testy if anyone called during the show. Music would tempt him out of doors, but not on stage – not yet. He went to see Ry Cooder and Simon & Garfunkel play, and met Bob Dylan during his residency at Earl's Court in the summer of 1981. "Bob asked him to sit in and he was, 'Oh no, I don't really want to do that'," recalls Dave Mattacks, who went with him to the concert. "It was a combination of shyness and... well, it must be very strange. It's like royalty, you fart and the world notices. He was very private."

Never party political in the mainstream sense – he showed definite right wing tendencies in several respects, but in general despaired of all politicians – he became more inclined towards grass roots activism. Fatherhood, too, no doubt gave him a more urgent perspective on the problems being handed on to the next generation. 'Save The World' had been an overt expression of his increasing sense that the earth was heading for disaster. "Sometimes I feel like I'm actually on the wrong planet," he said. "It's great when I'm in my garden, but the minute I go out the gate I think, 'What the hell am I doing here?'"[27]

He did go out of the gate, to march for Friends Of The Earth and for CND. He joined Greenpeace and invested in *Vole*, a magazine part funded by *Monty Python*'s Terry Jones and designed to highlight pressing ecological causes. Environmental issues, both global and local, were becoming a passion. He campaigned against the decision to close the only cinema in Henley-On-Thames, the Regal, to make way for a Waitrose supermarket. Protesting outside the building he told reporters that he wanted to "see the faces of these assassins" in the local planning office.[28]

He didn't want to remove himself from the world entirely, but he wanted the freedom to live in it on his own terms. His annual visits to the Chelsea Flower Show were decidedly low-key. He started taking helicopters to Brands Hatch for the Grand Prix. He declined a Freedom of the City Award from Liverpool. How he reacted to uninvited interaction depended on the place and his mood; he could be chatty and charming or overtly rude and abrasive. "George was a bit careful about his privacy," Joe Brown told me. "I just think he wanted to be a recluse, and he was a recluse, really." Olivia Harrison made the qualification that "he was only reclusive from the things we'd all like to escape from: traffic, pollution, noise, cities... but he nurtured friendships and his friends always felt they were close friends – they'd be surprised if they knew how much he thought about them."[29]

In Maui he became a well-liked fixture in the local community. He was a frequent visitor to the restaurant belonging to Bob Longhi, located on Front Street in Lahaina, and he made friends with neighbour Arnold Allencastre, a bulldozer operator who had helped clear the estate when he first bought it. The video for his 1988 single 'This Is Love' was shot at his house. "They used to go bulldozing together," said Olivia Harrison. "George really admired him." The Harrisons would often spend New Year's Eve at the Allencastres' home, playing guitars and ukuleles, singing and talking about their families. Music was a natural ice-breaker. "He got forced into the local community in Maui because he played the ukulele a lot," says Emil Richards. "He got into the community that way. He played all the time! He had his guitar in his hand all the time in the islands. Writing silly lyrics: 'Oh the IRS met the FBI...' and just on and on, it rhymed and made sense and was comical. He had things going all the time. I got to really respect that about him. He was a true musician, music was so important to him."

In Friar Park music was also the hub around which friendships revolved. The area was hardly short of jamming partners, often referred to collectively as the Henley Music Mafia: 'Legs' Larry Smith, Deep Purple's Jon Lord, Joe Brown, Mike Moran, session bassist Herbie Flowers, Irish blues guitarist Gary Moore, Ten Years After's Alvin Lee, Mott The Hoople and Bad Company guitarist Mick Ralphs and Rockpile's Dave Edmunds were among the regular guests who showed up at all hours. "We were always around one another's houses, playing guitars and ukes and God knows what else," said Brown. These were mostly wealthy men, now largely lacking in any great musical ambition, having unpretentious, unhurried, untaxing fun. "There would be Ray Cooper, Mike Moran, George's guitar tech, everyone," says Herbie Flowers. "Those times together were so convivial – he loved George Formby and absolutely loved the ukulele and the banjo. Some of the stuff we recorded, a lot of it must still be lying around in the cupboard. I once went to the house for Dhani's birthday in a Noddy outfit. I walked from the front gate all the way to the house dressed as Noddy. His whole life was completely beautiful. We would sit in the garden, tell silly jokes and lark about – it was heaven." It was an immersion in a very English kind of eccentricity, but also an extended diversion from serious work. He would often discuss "little projects he had in mind," says Flowers, while Palin recalled an idea for a musical "about a one-legged tap dancer."[30]

As time stretched out following Lennon's death, these sessions at Friar Park occasionally spilled into the public arena. Harrison would on rare occasions join the Pishill Artists, a loose collection of the Henley Music Mafia who would often play unannounced at the Crown Inn in nearby Pishill. He co-wrote two songs for Dick Clement's HandMade film *Water*, starring Michael Caine and Billy Connolly, and appeared with

Eric Clapton and Ringo Starr in the mocked-up concert for the film's finale, playing the revolutionary's anthem 'Freedom' and affectionately lampooning the Concert For Bangladesh. "That was a little coup, which we hoped would sell a few more tickets, although as often with these things it didn't make a lot of difference to the movie," says Clement. "It was a one-day shoot at Shepperton and he was quite shy, he didn't push himself forward." At the end of filming Harrison got his £40 fee in cash in a brown envelope. Further afield, on December 14, 1984 he joined Deep Purple on stage in Australia to jam 'Lucille', during a lengthy Antipodean trip to help Derek Taylor promote his book *Fifty Years Adrift (In An Open Necked Shirt),* also published by Genesis Publications.

As ever when the spotlight was diverted to friends, he was happy to use his Beatle superpowers to help. Live Aid, however, held at Wembley Stadium on July 13, 1985, was too large and exposed for him to seriously consider performing. The links between the event and the Concert For Bangladesh made Harrison an obvious choice to appear, but he was annoyed by the fact that there were attempts behind the scenes to get the remaining Beatles back together for the show. Harrison recalled that organiser Bob Geldof asked him to sing 'Let It Be' with McCartney "literally the day before the concert. And I don't know... well, I was jet-lagged for a start." In truth, he "didn't particularly want to go back into some situation that looked like the past. I don't want to be set up, put in a situation where I'm tricked into being a Beatle again."[31] He also wanted to make a point, whatever the cause: "Paul didn't want me to sing on it 10 years ago," he told Geldof. "Why does he want me now?"[32]

Underpinning these various prevarications was the fact that Harrison had no inclination to jump back on the treadmill at an event which would be watched live on television by two billion people. Those were scary figures. Beatle numbers.

Music remained integral to his life, but on a more intimate scale. "I've never stopped writing songs, and I've made hundreds of demos," he said.[32] He remained at heart a fan, and was often inspired to go into the studio at Friar Park after attending a concert. His lilting version of the classic ballad 'Let It Be Me', released in 2011 on the posthumous demos album *Early Takes Vol. 1*, was recorded by Harrison in the small hours after going to see The Everly Brothers reunion concert at the Royal Albert Hall on September 23, 1983. "He went back that night and decided to record an Everlys tribute on his own," says Giles Martin, who curated the *Early Takes* project. "He'd do things like that quite a lot. Very sweet. He was funny. I think he would often go into his studio and just record stuff and not be bothered about making a record. He used to wake Olivia up in the middle of the night because he wanted to do an overdub and he had no one to press the record button." He would record numerous Dylan songs for his own amusement: 'Abandoned Love', 'Every Grain Of Sand' or 'Mama You've Been On My Mind', often making elaborate overdubs and completing the track to releasable standard.

It was a Dylan song that finally marked a return to record-making. Dave Edmunds had been hired to produce the music for the soundtrack to *Porky's Revenge!*, the third in a series of dubious US high school sex comedies, and asked Harrison to provide a song. He chose 'I Don't Want To Do It', an obscurity dating back to the late Sixties which he had demoed acoustically during the *All Things Must Pass* sessions. "We recorded it in Record Plant in Los Angeles," says Chuck Leavell, who played organ on the song. "He was there for a couple of days, we did a few takes, and he was just fantastic. So sweet and engaging and down to earth." Though it did no business when it was released as a single in America in 1985, 'I Don't Want To Do It' was an encouraging piece of work: crisp, warm, direct, a million miles from the drifting dreaminess of *Gone Troppo*.

It signalled a gradual emergence from the musical shadows. Later that same year Dave Edmunds was again instrumental in persuading Harrison to play at a television tribute to his childhood hero Carl Perkins, joining a line-up that included Ringo Starr, Eric Clapton, Rosanne Cash and The Stray Cats. Harrison invited Perkins to Friar Park on the eve of the show, where they jammed for hours, and was a bag of nerves during the taping itself, but he got a huge kick out of it. Looking lean, enthused and animated, Harrison plugged back into the spirit of the Star Club as he sang and soloed, superbly, on 'Everybody's Trying To Be My Baby',

'Your True Love', 'Gone Gone Gone' and 'Whole Lotta Shakin' Goin'
On'. He was inching back into action.

★ ★ ★

At home, his son was growing up and turning into the spitting image of
his father. Dhani was enrolled at the local primary school, Badgemore
in Henley-On-Thames. Later he would be sent to the independent
Dolphin School nearby, and then to Shiplake College. He recalled the
day he became aware of who his father actually was. "I came home one
day from school after being chased by kids singing 'Yellow Submarine',
and I didn't understand why," Dhani said. "It just seemed surreal: why
are they singing that song to me? I came home and I freaked out on my
dad: 'Why didn't you tell me you were in The Beatles?' And he said, 'Oh,
sorry. Probably should have told you that.'"[34]

"Having a son was good for him," says Chris O'Dell, who remained
in touch. "But I don't know that it changed him that much. I think
he stayed pretty much the same." His was not an entirely cosy retreat
into fatherhood, domesticity and semi-retirement. His moods remained
unpredictable, and his sharp cynicism could be unexpected and
wounding. "He did become bitter about everything, which is a shame,"
says Chris Thomas. "I was conscious of that." Harrison had given
Thomas an acoustic guitar as a gift back in 1968 during the sessions for
The Beatles. Over a decade later, "I got a message from [engineer] Phil
MacDonald saying George wanted his guitar back. *What?* 'He wants his
guitar back.' I thought, Oh dear, that's a bit weird. What a strange thing
to do. Phil said, 'He'll give you some money for it.' I said, 'I don't want
any money for it!' You either give someone a present or you don't. He
was obviously not in a good space, which was a shame because he was
such a nice bloke, and funny. But he was obviously going through a sad
time."

Certain basic appetites also remained unchanged. Women were a
consistent source of intrigue. One industry friend recalls that on visits
to Los Angeles "George would usually call me on the way into town
and say, 'Is there any quim around?' He liked women, you know, and
there were always singers around or actresses from the studios." There

is a lurid published account of Harrison receiving oral sex from 'Liza' at a Hollywood party in the Eighties; he plays the ukulele throughout the entire encounter. On one foreign trip in the mid-Eighties he propositioned a famous, and married, young female television presenter. She was sitting on the floor with her back propped up against the legs of a friend, who recalls: "George said, 'Why are you sitting between his legs and not mine?' She said, 'Cos I love him.' And he said, 'But what's the use of being a Beatle if you're not going to fuck me?' She said, 'Well, John was always my favourite.' He said, 'Well he's not here so you best fuck me.'" Everyone was laughing, but as another friend points out, "the offer was definitely on the table."

His drinking could be heavy and his drug use fluctuated. Cocaine blew back into his life intermittently, while marijuana was an old and familiar friend. He gatecrashed the wedding of Slade drummer Don Powell and according to their roadie Graham Swinnerton "hid in the back and smoked joints."[35] The first time Neil Jordan met him, at a restaurant in Chelsea, "Ringo Starr came in and slipped him a little bit of dope."

During a rather sad and slightly drunken call from Sydney in the summer of 1985 Harrison told Michael Palin that he had given up all drugs and kicked (for now, in any case) cigarettes, but he had periods of indulgence much later than that. He told another old friend, Al Aronowitz, in the early Nineties that his excesses "got me to the point where I said, 'Jesus! I gotta do something here!'" The solution, he said, was meditation. "I had forgotten totally that that's what it was all about – to release the stress out of your system. And I got back into that. I do a double-dose now and it's like, say, whereas an alcoholic can't go through a day without going to AA or doing some kind of a program like that, for me it's the meditation program. In order to keep myself focused and keep the buoyancy, the energy, and also to realise that all this stuff that's going on is just bullshit."[36]

His spirituality had grown organically into an internalised and increasingly private affair. Prabhupada had died in 1977 but Harrison remained in contact with his friends in the Krishna movement, inviting them to Friar Park and visiting India in 1982 to see the construction of a new IKSCON temple in Mayapur. He chanted when he could but not obsessively, and while he still sung about his beliefs in songs such as 'Dear One', 'Life Itself' and 'Save The World', there was no evangelical cutting edge these days. It did not signify a lessening of intensity; simply a more pragmatic approach. "As the years have gone by I seem to have found myself more and more out on a limb as far as that kind of thing goes," he acknowledged. "I mean, even close friends of mine, they maybe don't want to talk about it."[37]

It had simply become part of who he was, and he seemed able to wear it more lightly. "As time went by he became so comfortable in his [spirituality] that it wasn't nearly so difficult to him as it was when he was younger," says O'Dell. At times his beliefs made everything, and everybody, seem almost comically insignificant. "One particular day I was late because the plane I was on was delayed," says Herbie Flowers. "When I got to the studio I said to George, 'Oh, I hate flying.' And George said, 'So what if it crashes? Who cares? Who do you think you are?' And I thought, Thank you George, you've hit the nail on the head! He didn't like flying much. He told me that the second before the plane landed he used to undo his safety belt. We laughed about that. I couldn't see the scientific advantage!"

Smoking was a vice which had taken nearly 30 years to conquer. Unfortunately, the experience of *Shanghai Surprise* made Harrison so stressed he started again. HandMade's first foray into the shark-infested waters of A-list American celebrity, the film starred husband-and-wife team Madonna and Sean Penn, arguably the most famous couple in the world in January 1986, when the lame screwball period comedy started shooting in Hong Kong.

Almost immediately word started filtering back to Cadogan Square that the actors, crew and director Jim Goddard were being abused and belittled by Penn in particular. "Penn and Madonna were being total bumholes," says Geoff Wonfor, who was on location directing the Making Of documentary, *HandMade In Hong Kong*. "They wouldn't let me film them and they wouldn't do an interview. Sean Penn said I was sending him 'negative waves'. I phoned George and said I was going to walk, there was nothing I could do. He was losing a lot of money, I had

e loved comedians because they, like him, had the ability to say the wrong thing at the right time." – Eric Idle. With Olivia, Idle and rry Gilliam, far right, at the premiere of *Monty Python And The Holy Grail*, Hollywood, July 1975. MIRRORPIX

e made musicians sound good without drawing attention to himself." – Paul Simon. Harrison and Simon in New York recording ngs for broadcast on *Saturday Night Live*, November 19, 1976. RICHARD E. AARON/REDFERNS

"He liked driving very fast. He was drawn to things, like Formula 1, that required a high level of excellence." – Russ Titelman. Harris[?] with his racing driver friends, including Jackie Stewart, far left, at the Spanish Grand Prix, May 8, 1977. PHIPPS/SUTTON IMAGES/CORL[?]

"There seemed to be parallels between Python and The Beatles, just different means of expression." – Olivia Harrison. Harrison appe[?] between Eric Idle and John Cleese for his brief cameo in the first HandMade film, *Monty Python's Life Of Brian*. IMAGE SHOT, 1979

eorge did not emerge all the time, then occasionally he would come down from Olympus and enthuse." – Dick Clement.
rrison performs at the end of Clement's 1985 HandMade film, *Water*, with Billy Connolly, Ringo Starr and Eric Clapton.
TORIAL PRESS LTD/ALAMY

eorge never lost sight that he was this kid who was very lucky
ho played guitar." – Lon Van Eaton. With Eric Clapton, right,
d childhood hero Carl Perkins, centre, 1985. MIRRORPIX

"I came home and I freaked out on my dad: 'Why didn't you tell me you were in The Beatles?'" – Dhani Harrison. Harrison with his wife and nine-year-old son at Friar Park, 1987. REX FEATURES

"I always thought of him as a musician, not a singer. That was my strong impression of George: how well he could play and how often he would put a guitar in his hand." – Emil Richards. Harrison at home with his guitar collection, 1987. RICHARD YOUNG/REX FEATURE

"George liked being in a band, and he was really so up for it. He really believed in it." – Jeff Lynne. With The Traveling Wilburys, 1988. PICTORIAL PRESS LTD/ALAMY

e disliked being in the public eye. I can remember some things ere George would say, 'God, I'm glad that's over'." – Herbie wers. Harrison and his wife Olivia appear on the Terry Wogan t show to promote the Romanian Angel Appeal, 1990. ARCHIVE/PRESS ASSOCIATION IMAGES

"I just hope that Denis doesn't turn out to be a madman." Harrison in the Eighties with his business manager and partner in HandMade Films, Denis O'Brien. HANDMADE FILMS PROMOTIONAL HANDOUT

here was no amicable interplay between them on stage at all. Eric had this block of ice around him. It was a strange vibe." – Steve rone. Harrison and Eric Clapton tour Japan, 1991. ROSS HALFIN

"Hallelujah, Hare Krishna, yeah, yeah, yeah: George Harrison!" Harrison, with Johnny Cash, Roger McGuinn, Bob Dylan and Donald 'Duck' Dunn, performing at Dylan's thirtieth anniversary concert in New York, October 16, 1992. KMAZUR/WIREIMAGE

"He had seen and completely understood his own mortality, and he was very comfortable with that." – Ken Scott. A reflective Harrison in the mid Nineties. MARTIN PHILBEY/REDFERNS

"I think the Concert For George closed a chapter for all of us. It a real connection, something we could give." – Tessa Niles. Oliv and Dhani Harrison attend a special screening in California of t Concert For George film, September 24, 2003.
FRAZER HARRISON/GETTY IMAGES

he degree of 'fame' officially bestowed on Harrison after his death would no doubt have amused him." Tom Petty, Jeff Lynne, Jim ltner, Paul McCartney, Olivia Harrison and Dhani Harrison at the unveiling of Harrison's star on the Hollywood Walk of Fame, s Angeles, April 14, 2009. MARK RALSTON/AFP/GETTY IMAGES

veryone who stayed at Friar Park worked on the garden. It was eflection of who he was, a beautiful creation." – Russ Titelman. ngo Starr and Olivia Harrison at 'A Garden For George' at the elsea Flower Show, May 19, 2008.
RIS JACKSON/GETTY IMAGES

"I have a son who needs a father, so I have to stick around for him as long as I can." Dhani Harrison performs on stage with his band Thenewno2 at Lollapalooza, Chicago, in 2012.
DANIEL BOCZARSKI/REDFERNS VIA GETTY IMAGES

"I have been convinced that George was one of the very few people I have ever met who was on a spiritual path." – John Barham. George Harrison in 1970. UPPA/PHOTOSHOT

a 19-man crew out there. They were also dreadful to Jim Goddard. It was dreadful to watch, actually, the manipulation."

Numerous tabloid headlines delighted in the trouble on set and the behaviour of the stars – it was damaging to the film, and to HandMade, and assuredly not what Harrison had got into film-making for. Finally he was forced to fly to Hong Kong to make peace. He felt he was being used as a pawn by both the HandMade money men and Madonna and Penn, and was angered to learn that there was so much banking on such an obviously poor piece of work. When the production moved to Shepperton in March he called a press conference in London in an attempt to draw a line under the episode. Madonna arrived an hour late; Penn didn't show at all. Again, Harrison was caught between a rock and a hard place: on one side the journalists, for whom he had nothing but contempt ("I did expect a certain amount of commotion from the press," he told then, "but I must admit I overestimated your intelligence..."); on the other, two people whom he felt obliged to publicly defend even though privately he despised their "star stuff: Penn is a pain in the ass [38]... and [Madonna] has to realise that you can be a fabulous person and humble as well."[39]

"That was the first time he'd really moved into Hollywood, and I think it was his last," says Wonfor. "It was terrible, they were dreadful – and the film! As he said, he was executive producer of one of the worst films to come out of Hollywood. It was a million miles outside his comfort zone, and George went through real nightmares with that. He was very committed to HandMade. He was meticulous."

It was indeed an awful film, which deservedly attracted stacks of mocking reviews and tanked at the box office. The budget was £17 million, a vast amount for HandMade. They were only saved from financial ruin because Denis O'Brien had presold the film to other territories, and thus ensured that the company had covered its outlay up front. But it had been a trial, and a risk, and for what? It was a portent of things to come. *Shanghai Surprise* was not the final act in Harrison's HandMade story but it was a turning point. *Withnail And I* aside, the films became less interesting, the hassles started mounting, and he became disillusioned and distanced from the process. In time, it would coalesce into a crisis.

Perhaps the only positive to be drawn from the experience was the music. Harrison wrote five pieces for the film: the vibrant Cab Calloway pastiche 'The Hottest Gong In Town', the eastern-flavoured title track, plus two ballads, 'Someplace Else' and 'Breath Away From Heaven', and the zippy big band throwback 'Zig Zag'. The original plan was for a soundtrack album to be released, but the failure of the film ensured that idea was quietly put to bed. It proved a blessing in disguise. The new songs gave him a head start on his first solo album in half a decade.

Be Here Now
Friar Park, September, 1987

George Harrison is back in business. His first album in five years is complete and will shortly be released to critical acclaim and platinum sales. A number one single is just around the corner. The scent of rejuvenation and success hangs over his career once more.

He is back in demand. Following the disappearing act of the past few years, Harrison consents to play his part in the promotional game. Today *Rolling Stone* magazine are at Friar Park to talk to him for a major feature. The interview with writer Anthony DeCurtis over, Harrison is now going through the rigmarole of being photographed for the cover. Sensing that he is not entirely entering into the spirit of the shoot – "I'm 44-years-old," he grumbles – the photographer's wife says playfully, "Don't you want to be on the cover of *Rolling Stone?*"

Harrison freezes. The camera shutter abruptly stops and the room falls into awkward silence. "Can I possibly tell you how little that means to me?" he says to everyone, including himself. "I've been on every magazine cover there is. I've been all over the world, and met every political and religious leader there is to meet, and none of them impressed me – let alone the world of pop music. The first person who ever impressed me was Ravi Shankar, because he helped show me a way beyond all that."

He pauses as if to digest the full ramifications of the question, and repeats it slowly. "'Don't I want to be on the cover of *Rolling Stone?*' I couldn't care less."[1]

CHAPTER 15

Travelling Man

"Everything gets easier," Harrison said in 1987. "I'm less worried about stuff."[1] An echo of that same, simple message is conveyed throughout the final album of original solo material he released in his lifetime, and also via the music he made with his superstar friends immediately afterwards. There is precious little dramatic tension or sense of struggle. He not only settled into a comfortable niche of tasteful, contemporary pop-rock, but for the first time in his solo career he was willing to explicitly reference the music he made with The Beatles. The songs are not without moments of disquiet or doubt, nor entirely free from condemnation, but the general spirit is upbeat, energised and positive. The eventual pay-off is a broadly even split between chugging blandness and joyful affirmation.

As the post-*Troppo* feeling of "what's the point?"[2] receded, Harrison returned to the spiritual notion that music was humanity's most direct expression of its better self – and for the first time since *George Harrison* he really gave that idea his full attention. He was also, crucially, willing to acknowledge external expectations, shaping his music to fit the times.

When he decided in the mid-Eighties that he wanted to record again, Harrison started looking for a partner who could enrich the experience, someone who "would understand me and my past, and have respect for that, who I have great respect for – and then I hit on Jeff Lynne."[3] It was an interesting choice. In his less charitable moments Harrison might easily have considered Lynne to be one of the legion of artists who had made hay from his reflected sunshine. As the creative force behind Electric Light Orchestra, Lynne was a craftsman whose lush, symphonic pop owed a considerable debt to The Beatles' recordings at the time of *Sgt Pepper* and *Magical Mystery Tour*. ELO's 1978 hit 'Mr Blue Sky' begins as an almost exact facsimile of the second section of 'A Day In The Life', while their use of strings, vocal harmony, humour and studio invention were highly evocative of Harrison's former band.

ELO bypassed punk completely and instead tied their sleek, tech-savvy aesthetic to the solid moorings of rock and roll classicism; little wonder that Harrison, with his love of "proper songs" with "good tunes", was seduced. 'Telephone Line' was a firm favourite on the jukebox at Friar Park long before he joined Lynne and the rest of the band in March 1986 for a surprise appearance at Heart Beat '86, one of many post-Live Aid charity concerts which had its roots in the Concert For Bangladesh. ELO drummer Bev Bevan had organised the event at the NEC in Birmingham in aid of the local children's hospital, and alongside the likes of Robert Plant and Denny Laine, Harrison turned up to lead the ensemble in an encore of 'Johnny B. Goode', with Jeff Lynne spurring him on to his right.

Dave Edmunds, who also appeared at Heart Beat '86 and had worked with Lynne on Edmunds' two most recent albums, facilitated the initial introduction, passing on the message that Harrison was interested in collaborating with the ELO front man. Inviting him to Friar Park, Harrison took Lynne for a spin in the boat around the lake, and sounded him out about a collaboration. The pair instantly hit it off. An upbeat, unaffected kind of rock star, Lynne's Birmingham accent is undiluted despite decades of LA living, and his sense of humour dry and mischievous. He was bloke-ish, without airs and graces – perfect for Harrison, who above all wanted his new music to be born of genuine friendship. He later said that he and Lynne "drank red wine [together] for a year and a half."[4]

"We got on great as luck would have it, it was like I'd known him forever," Lynne told me in 2012. "It was really easygoing. I went down to his house and he said, 'Do you want to come to the Grand Prix in Australia?' 'Yeah, I do actually!' So he said, 'Meet me in Hawaii in two weeks.'"

The visit, in late October 1986, "was a taste of things to come," said Lynne. "I met him in Hawaii and we flew off to Adelaide and got to the race in a helicopter. Into the middle of the track, into the pits, meeting all the teams. He knew them all. It was just magical. 'Wow, you can do anything with this guy – just go wherever you want!'" Being a Beatle remained the ultimate free pass. Steve Ferrone, who played drums for Harrison on his 1991 tour of Japan, recalls going to a Prince show at Wembley Arena with him. "We didn't have any tickets or anything," says Ferrone. "We got in this limousine to Wembley and George said to the driver, 'Just drive around to the back.' We slowly pull up to the two security guards at the gate, and they ask for credentials. George rolls down the window and says, 'It's okay, it's me!' And they said, 'Oh, okay, fine, park over there!' He looked at us with a little grin and said, 'It's good to play that Beatle card sometimes.' He didn't take it terribly seriously, but he was aware of the clout."

While in Australia Harrison and Lynne began their first collaboration for the new album. 'When We Was Fab', Lynne recalled, was "banged out on this old piano in this big old mansion in Australia, on an island off Queensland." On Hamilton Island Harrison "began the song on a little guitar someone loaned me... I got three or four chords into it when the string broke. We had to go to dinner but luckily there was a piano at the person's house where we went, so with people frying stuff in the background, we got on the piano and pursued three chords. They turned into the verse part."[5]

The song's working title was 'Aussie Fab', and when sessions began for the new album on January 5 at FPSHOT, now upgraded to a 24-track studio, it continued to evolve. More than any other track on what became *Cloud Nine*, 'When We Was Fab' captured the sea change in Harrison's mood and outlook. It didn't merely illustrate a new willingness to play around with The Beatles' myth and musical legacy; it also demonstrated a more open approach to recording. "Every so often we took the tape of 'Fab' out and overdubbed more, and it developed and took shape to where we wrote the words," Harrison said. "This was an odd experience for me; I've normally finished all of the songs I've done – with the exception of maybe a few words here and there – before I ever recorded them. But Jeff doesn't do that at all, he's making them up as he goes along."[6] Harrison was, encouragingly, "looking for a few new leaves to turn over."[7]

Lynne was a studio creature by inclination, never happier than when messing around with sounds and textures. Accustomed to shaping ELO records to his own precise specifications, he was a forceful presence who brought both enthusiasm and discipline, pushing Harrison to go the extra mile. "He's a craftsman, and he's got endless patience," said Harrison. "I tend to feel, 'Okay, that'll do', and go on, and Jeff'll still be thinking about how to tidy what's just been done."[8]

Not since Phil Spector had a producer influenced the sound of Harrison's music to such an overwhelming degree. "For me it was like, 'Now I'm back in a group'," he said. "We share responsibilities, we share ideas."[9] Lynne encouraged Harrison to put his guitar front and centre of the picture, with the result that his slide is prominent on over half of the songs on *Cloud Nine*, while his 12-string Rickenbacker is a key feature on several tracks. With this in mind, Harrison was "trying to write simple rockers."[10] Seeing Eurythmics at Wembley Arena shortly before starting work on the album made a strong impact. "I'd gotten into all these thick chord songs and I forgot, until I was watching the Eurythmics, how great that straight-from-the-gate force in rock rhythm is," he said. "I thought, 'God, I can do this!'"[11]

The pair played most of the music: Harrison on vocals, guitars and keyboards, Lynne on guitars, vocals, bass and keyboards. They were joined by the old gang: Ringo Starr and Jim Keltner on drums and Gary Wright on piano, and there were contributions from Eric Clapton, Ray Cooper and Jim Horn, as well as Elton John. The latter recalled "a lot of laughter... I remember staying up until eight o'clock in the morning recording and then asking him to play 'Here Comes The Sun'. And he did, and it was magical."[12]

The sessions were not continuous. Duane Eddy came to FPSHOT at the end of January 1987 to record two songs for his eponymous 1987 album, and in February Harrison was spotted at the Palomino Club in Los Angeles, where he gatecrashed a Taj Mahal concert alongside Bob Dylan, John Fogerty and Jesse Ed Davis. The usual staples were trotted out – 'Matchbox', 'Honey Don't', 'Blue Suede Shoes' and 'Peggy Sue' – while he and Dylan also had a shot at Dylan's 'Watching The River Flow'.

Despite these distractions, *Cloud Nine* was fast and happy work. Recording started in the first week of January and by August 25 Harrison was sitting in Mo Ostin's office at Warner Brothers' headquarters in Burbank with a mastered acetate of his first album in five years. Ostin, joined by Lenny Waronker, sat down with Harrison and listened through from start to finish.

They heard a clean, self-confident record with a strong, unified aesthetic. *Cloud Nine* was aimed at people who, like Harrison, had tired of what he regarded as the tyranny of computers and DX7s, the influence of which had turned the pop charts into "one big microchip... they're dehumanising music as they have with our cities and buildings."[13] He would grouch almost parodically about the rapper Tone-Loc ("Tone-Deaf more like...") and Kylie "Monologue". It was chastening to remember that he was still only 44. He was delighted that Dhani's favourite musicians were Chuck Berry, Jerry Lee Lewis and Little Richard.

The album's template sound was simple, direct rock and roll with a bright Eighties sheen – for all the grumbling about technology, the stabbing synth strings of 'This Is Love' time-stamps the music precisely, as does the bass and drum programming on several other tracks; the tinny, vacuous chorus of 'That's What It Takes'; and Lynne's signature dry, compressed drum sound which, following the success of *Cloud Nine*, seemed to spread all over the late Eighties like a rash.

Almost secondary to the prevailing air of renewed vigour, the songs themselves were a mixed bag. 'Got My Mind Set On You' was recorded spontaneously after Jim Keltner began playing a drum pattern which reminded Gary Wright of the old James Ray song which Harrison had bought on his first visit to the US in 1963. His version was a major overhaul, the loose, jazzy R&B of the original tightened up into a bright, syncopated rhythm track. 'Devil's Radio', inspired by a banner outside a church near Dhani's school, took aim at gossip-mongers and the press. "You wonder why I don't hang out much," he sings. "I wonder how you can't see." 'The Wreck Of The Hesperus' had a similar drive and a similar theme, veering off from Harrison's amusingly spirited stand against the onset of middle age to rail at "poison penmen" who "make up lies" and forced him to get "out of the line of fire".

The sound was pleasant, energetic, upbeat. Jeff Lynne knew how to shape a song for the radio, and had also steered Harrison, who was, lest anyone forget, a former member of the most famous pop group of all time, back towards his more accessible instincts as a writer. *Cloud Nine* was rarely terribly substantial, however, and at times Harrison's personality seemed to have been surgically removed, not least on the title track, a generic piece of throbbing minor-key blues-rock which would have sounded equally at home on an album by Eric Clapton – whose guitar is all over it – or Gary Moore.

The three ballads offered more heart and gravitas. 'Just For Today', an empathetic song about addiction, draws from the same deep well of exquisite sadness as 'Who Can See It' from *Living In The Material World*. Harrison also retooled two tracks from *Shanghai Surprise*. 'Someplace Else' is a stately song with a bittersweet slide hook about the inevitability of losing the ones we love. 'Breath Away From Heaven' is full of space and stillness, its Oriental motif betraying its origins. As it had 20 years before with *Wonderwall*, writing for film seemed to free Harrison. On 'Breath Away From Heaven' he wrote, unusually, entirely outside of his own experience, adopting a dramatic persona. The rich, poetic imagery and lack of autobiographical weight seems to make the song float on air.

'When We Was Fab' illustrates precisely what Lynne brought to the table, both positive and negative. The credits include humour, sonic innovation and a sure, modern pop touch – it was certainly Harrison's most inventive sounding single for many a year. On the other hand, Lynne allowed his rampant Beatle fandom to lurch unchecked into parody: the sawing cellos, the 'I Am The Walrus' whoops, the sitar coda and Ringo Starr's trademark drum fills are the sound of a man living out his fantasies with the added bonus of a real, live Beatle in tow. The video featured Harrison in a *Sgt. Pepper* suit, Starr playing the fool, and a man in a walrus costume who, Harrison claimed mischievously, might be Paul McCartney, a bit of sport on which McCartney swiftly poured cold water.

Though nothing comes quite so heavily freighted with resonance, 'When We Was Fab' is far from the only Beatles reference on the album. The 12-string Rickenbacker on two of its breezier pop songs, 'Fish On The Sand' and 'This Is Love', could have come straight off of *A Hard Day's Night*. Harrison had, not atypically, gone from one extreme to the other. Some found it a little rich that a man who had spent the past two decades aggressively distancing himself from The Beatles at every opportunity now seemed to want to dive in with both feet. As if to underline his reconciliation, before the album was released Harrison played smooth versions of 'While My Guitar Gently Weeps' and 'Here Comes The Sun' – "my two cute songs"[14] – at the Prince's Trust gala concerts at Wembley Arena on June 5 and 6, and joined in on Starr's rendition of 'With A Little Help From My Friends'. It was the first time he had played anything other than old rock and roll songs in public since his *Saturday Night Live* appearance over a decade before.

On the cover of *Cloud Nine* Harrison cradled his old Gretsch Duo Jet, the guitar he bought in 1961, but everything else had had a modern make-over. The font, the shirt, the *teeth*, the backdrop and the shimmering shades are all quintessentially Eighties. Gered Mankowitz, who shot the *Cloud Nine* photographs at his studio in Hampstead, recalls that Harrison happily participated in what people were now calling 'concepts'. "He was very sweet, very supportive of the whole idea – those big sky backgrounds, everything being very 'up' and slightly zany," says Mankowitz. "The whole vibe at the time was very 'up'. He was really pleased with the album, he brought a rough mix and played it to us."

Within two months of playing the newly mastered record to Warner's executives, Harrison had scored his first US number one single for nearly 15 years with 'Got My Mind Set On You'. Its driving rhythm and punchy vocal leapt out of the radio, while Gary Weiss' video was rarely off of television. In the UK the song reached number two, behind The Bee Gees' 'You Win Again'. Released on November 2, 1987, *Cloud Nine* reached the Top 10 in both major territories and quickly achieved platinum status in the US.

While the uncomplicated accessibility of the music naturally helped, the success was partly attributable to wider changes in music culture. Harrison emerged from his hiatus into a climate that was far more welcoming for a 40-something rock star in the doldrums than the one he had left five years earlier. The shock waves of punk had receded, and the rise of CDs had given fresh impetus to artists who had lost their way in the Eighties; back catalogues were now being lovingly curated, shedding fresh light and offering new perspectives on the careers of many, not least Bob Dylan, whose *Biograph* anthology was one of the first of its kind to appear in 1985 and set the benchmark for re-evaluating the work of musicians who otherwise were seen to be a little past their prime.

With the emergence of the 'legacy artist', it became a practical necessity for musicians to embrace the past and wrestle with its meaning. Harrison had shown with *Cloud Nine* that he wasn't averse to playing that game, while new magazines such as Q established a more forgiving critical context for the survivors of the Sixties. He also happened to release *Cloud Nine* hot on the heels of the twentieth anniversary of *Sgt. Pepper*, a landmark which had stirred up a remarkable amount of Beatles nostalgia in the media throughout the summer of 1987.

The mid-Eighties was not a particularly creatively vibrant time for rock's grandees, but they had found a home – clad in Armani and Ralph Lauren, they tended to huddle together for comfort, playing on each other's records, showing up at each other's gigs with their neat jeans and bad hair, doing their bit for charity, rehashing the past in glossy magazine articles. There was little critical kudos in it but it provided a workable context, and it sold. Harrison was, by association and perhaps by character, subsumed into this set. He was no longer a dark horse but part of the rock establishment. It wouldn't last, and it didn't necessarily suit him, but at the end of the Eighties it made him more popular than at any time since the early Seventies.

Crucially, he was also willing to promote the record. As if to make up for the past decade of relative indifference, he appeared anywhere and everywhere, acquiescing to a punishing media blitz which lasted several months and couldn't help but alert the four corners of the record-buying world that the most retiring ex-Beatle had a new album out. He weathered the inanities of breakfast television, prime-time chat shows and late night radio with blunt forbearance, and even assented to being interviewed live by Jonathan Ross in a south London pub, where between sips of beer he managed to subvert the whooping youth-orientated agenda by plugging Cab Calloway, Bessie Smith and Bob Dylan. He sat next to John Peel, two distinct galaxies briefly colliding.

But he could still be an awkward cog in the media machine. If Gered Mankowitz's recollection of the *Cloud Nine* shoot, where Harrison "was lovely to everybody – he was so nice, so normal, not remotely up himself," illustrated one side of his nature, the incident at the *Rolling Stone* photo session at Friar Park showed his less hospitable side. It was rarer these days, but not an isolated case. Appearing on the syndicated US radio show *Rockline* with Lynne, Harrison was audibly drunk and came across as haughty, superior and a little embarrassing. Responding to a fan who said he liked the album "quite a bit", Harrison replied: "*Quite* a bit? Well, get off the line, man, if you don't love it." He stumbled rather aimlessly through a medley of songs, including a wayward 'Here Comes The Sun', Dylan's 'Every Grain Of Sand' and 'Mr Tambourine Man' and the standard 'Let It Be Me', each performed in the manner of a man hogging a guitar at a party, oblivious to whether anyone wants to listen or not. He only agreed to play in the first place on the condition that he was allowed to keep the Gretsch he had borrowed from a member of the production team.

★ ★ ★

While he was making peace with the music of The Beatles, the reality of the band's affairs and internal dynamic was as complex as ever. Since a meeting in December 1983 between all three surviving members and Yoko Ono at the Dorchester Hotel in London, the momentum had slowly but steadily been moving towards a final settlement of all the various writs and contractual problems which continued to dog their existence. One recurring and particularly emotive issue was the fact that when McCartney re-signed to EMI in 1979 he had renegotiated his royalty rate on Beatles recordings, and was now receiving around two perc ent more than Starr and Harrison. When they found out, in 1985, the pair filed an $8.6 million lawsuit against McCartney, as much out of pique that he had broken the democratic bond of the band than for any material gain.

They struggled to dissociate the professional from the private. Just before *Cloud Nine* was released Harrison and Starr visited McCartney's house in St John's Wood for an amicable dinner, after which Harrison remarked that personal relations were as good as they been for years. A couple of months later, however, on January 20, 1988, when The Beatles were inducted into the Rock and Roll Hall of Fame in New York, McCartney refused to show up on principle because of certain "business differences" that remained unresolved. His non-appearance deeply irritated Harrison, whose initial instinct had also been to decline the invitation. He had been persuaded otherwise and had thoroughly enjoyed the night, for once deriving a sense of pride in the band's achievements when confronted with proof of what The Beatles meant to the public and his peers.

Attending the ceremony with an inebriated Starr, Harrison was humble and gracious, extending his "love" to McCartney. In a later interview he was less measured, suggesting that Paul had "put another nail in his own coffin as a person."[15] He was amusingly candid also in his opinion of McCartney's vanity project bomb *Give My Regards To Broad Street*, and in response to McCartney's suggestion that they might write together said, "It's pretty funny really, I've only been there about 30 years in Paul's life, and now he wants to write with me. But maybe it would be interesting to do that. There's a thing with Paul, one minute he says one thing and he's really charming and the next minute he's all uptight."[16] The overwhelming emotion nowadays was not of bitterness, but of philosophical resignation. From his new position of commercial and creative strength, Harrison seemed magnanimous, relaxed and in control; McCartney seemed churlish by comparison.

The unseemly brouhaha over the Hall of Fame ceremony almost certainly hastened the resolution of all their various legal disputes, with each other and their label. In November 1989 a final agreement between Apple, EMI and The Beatles was signed. "The settlement was about ten feet thick," said Harrison. "I don't think anybody but the lawyers read it. It's a good feeling to be done with it."[17]

They no longer had any business issues to resolve, but Harrison did not quite forget. Trust had been lost, and could not be easily regained. He muttered darkly about karma and being stabbed in the back. These factors would finally play out during the coming decade. For now, he had a new gang.

★ ★ ★

During his rather odd interview on *Rockline* in February 1988, Harrison had mentioned his desire to form a band called The Traveling Wilburys with "me and some of my mates."[18] 'Wilburys' was a joke word Lynne and Harrison had coined for obscure studio equipment. Though the formation of the band was later credited entirely to happenstance, the idea had certainly been in his mind during the making of *Cloud Nine*. Harrison had known Tom Petty & The Heartbreakers since the band had taken on the dubious honour of being Dylan's backing group on his Never-Ending Tour in the mid-Eighties. Subsequently, "I'd see George at Tom Petty's house quite frequently in LA," says Roger McGuinn. The pair became firm ukulele buddies, spending time together in Los Angeles or at Friar Park, often strumming through the night.

Harrison's contact with Roy Orbison was sporadic but stretched back to The Beatles' earliest UK tours in 1963. Both Orbison and Petty had recently started writing and working with Jeff Lynne; they were all in each other's orbits. Dylan, of course, was a close friend. "I'd been working on *Cloud Nine* for about three months or so," Jeff Lynne told me. "One night we were sitting back listening to what we were doing, having a few beers and that, and George said, 'You know what? You and me should have a group.' 'A group? Who should we have in it then?' 'Bob Dylan'. 'Bob Dylan? Oh, yeah, of course – what about Roy Orbison?' 'Yeah, great idea!' We both liked Tom, who we'd just been hanging out with on his tour with Dylan. We just had this little pipe dream session, and that was the Traveling Wilburys. Everyone wanted to be in it. Everyone wanted to join. It was amazing."

While Harrison and Lynne were in Los Angeles that spring an opportunity presented itself which allowed the idea to find its natural shape. Needing a new song for the 12-inch version of the third single from *Cloud Nine*, 'This Is Love', Harrison called Lynne and suggested that they could relive 'Instant Karma': he would start writing a song that night, and they would cut it the next day. Needing a place to record at short notice, they asked Bob Dylan if they could use the garage studio at his house in Malibu. "Come over tomorrow", he said. Harrison had left a guitar at Petty's house, so they invited him to join them; they'd had dinner with Orbison the night before. Either by serendipity or by sly design, Harrison suddenly had his dream band.

"George had half a song ready to go," says Lynne. "We finished it off in Bob Dylan's garage, recorded it there and then wrote the words after dinner." 'Handle With Care' – named after the stamp on a packing case in the studio – was done and dusted in around five hours, with three sections highlighting all five contributors: Harrison's distinctive descending melody line on the verses led to a rising bridge which was classically Orbisonian, and from there to a chugging middle section which principally fell to Petty and Dylan.

Harrison couldn't stop playing it. He took 'Handle With Care' to Mo Ostin at Warner Brothers, who immediately recognised that it was too good to disappear onto the wrong side of a 12-inch single. Presumably, he also saw dollar signs. Ostin suggested that the five men expand the idea and make an album together. Harrison needed little persuasion. Dylan, deep into his Never-Ending Tour, had the most immediately pressing schedule and was due back on the road in early June. If it was going to happen, they would have to work quickly.

They blocked off ten days beginning on May 7, 1988, and convened at Dave Stewart's home in Los Angeles while the Eurythmic was back in Britain. The weather was warm, and the doors to the large wooden house were left open. They would, Orbison recalled, "just sit outside and there'd be a barbecue and we'd all bring guitars and everyone would be throwing something in here and something in there, and then we'd go and put it down. Some days we'd finish just one song, some days two or three."[19]

Working with acoustic guitars, they set up chairs and microphones in the kitchen to create a makeshift studio, feeding the wires through to Stewart's small control room. "We'd usually go up and cut the backing track and take a break for dinner," said Petty. "We'd all eat around the same table, pass the lyrics around and work on them all through dinner. Then whoever drew the straw would sing it."[20] It was a cross between an upmarket *Basement Tapes* and a triple A-list version of the impromptu jams that Harrison had hosted at Friar Park, Maui and Los Angeles over the past decade. "We did the songs from scratch, and in ten days the whole album was finished, basic parts and rough vocals," says Lynne. "It was amazingly quick. Nobody's commitments were above the Wilburys!"

There was a lot of hero worship flying back and forth. They all idolised Orbison, one of the lode stars of American rock and roll, but none more so than Lynne. Meanwhile Harrison's reverence for Dylan was almost painfully obvious. He would surreptitiously film Dylan playing piano and listen back to it at night. "I think George frightened Bob," Petty laughed. "At the end of the first day, he said, 'We know that you're Bob Dylan and everything, but we're just going to treat you and talk to you like we would anybody else!'"[21]

After ten days they went their separate ways. Harrison and Lynne took charge of extra sessions at FPSHOT during the summer. Petty and Orbison came over, Jim Keltner added drums and Jim Horn saxophones. Arrangements were finessed, backing vocals added, but the freshness was carefully preserved. Released in October 1988, *Traveling Wilburys Vol. 1* was Harrison's second major album in 12 months, selling one million copies within a year and over five million in total. Transcending its cosy origins – which could be summarised as rich rock stars with their slippers on – at its best it transmitted a pure joy which was both disarming and infectious.

Each song was credited to all five members, re-enforcing the sense of an ego-free group enterprise, but in reality Harrison was the principal writer on three tracks. 'Handle With Care' reflected on the psychological fall-out from Beatlemania and was, in its way, as nakedly autobiographical as anything Harrison ever wrote. He also contributed the decidedly ELO-ish 'Heading For The Light', a breezy affirmation of his spiritual journey, and the rolling country-rocker 'End Of The Line'. All three possessed an easy, organic spontaneity that much of *Cloud Nine* lacked, and they remain among his most persuasive melodies. It was not a coincidence: Harrison was absolutely in his element. "George liked being in a band, and he was so up for it, he really believed in it," said Lynne. It conformed almost exactly to his ideal of what a group should be: a collection of equals playing for the love of it, every member contributing ideas and united by a sense of camaraderie – a bit like The Band in its earliest days or even the purest part of the early spirit of The Beatles. With The Traveling Wilburys he was, perhaps, able to right some of the wrongs of their dispiriting demise. Beyond the music he saw his role as preserving the five friendships, tending to the humour, the mutual love and affection, making sure above all that it never stopped being a pleasure. If they weren't laughing, why bother?

"George was kind of the kingpin, the driving force," Olivia Harrison told me. "'Come on, let's have some fun.' I didn't see any ego. I think all of them transcended that. If you can't be satisfied at that point in your life then you've got a problem. Nobody was there to try and prove anything. It was fun, but it was serious too! They wanted it to be good."

That the band was Harrison's baby is most evident in the way the album was presented. Each member was given a pseudonym – Harrison was 'Nelson Wilbury' on the first album and 'Spike' on the second. At his request Michael Palin wrote The Rutles-esque liner notes about "this great nomadic tribe of wandering musicians." It was Harrison's idea, too, to call the inevitable follow-up *Traveling Wilburys Vol. 3*.

Recorded almost exactly two years after the first, some of the spontaneity (and melody) departed the second time around, while Harrison's writing muse had very obviously deserted him. They were also without Roy Orbison, who had died suddenly of a heart attack on December 6, 1988, just days before the video shoot for 'End Of The Line'; in the film, an empty rocking chair takes his place. The Wilburys were all shocked by Orbison's death, but Petty was taken aback by Harrison's blunt reaction. "He called and said, 'Aren't you glad it's not you?'" Petty recalled. "He said, 'He'll be okay, he'll be okay, he's still around.' That was all he had to say about it."[22]

They toyed with inviting Del Shannon to join, and also sounded out Roger McGuinn. "I was in LA busy building the tracks for my *Back From Rio* album," says McGuinn. "George invited me to come and live at the house where they were all recording, it was around the corner: 'Come on over and hang out!' I said, 'I really can't, because I'm so busy with this pre-production for *Back From Rio*.' So that was that. You can draw your own conclusions what might have happened."

In the end they made the album as a four-piece, with a contribution from Gary Moore, who came in for the day to overdub lead guitar on 'She's My Baby'. During the same sessions they recorded a song for Olivia Harrison's Romanian Angel Appeal Foundation, set up in aid of the children afflicted by Nicolae Ceausescu's brutal neglect of Romanian orphanages in the Eighties. To support the cause, and his wife, Harrison made an uncomfortable appearance on the *Wogan* television chat show and also roped in many friends to contribute to an album released to raise funds for the foundation. The Traveling Wilburys' contribution was Lonnie Donegan's maudlin 1956 hit 'Nobody's Child', which Tony Sheridan had recorded with The Beatles as his backing band in Hamburg in 1961. Harrison called Joe Brown during the sessions in Los Angeles and asked him for the lyrics to the first verse; he simply made up the words for the second.

Creatively The Traveling Wilburys peaked early, but it never stopped being enjoyable. Harrison's friends from HandMade, Dick Clement and Ian Le Frenais, directed the video for 'Wilbury Twist' and were struck by the easy dynamic they all shared. "There was this sense of fun, and George was very much part of that," says Clement. "They were so happy just fooling around playing riffs to each other – that was how they communicated most of the day. There were a lot of egos in that group, but they seemed very tight, they were there because they wanted to be. He was definitely the captain of the team, he was the guy who pulled everything together. No one could say no to George."

'Wilbury Twist' was the final Traveling Wilburys' single – there was to be no more music, although a 2007 box-set combining the two albums went to number one in the UK. Nonetheless, Petty said that "for the rest of his life George considered himself a Wilbury,"[23] and every now and again after a drink or a smoke he would lose himself in loose, late night talk about future plans. "We had jokes about touring," Jeff Lynne told me. "George would say, 'Right, we're going to get an aircraft carrier and follow the sunshine. Play Hawaii, the Caribbean, all these lovely little spots.' We never did it, of course, but he was really looking into it big time. He was like, 'We could park in the dock and play on the deck, then hoist up the gang plank and off we'd go to the next one!'"

★ ★ ★

When Harrison did finally decide to tour again after 17 years it was a much more sedate affair, almost as though he had chosen to put his carefree Wilbury persona in mothballs and replace it with something much more safe and sensible.

Between February 5 and March 9, 1991, Eric Clapton played 24 nights at the Royal Albert Hall. During the run, Harrison dropped in to see his friend and afterwards went backstage. Talk turned to playing live and Clapton "more or less threw the gauntlet down," says Chuck Leavell, who played keyboards in Clapton's band. "He said, 'Come on George, you don't get out there in the trenches like the rest of us – you need to get out there and play.' George's response was, 'Well, I don't have a band.' Eric said, 'I have one, and you can have it. And you can have *me* – how's that?' He was backed into a corner." Clapton's drummer at the time, Steve Ferrone, recalls: "George turned around and said to us, 'Would you do that?' and we all said, '*Yes!*'"

The game was afoot, but Harrison's heart was never fully in it. Clapton recalled that he "was really scared to death, he changed his mind about five different times."[24] Feeling instinctively that it had become a now-or-never enterprise, he was convinced he had to try to master the art of touring before it was too late. Nonetheless, the parameters were strictly defined and the stakes considerably lower than they had been in 1974.

Even when playing the Prince's Trust concert, an event rarely mistaken for a rock and roll Valhalla, Harrison had been deeply affected by a fan near the stage "going absolutely bananas. He was so fanatical and kept staring at me with this manic glint in his eye. Even if I had been considering coming back to do large shows, the sight of this guy made me think twice."[25] Since The Beatles, and Lennon's murder, in Harrison's mind the more committed the fan, the greater the potential for imminent danger. His feelings of personal safety were further undermined when his wife started receiving death threats in the mail in 1989.

It was, therefore, decided that the tour would be restricted to Japan, where the crowds were always politely responsive yet carefully controlled, the reviews would be minimal and generally respectful, and the social environment would be strictly regimented. Rehearsals began in early November at Bray Studios near Maidenhead, a few miles east of Henley-On-Thames, with Clapton's touring group: Steve Ferrone (drums), Nathan East (bass), Greg Phillinganes (keyboards), Chuck Leavell (keyboards), and Tessa Niles and Katie Kissoon on backing vocals. To that line-up Harrison added – bafflingly, given that two of the greatest guitarists in the world were already in the band – a third guitarist, Andy Fairweather Low, and the ubiquitous Ray Cooper. It transpired that everything about the tour was designed to be super-safe: the country, the set and the band.

"He was very nervous, and very unsure," says Tessa Niles. "He was testing the waters, and we knew that he needed a lot of support." Clapton's group of flawless session pros were the perfect vehicle in that respect. "We were absolutely capable," says Ferrone. "He just jumped in there and sat back in a really comfy armchair." It proved an apt description of the polished but somewhat antiseptic shows that followed.

The song choices were an even split between Harrison's Beatles' compositions and his solo highlights, the latter spanning 'My Sweet Lord' to 'Cheer Down', his lively 1989 US single recorded for the *Lethal Weapon 2* soundtrack. All the hits were present and correct, as well as a handful of songs from *Cloud Nine*; the only real surprise was a sweetly funky take on 'Dark Horse'. The Beatles' songs 'Old Brown Shoe', 'I Want To Tell You', 'Taxman' and 'Piggies' were getting their first ever live outings. In the middle Clapton would perform a handful of his own songs, but it was very much Harrison's show.

They rehearsed six days a week, with Sundays off, for three weeks. He invited the band to Friar Park for a Thanksgiving Day dinner and would bring gifts to rehearsals: chocolates, flowers, cards. "He asked Jane Asher to make a cake which modelled everyone in the band out of marzipan," says Tessa Niles. "It went a bit wrong. They made Andy Fairweather Low black. We called him B.B. Low after that." On the final day Harrison invited family and friends, including Ringo Starr and Steve Winwood, to listen to the set.

Once in Japan Harrison and Clapton held a joint press conference on November 29 at the Capitol Tokyo Hotel, formerly the Tokyo Hilton, where The Beatles had stayed under luxurious house arrest in 1966. Japan was a country where something similar to Beatlemania was still alive and well – frustratingly, most of the questions, already stilted through translation, concerned his former band. The next day the party travelled the short distance to Yokohama to prepare for the opening concert.

Starting on December 1 and ending on December 17, the tour took in 12 shows in six venues: one in Yokohama, two in Osaka, one show apiece in Nagoya, Hiroshima and Fukouka, three more in Osaka, and three final performances at the Tokyo Dome Stadium. Each venue held between 10–12,000 people, and in a little over two weeks the sold-out tour grossed £\$9.7 million.

Indisputably a great set on paper, in execution the show offered little sense of excitement or risk. *Billboard*, the only western media outlet to review the tour, called the first night in Yokohama "entertaining if unspectacular,"[26] noting Harrison's obvious nervousness but commending his "sublime" slide playing. The concerts were tightly drilled, lacking much in the way of surprise or spontaneity. "We stuck to what we knew," says Niles. "I think he needed to know that things were in place every night to feel comfortable." Harrison attempted 'Fish On The Sand' and 'Love Comes To Everyone' at the first two concerts but they were swiftly dropped. Aside from that, the set list was unaltered each night.

The Beatles' songs were particularly well received and, says Leavell, "he seemed very comfortable in his skin playing them." Even in such a tame context, it was some small thrill to hear the strains of 'I Want To Tell You' ringing out as an opening song. During 'Piggies' in Osaka Steve Ferrone walked on stage wearing a fake pig's head, while throughout the tour Harrison sang an extra verse in the song, referencing George Orwell's *Animal Farm*. The lyrics to 'Taxman' were also updated to include the current Labour leader John Smith, British Prime Minister John Major, Boris Yeltsin and George Bush.

'Something' was an obvious crowd-pleaser most nights, although initially Harrison seemed unaware of its historical import. Peter Frampton describes the solo on *Abbey Road* as "phenomenal – one of the all-time best," yet when the band came to rehearse 'Something' at Bray Harrison played a completely different guitar break. "At the end George said, 'That was pretty good'," says Steve Ferrone. "I said, 'But you didn't play the solo.' He said, 'Yes I did, I played a solo.' I said, 'Yes, you played *a* solo, but you didn't play *the* solo.' I starting singing it and the whole band joined in and sang him the guitar solo. He was absolutely flabbergasted that the solo was an integral part of the song." It turned up present and correct in Japan.

The Beatles were in the air. The tour brought back not altogether comfortable memories of his last visit to the country with the band in 1966. "He said the hotel was exactly the same as when he was last holed up there," says Tessa Niles. "That was a bit weird for him. He was a bit shell-shocked, you could see he would get flashbacks about it." Harrison would also talk to the band about the 1974 tour. "He alluded that it was difficult to get through," says Leavell. "He didn't dwell on it, but he might say, 'Jeez, I hope we do this better than we did back then.' He was worried about his voice, which held up great in the end."

It was a harmonious few weeks, both on stage and off, at least between Harrison and the members of his band. He would invite them up to his suite to share mountainous plates of Chinese and Indian food, he organised birthday parties, gave them all gifts and was generally a thoughtful and attentive group leader. "It was very obvious," says Leavell, "That he liked being part of a band." At times he seemed oddly vulnerable in the modern world, such as on the few occasions he went to the gym with bass player Nathan East. "It was really sweet, he didn't know how it worked down there with the lockers," says East. "He was not used to public facilities. I had to explain: 'Here's the key, put your clothes in there...'"

He had time to shop and sight-see, and although he was recognised wherever he went, his space was respected. The entourage travelled by bullet train from city to city, and at each station a group of Hare Krishna devotees would appear, their bells gently chiming as they walked close by. When Harrison and the band boarded the train the Krishnas would hand everybody food through the windows. "It was their way of honouring George, it was very touching," says Tessa Niles. His spirituality, so strident and overt on his last tour, was now an almost entirely unspoken element of his life. "He didn't vocalise any of it, he didn't discuss it," Niles says. "He would light incense wherever he was. I think it was ritualistic, it wasn't just about the smell. You just knew that this was something that he carried in him. He was *kind*, and I think I was thrown by that. We were employees at the end of the day, but he was so much fun to be with, and very empathetic."

In Hiroshima Harrison organised for himself and the band to visit the Peace Memorial Park, and at one point considered climbing inside the huge Peace Bell and having someone ring it from the outside, "to see what it felt like," says Ferrone. "He was very moved," adds Niles. "It was refreshing that he wanted to do those things. I have to be honest, I think Eric went to Georgio Armani that day. Different strokes for different folks."

Indeed, the only sour note on the tour was a growing rift between Harrison and Eric Clapton. Although the entire enterprise was, essentially, a supremely generous gesture from one friend to another, something got lost between theory and practice. Struggling to deal with the aftermath of the tragic death of his four-year-old son Conor, who had died earlier in the year after falling from the 53rd floor of a Manhattan apartment building, Clapton was "experiencing tremendous feelings of anger and sadness."[27] He also seemed to be questioning the wisdom of lending his band to Harrison and then coming along for the ride in order to play second fiddle. "I was surprised [he did it], and when we started rehearsals I think it annoyed him a little bit," says Tessa Niles. When Harrison started shaping the band to his own specification, "that threw Eric," she says. "It was almost like renting your house out and someone coming in and moving the furniture. It was a brotherly relationship, but a difficult one at times."

Tensions deepened the day before they were all due to leave London for Japan, when Harrison had a falling out with Clapton's manager, Roger Forrester. The fall-out resulted in Forrester, who had been instrumental in setting up the tour, not coming on the trip. "It was weird," says Steve Ferrone. "There was tension between Roger and George, and Roger was Eric's manager so I guess Eric joined in. When Eric was on stage he barely acknowledged George through the entire tour until the very last gig. There was no amicable interplay between them on stage at all, Eric had this block of ice around him. It was a strange vibe. I don't like to second guess what people were thinking, but George was such a social person, and Eric is just not that kind of a person. I think maybe he felt a little bit threatened, or maybe he was feeling a bit disenfranchised. It wasn't bad blood, but it was uncomfortable."

Clapton toured Japan almost every year, and familiarity ensured there was a certain coolness from the media over his arrival; Harrison, on the other hand, was an ex-Beatle who hardly played *anywhere*, ever. His arrival was therefore a genuine event, and a tremendous fuss was duly made of him. Backing vocalist Katie Kissoon felt that as a result Clapton's "nose was a bit put out. The ego has to kick in there somewhere, otherwise you wouldn't go on stage at all. And everyone got on so well with George. I mean, we got on well with Eric, but I think there was a slight underlying thing there."

Lurking in the background was the latest, and last scene of the psychosexual soap opera which had linked the two friends since the late Sixties. Clapton and Pattie Boyd had divorced in 1988 after an increasingly fraught marriage had culminated in Clapton fathering children with two different women: Yvonne Kelly, with whom he had a daughter, Ruth, and the Italian television presenter Lory Del Santo, who was Conor's mother. Clapton and Del Santo were no longer in a relationship by the time of Conor's death, but she came to visit her ex-partner during the early stages of the Japanese tour. "Lory showed up out of the blue and just checked into our hotel," Clapton later said. "I couldn't handle it. Curiously enough, George stepped in and took control. They travelled around together and he seemed to have a calming influence on her."[28]

In fact, Del Santo later revealed that she and Harrison had a brief three-day affair while staying at the Sun Plaza Hotel in Hiroshima. The Italian felt that Harrison still had unresolved feelings about Clapton's pursuit of Boyd. "It could have started as a payback day," she later said of the affair. "It probably started because we both wanted revenge. We were hurting. We had this loneliness. But it turned out to be something special."[29] Shortly after Del Santo left, Olivia Harrison and 13-year-old Dhani arrived in Japan to accompany Harrison for the rest of the tour. On the final night, Dhani got up on stage and accompanied his father and the band on 'While My Guitar Gently Weeps' and 'Roll Over Beethoven'.

★ ★ ★

Throughout 1992 Harrison wrestled very visibly with the idea of throwing himself back into sustained live performance. There was certainly plenty of interest from the United States. Steve Ferrone remembers when he left Tokyo that there were "a lot of Americans on the plane back home who had come over to Japan just to see it." Meanwhile, everyone in the band was keen to prolong the experience.

"We were begging George," says Chuck Leavell. "'Bring this to the States, people would eat this up. We would work with you in a heartbeat with or without Eric.' He would just kind of smile and laugh and nod, but at the end of the day that wasn't what he wanted to do. We were terribly disappointed. He was nervous, but I think he was more comfortable doing it in Japan than he would have been in Europe or America." "We all wanted it to continue," says Tessa Niles. "We probably pushed him quite a lot, but deep down I think we knew it was a one-off."

Not quite. The tour party reconvened a final time on April 6, 1992, for a show at the Royal Albert Hall billed as 'The Natural Law Party

Presents George Harrison & Friends – Inspiration To The Youth Of Great Britain – Election Is A Celebration'. The cause behind Harrison's first ever solo concert in Britain raised more than a few eyebrows. He was finally breaking cover to play a benefit concert in aid of the Natural Law Party, the hastily assembled political wing of the TM movement which had been formed only three weeks earlier to fight for seats in the British general election, held three days after the concert on April 9.

For a long time Harrison had seemed detached from the real world, but in recent years he appeared more out of touch than ever. When discussing the problems of Brixton in south London, an inner-city area blighted by riots and racial tension in the late Seventies and Eighties, he said, "I don't know the answers. I think in the end, everybody has to go inside themselves and get spiritual. The more individuals there are with inner strength, then that will manifest itself in the external world."[30]

Key policies of the Natural Law Party included reducing health care costs by training citizens in 'self-pulse reading' and Yogic Flying. At a time of recession, political upheaval, nuclear threat and the Poll Tax riots, Harrison's public support of a party which sought to apply the principles of transcendental meditation to all aspects of government seemed conclusive confirmation that he was hopelessly cut adrift from the real world. Even his former band mates suspected as much. Harrison had called Paul McCartney the week before the election and asked him to stand – alongside him and Ringo Starr – as a Natural Law candidate for a seat in Liverpool. "He rang me from LA and said, 'I've been up all night and you may think this is a bit silly...'" When McCartney asked what they would do if they got in, Harrison replied, "We'll introduce meditation for everyone." McCartney recalled: "George was saying, 'You know places like Bradford and Blackburn or Southall where they have a big Indian community? They're going to bring in Indian guys, holy men, to be candidates.' He said, 'Well, they'll definitely win in all those Indian communities.'"[31] On election day all 310 Natural Law candidates lost their deposits, gaining 0.19 per cent of the total vote, and the Conservative party was voted in for a fourth term.

Before the concert Harrison issued a statement explaining his reasoning, ending with the claim that "the Natural Law Party is turning this election into a wonderful national celebration and I am with them all the way." A few years later, he remained unrepentant. "As far as I was concerned, in Britain, the left, the centre and the right were all really the same," he said. "Different shades of the same greyness. It was a long shot, the Maharishi tried to get these people to form together into a party... with consciousness as the basic thing... It can happen, but it's something that will take a long time, generations."[32]

The concert took some time to sell-out, despite a frisson of excitement among Beatle die-hards. The set was a reprise of the Japanese shows, with the same band minus, perhaps unsurprisingly, Eric Clapton, and the indisposed Nathan East. They were replaced by The Heartbreakers' Mike Campbell and American bassist Will Lee, while other guests included Zak Starkey, Joe Walsh and Gary Moore. Ringo Starr appeared at the end to play on 'While My Guitar Gently Weeps' and 'Roll Over Beethoven', to a predictably rapturous reception. The critical reaction was less easily prey to sentiment. "A middling performance," shrugged *The Times*, while the *Daily Express* summoned the spirit of '74 by complaining that Harrison shouted some words and "massacred" certain songs. The *Daily Telegraph* and *Evening Standard* were more positive.

There were a handful of other performances throughout the year, almost as though he was trying to talk himself into something more substantial; some were high profile, some low key. Between jumping on stage with a bewildering variety of acts, from Carl Perkins and Gary Moore to Eddie Van Halen, the major piece of business was his appearance at Bob Dylan's 30th anniversary concert at Madison Square Garden in October. For the show he ordered a supply of black T-shirts emblazoned with the slogan 'It's That Million-Dollar Bash!' Introduced by Chrissie Hynde with the words "Hallelujah, Hare Krishna, yeah, yeah, yeah: George Harrison!", he played 'If Not For You' with a look that transmitted sheer, unadulterated terror, before settling down for a fine version of 'Absolutely Sweet Marie'. The line-up included Lou Reed, Eric Clapton, Kris Kristofferson, John Mellencamp, Willie Nelson, Tom Petty, Johnny Cash, Tracy Chapman and Roger McGuinn, who joined Harrison for the ensemble finale and "had to teach him how to sing 'My Back Pages'. He had never done it before, and he was worried about how to do the phrasing on the verse that he was going to do. That was fun."

Fun, but ultimately not quite fun enough. In the end, the negatives of performing live outweighed the positives – 1992 was the last time Harrison did much of it. "I really enjoyed playing, but I have a conflict," he said. "I don't particularly want to play to audiences. It's unhealthy to be a star."[33]

There would be no US or European tour. Instead, there was a rather tepid souvenir of the Japanese shows in the form of the double live album, *Live In Japan*, released to almost complete indifference in the summer of 1992. He flew Steve Ferrone over first class from New York to London to record an overdub. "I got there and George told me there was *one* bass drum beat missing," says Ferrone. "All I had to do was hit a bass drum once. He must have spent about ten grand just to get me there. 'Well, it needed your sound!' I think he just wanted to hang out. He didn't quite want to let go of the guys yet."

Prophetic words.

Be Here Now
Friar Park, 2000

The new Millennium, and a spell of rough weather. In the past few years Harrison has survived the traumas of throat cancer, a knife attack, multi-million dollar fraud and, not least, a Beatles reunion. He no longer has a record deal and has released no new solo music in more than a decade. He asks himself a simple question: What would I miss if I were to leave today?

"I have a son who needs a father, so I have to stick around for him as long as I can," he says. "Other than that, I can't think of much reason to be here."[1]

CHAPTER 16

The Answer At The End

Harrison's decision to tour again, even in such a carefully orchestrated manner, was partly a reaction to some uncomfortable goings-on in his business life. Shortly after the bruising experience of *Shanghai Surprise* his relationship with HandMade began to sour. *Withnail And I*, written and directed by Bruce Robinson and released in 1987, was the last great film to come out of the stable, and also the last to bear its distinctive hallmarks of a literate script, terrific British actors and dark humour – it was another intelligent, eccentric and culturally resonant film for a discerning, if limited, audience.

HandMade had set up offices in New York and Los Angeles, at Denis O'Brien's insistence, and production began on several films which skewed the creative sensibility closer to Hollywood, and which proved to be both commercial and artistic disasters. The accountant-turned-producer was now exercising cineaste pretensions, with predictable results. "Later on Denis picked some very odd movies," says Dick Clement. "One or two were almost unreleasable."

David Leland was directing the misfiring comedy *Checking Out* for HandMade while Harrison was spending most of his time in Los Angeles promoting *Cloud Nine* and working with The Traveling Wilburys, whose first three videos Leland also directed. He intimated to Harrison that O'Brien was interfering in the creative process. Other directors were giving similar signals. "Denis O'Brien was very involved and quite a handful," says Richard Loncraine, who after making *The Missionary* worked again with HandMade on his 1987 film *Bellman And True*. "He was very charming when he wanted to be and a monster when he didn't want to be. I once said over lunch at San Lorenzo, 'The trouble with you, Denis, is that you're a cunt.' He was one of those big-shot kind of producers, but the thing that kept him alive is that every now and then he would have a good idea. But not often."

As goodwill dissipated and standards dropped, HandMade became a fulcrum for further headaches and hassles for Harrison. In 1988 they sued Cannon Films, their video distributor, for £1.6 million in unpaid fees, the case dragging on until 1991. The first public sign that something might be seriously amiss came via a cutting speech Harrison made at the party HandMade threw on September 23, 1988 at the Old House at Shepperton Film Studios, celebrating the company's tenth anniversary. The event cost £85,000, a substantial amount of which was spent on bringing over Carl Perkins to jam with Harrison on the night. Staff from the New York office were also flown in, and most of the leading lights of British film were in attendance.

Following a typically witty and gracious speech by Michael Palin, a drunkenly sardonic Harrison chose the moment to publicly vent his disaffection. "He got up on stage in front of hundreds of people and said how much he hated film people and what arseholes they were," recalls Richard Loncraine. "As the evening almost entirely consisted of film 'arseholes' – many of whom weren't – it was taken a rather dim view of. He called us all a lot of fucking wankers, used a lot of four-letter words, and the room went very quiet. I think there had been a drop to drink. He said, 'The only people I really care about are musicians, so now I'm going to play some music as it's my party.' It was not the most cool or elegant way to behave – in fact, it was incredibly rude. Sadly, that's my lasting memory of working with George."

Other choice phrases aired during the speech included: 'What are you fuckers doing here?' and 'Why am I spending all my money on you?' They were the words of a man from whose eyes the scales were slowly beginning to fall; the actions, too, of someone whose mean streak could be sharpened by alcohol. On another drunken occasion during this period Harrison adorned a treasured photograph of John Lennon and Yoko Ono hanging in the office of a Warner's executive with lewd graffiti, and captioned it "The Traveling Arseholes."

The simmering resentment behind his speech, which amounted to a indiscriminate Fuck You to the entire industry, did not dissolve with his hangover, however. A month after the party, on October 21, 1988, he sent a fax from Los Angeles to Cadogan Square in which he sacked everyone in the office, or at least everybody whose names he knew. It was not the cool, calculated act of a company director, but a rash gesture born out of personal anger.

In the end HandMade made ten redundancies from a staff of 35 and closed the office in New York. In an attempt to further alleviate their rapid financial decline – *Checking Out* eventually grossed a little over two per cent of its outlay; suicidal figures – the company brought in an accountant, John Reiss, to look into the books. Reiss very quickly discovered that Harrison was dangling at the end of a very precarious limb.

"I found documents to suggest that Denis had been telling George that he and George were equal partners in backing these films and that the bank guarantees would be signed by them both," Reiss later said. "But, in fact, Denis never signed them himself. So it was a single guarantee."[1] Harrison was, in effect, personally underwriting the entire operation, from paying for the coffee in the office to bankrolling multi-million dollar movies. While O'Brien was drawing a handsome salary from the company's funds, Harrison was solely responsible for all its mounting debts. When Reiss calculated the company's outgoings against Harrison's holdings and incomings he found a deficit of $32 million. With Friar Park and his stake in Apple among the assets used as collateral, the risk was enormous, even for a Beatle.

The Pythons had already expressed misgivings about O'Brien and his maze of front companies and financial smokescreens, but the scale and complexity of his deceit was beyond anyone's suspicions. When John Reiss found out the situation he told Ray Cooper, and together they visited Harrison at Friar Park one night in November 1988 to lay the facts on the line. "George really didn't want to know," said Reiss. "He virtually threw us out, even his old mate Ray. And that saddened me. I think he half-knew, he just didn't want to hear the terrible news."[2]

Harrison did not immediately act on the information he was given. Instead he watched as Reiss, then Ray Cooper, were sacked by O'Brien, and the production schedule slowed to a stop, although not before *Raggedy Rawney*, *Cold Dog Soup* and *Nuns On The Run* had made a mockery of the quality of the company's previous work. Finally, in the early Nineties, Harrison did instigate his own investigation into HandMade's finances. "I saw a lot of Denis O'Brien, he had a house in Encino," says Dick Clement. "I used to play tennis a lot of with Denis, Ian [Le Frenais] and Jeff Lynne. Then one day Jeff said to us, 'I can't play with you any more. I can't play with Denis because he has ripped George off for $18 million and George is my friend. I can't do it.' This was the first hint I'd had of any wrongdoing in that area. I never really saw George after that. It was a nasty feeling to think he had been exploited like that. It was a big blow."

Early in 1993 Harrison officially severed his 20-year business association with O'Brien, and in 1994 HandMade was sold to a Canadian company, Paragon, for a paltry $8.5 million – paid cash. Harrison then set to work chasing O'Brien and all his bad karma through the courts.

He found himself back in a depressingly familiar scene. While Allen Klein had never pretended to be anything other than a hard-nosed hustler – and despite everything, Harrison couldn't help but retain some affection for his former manager – O'Brien was a very different proposition. He had been a close friend, a partner, and had been shown complete trust. Harrison felt "bitter, betrayed, angry and let down," recalled Eric Idle. "He hated [O'Brien] with an intensity that was quite rare for George. It took him a long time to get over all that."[3] He wrote a song called 'Lying O'Brien' to let off steam, but for once it was hard to see the funny side. Yet another artistic endeavour born out of fun, friendship and good faith had crashed around his ears amid lawsuits, financial wrangles and bitter personal recrimination.

It seemed, on balance, an odd time to return to The Beatles.

★ ★ ★

It was Neil Aspinall who had first come up with the idea of making a Beatles documentary. He had worked on *The Long And Winding Road* throughout 1970, and by the following year had assembled a 90-minute cut which, given all the other Beatle-related drama ongoing throughout the Seventies, nobody quite had the time or inclination to deal with. Put on the back burner but never forgotten, *The Long And Winding Road* was resurrected by Aspinall in 1990, shortly after the dust had settled on all The Beatles' legal issues. They should not only revive the film, he said, but add up-to-date material from the archives, and perhaps even some new incidental music.

McCartney, Starr and Ono were not averse to the idea. Harrison was, as ever, entirely disinclined to delve into the past in general, and that part of it in particular. Appearing on television at the end of 1990 he had taken a swipe at McCartney, who had just completed a vast tour which played the Fab card with a vengeance. "He's decided to *be* The Beatles," said Harrison. "I'm not interested. For me, it's the past and, you know, 'be here now' is my motto."[4] As the extent of the problems at HandMade became apparent, however, a certain pragmatism crept into his decision-making process. The tour of Japan, with its big bucks and its Beatle-friendly set list, was one result. Signing up to the film project was another.

Apple's intention to make a definitive, authorised Beatles documentary was publicly announced in 1992. Geoff Wonfor, who had worked previously with both Harrison and McCartney, was appointed director: he started the project in a box room in the Apple office and ended in an edit suite in Shepherd's Bush. "I'd love to say it was five beautiful years but it wasn't," he says. "It was an immense amount of hassle and pressure."

The original idea was for the three surviving ex-Beatles and Yoko Ono to allow the film-makers access to their archives, providing rare photos, private film footage and perhaps some unheard music. As the project progressed, they all agreed to tape new interviews, and Harrison committed to a series of filmed conversations over a period of three years. His instinct was to treat the whole thing as a joke. The Rutles once again loomed large, while he told the director that he wanted the documentary to be made in the style of *Monty Python's Flying Circus*. "I said, 'I don't think I can do that, George!'" says Geoff Wonfor. "He told Ringo, and Ringo said, 'I watched a rerun of *Monty Python* and I didn't laugh once.' So even at that level it was difficult." Everything, from the title on down, became a potential flashpoint. The film was still titled *The Long And Winding Road* until objections were raised in certain quarters over the fact that it was named after a McCartney song. "That came from George – and Yoko," says Wonfor. For a long time it was simply *The Beatles Story*, and didn't become the *Anthology* until late on.

To keep the peace the three men were all interviewed separately, except on one occasion at Abbey Road and another when they spent a day together at Friar Park. The difficulties arose when they started viewing rough assemblies of each of the episodes.

"I would put something together, and then have to take it down to show Paul, then George, then send it to Ringo, and take the first programme out to [New York] and sit down with Yoko and get her version on it," says Wonfor. "A lot of my job at that stage was to stop them talking to each other, really, to keep them happy and not tell one what the other had said. There were items that were discussed and were originally in but I was made to take them out. George opened up totally about things, but especially with Yoko sometimes that didn't go down so well. They all had to agree before anything went out, it went back to their original contract."

Harrison was particularly exasperated when Yoko Ono insisted that John Lennon's great Beatles creation myth – his vision of a man on a flaming pie who had "said unto them 'From this day on you are Beatles with an 'A''" – was *literally* true. Even someone who voted for Yogic flying couldn't quite buy that one. "There were a lot of mind games," says Wonfor. "I had to come back to George and tell him what Yoko had said. He said, 'Well, that's her fucking opinion. There is no truth, really.' The whole film was the most nightmarish thing I ever had to do in my life. I really used to shake. Someone would do one thing and it would spark something off and you had to go back to the drawing board. George really kept my head straight. He was helpful, and he was fun. He could be very irreverent but that's what I loved about him."

During the filming Wonfor and Harrison, alongside Jools Holland, who was conducting many of the interviews, would occasionally go out to a restaurant, a show, and – just once – to the pub around the corner from the editing suite. On that occasion, says Wonfor, while Harrison was having a drink "a rather large lady came over and asked if she could have his autograph. He said, 'Sorry, ever since John signed Mark Chapman's book we just have something about giving autographs – we just don't do it.' She left, and I said, 'What if she had been 36-24-36?' And he said, 'I'd have signed her arse if she'd wanted me to!' The glint in his eye was fantastic, just beautiful." On another outing the director realised that Harrison didn't have the slightest idea how to use a payphone.

In tandem with the documentary, The Beatles sanctioned a vast sweep of their audio archive, collating lost tracks, alternate takes and demos dating back to The Quarry Men. Back in 1987 Harrison had taken a sober view of any material lying in the vaults. "What never came out was stuff that wasn't supposed to be a record," he said. "That is to say, if we were rehearsing things and someone happened to leave the tape running. It's not supposed to represent The Beatles or the music, but people want to scrape the barrel for anything they can find."[5] As late as 1993, George Martin expressed a similar opinion. "I've listened to all the tapes," he said. "There are one or two interesting variations, but otherwise it's all junk. Couldn't possibly release it."[6]

Almost overnight, this basement full of base metal somehow alchemised into a potential goldmine. The *Live At The BBC* album, released in 1994, had illustrated that there was still a vibrant market for unreleased Beatles music, and Martin dutifully began compiling and mixing material for what would become three triple albums of rarities. The impetus was a mix of clear-eyed corporate nous and a growing sense that they all had unfinished business. "When I met him in 1974 they still had a lot of sorting out to do, but time passes and you always remember the good times," Olivia Harrison told me. "Had the air not been cleared

I don't think they would have been able to do the *Anthology* the way they did. They were very relaxed, so relaxed, in those conversations."

Not always. But they were curious to see how it would play out. For Harrison, partly it was about filling in the blanks and trying to understand what all the fuss had been about the first time around, and where he fitted into it all. He had few distinct memories of certain landmarks in Beatles history – Shea Stadium, *Sgt. Pepper* – and "had never watched the [old] stuff," says Wonfor. "He'd watch footage and say things like, 'You know, Paul *was* a cute looking guy, really, wasn't he?'"

The timing was also right. In the UK the Britpop wave was beginning to crest, with Oasis leading the vanguard of new bands paying direct, if often uninspired homage to The Beatles and some idealised reimagining of Swinging London. Cast, The Boo Radleys, The Bluetones – on it went; even veterans like Paul Weller were enjoying a Sixties-scented second wind. The only group to explicitly reference Harrison's own oeuvre was Kula Shaker, the faintly preposterous psychedelic rockers led by Crispian Mills, son of English actress Hayley Mills.* Kula Shaker drew on Sanskrit verse and electrified Indian folk tunes for inspiration, and in the mid-Nineties scored their only Top 10 hit with 'Govinda', a song which shared both its title and general ethos with the second single Harrison produced for the Radha Krishna Temple in 1970. An alternate version was titled 'Govinda '97, Hari & St. George.' For the avoidance of any doubt, its B-side, 'Gokula', used the guitar riff from 'Ski-ing' from *Wonderwall Music*.

Oasis's biggest hit, 'Wonderwall', also drew from perhaps Harrison's most obscure piece of work, but he was unimpressed by the implied compliment. Feuding with the Gallagher brothers in the mid-Nineties became a national sport, and Harrison joined the fray after suggesting Oasis "weren't very interesting" and might be better off without their singer Liam Gallagher, "the silly one".[7] Gallagher responded by calling Harrison a "fucking nipple,"[8] and expanded on his theme in a later

---

* Coincidentally, a lifetime before, in March 1964, Harrison had accompanied Mills to the Regal Cinema in Henley-On-Thames for a charity midnight matinee.

interview. "Anyway, John and Ringo were The Beatles," he said. "Isn't It A Pity? It will be when I meet George Harrison. I'm gonna stand on his head and play golf. So who wants a fight?... I wanna meet you in the middle of Primrose Hill. Thursday afternoon, 12 o'clock, on the green."[9]*

Although one might reasonably have assumed that Harrison would approve of the rather proscriptive return to good old-fashioned "real music" forwarded by the likes of Oasis and Ocean Colour Scene, unlike McCartney he made no attempt to foster relationships with contemporary artists – the exact opposite, in fact. His fogeyish tendencies continued to deepen, publicised with statements such as "I listen to *Top Of The Pops* and after three songs I feel like killing someone,"[10] and "It seems to me music today is a pollution with no value at all. Rap stinks and techno is humanless music coming out of computers that brings you to madness."[11] Who did he like? "Dylan".

"He was the kind of man who didn't know who any of these bands were," says Geoff Wonfor. "It wasn't [an affectation]. He *really* didn't. It just wasn't on his wavelength, and yet ask him to play any George Formby song... He sat Dylan down in his lounge and made him sit through 'When I'm Cleaning Windows' six times. Dylan must have been thinking, What the fucking hell is this?" Harrison interrupted one *Anthology* meeting to call a friend to ask if they could remember the lyrics to Formby's 'Our Sergeant Major'. His tastes were set. He was fond of saying that "avant-garde is French for bullshit." Wonfor recalls: "We went to Ronnie Scott's one night, and there was this band on stage, real way-out jazz, and at the end of one number one of the guys went *briiiiiiing* on his guitar. George looked round and said, 'Oh, at last – a fucking chord!'"

★ ★ ★

The most contentious of all the aspects of the *Anthology* was the recording of new music. The idea of the 'Threetles', as they were now

---

* Liam's band mate and older brother Noel Gallagher enjoyed a more cordial brush with Harrison shortly before he died, at a bonfire party in Henley-On-Thames. Harrison offered him a can of Heineken and they talked about Carl Perkins.

being described in the press, working on entirely original material was a minefield. Whose song would it be? Who would sing it? And most significantly, how could it possibly be The Beatles without John Lennon? Throughout the Seventies Harrison had consistently batted away any talk of a full Beatles reunion, and after 1980 he would often comment that "while John Lennon remains dead" the entire premise of the question was ridiculous. The prospect of that obstacle being removed emerged with the suggestion that the remaining members could overdub their contributions onto unreleased Lennon material to make new Beatles music. McCartney attended Lennon's induction into the Rock and Roll Hall of Fame in New York in January 1994, and after the ceremony Yoko Ono gave him four unfinished songs from the Seventies in rough demo form: 'Free As A Bird', 'Real Love', 'Grow Old With Me' and 'Now And Then' (also known as 'Miss You' and 'I Don't Want To Lose You').

On February 11, 1994, at McCartney's studio, The Mill, in Sussex, the three surviving Beatles came together to make music for the first time in over 24 years. McCartney constructed a cutesy counter-factual narrative for the press in which the trio pretended that Lennon had gone off on holiday or popped out for a cup of tea, and had asked the rest of the band to finish off his songs. The reality was a little less cosy, and a good deal more pragmatic. The terms of engagement were hammered out as though the sessions were a Cold War summit: McCartney had home advantage, but Harrison had the strategic upper hand. His final – perhaps only – victory in The Beatles was to get Jeff Lynne to produce the new songs. It was a condition of his involvement. "George had said, 'This is the guy we should have,'" Lynne told me in 2012. "I didn't know Paul that well at that time. I don't know what would have happened if Paul had said, 'No, we'll have my bloke.'"

Lynne had already spent a considerable amount of time working on Lennon's original cassette demos, cleaning up the sound quality and transferring them to 48-track. Over the next fortnight the 'Threetles' added musical ballast to the frail outline of 'Free As A Bird', and wrote words to a bridge which Lennon's original version had barely sketched out. "It was just me and them, and I'm sitting there listening to all this amazing Liverpool folklore – Hamburg stories, just wonderful," said

Lynne. "There was no real tension – they would joke and take the piss, but it was good natured. I loved it, but it was really tough. Every morning I would wake up with half dread and half exhilaration. Doing it was the most thrilling thing you could imagine, but messing it up would be horrible. We all worked together on it diligently. I had a few tricks to get John's voice on the track and Paul was great with that, he ghosted John's voice underneath to give it more body."

They returned to The Mill again on June 22 to work on a second song, 'Now And Then'. This session was less successful. There were technical issues, the words weren't complete, and they ended up downing tools. The next day Starr and McCartney came to Friar Park, where the trio blew off steam in FPSHOT by playing some early rock and roll with just two acoustics and brushes, including Harrison's old audition number, 'Raunchy', as well as 'That'll Be The Day', 'Love Me Do', 'Blue Moon Of Kentucky' and 'Ain't She Sweet', the latter performed by the lake with Harrison strumming the ukulele.

Some of the sessions were filmed and what little footage has come to light shows three middle-aged men trying their best to have fun, but the underlying edge is apparent, particularly when compared to film of the Traveling Wilburys recording their first album, where everyone is clearly having a ball. At Friar Park Harrison was noticeably reluctant to respond to McCartney's more sentimental utterances – "Ah, it's been a lovely day, George" – and, off-camera, familiar niggles and veiled put-downs resurfaced. "George was mixing something down in his studio and McCartney came in," says Geoff Wonfor. "He said, 'Ah that sounds nice, George. When the fuck did you learn to do all this?' George looked up and said, 'Remember me? I was second on the right'." It was not a one way street. With Lennon no longer around, Harrison felt obliged to take on the role of agent provocateur; he was heard to utter heretical views about the quality of the raw material they were working with, and hoped that "someone does this with all my crap demos when I'm dead."[12] McCartney, pulling rank on baby Beatle, "personally thought that a little presumptuous."[13]

Throughout 1995 they worked on pulling together the various strands of the project: completing the new songs in further sessions in

February, March and May, overseeing the mixing and editing of the archive material, although George Martin did most of the spade work, and supervising the final cut of the documentary.

"It would be a lie to say they were all easy to work with – they weren't," says Wonfor. "The closer it got to the finish the more and more I didn't enjoy it. Although it was still pretty amicable, as soon as you went [back] to that time the issues that parted them were still there. They were all together once in the edit suite, which nobody knew about. That was one of the weirdest times in the whole *Anthology* – to sit down, just me and the three of them, and to hear what they thought about what I'd done. '*That* didn't happen like that.' 'Why did you say that?' – all that. Paul would get uptight, they'd get into an argument, and you wished a little fairy would come and take you out of your seat. McCartney wouldn't let me move: 'You sit down, you need to hear this.' But my heart started to pound quicker and quicker, and I wished that I really wasn't in that room." It was precisely the same reaction as Glyn Johns had experienced while working on what became *Let It Be* more than 25 years earlier.

The films were sold to ITV for £5 million and to ABC for $20 million, and were part of a Beatles blitz scheduled for the end of 1995. *Anthology* was broadcast on British television in six weekly hour-long episodes between November 26 and New Year's Eve. In the States it was shown in three two-hour episodes over five nights. The films presented a thorough but sanitised version of the story, offering just enough surface grit to avoid having to dig too deep. In both territories audience figures dropped off dramatically after a strong start. "I told George at the end I thought we could have been more forthright," says Wonfor. "He said, 'Yes, but you got as close as anybody will ever get.' George was basically such a nice man that he wanted to give the fans [the] dream."

The first triple album, *Anthology 1*, was released on November 21, to almost instantaneous multi-platinum success. 'Free As A Bird' followed two weeks later, the first new Beatles song for a quarter of a century, and their first ever single credited to all four members. It was, in the end, a failure, as it had to be, but a democratic one at least. Perhaps that carefully calibrated democracy was part of the problem. After the opening thwack of Starr's drums the first sound on the song is Harrison's unmistakeable swooping slide, placed centre stage – but it is the sound of solo George, not Beatle George, a fact that McCartney wasn't shy in pointing out. "I thought, 'Oh, it's 'My Sweet Lord' again'."[14] The tempo dragged, and Starr's trademark drum sound was neutered by Jeff Lynne into a dry, compressed clomp. Perhaps the final cosmic joke Harrison wished to play on his old band was to make their celebrated comeback sound like a Traveling Wilburys B-side. He sang the second bridge and added harmonies, the one element of the song that succeeded in evoking some recognition of former glories.

The first single was followed in March 1996 by a second, the more immediate 'Real Love', which was, comically, not playlisted by Radio One, thus officially consigning The Beatles to oldies status. Over the next 12 months *Anthology 2* and *Anthology 3* also appeared. There was much that appeared on the nine albums of specific interest to Harrison fans: the historic 'In Spite Of All The Danger', with its careful little solo; his lead vocals on songs taken from the Decca demos in early 1962; the previously unheard 'You'll Know What To Do'; different takes of 'Taxman', 'Only A Northern Song' and 'Norwegian Wood (This Bird Has Flown)', the latter with much busier sitar; an instrumental 'Within You Without You'; the infamous take 102 of 'Not Guilty'; the Esher demo of 'Piggies'; the exquisite first attempt at 'While My Guitar Gently Weeps'; and his equally fine 'birthday demos', taped on February 25, 1969, of 'All Things Must Pass', 'Something', and 'Old Brown Shoe'. Cumulatively, they added significant shade and nuance to the existing, perhaps rather rudimentary portrait of Harrison as a Beatle.

In contrast to volumes one and two, *Anthology 3* lacked a new Beatles song. The intention had been to make 'Now And Then' the third single, but according to McCartney, Harrison "didn't want to do it."[15] "There was a third song, and Paul always says that George went off it," Lynne told me, adding "I think he probably did." A mooted Harrison-McCartney composition, 'All For Love', also never quite got off the ground. Deep down the pair remained an awkward fit, especially if Starr wasn't around to neutralise their core differences: the friction between

McCartney's hectoring ebullience and Harrison's somewhat wearing ambivalence had only increased with time. "George has some business problems, and it didn't do a lot for his moods over the last couple of years." McCartney rationalised. "He's not been that easy to get on with."[16]

His moods could indeed be bleak. During the making of *Anthology* Harrison was getting to grips with the fall-out, both financial and emotional, of his dealings with Denis O'Brien. Early in 1995 he sued his former manager for $25 million for the "enormous losses and liabilities [suffered] as a result of O'Brien's improper and inept management and deceitful conduct." The 18-page submission sent to the Los Angeles County Superior Court outlined how enormously betrayed Harrison felt on a personal level: "This case involves the tortious misconduct of a faithless manager. Pretending to serve the interests of his musician client, he misused his position and his client's assets and credit to finance secret profit and a lavish international lifestyle for himself, while subjecting his trusting client to massive economic risks and losses."

O'Brien defended himself against all the allegations. When, in January 1996, Harrison was awarded $11 million in damages, O'Brien immediately appealed. In February 1998 the Californian Court of Appeal ruled that the original award of $11 million would stand. By now O'Brien had been declared bankrupt, and had left a sufficiently Byzantine paper trail in his wake to ensure that Harrison would struggle to ever receive what he was owed. The financial aspect was not insignificant but it was a secondary concern. Media reports that Harrison might be "down to his last £10 million" suggested the wolf wasn't quite pawing at the gates of Friar Park, while Olivia Harrison's announcement that a seven-figure sum from the profits for the *Anthology* would be donated to the Romanian Angel Appeal Foundation underlined that Harrison would never be destitute.*

The damage to his already rather tenuous faith in human nature, however, was immense. There were other black clouds hovering. A

---

* Following the flood of income from The Beatles' later projects, he left a little over £99 million in his will.

long and rather ugly disagreement over his home in Hana ended up in a Maui courtroom in July 1993. The dispute centred on a path which offered his neighbours a safe route to the shoreline, and which ran across his land, at one point within 30 metres of his bedroom. Locals claimed that they had historical access rights to the path that were being denied after Harrison had padlocked the gate in the mid-Eighties. "He was pretty much under the opinion that it didn't matter," said one local man, Scott Whitney.[17] "Like 'I'm George Harrison and you're not.'" Harrison claimed that his privacy was being violated. "Have you ever been raped?" he said to the press after testifying. "I'm being raped by all these people. My privacy is being violated."[18] Two men later sued him for defamation. The court finally ruled against Harrison, who appealed, and a settlement was only reached a matter of months before he died. In Australia, meanwhile, Hamilton Island had also become tainted. Tourism in the area was growing and word had got around that among all the other exotic wildlife in the area a rare species of Beatle could sometimes be spotted on the shoreline, a fact loudly announced by boat tours as they passed. Paradise, Harrison complained, had turned into "wallyworld."

In the technological age the world was shrinking for everyone, but for Harrison more rapidly than most. Just as nobody appeared to be truly trustworthy, so nowhere he went seemed quite remote enough. In a new song called 'Run So Far' he wrote, "There's no escape, can only run so far." Terry Gilliam noted the change in him. When the Python saw Harrison in the mid-Nineties he thought "it looked like he's aged ten years."[19]

★ ★ ★

It was not all doom and gloom. Harrison was ahead of the curve when it came to a guest appearance on *The Simpsons*, taping a brief cameo for 'Homer's Barbershop Quartet' in which he pointed Homer Simpson in the direction of the chocolate brownies. Anyone fearing for his financial health, meanwhile, would have been reassured at his outlay of £540,000 on a ludicrously exclusive McLaren Formula 1 'supercar' which could travel at 230 mph. According to the designer, Gordon Murray, Harrison liaised closely with the build team and had "at least 14 Indian symbols included in the build. One item was actually laid up in the construction of the chassis."[20] He was still a fixture in the pits at Grand Prix around the world, and had become friends with a new generation of drivers, including British world champion, Damon Hill. Hill was one of the first people on the planet to hear 'Free As A Bird' while attending the Australian Grand Prix on November 12.

Though the tensions of the *Anthology* project and his business worries dominated much of the Nineties, he was capable of switching off. Friends would be invited to Friar Park for a swim, a cup of tea in the gardens, a chat and a jam. After *Cloud Nine* his five-album deal with Warner's had run its course, and he had no particular desire for a new one. "There was no urgency for him," his son Dhani said. "Occasionally he'd get motivated."[21]

Father and son were as close as they looked, and shared a particularly strong bond over music. Harrison had shown Dhani guitar chords at a young age, and he had blossomed into a fine player. He had even grown to love the ukulele. When Harrison made a surprise appearance at a George Formby fan convention in Blackpool in the early Nineties, playing 'In My Little Snapshot Album', Harrison Jnr went along for the ride. They would frequently disappear into FPSHOT together. "Oh, we had some great times," Dhani later said. "Some days it would be me in there pressing 'play' and 'stop', and some days we'd have engineers, so we could play together. It was very relaxed, just me and him at home in the studio."[22] Harrison was still writing and recording, but mostly he was content to play new songs for his friends on one of his scores of ukuleles.

He escaped the worst of the hype surrounding the second coming of The Beatles by travelling to Australia at the end of 1995, and then to India. In March 1996 he returned to Vrindavan, the holiest of Krishna cities, with his devotional friends Shyamasundar Das and Mukunda Das, making a pilgrimage to the temples and sacred places. While in the country he started work on a new collaboration with Ravi Shankar, *Chants Of India*, a serene album which put aside the sitar in favour of setting Sanskrit chants, mantras and prayers from ancient Hindu scriptures to drifting music.

The sessions moved back to FPSHOT in the summer of 1996. John Barham, once again working as string arranger, notes that in the times he and Harrison had worked together in the past George had seemed "happier and more outgoing than in his latter years. I think he experienced anguish as a consequence of the disloyalty of some of the people who took advantage of his trust in them."

Released in May 1997, *Chants Of India* was the kind of worthy cause Harrison felt inspired to promote. With Shankar and his wife Sukanya, in New York on May 14 he taped the VH-1 special *George Harrison & Ravi Shankar: Yin & Yang,* which aired in July. His long hair was streaked with grey and fell over his shoulders – sporting a short, neat beard, linen jacket and loose trousers; he looked weathered but well. He consented to sing a few songs on acoustic guitar, but was clearly nervous and spent a long time prevaricating. Eventually Harrison played The Traveling Wilburys' 'If You Belonged To Me', originally sung on *Volume 3* by Bob Dylan, a short, folksy 'All Things Must Pass', 'Prabhujee', from *Chants Of India*, with Shankar, and the breathless 'Any Road', a new song with a torrential, skifflish melody.

It was to be his last appearance as a performing musician. With host John Fugelsang he discussed The Beatles and the Concert For Bangladesh, but mainly focused on the profound influence Shankar had had on him, and his spiritual life in general. Though he now rarely spoke publicly of his beliefs, on this occasion it seemed appropriate. He talked about attaining "pure consciousness, pure awareness," and spelled out his dislocation from modern life and transient obsessions. "I get confused when I look around at the world, and I see everybody's running around," he said. "And you know, as Bob Dylan said, 'He not busy being born is busy dying,' and yet nobody's trying to figure out what is the cause of death and what happens when you die. I mean, that to me is the only thing really that's of any importance. The rest is all secondary."[23]

He was about to be presented with an unwelcome opportunity to conduct some primary research into the subject. Shortly after taping *George Harrison & Ravi Shankar: Yin & Yang*, Harrison discovered a lump on his neck while gardening at Friar Park. It was quickly removed, but in August he entered the Princess Margaret private hospital in Windsor, registered under the name of Sid Smith, to undergo surgery for throat cancer. Following the removal of several lymph nodes, he spent a fortnight receiving radiation treatment at the Royal Marsden Hospital in Chelsea, and returned for a further dose in September.

Serious illness suddenly seemed endemic among The Beatles' inner circle. Following Maureen Starkey's death in 1994, within 12 months of his own initial diagnosis Harrison lost his dear friend Derek Taylor, who had rejoined Apple in the Nineties to help with the *Anthology* projects. Taylor succumbed to throat cancer while a year later Linda McCartney passed away from breast cancer. Carl Perkins, Harrison's friend and boyhood hero, also died from throat cancer. He attended services for all three, playing a brief burst of 'Your True Love' at Perkins' funeral.

He seemed to have had better luck. In January 1988, and again in May, Harrison visited the Mayo Clinic in Rochester, Minnesota, for full check-ups, and was told that his cancer had not returned. It was only when he was spotted leaving the hospital in May that the news of his illness broke in the media, with rumours spreading that he was dangerously ill. Back in Britain in June, Harrison came out to the front gates at Friar Park and very calmly talked to waiting reporters, calling for a little perspective and no hysteria. "I'm not going to die on you just yet," he said, adding, "[I know] it makes a good story." He clarified the state of his health. "I got [cancer] purely from smoking," he said. "I gave up cigarettes many years ago, but had started again for a while and then stopped in 1997. Luckily for me they found that this nodule was more of a warning than anything else. There are many different types of cancerous cells and this was a very basic type."[24] He looked healthy enough. With his hair now cut short and swept back, Harrison resembled a slightly greyer incarnation of the Kaiserkeller kid of almost 40 years before.

He entered a period of quiet convalescence. Spurning the modern advancements of email, mobile phones and computers, he found peace in the garden, where he could not easily be disturbed. He went to see Ravi Shankar play at the Barbican, and towards the end of the year broke cover in New York at a club show by his old friends Dave Mason and Jim Capaldi. "That was the last time I saw him before he died," says Mason. "We asked him, but he didn't come up and play."

He was anxious to attend to his musical archive. In a 1999 interview with *Billboard* Harrison revealed that as well as continuing to work on new songs, he was contemplating a box-set of outtakes and demos, as well as a reissue campaign for his solo albums, each one released with bonus tracks. He was also hoping to tidy up the *Concert For Bangladesh* album and film for re-release in modern formats.

The first order of business was to return to *All Things Must Pass*, in preparation of its thirtieth anniversary in November 2000. "He contacted me out of the blue, I hadn't spoken to him for donkey's years," says Ken Scott, engineer on the original album. "We talked for an hour, easily, and then I went over and met him the next day at a hotel in Los Angeles. This was after his first bout of cancer. He had been in his shell for a bit after that, but he came out of it – he was great, amazing. We were set to start things a short time later.

"Then, of course, he gets attacked in his house."

★ ★ ★

For some time Harrison had felt that the world was encroaching more and more on his fiercely protected privacy. After the disputes in Maui and the annoyances of Hamilton Island, there were further intrusions. In 1998 thieves broke into the grounds of Friar Park and stole from the gardens two bronze busts of monks worth £50,000. Late in 1999, while he was in Henley, he received the news that a stalker had broken into his home in Hana. Cristin Kelleher, a 27-year-old woman with mental health issues, had entered the house, taken a pizza from the freezer, cooked and eaten it, and was busy doing her washing when the police arrived. She told them she had a "psychic connection with George."

These were mere trifles compared to the brutal and terrifying attack which took place at Friar Park in the early hours of December 31, 1999. Having watched a film on television, Harrison and his wife had gone to bed around 2 a.m. Dhani and a friend were staying in one of the lodges, while Olivia's mother was sleeping elsewhere in the house. Most of the staff had gone home for the holidays.

At around 3 a.m. Michael Abram managed to enter the grounds at one of the many points where the perimeter fence was broken, away from the security cameras. Abram was a 34-year-old paranoid schizophrenic from Liverpool with a history of drug addiction, who had become fixated with The Beatles as "witches". He had recently made several visits to Henley-On-Thames to make inquiries about Harrison's house, and on Thursday, December 30, travelled down from Liverpool for the final time.

Once in the grounds of Friar Park he made his way to the house and used a statue of St George and the Dragon to smash the patio doors to the kitchen. The burglar alarm failed to activate, but Olivia Harrison was woken by the noise and alerted her husband, who went to investigate. From the top of the stairs on the first floor Harrison saw Abram in the hall below armed with the spear from the statue in one hand and a knife in the other. Trying to retreat back into the bedroom but finding the key jammed, Harrison decided to confront the man. Chanting 'Hare Krishna' in an attempt to appease Abram, he only managed to further provoke the intruder, who started screaming at him before racing up the stairs. He jumped on top of Harrison and began attacking him as they lay on the ground.

A 20-minute struggle ensued on the gallery that ran around the Great Hall below. Abram rained down blows as Harrison tried to defend himself. Having phoned for help, Olivia Harrison emerged from the bedroom, grabbed a heavy brass poker and started hitting the attacker on the head, at which point Abram started attacking her. Harrison, now with several knife wounds and bleeding profusely, roused himself with difficulty to challenge Abram again. Once more he was overpowered, and stabbed in the right side of his chest, this time deeply. He later told Olivia Harrison in hospital that his recurring thought was, "I can't believe after everything that's happened to me I'm being murdered in my own home."[25] At the same time as instinctively fighting to save himself and his wife, he was also trying to prepare mentally for the moment he had been working towards for the past 30 years: the point when the soul leaves the body.

Olivia Harrison hit Abram with a lamp but it seemed to do little good. Her assailant seized it and attacked Harrison again, before pursuing Olivia. Just when there seemed to be little prospect of escape, two police officers appeared and quickly brought Abram under control. Dhani arrived at the house shortly afterwards and was convinced his father, covered in blood, losing consciousness and struggling to breathe, was about to die. The paramedics arrived at 4 a.m. and spent 20 minutes treating his stab wounds, stabilising the blood flow, and putting him on a saline drip. Harrison and his wife were then taken in wheelchairs to the nearest NHS hospital, the Royal Berkshire in Reading.

In the end he was lucky. The most serious injuries were a punctured lung and a one-inch stab wound just below the collarbone which required 12 stitches – had the latter been half an inch to the side, it would have ruptured a blood vessel connecting the heart and head and he would have died within minutes. As it was, the executive of the Royal Berkshire, Mark Gritten, quickly reassured the public that it was not a life-threatening wound. Olivia Harrison was treated for cuts and bruises. Later that day Harrison was transferred to Harefield Hospital in Uxbridge, and by the evening of the first day of the new Millennium he was allowed back home.

As gruesome front page headlines appeared around the world, friends rallied. Eric Idle flew back immediately from the States to visit Friar Park. Starr and McCartney offered messages of support. Tom Petty sent a fax: "Aren't you glad you married a Mexican girl?" Harrison joked to Mark Gritten that, whoever he was, the intruder "wasn't a burglar and certainly wasn't auditioning for the Traveling Wilburys."[26] So who *was* Abram, and what was his motivation? In an interview with the *Liverpool Echo* shortly after the attack his mother described how her son was a former heroin addict with numerous mental health problems. Abram had been treated at a psychiatric unit but had largely been left to fend for himself, and had recently become obsessed with the music of The Beatles. "He has been running into pubs shouting about The Beatles," she said. "He started to wear a Walkman to play music to stop the voices in his head. He talked about Paul McCartney more than George Harrison."[27]

Abram was charged with two counts of attempted murder. When the case came to trial at Oxford Crown Court on November 14,

2000, Harrison was spared the ordeal of appearing, instead submitting a written account of the attack. Olivia Harrison, in court with Dhani, gave graphic and powerful testimony of the events that night and the effect it had on her family. On the second day of the trial the jury found Abram not guilty on grounds of insanity. The judge ordered that he be treated indefinitely in a secure psychiatric unit, and he was moved to the Scott Clinic in Rainhill, near Liverpool. The Harrisons' QC, Geoffrey Robertson, asked to be notified should there be any prospect of Abram being released, but the judge regretted that he had no power to do so. Afterwards Dhani Harrison, aged 22 and making his first high profile public appearance, stood outside the court room and expressed, passionately and with impressive eloquence, the family's anger at the verdict. "The prospect of him being released into society is abhorrent," he said. Within 30 months their concerns were realised, and an apparently rehabilitated Abram was freed.

Deep down Harrison always suspected that what he perceived as the huge waves of karma created by The Beatles' immense fame would one day ricochet back at him. All those terrors on tour, all those screaming fans and death threats, all the intrusion and paranoia had already left him, said his wife, "literally shell-shocked"[28] for the rest of his life. Now his worst fear had come to pass, at the age of 56, in his own home. "They used us as an excuse to go mad, the world did," he said on the *Anthology*. Some people were still doing so. He discounted out of hand the idea of leaving Friar Park and tried not to let the unimaginable psychological horrors of the attack overpower him, but many of his friends believe it took years off of his life, particularly coming at a time when his health was especially vulnerable. "The trauma that George had, the break-in, nobody will know what that did," says Geoff Wonfor. "It was a dreadful, dreadful time. He never quite recovered from that."

★ ★ ★

Shortly afterwards, in the dawning days of the new Millennium, Harrison went underground. He and Olivia took a holiday in Barbados with Joe Brown and his wife Manon to recuperate while the considerable media fuss died down, and then to Ireland to stay at Ronnie Wood's home in County Kildare, from where they expressed thanks at the goodwill messages they had received, directly and indirectly, from around the world. Shortly afterwards he retreated to the remotest part of the remotest island on Fiji and finally ended up in Australia, where in March he made his first public appearance since the attack at the Grand Prix. At Montreal in June, at another Grand Prix, bundled up under an old hat and raincoat and clearly less than thrilled at being cornered by a TV camera, Harrison looked gaunt, grey and a little frail.

He was still working on new music and the reissue of *All Things Must Pass*. "My immediate reaction [after the attack] was, he's never going to come out of his shell again now," says Ken Scott. "But as soon as he was able he called up and we set it up and started. It was great. I went over to Friar Park and was in the studio with him, and we looked at each other and burst out laughing. For two reasons: one, here we were 30 years later in exactly the same position listening to exactly the same tapes. The other thing was all the reverb – how could we possibly have ever liked it like that? It was just so overboard. The initial plan was to work on the remaster of *All Things Must Pass* for the thirtieth anniversary, then get all the Dark Horse stuff together, and after that we were going to be working together on the new album."

The reissue of *All Things Must Pass*, released on November 21, 2000, featured five additional tracks: the charming session outtake 'I Live With You', the acoustic demo of 'Beware Of Darkness', a rough mix of 'What Is Life', a 1970/2000 hybrid of 'Let It Down', and most intriguingly, a new version of 'My Sweet Lord', featuring Dhani, Ray Cooper and Joe Brown's daughter, Sam. It showed that the lawsuit over the song still rankled with Harrison even now: he purposely adapted the melody so that the notorious "Motif A" and "Motif B" were no longer there. "I enjoyed singing the song again and not singing those notes in that order," he admitted. "And [I wanted] to play a better slide guitar solo."[29]

The classic cover photograph was now colourised, and the individual CD cases inside the box were further adapted to show a modern housing block, a flyover and gas towers looming over Friar Park. It was a none too subtle statement from a man whose sense of privacy, both mental and physical, had been battered in recent times, and who found modernity increasingly ugly and nerve-shredding. It was, he said, "a little dig at the way our planet has gone in the last 30 years – it's just turning into a big concrete block."[30]

His playful side was still evident, however, as was his penchant for hatching madcap musical schemes. "We had plans to do more stuff, believe me," says Emil Richards. "George wanted Ray Cooper and I to get together to form a band. He loved Spike Jones, and he wanted to do a Spike Jones type of band. We were actually preparing for it – we would have done that if things had worked out."

Jim Keltner also revealed that he had been at FPSHOT and had "put drums on a tremendous amount of stuff. Some of the songs I played on were absolutely wonderful."[31] Harrison planned to go into the studio with Jeff Lynne in March 2001, but events conspired against him. Cancer had returned, this time in his lung. In the spring he was operated on at the Mayo Clinic, where a large part of the lung was removed. A statement from Harrison's lawyers put on a brave face. "The operation was successful and George has made an excellent recovery. He is in the best of spirits and on top form – the most relaxed and free since the attack on him in 1999. Although All Things Must Pass Away, George has no plans right now and is still Living In The Material World, and wishes everyone all the very best, God Bless and not to worry."

In reality, the prognosis did not look good. He was apparently at ease with the news, and the consequences. "I was blessed to spend a fair amount of time with him before his passing," says Ken Scott. "He was very positive. He had seen and completely understood his own mortality, and he was very comfortable with that." There was no major shift in perspective. The illusion of physical death, after all, was a subject he had been contemplating since his early twenties. "The soul keeps on going," he said. "I know that to be true. It's not something I just made up to make myself feel good."[32]

The animal instinct to preserve life is a powerful one, however, and he did not resign himself to his fate. In early summer Harrison travelled to Switzerland for treatment under Professor Franco Cavalli, one of Europe's top cancer specialists, at the Oncology Institute of Southern Switzerland. He bought a £10 million, 14-room villa, Collina d'Oro, in nearby

Montagnola in the canton of Ticino, near the Italian border, with beautiful gardens and views of Lake Lugano and the Swiss Alps. And he continued to work on music, much of it ending up on his posthumously released album *Brainwashed*. "The final recording material came from Switzerland," said Dhani Harrison. "It was the most recent stuff that my dad and I worked on. He would work in the studio a lot by himself wherever we were. We lived in Switzerland for a while, and we had a home studio there: Swiss Army Studios. A lot of the album was done there."[33]

"He was editing all this stuff he had done with the intention that Dhani and Olivia would put it all out," says Emil Richards. "He knew he was going, but he was working on music right to the end." The last thing Harrison ever recorded, on October 2, was a vocal overdub for 'Horse To The Water', a composition written by him and Dhani for inclusion on *Small World Big Band*, an album by Jools Holland's Rhythm & Blues Orchestra. Over a brassy, bluesy backing track that briefly recalled the glory days of 'Bangla Desh', Harrison sounded weak but spirited as he sang an intriguing Dylanesque narrative on an enduring theme: the inability or unwillingness of those who were floundering in life to embrace "God realisation." The song was credited to Harrison's new publishing company, R.I.P. Music Ltd.

Friends such as Holland and Ringo Starr, who made his emotional final farewell to Harrison in Switzerland, made positive noises in the press, but in private he was ailing as the cancer spread from his lung to his brain. He resigned from Apple and from Harrisongs, with his wife taking his place. In a final swipe at the Taxman, he was fast-tracked as a Swiss resident.

As his condition deteriorated Harrison flew to New York for treatment at the Staten Island University Hospital. The unit specialised in fractionated sterotactic radiosurgery, an experimental cancer therapy which focuses beams of radiation directly at the tumour, avoiding as much healthy brain tissue as possible; the beam is also rotated around the body so it can attack the tumour from all directions. "He had been trying all kinds of different things," says Emil Richards. "Different things, different doctors." It was in New York that Harrison said a last goodbye to Paul McCartney, some 45 years after they had first met in Speke on the top deck of the 86 bus. They held hands, laughed and wept, and parted in love. Harrison's sister Louise drove from Illinois to see her youngest brother for the first time in many years. A rift had developed between them in the Nineties over Harrison's belief that she had exploited her associations with The Beatles. They were now reconciled.

The pressing priority became the issue Harrison had explicitly addressed in song 30 years earlier, and one to which he had dedicated much of his adult life: the art of dying. He was not always assisted in his task by the actions of others. In a lawsuit filed in 2004, the Harrison family alleged that Dr Gilbert Lederman, the director of radiation oncology at the University Hospital, had taken two of his children to the Staten Island house where Harrison was living, made him listen to his son play guitar, and then coerced him into signing the instrument as well as autographing other pieces of paper. According to the suit, "Mr. Harrison, who was weak and exhausted, resisted and said, 'I do not even know if I know how to spell my name any more.' Dr. Lederman reached out to hold Mr. Harrison's hand to help him write and said, 'Come on, you can do this,' and spelled out Mr. Harrison's name for him beginning with the letter "G" and continuing to spell the entire name, "E-O-R-G-E H-A-R-R-I-S-O-N."[34] The suit also alleged that Lederman's courting of the media had been a breach of confidence which had made Harrison's last weeks needlessly stressful.*

★ ★ ★

It is difficult at times not to turn Harrison's final years into a sorrowful tale. He suffered a number of cruel blows: serious and recurring illness, extreme violence, personal invasion and shocking breaches of trust and good faith, of which Dr Lederman's was merely the latest. His illness was a major news story, and he did not always get the privacy he craved. "I'll tell you, the media wasn't very sweet in the last year of his life," said Tom Petty. "Especially in Europe, he never got a moment's peace. He would

---

* The case was settled in 2004 when Lederman agreed to "dispose of" the guitar and autographs. No payment was made. The Harrison estate put on record that the quality of medical care "was not an issue."

have helicopters follow him when he left the house."[35] He was also persuaded into once again "getting caught up in this big tangle" that was The Beatles, and "creating more and more karma" for himself.[36]

If these struggles to free himself of the intrusions of the physical world and the chains of the past were a test of his resolve, those closest to him insist that he passed it, and that his final days were serene, settled and free of bitterness – even if some of the last songs he wrote, such as 'Stuck Inside A Cloud' and 'Looking For My Life', reflect a more anguished, conflicted view of his life and the impending separation of soul and body.

Now as the time drew close, locations became significant. He had bid his final farewell to India a few months before, when he summoned the strength to make a trip to Benares, bathing one last time in the Ganges, visiting the holy Krishna temple, and pledging a final donation to IKSCON. He didn't want to die in hospital. Landing at Maui's small but very public airstrip would attract too much attention. England was too exposed, and in any case there were now residency issues. Instead, in mid-November Harrison flew through the night by private jet to Los Angeles, where he was administered by Dr Lee S. Rosen, chief oncologist at UCLA Medical Center. It was purely palliative care, attempting to strike the tricky balance between pain relief and maintaining awareness: he wanted to be conscious and alert at the moment of his death.

He spent his final days at 9536 Heather Road in Beverly Hills, at a house owned by Paul McCartney.* "Olivia called us and said, 'I think you better get over here right away, he's not going to last the night,'" says Emil Richards. "That was at Paul's house in Los Angeles."

George Harrison died shortly before 1.30 p.m. Pacific time, on November 29, 2001, aged 58, with his wife and son at hand and a few important, close friends nearby, chanting, singing and praying. It was a moment, said Olivia Harrison of "profound beauty... he longed to be with God." Within 20 minutes staff from the Hollywood Forever

---

* His original death certificate initially stated that he had died at 1971 Coldwater Canyon Road in Beverly Hills, a false address intended to put the media off the scent. It was later amended.

Cemetery arrived to collect Harrison's body, which had been covered in scented oils and holy water and wrapped in a silk blanket. He was taken in an unmarked white van to UCLA Medical Center, and within ten hours his body had been cremated in a simple Hare Krishna service, accompanied by a reading from the *Bhagavad Gita*.

By the time the news of his death had broken, Olivia and Dhani Harrison were already leaving for Switzerland with his ashes. These were later scattered, in a secret ceremony delayed to avoid the intrusion of fans and media, at Allahabad, the meeting place of Hinduism's three most sacred rivers: the Ganges, Yamuna and Saraswati.

His ashes were also distributed at nearby Benares, the place where Harrison's spiritual journey could be said to have truly begun in the late summer of 1966, when he visited with Ravi Shankar on a trip which revealed a life-changing glimpse of the kind of "bliss" that fame, wealth, pop music and John, Paul and Ringo could never quite offer. For those who believed in reincarnation and souls "nipping through the astral plane"[37] he was finally home. For those of a more sceptical bent, if nothing else Harrison's final journey to the holy city of Benares, more than 35 years after his first, spoke of an admirable commitment to the quest to attain self-knowledge. Few rock stars asked as many awkward questions – of themselves, of God, of life itself. He was ready to hear some answers.

"When I met George he said his ambition was to have no ambition," Olivia Harrison said. "And I think he achieved that. For the last five years he felt like that. He was free to go."[38]

EPILOGUE

Everyone's Got To Be Somewhere

Paying tribute to George Harrison on the front page of the *Guardian* on December 1, 2001, Richard Williams, who had made such a sage assessment of the merits of *All Things Must Pass* exactly 31 years earlier, recalled "a sensitive but uneducated boy confronted by unimaginable fame and wealth, and trying to find a satisfactory response."

Harrison's failing health had been widely telegraphed in the previous months and indeed years – his death did not elicit the sudden, lurching sense of shock felt by the world on hearing of John Lennon's murder, nor the same sense of cultural bereavement. In their place was something more intimate and thoughtful. Small crowds gathered at Abbey Road and Friar Park, many leaving flowers; in New York, similar congregations headed for Strawberry Fields in Central Park to talk, play and sing. Bob Dylan was moved to rare comment and an even rarer mode of expression. "He inspired love and had the strength of a hundred men," his statement read. "He was like the sun, the flowers and the moon, and we will miss him enormously. The world is a profoundly emptier place without him."

Implicit in all the words and gatherings, and in many of the thousands of obituaries, eulogies, magazine features, special issues, news reports, film clips, interviews and musical tributes that followed, was a very personal form of recognition. More so than the music he made, Harrison's struggle to make sense of the path down which his life had been diverted at an early age struck a chord on a purely human level.

In many ways he had been the everyman Beatle. It was not easy to truly fathom the complex mixture of ego, ambition, loss and, dare one say, genius which drove Lennon and McCartney to such remarkable heights. Starr was something else again, a carnival personality, unique and inimitable. But Harrison? George just wanted to play guitar. "He never lost sight that he was this kid who was very lucky who played guitar," says Lon Van Eaton. "When it really came down to it that's who he was. Even though he went through all that stuff and played the games and wore the fancy heart glasses, when he was really just at one with things was when he was making songs and playing the guitar. That was his heart and soul."

With a large slice of luck and a following wind, it is not impossible to see ourselves in Harrison's skin, in that band, exhilarated and clinging on for dear life. Possible too to imagine the difficulty in trying to find a way out. This subliminal connection partly explained why he was the favourite Beatle of so many for so long, and the deep, quiet sadness that was widespread at his passing.

'My Sweet Lord' returned to the top of the British singles charts at the end of January 2002, one final twist in the song's remarkable life story. In the month after his death My Morning Jacket's Jim James recorded *A Tribute To...*, a hazy, heartfelt six-song EP of Harrison songs, eventually released in 2009, and in April 2002 Sting, James Taylor and Elton John used the first hour of the Rainforest Foundation benefit concert at New York's Carnegie Hall to honour his music, performing a handful of Harrison songs before being joined by Ravi Shankar and daughter Anoushka for a final 'My Sweet Lord'.

Away from music, in February 2002 Harrison's contributions to independent film making were honoured at the British Independent Film Awards. Eric Idle's speech on the occasion of Harrison's induction into the Hollywood Bowl Hall of Fame on June 28 of that year similarly emphasised his hinterland, remembering a man "with an extraordinary capacity for friendship... he was a gardener, he grew beauty in everything he did, in his life, in his music, in his marriage and as a father."

The legacy of the Concert For Bangladesh also grew. In 2005 UNICEF reaffirmed their relationship with Harrison when then UN Secretary General Kofi Annan approached Olivia Harrison with the idea of setting up the George Harrison Fund For UNICEF, which now provides support not just to Bangladesh but to children around the world.

The point was made frequently by friends that music was only a single strand in Harrison's life, but for most people it remained the most prominent. A little under a year after his death, on November 18, 2002, his final studio album was released. Having shed its working title *Portrait Of A Leg End*, a characteristic groaning pun, it was now called, equally pointedly but less humorously, *Brainwashed*.

"George bequeathed it," said Jeff Lynne[1], who took delivery of the tapes from Dhani Harrison four months after Harrison died. The songs were in demo form, but already fleshed out with Jim Keltner's drums and Harrison's vocals, guitar parts, keyboards and harmonies. Lynne and Dhani, working to detailed notes, added bass, piano, vocals, additional keyboards and acoustic guitars, as well as string arrangements, trying to join the dots without leaving a trace of their fingerprints.

In the end Lynne only half-delivered on Harrison's final instruction: "Don't make it too posh!" *Brainwashed* was almost certainly a slicker, sleeker version of the more dressed-down album Harrison had envisaged, but there remained an appealing campfire flavour to much of it. Despite the occasional intrusions of Lynne's bombastic signature sound, the default setting was warm, relaxed folk-pop, characterised by the almost skifflish 'Any Road', mixed in places with a laid-back atmosphere redolent of Ry Cooder. The South Seas blues of 'Rocking Chair In Hawaii' felt like an older, slower incarnation of 'For You Blue'. Harrison's version of 'Between The Devil And The Deep Blue Sea', made famous in 1931 by Cab Calloway, dated back to the early Nineties, recorded originally for Jools Holland's film *Mr Roadrunner*. Featuring Ray Cooper, Herbie Flowers and Joe Brown, it offered a window into those loose, just-for-fun sessions held at Friar Park during the Eighties and Nineties, and captured the spirit of the kind of music Harrison most loved playing and listening to in his later years.

Yet there was, unsurprisingly, an elegiac tone to much of *Brainwashed*. The end-of-the-line despair of 'Stuck Inside A Cloud' and hard-won wisdom of 'Looking For My Life' may well have been sweetened by his most memorable melodies for decades, but there was no disguising the bruising on either, nor the deep sense of sadness pervading the instrumental 'Marwa Blues'.

Much of the rest were glass-half-empty musings, directed at the wider world but also closer to home. Harrison explored his own eternally conflicted nature in 'Pisces Fish' ("One half's going where the other half's just been") and there was a last jab at the Catholic Church in the chugging 'P2 Vatican Blues'. 'The Rising Sun' deployed several of The Beatles' most recognisable musical tropes circa 1967 – queasy minor-chord falls, low cellos and swooping guitar – to better emphasise the apparently drastic personal cost to Harrison of being in the band in the first place ("I was almost a statistic inside a doctor's case"), before he offered gratitude at finding an alternate path.

Before his death he had made it clear that the title track should be his final musical statement. Its world-weariness was unequivocal. At its centre was a litany of the ills of life on 'Bullshit Avenue', delivered in Harrison's most unlovely, stridently nasal voice. Denis O'Brien for one may have felt the hot breath of fury on his back. Between the seemingly unending horrors of the modern world were interpolated cries of "God, God, God, won't you lead us through this mess," and a reading from *How To Know God (The Yoga Aphorisms of Patanjali)*. The song ended, becalmed, with chants of "Hare Hare" and "Shiva Shiva" drifting over burbling tabla. It seemed only fitting that the last song on Harrison's last album should be an archetypal mix of the sour, spiritual and sublime.

'Brainwashed' concluded a brave and characteristically honest record, both warm and spiky, and satisfying in its refusal to shirk the hard questions or neatly tie up all the loose ends. Harrison remained contrary to the last, and with time *Brainwashed* has staked a persuasive claim to being perhaps his most enjoyable solo record since the mid-Seventies.

It was sympathetically reviewed but sold modestly, underlining the hard truth that while many people held Harrison in great affection, few were now moved to listen to his music on a regular basis.

★ ★ ★

On November 29, a little over a week after the release of *Brainwashed*, Harrison's life and music were celebrated in the Concert For George, a tribute held at the Royal Albert Hall on the first anniversary of his death. Guests included Paul McCartney, Ringo Starr, Jeff Lynne, Tom Petty & The Heartbreakers, Jools Holland, Billy Preston, Ravi Shankar, Joe Brown, Ray Cooper, Jim Keltner, Klaus Voormann, members of Monty Python and Tom Hanks. Eric Clapton was musical director. Bob Dylan couldn't make it but had played 'Something' as a tribute at his Madison Square Garden show a fortnight earlier, on November 13, 2002. The lack of any representatives from more recent generations of artists was hardly surprising but worthy of comment.

Incorporating ideas that stretched back to the Concert For Bangladesh and the 1974 US tour, the show opened with an Indian music section, featuring a new composition by Ravi Shankar, performed by his orchestra and his daughter Anoushka. Jeff Lynne later joined the Indian musicians to sing 'The Inner Light'. After the intermission there was a comic interlude courtesy of the Monty Python team, aided by Hanks, which included 'The Lumberjack Song', before the all-star cast ran through a selection of Harrison's best-known songs. The revival of some – 'I Need You', perhaps, delivered with sweet-hearted sincerity by Tom Petty – might well have made Harrison wince, but the performance of 20 of his compositions by a range of artists amounted to an impressive précis of a catalogue which lacks strength-in-depth but is full of character and front-loaded with several gems. Tellingly, the only songs post-dating 1973 were 'That's The Way It Goes' (from *Gone Troppo*), 'Handle With Care' and 'Horse To The Water'.

Olivia Harrison lit incense and Dhani Harrison stayed on stage for almost the entire evening, playing guitar, anxious not to miss a second. Near the end Paul McCartney, cleared moved but equally clearly a little unsure of quite how and where to position himself amongst Harrison's closest friends, gestured to Dhani and said: "It looks like George stayed young and we all got old."

As part of his short set McCartney played 'Something' on the ukulele, an appropriately low-key deconstruction, before Clapton joined in and reunited the song with its original stately grandeur. The pair then duetted on 'While My Guitar Gently Weeps'. Starr bashed through a now truly poignant 'Photograph' and announced: "I loved George, George loved me." Preston performed 'What Is Life' and 'My Sweet Lord', and at the request of Olivia Harrison, Joe Brown and his ukulele provided a wonderfully bittersweet finale, singing the 1924 popular song 'I'll See You In My Dreams' as rose petals fell from the heavens of the hall, and an image of Harrison as many still remembered him and perhaps always will – young, beautiful, suited and serious as Beatle George – was frozen on the screen.

It was a moving end to a perfectly pitched evening – intimate but powerful, utterly genuine and filled with warmth and memories. The night fell somewhere between a celebration and a memorial, and for those involved the rehearsals and concert itself provided both a focus for their grief and the opportunity to move on. "I think it closed a chapter for all of us, particularly Eric," says Tessa Niles, who sang backing vocals with Katie Kissoon. "Eric was musical director for Concert For George and he handled that extremely well. He really wanted to do that for George and Olivia. People would show up outside the rehearsal rooms with their guitars and ask, 'Can we join in?' It was a real connection, something we could give."

The Concert For George, filmed by David Leland and later released on DVD, was part of a careful cultivation of Harrison's legacy, encompassing his music, his humanitarian work and other aspects of his life.

Attempts at anything too brash, or hasty, or perceived to be out of sync with his image were quietly but robustly resisted. A BBC tribute programme scheduled for broadcast over Christmas 2001, just a month after his death, was scrapped at the family's request. There was a rather more protracted contretemps with Henley Town Council over plans for a permanent memorial. First, Olivia Harrison asked the council not to build a new park in Harrison's name opposite Friar Park. Perhaps mindful of Michael Abram – who had been released from secure hospital in July 2002, much to the family's distress – she did not want the area immediately surrounding her home to become a place of pilgrimage for Beatles fans.

She then asked the council to reconsider their Plan B, which was to rename Red Lion Lawn, a prominent local riverside landmark, after Harrison. In a letter she explained that "George's favourite spots were away from the town centre and traffic and I hope one day a more appropriate, quiet place will present itself as a fitting memorial to a man who enjoyed nature and solitude." In the ensuing decade nothing did. In 2013 Olivia put an end to a campaign to have a statue of Harrison erected in the town, saying she would prefer to have her late husband associated with a local community project.

The same year, in May, a memorial garden was opened at Bhaktivedanta Manor, 40 years after Harrison had bought the property for the Hare Krishna movement. The ceremony, which began with a sitar recital, was conducted by Olivia Harrison and television gardener Monty Don. The garden, situated in the woodland dell behind the main building, is intended to be set aside for prayer and contemplation.

The treatment of Harrison's music has been equally assiduous. In 2004 came *The Dark Horse Years: 1976–1992*, a box-set which Harrison had been working on prior to his death containing his six post-EMI solo albums, each with a handful of outtakes, and a DVD of selected videos. In the same year he was inducted posthumously into the Rock and Roll Hall of Fame as a solo artist by fellow Wilburys Jeff Lynne and Tom Petty. In 2006 he was also inducted into the Madison Square Garden Walk of Fame in recognition of the Concert For Bangladesh, which was also reissued on CD and DVD. Not a concept he was drawn towards in his lifetime, the variety and degree of "fame" officially bestowed on Harrison after his death would no doubt have amused him. In 2009 he was awarded a star on the Hollywood Walk of Fame in front of the Capitol Records building in Los Angeles. Paul McCartney, Lynne and Petty were present, Tom Hanks and Eric Idle made speeches, and Dhani recited the Hare Krishna mantra.

A new Best Of album was released the same year. *Let It Roll: Songs By George Harrison* aimed to right some of the wrongs of that first mongrel compilation, issued in 1976. The only Beatles-era songs included this time were three live recordings taken from the *Concert For Bangladesh*. "I instigated it, and I consulted lots of friends and family until it was just the problem of diversity," Olivia Harrison told me in 2009. "It had started out as a larger collection. I had deeper tracks that I wanted on there and to me it's missing huge chunks, and yet I think it's a great way for people to get reacquainted with George's music for those who don't know it. It represents many aspects of George."

Two years later came Martin Scorsese's vast authorised documentary, *Living In The Material World*, a partial and oddly uneven but nevertheless welcome attempt to add more colour and depth to the general perception of the man and his music.

★ ★ ★

The overall aim of all this carefully calibrated activity was clear: to not only preserve but to quietly bolster Harrison's perhaps rather undernourished legacy. Even after his death, the majority of his songs remain under-known and under-played. Whether they are underrated is another matter.

The nature and extent of Harrison's talent are issues which continue to divide opinion. There are those for whom the fact that he was a Beatle is enough, as though being at one time a member of that band is all but conclusive proof of genius and near sainthood. There are others who will always see Harrison as a man raised by sheer good fortune to a position considerably more exalted than his gifts merited; but for a twist of fate here or there he would probably have eked out an unremarkable career – possibly quite contentedly – in any number of Merseybeat also-rans.

A more considered assessment might correspond more closely with Harrison's own clear-eyed reckoning of what he could and could not do, and what he aspired to. It would argue that he was talented and conscientious but all too rarely inspired; that his range was narrow, his lyrical vision myopic, and his voice limited. It might recall that the only real success he enjoyed as a solo artist in his final 25 years was with two songs about The Beatles and a cover version, and that his default position as a writer was to present a jaundiced view of the world which often jarred unpleasantly with his privileged position in it. Harrison seemed almost incapable of telling a lie: an admirable, if challenging trait in life, but a handicap for a songwriter.

Such an assessment must also point out, however, that Harrison was responsible for perhaps six or eight songs which have deservedly entered the popular songbook, and a further eight or ten which have lasting value; that he sang on, played on, and on occasion wrote some of the greatest pop music ever made, as well as being responsible for one truly superb solo album. It would note that he composed an enviable number of memorable riffs; that his restraint, taste and economy influenced as many guitarists as Jimi Hendrix, and that he created a slide guitar sound which is his and his alone. His early adoption of Indian music and its attendant philosophy made a worthy contribution to widening cultural horizons in the Sixties and Seventies, and he did much to engender a sense of moral and social responsibility in popular music. He wrote songs that no one else would have written, with unusual chord structures and challenging time signatures, while his dedication to melody rarely wavered.

It's a chequered but far from insubstantial legacy. Whether it could have been greater remains open to question. Harrison's distaste for the limelight saw him retreat at the moment of his greatest triumphs, while his cautious nature meant he did not always take the kind of chances that, post-Beatles, might have pushed his music to more exciting places. In bootleg recordings a raw spontaneity exists which is ironed out on the majority of his final product. *Early Takes Vol. 1*, an album originally included as part of the deluxe DVD edition of Martin Scorsese's documentary, and later released in its own right in 2012, makes a compelling case in support of those who feel Harrison did not always play to his strengths.

A deceptively simple affair, the album comprises ten tracks of unadorned demos, most featuring just Harrison and his acoustic guitar, occasionally with rudimentary bass and guitar backing. Producer Giles

Martin compiled *Early Takes* with the hope that it would provide a "different way of listening" to Harrison. "There was a singer-songwriter thing I wanted to get to, I was trying to bring him as close as possible," he told me. "It's nice to be able to hear him singing and accompanying himself at the same time – you never really hear that on his records. On this record you can hear George's personality: his frailty, his cockiness, all that. The more things that are added the less it's him."

Early Takes is indeed a glimpse into a side of Harrison we were rarely allowed to see. And it is fascinating and wonderful: the raw, soulful, uncensored ease of expression seems to reflect back the nature of the man more clearly and completely than almost anything else he did. In the vaults at FPSHOT are many more evocations of the richness of Harrison's life which his released music, however honest, often only hints at. There are entire radio comedy programmes preserved on tape, and the ghosts of F1 cars roaring past at the British Grand Prix. There is a recording of a confused, spiritually famished young man being given his very first sitar lesson from Ravi Shankar; and not much later the same man playing in a hotel room in Jaipur. There are joke songs from Hawaii, Dylan covers, father-and-son recordings, island songs, instrumentals, endless ukulele strums, voices from the past and echoes of people that are now gone.

In the end most of that music was made for personal pleasure and given to just a few – to family, and to his many friends – just as the contradictory life it mirrors, with all its complex counter-narratives and parallel plot lines, was lived for its own sake and its own rewards. Harrison may have appeared naïve and even foolish at times through the expression of his beliefs. He may have grown detached from the world and oddly embittered by it, but he was never hoodwinked into believing that the pursuit of fame – or indeed even its less seductive cousin, mere success – mattered more than his determination to lead some semblance of an ordinary existence.

In his speech at the Hollywood Bowl in 2002 Eric Idle reflected: "What made George special, apart from his being the best guitarist in The Beatles, was what he did with his life after they achieved everything... I was on an island somewhere when a man came up to him and said,

405

'George Harrison! Oh my God, what are you doing here?' And he said, 'Well, everyone's got to be somewhere.'"

Perhaps Harrison's greatest achievement was striving to find fulfilment each day in the rudimentary joys of being "somewhere", rather than regarding any place beyond the parameters of a stage, a studio, a penthouse suite and a private plane as "nowhere". One of his final notebook entries read: "Sort out middle of *Brainwashed*. Cut down yew trees at back of lodge."

The difficulty would have been deciding which to do first, rather than which mattered most.

Acknowledgements

I would like to thank everyone who agreed to answer my questions about George Harrison. They include: David Acomba, John Barham, Pattie Boyd, Tony Bramwell, Dick Clement, Nathan East, Bill Elliott, Steve Ferrone, Herbie Flowers, Ben Fong-Torres, Robben Ford, Peter Frampton, Bill Harry, Garth Hudson, Glyn Johns, Bobby Keys, Al Kooper, Danny Kortchmar, Bernie Krause, Sam Leach, Chuck Leavell, Will Lee, Jackie Lomax, Richard Loncraine, Gered Mankowitz, Dave Mason, Dave Mattacks, Roger McGuinn, Andy Newmark, Tessa Niles, Rick Nowels, Chris O'Dell, Jerry Pompili, Emil Richards, Robbie Robertson, Leon Russell, Ken Scott, Ravi Shankar, Chris Spedding, Jon Taplin, Alvin Taylor, Ted Templeman, Chris Thomas, Russ Titelman, Lon Van Eaton, Allan Williams, Bobby Whitlock, Geoff Wonfor and Roy Young. Thanks, too, to those who agreed to speak off the record.

Thanks also to Spencer Leigh and Jamie Bowman for Liverpool knowledge, to Al Bainbridge and Tom Brennan for Splinter, to Kristen O'Brien, Carol Young, David Cavanagh, Mog Yoshihara, Rod Davis and Mary Hopkin; to Ronnie Hodge at Merseycats, to David Dalton and Richard DiLello, and to Colin Harper.

A more general note of thanks to everyone who shared their knowledge of The Beatles and George Harrison, and to the numerous kind souls who forwarded emails, passed on phone numbers, placed the right words in the right ears, and in doing so helped make easier the often arduous process of establishing contacts and arranging interviews.

Particular thanks are due to my editor, Chris Charlesworth, for providing the initial spark for this book, and for his perspicacious suggestions and encouragement throughout the long process of writing it. I am also very grateful for his patience, which at times I'm sure was sorely tested. Thanks to Andy Neill and to Johnny Rogan for comments which never failed to improve the text, and to Dave Brolan for help with obtaining the cover photograph.

Finally, as ever, I owe an enormous debt of thanks to all my family, especially my mother, Kathleen, for her unswerving support, and most of all to my wife, Jen, and our three children, for their love, patience, help and understanding, without which I can confidently state that this book could never have been written.

Notes and Sources

All quotations are derived from interviews conducted by the author exclusively for this book unless indicated otherwise in the text or marked with a reference number corresponding to the sources listed below.

All footnotes are denoted by an asterisk and are listed at the bottom of the relevant page.

PROLOGUE:
1. *Harrison, By The Editors of Rolling Stone*, Simon & Schuster, 2002
2. *Yin & Yang: George Harrison and Ravi Shankar*,VH1, May 14, 1997

CHAPTER 1:
1. *I Me Mine*, George Harrison, Chronicle Books
2. *ibid*
3. *Good Morning Australia*, April 19, 1982
4. *I Me Mine*, George Harrison, Chronicle Books
5. *Beatles Book Monthly*, October 1966
6. *The Beatles*, Hunter Davies, Ebury, 2009
7. *Living In The Material World* (film), Dir: Martin Scorsese, 2011
8. *I Me Mine*, George Harrison, Chronicle Books
9. *Lowside Of The Road: A Life Of Tom Waits*, Barney Hoskyns, Faber & Faber, 2010
10. *The Beatles*, Hunter Davies, Ebury, 2009
11. Press conference in New Zealand, 1984

12. *Living In The Material World* (film), Dir: Martin Scorsese, 2011
13. *The Beatles Anthology*, The Beatles, Cassell & Co, 2000
14. *Saturday Evening Post*, March 1964
15. *The Beatles Anthology*, The Beatles, Cassell & Co, 2000
16. *George Harrison: The Quiet One* (documentary)
17. *ibid*
18. See *George Harrison: 1943–2001*, Alan Clayson, Sanctuary, 2001
19. *The Beatles*, Hunter Davies, Ebury, 2009
20. *I Me Mine*, George Harrison, Chronicle Books
21. *The Beatles Anthology*, The Beatles, Cassell & Co, 2000
22. See *Dark Horse*, Geoffrey Giuliano, Da Capo Press, 1997
23. *Living In The Material World* (film), Dir: Martin Scorsese, 2011
24. *George Harrison: 1943–2001*, Alan Clayson, Sanctuary, 2001
25. *I Me Mine*, George Harrison, Chronicle Books
26. *Living In The Material World* (film), Dir: Martin Scorsese, 2011
27. *MOJO*, November 2011
28. *The Beatles Anthology*, The Beatles, Cassell & Co, 2000
29. *ibid*
30. *George Harrison: The Quiet One* (documentary)
31. *I Me Mine*, George Harrison, Chronicle Books
32. *Paul McCartney: Many Years From Now*, Barry Miles, Vintage Books, 1997
33. *I Me Mine*, George Harrison, Chronicle Books
34. *ibid*
35. *ibid*
36. *The Beatles*, Hunter Davies, Ebury, 2009
37. *George Harrison: The Quiet One* (documentary)
38. *Melody Maker*, September 9, 1967
39. *The Beatles*, Hunter Davies, Ebury, 2009
40. *I Me Mine*, George Harrison, Chronicle Books

CHAPTER 2:
1. *The Beatles Book Monthly*, November 1964
2. *The Beatles Anthology*, The Beatles, Cassell & Co, 2000
3. *ibid*
4. *The Beatles*, Hunter Davies, Ebury, 2009
5. *The Beatles Anthology*, The Beatles, Cassell & Co, 2000
6. *George Harrison: Reconsidered*, Timothy White, Larchwood & Weir, 2013
7. *The Beatles*, Hunter Davies, Ebury, 2009
8. *The Beatles Anthology*, The Beatles, Cassell & Co, 2000
9. *New Musical Express*, August 16, 1963
10. *The Beatles*, Hunter Davies, Ebury, 2009

11. *The Beatles Anthology*, The Beatles, Cassell & Co, 2000
12. *ibid*
13. *Living In The Material World* (film), Dir: Martin Scorsese, 2011
14. *The Beatles*, Hunter Davies, Ebury, 2009
15. *The Beatles Anthology*, The Beatles, Cassell & Co, 2000
16. *The Beatles*, Hunter Davies, Ebury, 2009
17. *The Love You Make: An Insider's Story Of The Beatles*, Peter Brown and Steven Gaines, McGraw-Hill, 1983
18. *I Me Mine*, George Harrison, Chronicle Books, 2002
19. *The Beatles Anthology*, The Beatles, Cassell & Co, 2000
20. *Living In The Material World* (film), Dir: Martin Scorsese, 2011
21. *Crawdaddy*, February, 1977
22. *The Complete Beatles Recording Sessions*, Mark Lewisohn, EMI Records, 2006
23. *A Hard Day's Write*, Steve Turner, Carlton Books, 2010
24. *New Musical Express*, August 16, 1963
25. *The Beatles*, Hunter Davies, Ebury, 2009
26. *New Musical Express*, July 29, 1966
27. *The Beatles*, Hunter Davies, Ebury, 2009
28. *The Mirror*, October 6, 2012
29. http://sentstarr.tripod.com/beatgirls/caldwell.html
30. *The Beatles*, Hunter Davies, Ebury, 2009
31. *The Mirror*, October 6, 2012
32. *ibid*
33. *The Beatles Anthology*, The Beatles, Cassell & Co, 2000
34. *ibid*
35. *New Musical Express*, August 16, 1963
36. *Liddypool: Birthplace Of The Beatles*, David Bedford, Dalton Watson, 2009
37. *The Beatles Anthology*, The Beatles, Cassell & Co, 2000
38. *ibid*

CHAPTER 3:
1. *The Beatles Anthology*, The Beatles, Cassell & Co, 2000
2. *ibid*
3. *ibid*
4. *Goldmine*, November 25, 1994
5. *Guitar World*, December 1992
6. *ibid*
7. Radio interview, Chicago, August 13, 1966
8. *The Beatles Anthology*, The Beatles, Cassell & Co, 2000
9. *ibid*
10. *ibid*

11. *Crawdaddy*, February, 1977

12. *Living In The Material World* (film), Dir: Martin Scorsese, 2011

13. *The Beatles*, Hunter Davies, Ebury, 2009

14. *ibid*

15. *The Beatles Anthology*, The Beatles, Cassell & Co, 2000

16. *ibid*

17. *Living In The Material World* (film), Dir: Martin Scorsese, 2011

18. *Goldmine*, November 25, 1994

19. See *All Things Must Pass,* Marc Shapiro, Virgin Books, 2002

20. *MOJO*, November 2011

21. *The Beatles*, Hunter Davies, Ebury, 2009

22. *Crawdaddy*, February, 1977

23. *The Beatles Anthology*, The Beatles, Cassell & Co, 2000

24. *Guitar World*, December 1992

25. *John Lennon: The Life*, Philip Norman, Harper Collins, 2008

26. *Magical Mystery Tours: My Life With The Beatles*, Tony Bramwell with Rosemary Kingsland, Portico, 2009

27. *ibid*

28. http://www.bbc.co.uk/news/entertainment-arts-19800059

29. *The Beatles: The Biography*, Bob Spitz, Aurum Press, 2005

30. *The Beatles Anthology*, The Beatles, Cassell & Co, 2000

31. *ibid*

32. *ibid*

33. *I Me Mine*, George Harrison, Chronicle Books

34. *The Beatles Anthology*, The Beatles, Cassell & Co, 2000

35. *ibid*

36. *Living In The Material World* (film), Dir: Martin Scorsese, 2011

37. *The Love You Make: An Insider's Story Of The Beatles*, Peter Brown and Steven Gaines, McGraw-Hill, 1983

38. *The Beatles: An Oral History*, David Pritchard & Alan Lysaght, Hyperion, 1999

BE HERE NOW, 1963

1. *Living In The Material World* (film), Dir: Martin Scorsese, 2011

CHAPTER 4:

1. *The Beatles Anthology*, The Beatles, Cassell & Co, 2000

2. *Record Mirror*, February 2, 1963

3. *All We Are Saying*, David Sheff, Pan Books, 2001

4. *Veronica Broadcasting Association*, November 1976

5. *Globe*, September 1969

6. *The Beatles Anthology*, The Beatles, Cassell & Co, 2000

7. *ibid*
8. *Beatles Book Monthly*, November 1964
9. *Love Me Do*, Michael Braun, Penguin, 1964
10. *The Beatles Anthology*, The Beatles, Cassell & Co, 2000
11. *New Musical Express*, August 16, 1963
12. *ibid*
13. *ibid*
14. *Can't Buy Me Love*, Jonathan Gould, Piatkus, 2007
15. *Melody Maker*, May 1, 1965
16. *Saturday Evening Post*, March 1964
17. *Melody Maker*, May 1, 1965
18. *Beatles Monthly*, March 1983
19. *Beatles Book Monthly*, November 1964
20. *The Beatles Anthology*, The Beatles, Cassell & Co, 2000
21. *Melody Maker*, May 1, 1965
22. *Beatles Book Monthly*, November 1964
23. *New Musical Express*, September 29, 1963
24. *ibid*
25. See *George Harrison: 1943–2001*, Alan Clayson, Sanctuary, 2001
26. *The Beatles Anthology*, The Beatles, Cassell & Co, 2000
27. *Before He Was Fab: George Harrison's First American Visit*, Jim Kirkpatrick, Cache River Press, 2000
28. *ibid*
29. *The Beatles Anthology*, The Beatles, Cassell & Co, 2000
30. *George Harrison: Reconsidered*, Timothy White, Larchwood & Weir, 2013
31. *Revolution In The Head*, Ian MacDonald, Fourth Estate, 1994
32. *Love Me Do*, Michael Braun, Penguin, 1964
33. *The Beatles Anthology*, The Beatles, Cassell & Co, 2000
34. *MOJO*, November 2011
35. *Sarasota Herald-Tribune*, November 28, 2011
36. *Saturday Evening Post*, March 1964
37. Beatles Press Conference: Sydney, Australia, November 6, 1964
38. http://sentstarr.tripod.com/beatgirls/farrell.html
39. *ibid*
40. *Rolling Stone*, January 21, 1971
41. *Here Comes The Sun*, Joshua M Greene, Bantam Books, 2006
42. *Wonderful Tonight,* Pattie Boyd with Penny Juror, Harmony Books, 2007
43. *MOJO*, November 2011
44. *Wonderful Tonight,* Pattie Boyd with Penny Juror, Harmony Books, 2007
45. *Love Me Do*, Michael Braun, Penguin, 1964

BE HERE NOW, 1964
1. *KRLA Beat*, May 12, 1965
2. *The Beatles Anthology*, The Beatles, Cassell & Co, 2000

CHAPTER 5:
1. *Here Comes The Sun*, Joshua M Greene, Bantam Books, 2006
2. *Living In The Material World* (film), Dir: Martin Scorsese, 2011
3. Interview with Michael Lydon, March 1966, previously unpublished, via *Rock's Back Pages*
4. *Melody Maker*, November 7, 1964
5. *MOJO*, November 2011
6. *Disc*, November 24, 1962
7. *Saturday Evening Post*, March 1964
8. *MOJO*, November 2011
9. *I Me Mine*, George Harrison, Chronicle Books, 2002
10. *The Beatles Anthology*, The Beatles, Cassell & Co, 2000
11. http://www.beatlemania.ca/toursworld/64australia.htm
12. Beatles Press Conference: Sydney, Australia, November 6, 1964
13. *Rolling Stone,* January 17, 2002
14. *The Beatles Anthology*, The Beatles, Cassell & Co, 2000
15. *Melody Maker*, November 7, 1964
16. *Rolling Stone,* January 17, 2002
17. *Living In The Material World* (film), Dir: Martin Scorsese, 2011
18. *The Beatles Anthology*, The Beatles, Cassell & Co, 2000
19. *Melody Maker*, February 27, 1965
20. *Record Mirror*, May 3, 1965
21. *Sunday Mirror*, January 7, 2001
22. *KRLA Beat*, May 15, 1965
23. *Evening Standard*, March 18, 1966
24. *Rolling Stone*, January 21, 1971
25. *Beatles Down Under: The 1964 Australian & New Zealand Tour*, Glenn A Baker, Magnum Imprint, 1996
26. *John Lennon: The Life*, Philip Norman, Harper Collins, 2008
27. *Magical Mystery Tours: My Life With The Beatles*, Tony Bramwell with Rosemary Kingsland, Portico, 2009
28. *Beatles Down Under: The 1964 Australian & New Zealand Tour*, Glenn A Baker, Magnum Imprint, 1996
29. *Evening Standard*, March 18, 1966
30. *ibid*
31. *Wonderful Tonight,* Pattie Boyd with Penny Juror, Harmony Books, 2007
32. *Beatles Book Monthly*, October 1966

33. *I Me Mine*, George Harrison, Chronicle Books, 2002
34. *Beatles Book Monthly*, October 1966
35. See *Can't Buy Me Love*, Jonathan Gould, Piatkus, 2007
36. *All We Are Saying*, David Sheff, Pan Books, 2001
37. *Saturday Evening Post*, March 1964
38. *Northern Songs: The True Story of The Beatles Publishing Empire*, Brian Southall, Omnibus Press, 2007
39. *Living In The Material World* (film), Dir: Martin Scorsese, 2011
40. *I Me Mine*, George Harrison, Chronicle Books, 2002
41. *ibid*
42. *Disc*, July 16, 1966
43. *I Me Mine*, George Harrison, Chronicle Books, 2002
44. http://www.beatlesinterviews.org/db1966.0819.beatles.html
45. *I Me Mine*, George Harrison, Chronicle Books, 2002

BE HERE NOW, 1966

1. *Here Comes The Sun*, Joshua M Greene, Bantam Books, 2006

CHAPTER 6:

1. *The Complete Beatles Chronicle*, Mark Lewisohn, Chicago Review Press, 1992
2. *The Beatles Anthology*, The Beatles, Cassell & Co, 2000
3. *The Beatles*, Hunter Davies, Ebury, 2009
4. *The Beatles Anthology*, The Beatles, Cassell & Co, 2000
5. *ibid*
6. *My Music, My Life*, Ravi Shankar, Mandala Publishing Group, 2008
7. *The Beatles Anthology*, The Beatles, Cassell & Co, 2000
8. *ibid*
9. See *Here Comes The Sun*, Joshua M Greene, Bantam Books, 2006
10. *Detroit Free Press*, August 19, 1966
11. *I Me Mine*, George Harrison, Chronicle Books, 2002
12. *The Dawn of Indian Music in the West*, Peter Lavezzoli, Continuum, 2007
13. *The Complete Beatles Recording Sessions*, Mark Lewisohn, EMI Records, 2006
14. *The Dawn of Indian Music in the West*, Peter Lavezzoli, Continuum, 2007
15. *The Beatles Anthology*, The Beatles, Cassell & Co, 2000
16. *Yin & Yang: George Harrison and Ravi Shankar*, VH1, May 14, 1997
17. *My Music, My Life*, Ravi Shankar, Mandala Publishing Group, 2008
18. http://www.gadflyonline.com/12-3-01/music-lifeofgeorge.html
19. *The Beatles Anthology*, The Beatles, Cassell & Co, 2000
20. *ibid*
21. *Living In The Material World* (film), Dir: Martin Scorsese, 2011
22. *The Beatles*, Hunter Davies, Ebury, 2009

23. *International Times*, May 19, 1967
24. *The Mirror*, November 11, 1966
25. *Paul McCartney: Many Years From Now*, Barry Miles, Vintage Books, 1997
26. *Rolling Stone*, October 22, 1987
27. *MOJO*, October 1996
28. *The Beatles Anthology*, The Beatles, Cassell & Co, 2000
29. *Making Music*, June 1987
30. See *All Things Must Pass*, Marc Shapiro, Virgin Books, 2002
31. *Detroit Free Press*, August 19, 1966
32. *Melody Maker*, September 2, 1967
33. *International Times*, May 19, 1967
34. *ibid*
35. *Q*, May 1994
36. *Melody Maker*, September 2, 1967
37. *The Beatles Anthology*, The Beatles, Cassell & Co, 2000
38. *International Times*, May 19, 1967
39. *The Beatles Anthology*, The Beatles, Cassell & Co, 2000
40. *ibid*
41. Press conference, Bangor, August 27, 1967
42. *Western Daily News*, August 28, 1967
43. *The Beatles*, Hunter Davies, Ebury, 2009
44. *The Beatles Anthology*, The Beatles, Cassell & Co, 2000
45. *The George Harrison Encyclopaedia*, Billy Harry, Virgin Books, 2003
46. *George Harrison: Reconsidered*, Timothy White, Larchwood & Weir, 2013
47. *ibid*
48. *Melody Maker*, March 9, 1968
49. *The Beatles Anthology*, The Beatles, Cassell & Co, 2000
50. *The Beatles*, Hunter Davies, Ebury, 2009
51. *Paul McCartney: Many Years From Now*, Barry Miles, Vintage Books, 1997
52. http://www.elsewhere.co.nz/film/3852/joe-massot-interviewed-2001-and-after-all-youre-my-wonderwall
53. *The Beatles Anthology*, The Beatles, Cassell & Co, 2000
54. *International Times*, September 11, 1969

BE HERE NOW, 1968
1. *The Longest Cocktail Party*, Richard DiLello, Canongate, 2000

CHAPTER 7:
1. *Paul McCartney: Many Years From Now*, Barry Miles, Vintage Books, 1997
2. *The Beatles Anthology*, The Beatles, Cassell & Co, 2000
3. *Rolling Stone*, April 1979

4. *George Harrison: Reconsidered*, Timothy White, Larchwood & Weir, 2013
5. Interview with the author on *The Arts Desk*, May 14, 2012
6. See *The Beatles Diary – Vol. 2: After The Break Up 1970–2001*, Keith Badman, Omnibus Press, 2001
7. *The Beatles Anthology*, The Beatles, Cassell & Co, 2000
8. *Rolling Stone*, January 21, 1971
9. *The Beatles Anthology*, The Beatles, Cassell & Co, 2000
10. *Eric Clapton: The Autobiography*, Eric Clapton with Christopher Simon Sykes, Century, 2007
11. *Yin & Yang: George Harrison and Ravi Shankar*, VH1, May 14, 1997
12. *I Me Mine*, George Harrison, Chronicle Books, 2002
13. *You Never Give Me Your Money*, Peter Doggett, Vintage Books, 2009
14. *ibid*
15. *Fifty Years Adrift*, Derek Taylor, Genesis Publications, 1984
16. *The Beatles Anthology*, The Beatles, Cassell & Co, 2000
17. Capitol A&R man Ken Mansfield in an interview with James Rosen, December 4-5, 2007: http://www.foxnews.com/story/0,2933,317539,00.html#ixzz2SjypaohH
18. *George Harrison: Reconsidered*, Timothy White, Larchwood & Weir, 2013
19. *Down The Highway: The Life Of Bob Dylan*, Howard Sounes, Doubleday, 2001
20. *George Harrison: Reconsidered*, Timothy White, Larchwood & Weir, 2013
21. *ibid*
22. *The Beatles Anthology*, The Beatles, Cassell & Co, 2000

CHAPTER 8:
1. *Rolling Stone*, July 7, 1970
2. *Creem*, December 1987
3. *Paul McCartney: Many Years From Now*, Barry Miles, Vintage Books, 1997
4. *The Beatles Anthology*, The Beatles, Cassell & Co, 2000
5. See *You Never Give Me Your Money*, Peter Doggett, Vintage Books, 2009
6. *ibid*
7. *Fifty Years Adrift*, Derek Taylor, Genesis Publications, 1984
8. *Living In The Material World* (film), Dir: Martin Scorsese, 2011
9. *Wonderful Tonight,* Pattie Boyd with Penny Juror, Harmony Books, 2007
10. *I Me Mine*, George Harrison, Chronicle Books, 2002
11. *ibid*
12. http://www.gadflyonline.com/12-3-01/music-lifeofgeorge.html
13. *ibid*
14. *Eric Clapton: The Autobiography*, Eric Clapton with Christopher Simon Sykes, Century, 2007
15. *Scene And Heard*, BBC Radio One, October 1969
16. *The Beatles Anthology*, The Beatles, Cassell & Co, 2000

417

17. *The Beatles*, Bob Spitz, Little, Brown, 2005
18. *I Me Mine*, George Harrison, Chronicle Books, 2002
19. *Scene And Heard*, BBC Radio One, October 1969
20. *Saturday Review*, October 25, 1969
21. *Scene And Heard*, BBC Radio One, October 1969
22. *Here Comes The Sun*, Joshua M Greene, Bantam Books, 2006
23. *Melody Maker*, December 6, 1969

BE HERE NOW, 1970
1. *While My Guitar Gently Weeps: The Music Of George Harrison*, Simon Leng, Firefly, 2003

CHAPTER 9:
1. *Eric Clapton: The Autobiography*, Eric Clapton with Christopher Simon Sykes, Century, 2007
2. *All Things Must Pass*, Marc Shapiro, Virgin Books, 2002
3. *George Harrison: Reconsidered*, Timothy White, Larchwood & Weir, 2013
4. See http://www.beatlesbible.com/people/george-harrison/songs/my-sweet-lord
5. *The Beatles Anthology*, The Beatles, Cassell & Co, 2000
6. *Scene And Heard*, BBC Radio One, October 1969
7. *Disc & Music Echo*, April 11, 1969
8. *Here Comes The Sun*, Joshua M Greene, Bantam Books, 2006
9. *Living In The Material World* (film), Dir: Martin Scorsese, 2011
10. *I Me Mine*, George Harrison, Chronicle Books, 2002
11. *Daily Express*, October 11, 1969
12. *Wonderful Tonight,* Pattie Boyd with Penny Juror, Harmony Books, 2007
13. *Scene And Heard*, BBC Radio One, October 1969
14. *Living In The Material World* (film), Dir: Martin Scorsese, 2011
15. *Rolling Stone*, October 22, 1987
16. *George Harrison: Reconsidered*, Timothy White, Larchwood & Weir, 2013
17. See http://www.beatlesbible.com/people/george-harrison/songs/my-sweet-lord
18. *George Harrison: Reconsidered*, Timothy White, Larchwood & Weir, 2013
19. *ibid*

BE HERE NOW, 1971
1. *Yin & Yang: George Harrison and Ravi Shankar*, VH1, May 14, 1997

CHAPTER 10:
1. *I Me Mine*, George Harrison, Chronicle Books, 2002
2. *ibid*
3. http://www.rockcellarmagazine.com/2011/06/03/did-delaney-bramlett-really-write-my-sweet-lord

4. *ibid*
5. *ibid*
6. *Melody Maker*, September 4, 1971
7. *Rolling Stone*, April 19, 1979
8. *Rolling Stone*, January 21, 1971
9. *Paul McCartney: Many Years From Now*, Barry Miles, Vintage Books, 1997
10. *John Lennon: For the Record*, Peter McCabe and Robert Schonfeld, Bantam, 1984
11. *I Me Mine*, George Harrison, Chronicle Books, 2002
12. *Yin & Yang: George Harrison and Ravi Shankar*, VH1, May 14, 1997
13. *ibid*
14. *I Me Mine*, George Harrison, Chronicle Books, 2002
15. *George Harrison: Reconsidered*, Timothy White, Larchwood & Weir, 2013/ *I Me Mine*, George Harrison, Chronicle Books, 2002
16. *Yin & Yang: George Harrison and Ravi Shankar*, VH1, May 14, 1997
17. *George Harrison: Reconsidered*, Timothy White, Larchwood & Weir, 2013
18. *Village Voice*, August 5, 1971
19. *George Harrison: Reconsidered*, Timothy White, Larchwood & Weir, 2013
20. *Village Voice*, August 5, 1971

CHAPTER 11:
1. *Disc and Music Echo*, December 4, 1971
2. *I Me Mine*, George Harrison, Chronicle Books, 2002
3. *Crawdaddy*, February 1977
4. *While My Guitar Gently Weeps: The Music Of George Harrison*, Simon Leng, Firefly, 2003
5. *George Harrison: Reconsidered*, Timothy White, Larchwood & Weir, 2013
6. *Living In The Material World* (film), Dir: Martin Scorsese, 2011
7. *I Me Mine*, George Harrison, Chronicle Books, 2002
8. *Living In The Material World* (film), Dir: Martin Scorsese, 2011
9. *Chant And Be Happy: The Power of Mantra Meditation*, A. C. Bhaktivedanta Prabhupada, The Bhaktivedanta Trust, 1999
10. http://www.youtube.com/watch?v=4Te_xgy-8c4
11. *ibid*
12. *ibid*
13. *The Beatles*, Hunter Davies, Ebury, 2009
14. See *George Harrison: 1943-2001*, Alan Clayson, Sanctuary
15. *The Beatles Forever*, Nicholas Schaffner, Cameron House, 1978
16. *Rolling Stone*, July 19, 1973
17. *The Beatles Forever*, Nicholas Schaffner, Cameron House, 1978
18. *Living In The Material World*, CD reissue
19. *I Me Mine*, George Harrison, Chronicle Books, 2002

20. *ibid*
21. *Record Mirror,* April 15, 1972
22. *Crawdaddy,* February 1977
23. *Living In The Material World* (film), Dir: Martin Scorsese, 2011
24. *Crawdaddy,* February 1977
25. *Eric Clapton: The Autobiography*, Eric Clapton with Christopher Simon Sykes, Century, 2007
26. *Living In The Material World* (film), Dir: Martin Scorsese, 2011
27. *Crawdaddy,* February 1977
28. *Undercover,* 1996
29. *Crawdaddy,* February 1977

CHAPTER 12:
1. Press conference, Beverly Wilshere Hotel, Los Angeles, October 23, 1974
2. *Rolling Stone,* December 19, 1974
3. See *The Beatles Diary – Vol 2: After The Break Up 1970–2001*, Keith Badman, Omnibus Press, 2001
4. *Rolling Stone,* April 19, 1979
5. *Living In The Material World*, Olivia Harrison, Abrams, 2011
6. *I Me Mine*, George Harrison, Chronicle Books, 2002
7. *Circus Raves,* March 1975
8. *Biograph* liner notes, 1985
9. *New Musical Express*, December 1, 1976
10. *Rolling Stone,* December 19, 1974
11. *ibid*
12. *ibid*
13. *Circus Raves,* March 1975
14. *Rolling Stone,* December 19, 1974
15. *ibid*
16. *Rolling Stone,* April 19, 1979
17. *The Beatles After the Break-up*, David Bennahum, Omnibus Press, 1992
18. *Melody Maker*, March 8, 1975
19. *ibid*
20. *ibid*
21. *The Beatles Diary – Vol 2: After The Break Up 1970–2001*, Keith Badman, Omnibus Press, 2001
22. *Swank*, 1977
23. *The Beatles After the Break-up*, David Bennahum, Omnibus Press, 1992
24. *Rolling Stone,* April 19 1979
25. *Rolling Stone,* January 30, 1975
26. *ibid*

CHAPTER 13:
1. *Sunday Times*, October 12, 2003
2. *Living In The Material World* (film), Dir: Martin Scorsese, 2011
3. Radio interview with WNEW, 1975
4. *Rolling Stone*, February 13, 1975
5. *New Musical Express*, December 21, 1974
6. *George Harrison: Reconsidered*, Timothy White, Larchwood & Weir, 2013
7. *ibid*
8. *New Musical Express*, December 21, 1974
9. *I Me Mine*, George Harrison, Chronicle Books, 2002
10. *Rolling Stone*, April 19 1979
11. *Rockweek*, Radio One, September 6, 1976
12. *ibid*
13. *I Me Mine*, George Harrison, Chronicle Books, 2002
14. *Rockweek*, Radio One, September 6, 1976
15. *Crawdaddy*, February 1977
16. *While My Guitar Gently Weeps: The Music Of George Harrison*, Simon Leng, Firefly, 2003
17. *I Me Mine*, George Harrison, Chronicle Books, 2002
18. *Rockweek*, Radio One, September 6, 1976
19. A Personal Music Dialogue with George Harrison, 1976 promo LP
20. *Rockweek*, Radio One, September 6, 1976
21. *The Beatles Diary – Vol 2: After The Break Up 1970–2001*, Keith Badman, Omnibus Press, 2001
22. *ibid*
23. *I Me Mine*, George Harrison, Chronicle Books, 2002
24. A Personal Music Dialogue with George Harrison, 1976 promo LP
25. http://www.blacklistedjournalist.com/column66a.html
26. *Rolling Stone*, December 30, 1976
27. *ibid*
28. See *The Beatles Diary – Vol 2: After The Break Up 1970–2001*, Keith Badman, Omnibus Press, 2001
29. *I Me Mine*, George Harrison, Chronicle Books, 2002
30. *Harrison, By The Editors of Rolling Stone*, Simon & Schuster, 2002
31. *ibid*
32. *Crawdaddy*, February 1977
33. *Rolling Stone*, April 19, 1979
34. *Sunday Times*, October 12, 2003
35. *Rolling Stone*, April 19, 1979
36. *The Python Years: Diaries 1969–1979*, Michael Palin, Phoenix, 2006
37. Radio KHJ 930 AM, December 21, 1974

38. *Rolling Stone*, April 19, 1979
39. *ibid*
40. *Winning Is Not Enough*, Jackie Stewart, Headline, 2007
41. *Rolling Stone*, April 19, 1979
42. *Maui Times*, August 9, 2012
43. *Rolling Stone*, April 19, 1979
44. *ibid*
45. *ibid*
46. *ibid*

CHAPTER 14:
1. Howard Worth talks about *Raga*, https://www.youtube.com/watch?v=-VVi6sC54kA
2. The *Observer*, October 30, 2011
3. *The Python Years: Diaries 1969–1979*, Michael Palin, Phoenix, 2006
4. Speech at the Hollywood Bowl, Los Angeles, June 28, 2002
5. *Always Look On The Bright Side Of Life: The Inside Story Of HandMade Films*, Robert Sellers, John Blake, 2003
6. http://en.wikipedia.org/wiki/The_Rutles
7. *Film Comment*, May/June 1988
8. Speech at the Old House, Shepperton studios, September 23, 1988
9. *Film Comment*, May/June 1988
10. *ibid*
11. *ibid*
12. *Living In The Material World* (film), Dir: Martin Scorsese, 2011
13. *Halfway To Hollywood: Diaries 1980-1988*, Michael Palin, Phoenix, 2009
14. *Always Look On The Bright Side Of Life: The Inside Story Of HandMade Films*, Robert Sellers, John Blake, 2003
15. *Film Comment*, May/June 1988
16. *Creem*, December 1987
17. *Time Out*, October 19, 1989
18. *Rolling Stone*, October 22, 1987
19. See *Dark Horse*, Geoffrey Giuliano, Da Capo Press, 1997
20. *Rolling Stone*, October 22, 1987
21. *Playboy*, January 1981
22. *West 57th Street*, CBS, 1987
23. *Rolling Stone*, October 22, 1987
24. *Here Comes The Sun*, Joshua M Greene, Bantam Books, 2006
25. *Daily Mirror*, December 31, 1999
26. *Architectural Digest*, August 2007
27. *Brainwashed* EPK
28. *Henley Standard*, July 1986

29. *Sunday Times*, October 12, 2003
30. *Halfway To Hollywood: Diaries 1980-1988*, Michael Palin, Phoenix, 2009
31. *Rolling Stone*, October 22, 1987
32. *The Eighties: One Day, One Decade*, Dylan Jones, Preface, 2013
33. *People*, October 9, 1987
34. https://www.rutherford.org/publications_resources/john_whiteheads_commentary/ george_harrison_living_in_the_material_world
35. *Look Wot I Dun: Don Powell Of Slade*, Don Powell, Omnibus Press, 2013
36. http://www.blacklistedjournalist.com/column66a.html
37. *Yin & Yang: George Harrison and Ravi Shankar*, VH1, May 14, 1997
38. *Always Look On The Bright Side Of Life: The Inside Story Of HandMade Films*, Robert Sellers, John Blake, 2003
39. *ibid*

BE HERE NOW, 1987

1. *Rolling Stone*, October 22, 1987

CHAPTER 15:

1. *The Midday Show*, 1988
2. *Rolling Stone*, October 22, 1987
3. *Musician,* November, 1987
4. *Guardian*, November 8, 1988
5. *George Harrison: Reconsidered*, Timothy White, Larchwood & Weir, 2013
6. *ibid*
7. *ibid*
8. *ibid*
9. *Rolling Stone*, October 22, 1987
10. *BBC Breakfast Time*, October 1987
11. *George Harrison: Reconsidered*, Timothy White, Larchwood & Weir, 2013
12. *Harrison, By The Editors of Rolling Stone*, Simon & Schuster, 2002
13. *Daily Mirror*, November 11, 1988
14. Backstage interview at Wembley Arena, June 5, 1987
15. *The Midday Show*, 1988
16. Toronto press conference, March 28, 1988
17. *Musician*, March 1990
18. *Rockline*, KLOS LA, February 10, 1988
19. See *Dylan: Behind The Shades*, Clinton Heylin, Viking, 1991
20. *BAM*, May 5, 1989
21. *Harrison, By The Editors of Rolling Stone*, Simon & Schuster, 2002
22. *Living In The Material World* (film), Dir: Martin Scorsese, 2011
23. *Harrison, By The Editors of Rolling Stone*, Simon & Schuster, 2002

24. *The Beatles Diary – Vol 2: After The Break Up 1970–2001*, Keith Badman, Omnibus Press, 2001
25. *The Sun*, October 2, 1987
26. *Billboard,* December 2, 1991
27. *Eric Clapton: The Autobiography*, Eric Clapton with Christopher Simon Sykes, Century, 2007
28. *ibid*
29. *Daily Mirror,* August 11, 2007
30. *Rolling Stone*, October 22, 1987
31. *Paul McCartney: Many Years From Now*, Barry Miles, Vintage Books, 1997
32. *Yin & Yang: George Harrison and Ravi Shankar,* VH1, May 14, 1997
33. RCD Vol 1–4, 1992

BE HERE NOW, 2000
1. *Living In The Material World* (film), Dir: Martin Scorsese, 2011

CHAPTER 16:
1. *Always Look On The Bright Side Of Life: The Inside Story Of HandMade Films*, Robert Sellers, John Blake, 2003
2. *ibid*
3. *ibid*
4. *Rapido*, December 5, 1990
5. *Globe and Mail*, September 26, 1987
6. *The Times,* August 8, 1993
7. *Le Figaro,* July 12, 1997
8. MTV, 1997
9. GQ, February 1, 1998
10. See *The Beatles After the Break-up,* David Bennahum, Omnibus Press, 1992
11. *Le Journal De Dimanche,* July 15, 1997
12. *Today Tonight*, November 1995
13. *The Times*, November 11, 1995
14. Q, December 1995
15. *The Beatles Diary – Vol 2: After The Break Up 1970–2001*, Keith Badman, Omnibus Press, 2001
16. *Arena*, winter 1995
17. *People,* August 1993, Vol. 40, No. 6
18. *ibid*
19. *Always Look On The Bright Side Of Life: The Inside Story Of HandMade Films*, Robert Sellers, John Blake, 2003
20. http://www.carmagazine.co.uk/Community/Car-Magazines-Blogs/Tim-Pollard-Blog2/Twelve-things-you-may-not-know-about-the-McLaren-F1

21. *MOJO*, December 2002
22. *Guitar World*, January 2003
23. *Yin & Yang: George Harrison and Ravi Shankar*, VH1, May 14, 1997
24. *Independent*, June 29, 1998
25. *Living In The Material World* (film), Dir: Martin Scorsese, 2011
26. *Guardian*, December 31, 1999
27. *New York Times*, December 31, 1999
28. *Architectural Digest*, August 2007
29. A Conversation with George Harrison, promo CD: February 15, 2001
30. *ibid*
31. See *The Beatles Diary – Vol 2: After The Break Up 1970-2001*, Keith Badman, Omnibus Press, 2001
32. *Rapido*, December 5, 1990
33. *Guitar World*, January 2003
34. *New York Times*, January 7, 2004
35. *Harrison, By The Editors of Rolling Stone*, Simon & Schuster, 2002
36. RCD Vol 1–4, 1992
37. *I Me Mine*, George Harrison, Chronicle Books, 2002
38. *Sunday Times*, October 12, 2003

EPILOGUE:
1. http://www.ezfolk.com/uke/news/110902gh/110902gh.html

Olivia Harrison interview conducted by the author in May 2009 for a feature in the *Observer Music Monthly*, issue dated June 2009

Leon Russell interview conducted by the author for the article *Leon's back with a little help from his friends*, published in *The Herald*, June 30, 2011

Jonathan Clyde interview conducted by the author in July 2011 for the article *The Concert for Bangladesh and its charity pop legacy*, published in the *Guardian*, July 28, 2011

Giles Martin interview conducted by the author for the feature *George Harrison: Behind The Locked Door*, published on *The Arts Desk*, May 14, 2012

Joe Brown interview conducted by the author in September 2012 for *The Arts Desk*

Jeff Lynne interview conducted by the author in March 2013 for the feature *Jeff Lynne: Album By Album*, published in *Uncut*, May 2013

Robbie Robertson interview conducted by the author for the feature *Music From Big Pink: The Inside Story*, published in *Uncut*, August 2013

SELECTED BIBLIOGRAPHY

A vast number of newspapers, magazines, web pages, television programmes and films were enormously helpful during the process of writing of this book. They are far too numerous to list individually, but many of the most enriching can be found in the notes and sources.

Among the almost equally numerous books used as references, the following proved particularly useful:

Allison, Dale C Jr. *Love There That's Sleeping: The Art And Spirituality Of George Harrison, The* (Continuum, 2006)

Badman, Keith. *Beatles Diary: Vol 2: After The Break Up 1970-2001, The* (Omnibus Press, 2001)

Badman, Keith. *Beatles Off The Record: Outrageous Opinions & Unreleased Interviews, The* (Omnibus Press, 2007)

Baker, Glenn A., *Beatles Down Under: The 1964 Australian And New Zealand Tour* (Magnum Imprint, 1996)

Beatles, The. *Beatles Anthology, The* (Cassell & Co, 2000)

Bedford, Carol. *Waiting For The Beatles: An Apple Scruff's Story* (Blandford Press, 1984)

Boyd, Pattie, with Junor, Penny. *Wonderful Tonight* (Harmony Books, 2007)

Bramwell, Tony, with Kingsland, Rosemary. *Magical Mystery Tours: My Life With The Beatles* (Portico, 2009)

Braun, Michael. *Love Me Do* (Penguin, 1964)

Brown, Peter and Gaines, Steven. *Love You Make: An Insider's Story Of The Beatles, The* (McGraw-Hill, 1983)

Clapton, Eric, with Simon Sykes, Christopher. *Eric Clapton: The Autobiography* (Century, 2007)

Clayson, Alan. *George Harrison: 1943-2001* (Sanctuary, 2001)

Connolly, Ray. *John Lennon: 1940-1980* (Fontana, 1981)

Creasy, Martin. *Beatlemania: The Real Story Of The Beatles' UK Tours* (Omnibus Press, 2011)

Davies, Hunter. *Beatles, The* (Ebury, 2009)

Dawson, Hulian. *And On Piano... Nicky Hopkins* (Deserthearts, 2011)

DiLello, Richard. *Longest Cocktail Party, The* (Canongate, 2000)

Doggett, Peter. *You Never Give Me Your Money* (Vintage Books, 2009)

Goldman, Albert. *Lives Of John Lennon, The* (Bantam, 1988)

Gould, Jonathan. *Can't Buy Me Love* (Piatkus, 2007)

Greene, Joshua M. *Here Comes The Sun* (Bantam Books, 2006)

Guiliano, Geoffrey. *Dark Horse* (Da Capo Press, 1997)

Harrison, George. *I Me Mine* (Chronicle Books, 2002)

Harrison, Olivia. *Living In The Material World* (Abrams, 2011)

Harry, Bill. *George Harrison Encyclopaedia, The* (Virgin Books, 2003)

Heylin, Clinton. *Dylan: Behind The Shades* (Viking, 1991)

Hoskyns, Barney. *Across The Great Divide: The Band And America* (Pimlico, 2003)

Hoskyns, Barney. *Lowside Of The Road: A Life Of Tom Waits* (Faber & Faber, 2010)

Kilpatrick, Jim. *Before He Was Fab, George Harrison's First American Visit* (Cache River Press, 2000)

Lavezzoli, Peter. *Dawn of Indian Music in the West, The* (Continuum, 2007)

Leavell, Chuck, with Craig, J Marshall. *Between Rock And A Home Place* (Mercer University Press, 2004)

Leng, Simon. *While My Guitar Gently Weeps: The Music Of George Harrison* (Firefly, 2003)

Lewisohn, Mark. *Complete Beatles Chronicle, The* (Octopus, 1992)

MacDonald, Ian. *Revolution In The Head* (Fourth Estate, 1994)

Madinger, Chip and Easter, Mark. *Eight Arms To Hold You: The Solo Beatles Compendium* (44.1 Productions, 2001)

Miles, Barry. *Beatles Diary: Vol 1: The Beatles Years 1970-2001,* (Omnibus Press, 2001)

Miles, Barry. *Paul McCartney: Many Years From Now* (Vintage Books, 1997)

Norman, Philip. *John Lennon: The Life* (Harper Collins, 2008)

Norman, Philip. *Shout!* (Elm Tree, 2001)

O'Dell, Chris, with Ketcham, Katherine. *Miss O'Dell* (Simon & Schuster, 2009)

Palin, Michael. *Halfway To Hollywood: Diaries 1980-1988* (Phoenix, 2009)

Palin, Michael. *Python Years: Diaries 1969-1979, The* (Phoenix, 2006)

Peebles, Andy (ed). *Lennon Tapes, The* (BBC, 1981)

Richards, Keith. *Life: Keith Richards* (Weidenfeld & Nicholson, 2010)

Scott, Ken, with Owsinski, Bobby. *Abbey Road To Ziggy Stardust* (Alfred Music Publishing, 2010)

Sellers, Robert. *Always Look On The Bright Side Of Life: The Inside Story Of HandMade Films* (John Blake, 2003)

Shankar, Ravi. *My Music, My Life* (Mandala Publishing Group, 2008)

Shapiro, Marc. *All Things Must Pass* (Virgin Books, 2002)

Sounes, Howard. *Down The Highway: The Life Of Bob Dylan* (Doubleday, 2001)

Spitz, Bob. *Beatles: The Biography, The* (Aurum Press, 2005)

Various, as told to Joanna Parrent. *You'll Never Make Love In This Town Again* (Dove Books, 1995)

Various. *Harrison, By The Editors Of Rolling Stone* (Simon & Schuster, 2002)

White, Timothy. *George Harrison: Reconsidered* (Larchwood & Weir, 2013)

Whitlock, Bobby, with Roberty, Marc. *A Rock 'N' Roll Biography: Bobby Whitlock* (McFarland & Company, 2011)

Index

Singles releases are in roman type and single inverted commas. Albums and films are in italics.

435